The

HABSBURGS

Also by Martyn Rady

The Habsburg Empire: A Very Short Introduction

Customary Law in Hungary: Courts, Texts, and the Tripartitum

Romania in Turmoil: A Contemporary History

Nobility, Land, and Service in Medieval Hungary

The Emperor Charles V

Medieval Buda

MARTYN RADY

The

HABSBURGS

TO RULE THE WORLD

BASIC BOOKS

New York

Basic Books
Hachette Book Group
1290 Avenue of the Americas, New York, NY 10104
www.basicbooks.com

Printed in the United States of America

First Edition: May 2020

Published by Basic Books, an imprint of Perseus Books, LLC, a subsidiary of Hachette Book Group, Inc. The Basic Books name and logo is a trademark of the Hachette Book Group.

The publisher is not responsible for websites (or their content) that are not owned by the publisher.

Print book interior design by Amy Quinn.

Library of Congress Cataloging-in-Publication Data
Names: Rady, Martyn C., author.
Title: The Habsburgs : To Rule the World / Martyn Rady.
Description: First edition. | New York, NY : Basic Books, 2020. | Includes
    bibliographical references and index.
Identifiers: LCCN 2019042154 | ISBN 9781541644502 (hardcover) | ISBN
    9781541644496 (ebook)
Subjects: LCSH: Habsburg, House of. | Austria—Kings and rulers. |
    Austria—History. | Europe—History.
Classification: LCC DB36.3.H3 R335 2020 | DDC 929.7/36—dc23
LC record available at https://lccn.loc.gov/2019042154

ISBNs: 978-1-5416-4450-2 (hardcover), 978-1-5416-4614-8 (ebook)

LSC-C

10 9 8 7 6 5 4 3 2 1

For Howard and Mary

CONTENTS

List of Maps		ix
The Habsburg Family Tree		xi
A Note on Names		xvii
	Introduction: An Emperor's Library	1
1.	Castle Habsburg and the 'Fortinbras Effect'	11
2.	The Holy Roman Empire and the Golden King	21
3.	Losing Place and Forging a Past	31
4.	Frederick III: Saturn and Mars	41
5.	Maximilian and the Colour-Coded Kings	51
6.	Charles V: Ruler of the World	63
7.	Hungary, Bohemia, and the Protestant Challenge	75
8.	Philip II: The New World, Religious Dissent, and Royal Incest	85
9.	Don John and the Galleys of Lepanto	97
10.	Rudolf II and the Alchemists of Prague	107
11.	The Triumph of the Heretics	117
12.	Ferdinand II, the Holy House, and Bohemia	127
13.	The Thirty Years 'World War'	137

14. The Abnormal Empire and the Battle for Vienna   147

15. Spain's Invisible Sovereigns and the Death of
     the Bewitched King   159

16. The Theatre of the Baroque   169

17. Maria Theresa, Automata, and Bureaucrats   179

18. Merchants, Botanists, and Freemasons   189

19. Vampirism, Enlightenment, and the
     Revolution from Above   199

20. Archduchesses and the Habsburg Low Countries   209

21. Censors, Jacobins, and *The Magic Flute*   219

22. Metternich and the Map of Europe   229

23. 1848: Von Neumann's Diary and Radetzky's March   243

24. Franz Joseph's Empire, Sisi, and Hungary   255

25. Maximilian, Mexico, and Royal Deaths   269

26. The Politics of Discontent and the 1908 Jubilee   279

27. Explorers, Jews, and the World's Knowledge   291

28. The Hunter and the Hunted: Franz
     Ferdinand and Bosnia   301

29. World War and Dissolution   313

     Conclusion   325

     Acknowledgments   331

     Credits for Illustrations   333

     Abbreviations   335

     Further Reading   337

     Notes   345

     Index   377

LIST OF MAPS

Southern Swabia, c. 1200   16
Habsburg Territories in Europe, 1555   73
Habsburg Possessions in 1600   89
Habsburg Territories in Central Europe, 1648   145
Austria-Hungary in 1914   311

THE HABSBURG FAMILY TREE

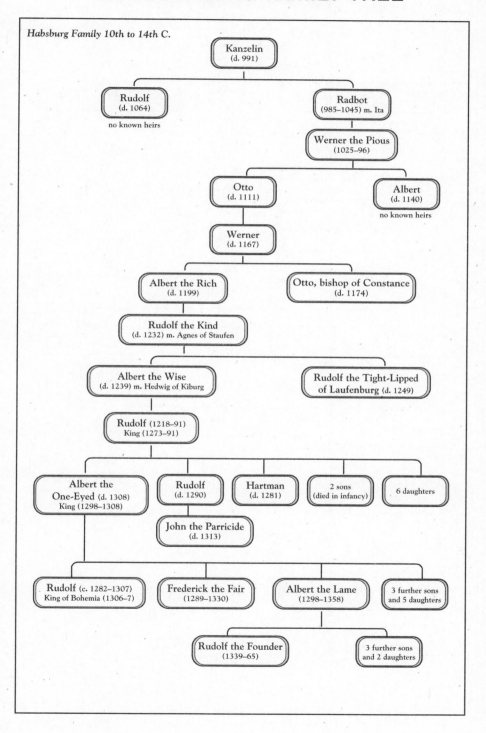

Habsburg Family 10th to 14th C.

Kanzelin
(d. 991)

Rudolf
(d. 1064)
no known heirs

Radbot
(985–1045) m. Ita

Werner the Pious
(1025–96)

Otto
(d. 1111)

Albert
(d. 1140)
no known heirs

Werner
(d. 1167)

Albert the Rich
(d. 1199)

Otto, bishop of Constance
(d. 1174)

Rudolf the Kind
(d. 1232) m. Agnes of Staufen

Albert the Wise
(d. 1239) m. Hedwig of Kiburg

Rudolf the Tight-Lipped
of Laufenburg (d. 1249)

Rudolf (1218–91)
King (1273–91)

Albert the
One-Eyed (d. 1308)
King (1298–1308)

Rudolf
(d. 1290)

Hartman
(d. 1281)

2 sons
(died in infancy)

6 daughters

John the Parricide
(d. 1313)

Rudolf (c. 1282–1307)
King of Bohemia (1306–7)

Frederick the Fair
(1289–1330)

Albert the Lame
(1298–1358)

3 further sons
and 5 daughters

Rudolf the Founder
(1339–65)

3 further sons
and 2 daughters

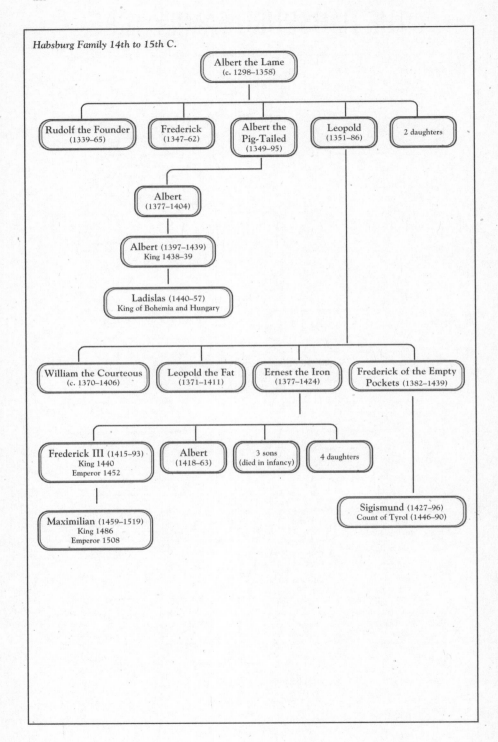

Habsburg Family 14th to 15th C.

Albert the Lame (c. 1298–1358)

Rudolf the Founder (1339–65) — Frederick (1347–62) — Albert the Pig-Tailed (1349–95) — Leopold (1351–86) — 2 daughters

Albert (1377–1404)

Albert (1397–1439) King 1438–39

Ladislas (1440–57) King of Bohemia and Hungary

William the Courteous (c. 1370–1406) — Leopold the Fat (1371–1411) — Ernest the Iron (1377–1424) — Frederick of the Empty Pockets (1382–1439)

Frederick III (1415–93) King 1440 Emperor 1452 — Albert (1418–63) — 3 sons (died in infancy) — 4 daughters

Maximilian (1459–1519) King 1486 Emperor 1508

Sigismund (1427–96) Count of Tyrol (1446–90)

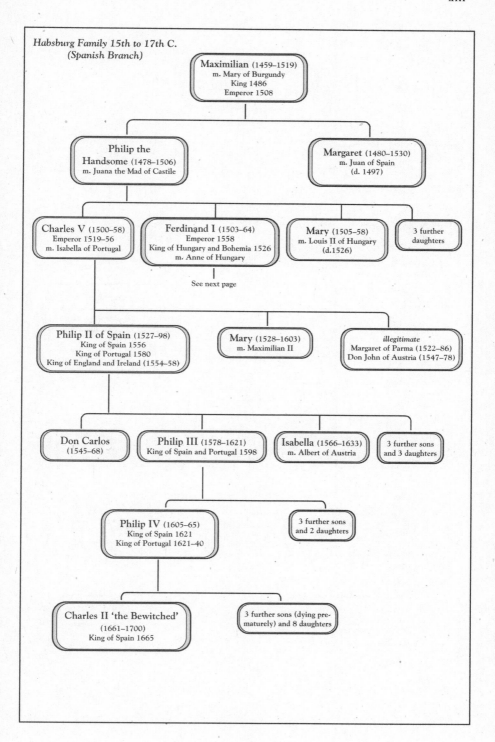

Habsburg Family 15th to 17th C.
(Spanish Branch)

Maximilian (1459–1519)
m. Mary of Burgundy
King 1486
Emperor 1508

Philip the Handsome (1478–1506)
m. Juana the Mad of Castile

Margaret (1480–1530)
m. Juan of Spain
(d. 1497)

Charles V (1500–58)
Emperor 1519–56
m. Isabella of Portugal

Ferdinand I (1503–64)
Emperor 1558
King of Hungary and Bohemia 1526
m. Anne of Hungary

Mary (1505–58)
m. Louis II of Hungary
(d.1526)

3 further daughters

See next page

Philip II of Spain (1527–98)
King of Spain 1556
King of Portugal 1580
King of England and Ireland (1554–58)

Mary (1528–1603)
m. Maximilian II

illegitimate
Margaret of Parma (1522–86)
Don John of Austria (1547–78)

Don Carlos (1545–68)

Philip III (1578–1621)
King of Spain and Portugal 1598

Isabella (1566–1633)
m. Albert of Austria

3 further sons and 3 daughters

Philip IV (1605–65)
King of Spain 1621
King of Portugal 1621–40

3 further sons and 2 daughters

Charles II 'the Bewitched'
(1661–1700)
King of Spain 1665

3 further sons (dying prematurely) and 8 daughters

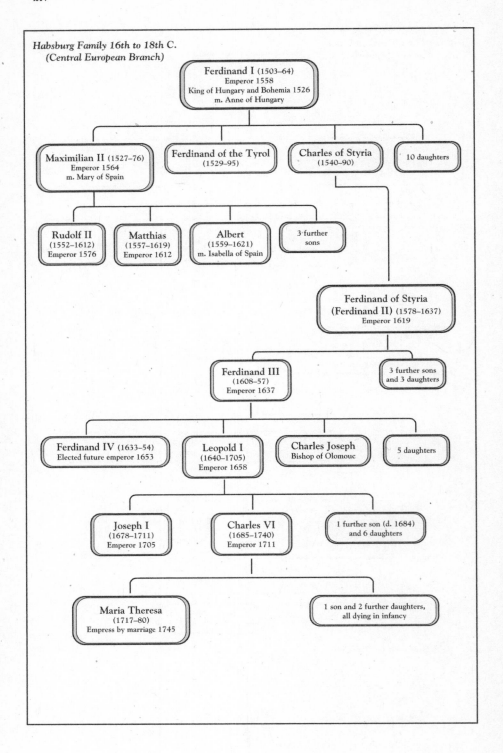

Habsburg Family 16th to 18th C.
(Central European Branch)

Ferdinand I (1503–64)
Emperor 1558
King of Hungary and Bohemia 1526
m. Anne of Hungary

Maximilian II (1527–76)
Emperor 1564
m. Mary of Spain

Ferdinand of the Tyrol
(1529–95)

Charles of Styria
(1540–90)

10 daughters

Rudolf II
(1552–1612)
Emperor 1576

Matthias
(1557–1619)
Emperor 1612

Albert
(1559–1621)
m. Isabella of Spain

3 further
sons

Ferdinand of Styria
(Ferdinand II) (1578–1637)
Emperor 1619

Ferdinand III
(1608–57)
Emperor 1637

3 further sons
and 3 daughters

Ferdinand IV (1633–54)
Elected future emperor 1653

Leopold I
(1640–1705)
Emperor 1658

Charles Joseph
Bishop of Olomouc

5 daughters

Joseph I
(1678–1711)
Emperor 1705

Charles VI
(1685–1740)
Emperor 1711

1 further son (d. 1684)
and 6 daughters

Maria Theresa
(1717–80)
Empress by marriage 1745

1 son and 2 further daughters,
all dying in infancy

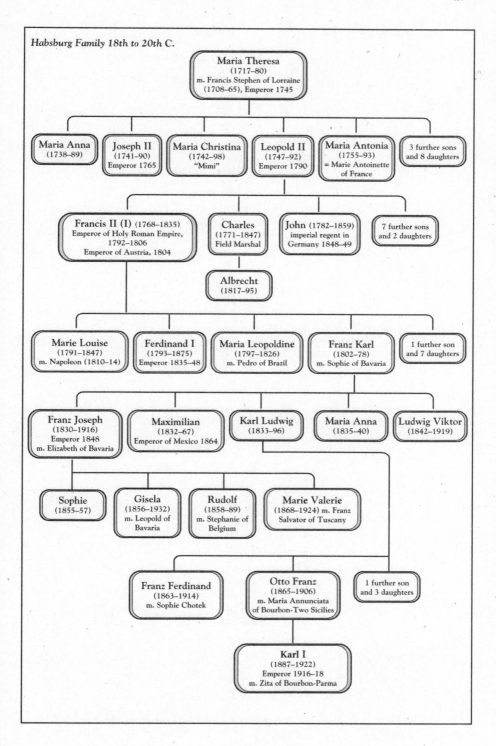

Habsburg Family 18th to 20th C.

Maria Theresa (1717–80) m. Francis Stephen of Lorraine (1708–65), Emperor 1745

- **Maria Anna** (1738–89)
- **Joseph II** (1741–90) Emperor 1765
- **Maria Christina** (1742–98) "Mimi"
- **Leopold II** (1747–92) Emperor 1790
- **Maria Antonia** (1755–93) = Marie Antoinette of France
- 3 further sons and 8 daughters

- **Francis II (I)** (1768–1835) Emperor of Holy Roman Empire, 1792–1806 Emperor of Austria, 1804
- **Charles** (1771–1847) Field Marshal
- **John** (1782–1859) imperial regent in Germany 1848–49
- 7 further sons and 2 daughters

- **Albrecht** (1817–95)

- **Marie Louise** (1791–1847) m. Napoleon (1810–14)
- **Ferdinand I** (1793–1875) Emperor 1835–48
- **Maria Leopoldine** (1797–1826) m. Pedro of Brazil
- **Franz Karl** (1802–78) m. Sophie of Bavaria
- 1 further son and 7 daughters

- **Franz Joseph** (1830–1916) Emperor 1848 m. Elizabeth of Bavaria
- **Maximilian** (1832–67) Emperor of Mexico 1864
- **Karl Ludwig** (1833–96)
- **Maria Anna** (1835–40)
- **Ludwig Viktor** (1842–1919)

- **Sophie** (1855–57)
- **Gisela** (1856–1932) m. Leopold of Bavaria
- **Rudolf** (1858–89) m. Stephanie of Belgium
- **Marie Valerie** (1868–1924) m. Franz Salvator of Tuscany

- **Franz Ferdinand** (1863–1914) m. Sophie Chotek
- **Otto Franz** (1865–1906) m. Maria Annunciata of Bourbon-Two Sicilies
- 1 further son and 3 daughters

- **Karl I** (1887–1922) Emperor 1916–18 m. Zita of Bourbon-Parma

A NOTE ON NAMES

All names of places are given by reference to their current names in use. The exception is Budapest, where Buda and Pest are used separately up until 1873, when the two cities merged.

The names of people follow no consistent scheme. Generally, the names given are the ones most often used in the current historical literature—so Archduke Ludwig but Archduke John. Where there is no consensus, names have been anglicized. The German *-f* ending in proper names has generally been rendered *-ph*.

Introduction

AN EMPEROR'S LIBRARY

T
he Hofburg was the winter palace of the Habsburgs and is now Vienna's main tourist attraction. Horse-drawn carriages take sightseers through its arches and along the narrow streets of the neighbouring old city. Crowds press through tight alleys, spilling carelessly into the traffic when they spot the white noses of the Lipizzaner horses in their stables. Apart from the green-domed St Michael's wing, built in the nineteenth century, the palace exterior is unimpressive, comprising consecutive courtyards, now used as carparks, with surrounding facades in a generally subdued Baroque style.

At least today's Hofburg is in good repair. Photographs and lantern slides from the time before 1918, when it was still a 'working palace', show fallen masonry, cracked walls, and broken windows. For much of its history, the Hofburg has been a building site. Successive emperors added on wings, tore down obstacles to improvement, and rebuilt in stone rather than wood. Until the late seventeenth century, the Hofburg was also integral to the city's defences and rested against one of Vienna's bastioned walls. The Ottoman Turks last set siege to the city in 1683. With their defeat, it was finally possible for Habsburg emperors to conceive of the Hofburg as a palace and ceremonial stage and not as a fortified residence.

At the heart of the Hofburg is the so-called Old Fort (Alte Burg). The reconstruction of the palace in the late seventeenth and eighteenth centuries has built over it so that little trace of the original fabric of the Old Fort is visible today. Put up in the first half of the thirteenth century, the Old Fort was a massive stone keep, 50 metres (160 feet) square, with four towers, each topped with high-gabled roofs and finials. Despite its size, the interior of the Old Fort was bleak. Visitors complained of the courtyard within, which was insufficiently broad for a cart to turn, of the cramped chambers, mouldy staircases, and lack of tapestries on the walls. But the purpose of the Hofburg's Old Fort was not to impress by the luxury of its accommodation. It was intended to overawe the city and countryside beyond and to communicate a message of power.[1]

The Old Fort became the first Habsburg emblem. In origin the Habsburgs were a Central European dynasty and Austria was their heartland. But in the sixteenth and seventeenth centuries, they were also rulers of Spain and of Spain's possessions in the Low Countries, Italy, and the New World. Although by then militarily obsolete, the design of the Old Fort was reproduced in the great castles that the Habsburgs either commissioned or rebuilt in Spain—in Toledo and Madrid—and it was carried to the Americas. In Mexico, the block house with four towers was a mark of the power wielded by the first royal governors—lesser men had to be content with just two towers. In the Holy Roman Empire, over which the Habsburgs ruled as emperors, and which is very roughly where Austria, Germany, and the Czech Republic are today, ambitious princes also built four-tower keeps, as a way of communicating their own prestige.[2]

The Habsburgs were the first rulers whose power encompassed the world, and they achieved greatness by luck and by force. The four-tower keep was in the sixteenth century an expression of their physical mastery of a part of Europe and, by its reproduction overseas, evidence of their global dominion. But it was only one symbol among many that the Habsburgs deployed, for they conceived of their power as both something that they had been predestined for and part of the divine order in which the world was arranged. This required a subtler symbolism than a threat in stone.

The rebuilding of the Hofburg in the early eighteenth century, which saw the Old Fort finally disappear from the horizon, included the construction of the Court Library (Hofbibliothek). Previously, the imperial library had been housed in an abandoned friary in Vienna, in the wing of a private palace, and in a wooden structure in the shadow of the Old Fort (on today's Josefsplatz). The librarians complained of the damp, the dust from the street, the inadequate lighting, and the fire hazard. But it was only during the long reign of Charles VI (1711–1740) that the Imperial Library found a permanent home on a space immediately south of what had been the Old Fort.[3]

The new library building was put up in the 1720s, and it remains much the same today, as Emperor Charles VI intended. Some two hundred thousand books and manuscripts were shelved in a single hall, 75 metres (250 feet) long. By this time, the collection included works on theology, church history, law, philosophy, science, and mathematics, and bound manuscripts written in Greek, Latin, Syriac, Armenian, and Coptic. Charles opened his library to scholars, although they had to apply for permission, and visiting hours were restricted to mornings. In return for this act of generosity, Charles imposed a tax on newspapers. Originally temporary, to cover the cost of building, the tax soon became permanent, being ostensibly dedicated to future acquisitions. Printers were also expected to furnish the library with copies of every book they produced. Since many Viennese printers also dealt in pornography, this was an obligation that was often shirked.[4]

In the centre of the library stands a life-size marble statue of Charles VI, portrayed as Hercules of the Muses. The domed ceiling above depicts his apotheosis or elevation to the heavens and celebrates his achievements with allegorical figures. Unlike George Washington, whose apotheosis is shown on the rotunda of the United States Capitol Building, no portrait of Emperor Charles stares down at us from the ceiling. Charles was still alive when the artist began work and so not yet received in heavenly glory. But a floating figure bearing a laurel crown waits for him, leaving us in no doubt that Charles will at his life's end be received in the company of the angels and will sit among them in the clouds.

The marble statue of Charles VI was joined on the floor of the library by sixteen statues of Habsburg emperors, kings, and archdukes, starting with the thirteenth-century King Rudolf and finishing with Charles II of Spain, who died in 1700. Marble statues are expensive items to commission, so most were taken from the Hofburg's store rooms and gardens. Over time, they were added to and swapped with statues in other imperial palaces. The earliest historian of the Court Library was critical of the original selection, for he considered too many of the sixteen statues to recall Habsburg rulers who had shown no special interest in study or learning. Clearly, he imagined that a library should have something to do with books and scholarship. But this was a Court Library, and its purpose was different: to make a statement about the Habsburgs and their place in the divine ordering of the universe.[5]

The entire decoration of the library, including its ceiling, wall frescoes, and furniture, speaks to the greatness of the Habsburgs and to their limitless power. So the four large globes of the earth and heavens that stand beneath the central cupola are metaphors for the reach of Habsburg ambition. Each bookcase is flanked by double pillars, and the motif of the twin pillars is evident throughout the library's construction, most notably in the white marble and gilt columns at each end of the hall as well as on the building's exterior facade. They stand for the Pillars of Hercules and the Habsburg watchword 'Still Further', and thus for a dominion that was unconstrained by physical geography. Above, in the fresco of the apotheosis, are three classical goddesses, who bear a banner on which is written AEIOU. The acrostic can stand for many things, and scholars have suggested that there may be as many as three hundred different solutions and combinations. But all of them point to the greatness of the Habsburgs of Austria—hence in the acrostic's most common reading, 'Austria is to rule the whole world' (in Latin, *Austria Est Imperare Orbi Universae* or, in German, *Alles Erdreich Ist Österreich Untertan*).[6]

This was not, however, a vision of worldly dominion rooted in the exercise of political power and in physical coercion. Charles poses in his library as the patron of the sciences and arts, not as a warrior bent on conquest. The apotheosis celebrates Charles's virtues—his magnanimity, fame, splendour, and steadfastness. His martial victories are hinted at by showing the three-headed dog, Cerberus, crushed beneath the feet of Hercules, but otherwise Charles's military achievements are passed over. Even the frescoes on the theme of war are understated, extolling its opposites—harmony, order, and knowledge. Above all else, Charles intended to be celebrated as the author of peace and promoter of learning. The trompe l'oeil beneath the rotunda shows realistic figures in conversation, with each cluster representing one of the branches of knowledge to which Charles had brought life—anatomy, archaeology, botany, hydraulics, heraldry, numismatics, and even gnomonology, which is the art of making sundials.

The same historian who imagined that a library should be for books also considered the rotunda and frescoes to be an allegory of a library. It may well be, but allegories in the Baroque Age often contained several hidden messages. With its statues of Habsburg emperors and champions, the repetitive double pillars, and the artfully placed globes, the library and its furnishings are also an allegory of the unlimited and timeless dominion of the Habsburg dynasty. But, the frescoes tell us, the world for which the dynasty strives is not only to be found in the bonds of earth but also in the transcendent world of knowledge and scholarly endeavour. Like the acrostic AEIOU, no single solution explained the complexity of the Habsburg mission or exhausted its possibilities.[7]

The Habsburgs' idea of their role in the world was built up gradually, with different episodes in the dynasty's history yielding new aspirations, all of which were woven together in a single skein of ideological assumptions. It was first conceived in religious terms. Back in the thirteenth century, King Rudolf of Habsburg (reigned 1273–1291) was known as a sacker of churches and despoiler of nunneries. But just two or three decades after his death, the tale circulated that Rudolf had one day chanced upon a priest hastening to bring the Host (Holy Communion or eucharist) to a dying man and had given him his horse. The story was repeated and embellished over the succeeding centuries, so that in recompense for his horse Rudolf received an earthly crown, with the eucharistic bread and wine now mystically anointing him at his coronation. Biblical passages were also seized upon to show that in return for speeding the Host on its way, Rudolf's heirs would themselves be nourished by the eucharist in accordance with a divine plan first explained in the Old Testament.[8]

Veneration of the Host lay at the centre of the Habsburg dynasty's religious observance, being played out in processions, pilgrimages, and church festivals. Any hurrying priest spotted by a Habsburg was likely to have a horse or carriage forced upon him. During the religious struggles of the sixteenth and seventeenth centuries, the meaning and significance of the eucharist was disputed by Protestants. The exaggerated respect for the Host demonstrated by successive Habsburg rulers stood as a symbol of their dedication to the Catholic Church and of their continued service as divine instruments on earth. Even in the final years of the Habsburg Empire, the association of the dynasty with the eucharist endured, being recalled not only in ritual observance but also in more mundane contexts. When asked in 1912 to provide a trophy for a Swiss rifle club, Emperor Franz Joseph sent a figurine of Rudolf dismounting from his horse to speed the priest's journey.[9]

The Habsburgs were intermittently rulers of the Holy Roman Empire after 1273 and almost continuously so from 1438 until the empire's demise in 1806. The Holy Roman Empire had been founded by Charlemagne in 800 CE but was considered the continuation of the Roman Empire of classical antiquity. To begin with, it was known simply as 'the Roman Empire'— the adjective 'Holy' was added in the thirteenth century, but there was never much consistency in usage. The Holy Roman Empire was reconstituted in the tenth century as a largely German empire, but this did not diminish the prestige attaching to the imperial title. The emperor continued to be seen as the direct successor of the Roman emperors of antiquity, as being in some way the counterpart of the pope in Rome, and as possessed of an authority that marked him out as superior to all other monarchs. Medieval prophecies that foretold an impending war between the angels and the devil's apprentice, the Antichrist, and of how 'the last emperor' would usher in a millennium of godly rule, added to the lustre of the imperial office. On this the Habsburgs built, extolling their future role in the imminent apocalypse. Emperor Maximilian I (ruled as king 1486–1508, as emperor 1508–1519) had his portrait duly painted to give him the reputed features of the last emperor, whom prophecies foretold would have 'a lofty forehead, high eyebrows, wide eyes, and an aquiline nose.'[10]

The last emperor was expected not only to take on the Antichrist but also to vanquish the Turks, liberate Istanbul (Constantinople) from their clutches, and free the holy city of Jerusalem from Muslim rule. Successive emperors advertised their commitment to a crusade against the infidel, by which they might not only fulfil prophecy but also demonstrate their leadership of Christendom and dedication to the ideals of Christian knighthood. In the Habsburg imagination, the war against the unbeliever was joined in the sixteenth century to a war against misbelief. Successive Habsburg emperors and rulers cracked down on the spread of Protestant doctrines, which challenged the authority of the Catholic Church. In the religious observance of the Spanish Habsburgs, the mission to cleanse the faith was as much marked by the choreographed burning of heretics as by ostentatious dedication to the eucharist.

As part of the general renewal of learning and the arts known as the Renaissance, the study of classical texts intensified in the fifteenth and sixteenth centuries. Renaissance literary scholars or humanists looked back to ancient Rome for inspiration and guidance. Many borrowed from Roman antiquity the belief in a hierarchically arranged order, headed by an emperor, whose task was to mediate between rulers and usher in a reign of peace. Humanists often saw the Habsburgs as uniquely gifted by the office of emperor to restore order and harmony. They spoke thus of a 'world empire' and 'universal monarchy', shepherded by Habsburg rulers, and they recast classical epics to portray Habsburg emperors in the manner of Roman Caesars. To reinforce their message, they also included elaborate speeches by classical gods which referred to a Habsburg destiny and described how Habsburg rulers were invested with shields that bore maps of the whole known world.[11]

Erasmus of Rotterdam, the greatest of Renaissance humanists, had no time for this erudite nonsense. Observing that 'kings and fools are born, not made', he foresaw that a universal monarch was likely to be a universal tyrant—'the enemy of all and all are his enemies.' But the Habsburgs came close to realizing the 'world monarchy' that Erasmus feared. The imperial office was elective, with the emperor chosen by seven leading princes of the Holy Roman Empire. Besides being Holy Roman Emperors, however, the Habsburgs ruled provinces and territories within the empire by hereditary right, as their own private possessions rather than ones that fell beneath their sway because they were emperors. To begin with, these private, family dominions were in the area of the Upper Rhine, but by the thirteenth century, the Habsburgs were amassing a body of lands in Central Europe, roughly where Austria and Slovenia are today. Then, in a period of just half a century, beginning in the 1470s, the Habsburg lands exploded outwards— to take in the Low Countries, Spain, Bohemia, Hungary, and most of Italy. Hungary, which was an independent kingdom and, unlike Bohemia, not a part of the Holy Roman Empire, extended Habsburg power 450 miles (700 kilometres) eastwards to what is now Ukraine. But Spain was an even greater prize, for along with it came the New World and a colonial enterprise that looked to the Pacific Ocean and Asia. The Habsburg dominions were the first empire on which the sun never set.[12]

The official title of Emperor Charles V in 1521 gives some idea of the spread of Habsburg possessions:

Charles, by the grace of God, elected Holy Roman Emperor, at all times Enlarger of the Empire etc., King in Germany, of Castile, Aragon, León, both Sicilies, Jerusalem, Hungary, Dalmatia, Croatia, Navarre, Granada, Toledo, Valencia, Galicia, the Balearic Islands, Seville, Sardinia, Cordoba,

Corsica, Murcia, Jaén, the Algarve, Algeciras, Gibraltar and the Canary Islands, and also the Islands of the Indies, and the mainland of the Ocean Sea etc; Archduke of Austria, Duke of Burgundy, Lorraine, Brabant, Styria, Carinthia, Carniola, Limburg, Luxembourg, Gelders, Württemberg, Calabria, Athens, Neopatras etc; Count of Flanders, Habsburg, the Tyrol, Gorizia, Barcelona, Artois, and Burgundy; Count Palatine of Hainaut, Holland, Zealand, Ferrette, Kiburg, Namur, Roussillon, Cerdagne, and Zutphen; Landgrave in Alsace; Margrave of Oristano, Goceano, and of the Holy Roman Empire; Prince of Swabia, Catalonia, Asturias etc; Lord in Friesland, on the Windisch Mark, of Pordenone, Vizcaya, Molins, Salins, Tripoli, and Mechlin etc.[13]

The list is a jumble and includes places that were no longer or never had been in the Habsburgs' possession (Jerusalem, Athens, and so on) but to which they continued to lay dubious claim. Others were added precisely because they were contested, but plenty more were left out as the succession of 'et ceteras' hints. Nevertheless, the itemized arrangement suggests a feature of Habsburg rule that would largely persist into the nineteenth and twentieth centuries. The parts were not unified but retained their own governments, laws, nobilities, patricians, and parliaments or diets. To that extent, they were almost independent countries, brought together only by the person of the ruler. Given the distances between the parts, disunity was to an extent inevitable, but it was also a deliberate act of policy that was intended to keep very different peoples reconciled to rule by an absent sovereign. As a Spanish jurist explained to Charles V (ruled as emperor 1519–1556), to maintain the loyalty of his dominions, he should treat them separately, 'as if the king who keeps them together were only the king of each.'[14]

The Habsburgs embraced a vast, all-encompassing vision of a world united under the ethereal sway of a single sovereign, who was dedicated to the service of religion, peace among Christians, and war against the unbeliever. But this was never converted into a political programme even within the territories that the Habsburgs ruled. All monarchies have started off as composite states, constructed from diverse territories, which were then welded together and made uniform. Even states built out of several kingdoms have tended, over time, to become more metropolitan, with the singularity of the constituent parts gradually effaced so that they lose their independent character and institutions. The Habsburgs never accomplished this—indeed, except for brief interludes, they never even really tried. Despite some unification of the administrative and legislative apparatus in the eighteenth and nineteenth centuries, their dominions continued to be ruled as if the sovereign were only the lord of each rather than a super-monarch with limitless authority. Whereas an eighteenth-century French sovereign was styled simply as 'king of France and Navarre', and not listed as duke of Aquitaine and Brittany, count of Toulouse, duke of Normandy, et cetera, right through to the twentieth century the Habsburg imperial style enumerated each part of the whole as a separate unit.

Historians write with the benefit of hindsight. Because they know the future to belong to the centralized nation state, political conglomerations which rest on principles of decentralization and dissimilarity must be bound to failure. 'Ramshackle', 'anachronistic', and 'accidental' are the terms they most frequently use to describe the later Habsburgs and their empire. But the Habsburgs cannot be judged so simply. Theirs was a vision woven of many strands, which looked beyond territory and intimidating stone keeps. It was, as Charles VI's library explains, rooted in complementary ideals and aspirations—in history and inheritance, in the Rome of the Caesars and of the Catholic faith, in beneficent leadership, and in a quest for knowledge, the immutable, and heavenly glory.

Of course, politics intruded, confounding the mystique of Habsburg monarchy and often rendering its manifestations redundant or banal. But something remained of the vision, even as the Habsburgs entered the last decades of their rule, little more than a century ago. It is the purpose of this book to explain their empire, their imagination as well as the ways in which they were imagined, and their purposes, projects, and failures. For half a millennium, from the fifteenth to the twentieth centuries, the Habsburgs counted among the most important dynasties of Europe, and for several centuries their dominions reached to the New World and beyond, making their empire the first global enterprise. What follows is partly their story, but it is partly, too, a reflection on what it meant for a Habsburg to rule the world.

1

CASTLE HABSBURG AND THE 'FORTINBRAS EFFECT'

*A*t the beginning of the last century, an unusually diligent student set himself the task of establishing the descent of Archduke Franz Ferdinand, who was at that time Emperor Franz Joseph's heir. The genealogy he established ran to thirty-three tables and listed more than 4,000 of Franz Ferdinand's ancestors, going back to the sixteenth century. On account of intermarriage, however, there were so many overlaps that the student found only 1,500 separate individuals, for many husbands were also cousins, and wives were often nieces several times over. So Franz Ferdinand was related to the sixteenth-century Emperor Ferdinand I through more than a hundred separate descents and to Ferdinand's distant cousin, the unmemorable but deeply pious Renate of Lorraine, by twenty-five.[1]

Dedicating his research to Franz Ferdinand, the student glossed over the extent of Habsburg intermarriage by demonstrating statistically that all the ruling families of Europe had in the past been equally incestuous. He also apologized that he had been unable to take his investigations further back into the Middle Ages. But had he tried to track the archduke's descent back to the eleventh century, he would have had to fill in the names of several hundred thousand ancestors, for every generation back yields double the number of forebears. Even so, our student's task would in some ways have been made easier the further back he dug, for the written record becomes correspondingly sparser and the blanks accumulate. By the tenth century, the ancestry of the Habsburgs contracts from, in theory, the hundreds of thousands to, in practice, just a few shadowy individuals.

Books on early Habsburg history often read like mystery thrillers, with speculations that trace a Habsburg bloodline back through the shadowy Etichonid family of Alsatian counts to the French Merovingian kings, whose mythical fifth-century progenitor was a quinotaur, or bull with five horns. In fact, the earliest Habsburgs can only be tracked back to the late tenth century, when they lived in the region of the Upper Rhine and Alsace, on the present border between France and Germany, and in the Aargau, in today's northern Switzerland. All this territory constituted a part of the Holy Roman Empire, belonging to the duchy of Swabia, and was divided into largely self-governing counties or *gaus*, each with several counts. The first Habsburg of whom we have definite knowledge was a certain Kanzelin (sometimes given as Lanzelin), who is associated in later accounts with a small fort at Altenburg, near the town of Brugg in the Swiss Aargau.[2]

On Kanzelin's death around 990, his two sons, Radbot (985–1045) and Rudolf, divided up his lands. Among Radbot's possessions was the village of Muri, twenty-five kilometres (fifteen miles) south of Altenburg. Upon his marriage, Radbot gave Muri as a wedding gift to his bride, Ita (Idda), who in 1027 founded there an abbey of Benedictine monks. Ita's piety was rewarded with a resting place next to the altar of the abbey church. Notwithstanding the sack of the abbey by Protestant Berne in 1531, Ita's grave survives to this day. She is joined there in death by the partial presence of the last Habsburg emperor and empress, Karl and Zita, whose hearts are kept in urns in a chapel by the altar. Since it was not allowed to be returned to Austria after the First World War, the rest of Karl's body is on the Portuguese island of Madeira, where he died in 1922, although Zita's is in the Capuchin Crypt in Vienna.

The abbey at Muri prospered from the generosity of the faithful and of its founders. It accumulated property in more than forty neighbouring villages as well as a treasury of relics, which included the bones of over a hundred saints and martyrs as well as fragments of the True Cross, of the tablets on which the Ten Commandments had been written, and of the pillar beside which Pontius Pilate had judged Christ. Radbot and Ita's descendants considered all this, however, to be their own. Established and made rich by their family, the abbey counted as a 'proprietary monastery'—a place of burial where masses were said for their forebears and over which they appointed an abbot of their choosing. They also assumed the duties of protector or *Vogt* (sometimes rendered as 'steward' or 'advocate'), in return for which they extracted an income from the abbey.[3]

Radbot's son, Werner (1025–1096), later called 'the Pious', was alert to the new trends in monastic life emanating from the great abbeys of Cluny and Hirsau, which favoured obedience, continuous prayer, and disengagement from the world. Disappointed by the brothers of Muri, who (we are told) came and went as they pleased, Werner brought to Muri disciplined monks from the Black Forest to set an example. But Werner's reverent act backfired. The monastic reform movement was never concerned only with monkish morals. It also stressed the right of ecclesiastical superiors to oversee religious houses, and it opposed the practice of having laymen treat monasteries as their own private property. This directly affected the interests of Werner, who foresaw that he would lose all control over a monastery in whose foundation his family had invested.[4]

During the mid-1080s, Werner forged a charter, which he pretended had been written six decades earlier by his uncle (or possibly, great-uncle), Bishop Werner of Strasbourg. The charter gave its alleged author, the bishop, credit for founding the abbey and vested the office of Vogt in perpetuity in his family. The fake charter was recorded at an assembly of the principal men of the Aargau and later confirmed in Rome by the College of Cardinals. To add credence to their story, a group of monks loyal to Werner composed a necrology, which listed the dead for whom masses should be said. The necrology highlighted in red Bishop Werner but omitted Ita entirely. The foundation of the abbey was thus linked not to Ita but to the bishop and so, by implication, to the rights enumerated in the charter that had been forged in his name.[5]

The terms of the fake charter were approved in 1114 by the Holy Roman Emperor, Henry V. On this occasion, however, the emperor added the proviso that the abbey's protectors should neither profit from their duties nor interfere in the running of the abbey. From this point onwards, Werner's heirs were gradually stripped of their powers over the abbey. In order to make sure that they did not go off with the abbey's property in the meantime, the monks composed a detailed list of their lands and itemized their precious relics. They also put together an account of Muri's early history, which depicted its founding family as plunderers and thieves, who had given land to the abbey to relieve their guilty consciences. Although there may be some truth in the stories the monks of Muri told, their work fostered the belief that the earliest Habsburgs were no more than robber barons, who in one modern description 'rode across the countryside, murdering and looting.'[6]

Landowners founded monasteries as prayer factories where masses would be endlessly rehearsed to speed their souls through Purgatory. To protect themselves on this Earth they built castles. Whereas fortifications had in the past been mostly earthworks, the fashion from the eleventh century onwards was for keeps of wood and stone. Their purpose was to defend, dominate, and overawe the surrounding countryside, but castles also stood as symbols of the increasingly independent power of counts and lords. The Swiss Aargau had one of the densest concentrations of castles in medieval Europe. One late-nineteenth-century antiquary counted no fewer than seventy stone forts, most of which had their origin before 1300, in an area of just 1,400 square kilometres (550 square miles). The Aargau needed them, for its rich pastures and control over the roads leading through the Alps made it the prey of avaricious neighbours.[7]

Legend has it that Radbot was out hunting one day when he lost his favourite hawk. Searching for it, he came by chance on a rocky outcrop, next to the River Aare, on the very edge of his properties, which seemed an ideal site for a stronghold. Radbot named the fort that he built there the Habichtsburg or Hawk's Castle (in Old High German, a hawk is a *Habicht* or *Habuh*). This, in the contracted form of Habsburg, became its name and thus, over time, the toponymic embraced by Radbot's heirs. Centuries later, the tale of Radbot's hawk and of the castle's origins still excited the romantic imagination. The earliest English historian to write a history of the Habsburgs, Archdeacon William Coxe (1748–1828), ascribed his own inspiration to the sight of Castle Habsburg and likened himself to Edward Gibbon surveying the ruins of the Roman Forum.[8]

Set on a steep escarpment, Castle Habsburg is still an imposing structure, notwithstanding its conversion into a restaurant, with parasols on the battlements. The story, however, of Radbot's hawk is plainly borrowed from elsewhere. The name of Habichtsburg first occurs only in the 1080s. In origin, it probably had nothing to do with a hawk, but instead with a ford or *Hafen*, the castle being located close to a crossing point on the River Aare.

Moreover, 'Habsburg' in its various early forms (Havechisburg, Havichs-berg, Havesborc, and so forth) was only one of several places referred to in the family's preferred list of titles. Once the family began to accumulate properties elsewhere, reference to the Habsburg slid down the list, eventually to be lost in the thicket of the family's other properties and possessions. The name of Habsburg was revived only in the eighteenth century, at a time when it was fashionable to recall ancestral origins, and it became common currency with Schiller's popular historical ballad, 'The Count of Habsburg' (1803). Until that time, the only family to have consistently embraced the name of Habsburg were the earls of Denbigh from Warwickshire in England. Complete parvenus, they made up ambitious descents and cultivated spurious foreign titles in the hope of adding lustre to their name.[9]

Castle Habsburg was not a 'robbers' nest' but intended to be a home as much as a military stronghold. The original heart of the castle was a rectangular stone keep, measuring over eighteen metres by thirteen metres (sixty by forty feet), with walls almost two metres (six feet) thick at the base. Over this was later built a four-storey residence, which was connected on its north-eastern side to a square tower. In the late twelfth century, both the keep and the tower were surrounded by a long flanking wall, which served also to create a courtyard. A second tower was constructed around this time to the west of the main keep, which subsequently became the kernel of a separate complex, to which a hall and living quarters were attached. It is this more recent construction that tourists now visit, the rest consisting only of heaps of stones.

During the second half of the thirteenth century, the Habsburgs relinquished the castle, preferring the Lenzburg, which lay ten kilometres to the south. But they also had seats at Brugg, where Werner's great-grandson, Albert the Rich (died 1199), had previously built the so-called Black Tower (which survives) and later the hilltop castle at Baden in Aargau (which is a ruin). Both Brugg and Baden were preferable to Castle Habsburg as residences, since their proximity to marketplaces made their provisioning easier. Meanwhile, the old Castle Habsburg was assigned to vassals of the Habsburgs, being subsequently divided into two separate redoubts. It was finally captured by the city of Berne in 1415.

The Habsburg heartland lay around the confluence of the Aare, Limmat, and Reuss, all of which were in the Middle Ages navigable rivers. The region was also situated at a crossroads that connected the mountains of Inner Switzerland to the lowlands of the plain. The opening of the Alpine

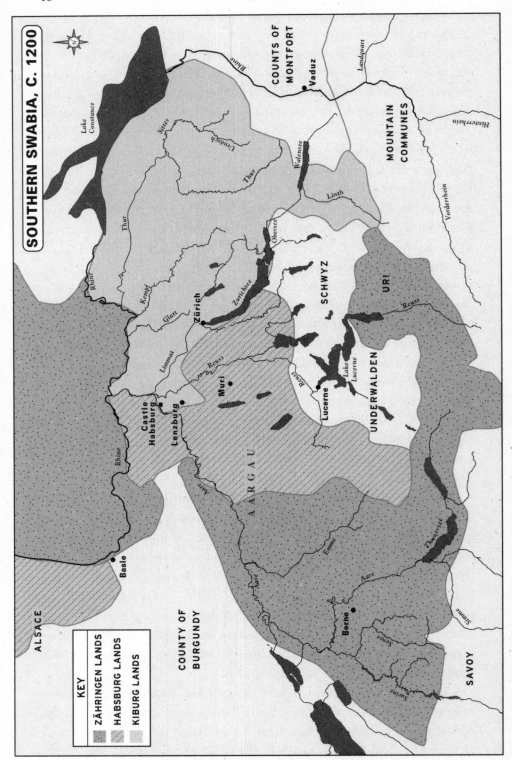

SOUTHERN SWABIA, C. 1200

KEY

ZÄHRINGEN LANDS

HABSBURG LANDS

KIBURG LANDS

COUNTS OF MONTFORT

MOUNTAIN COMMUNES

ALSACE

COUNTY OF BURGUNDY

SAVOY

SCHWYZ

URI

UNDERWALDEN

AARGAU

Vaduz

Zürich

Muri

Castle Habsburg

Lenzburg

Lucerne

Basle

Berne

Lake Constance

Walensee

Linth

Obersee

Zürichsee

Lake Lucerne

Thunersee

Landquart

Hinterrhein

Vorderrhein

Rhine

Sitter

Urnäsch

Thur

Thur

Rhine

Kempf

Glatt

Limmat

Reuss

Reuss

Reuss

Reuss

Aare

Aare

Aare

Emme

Sense

Sense

Sarne

Simme

Simme

St Gotthard Pass at the beginning of the thirteenth century drew the commerce of northern Italy through Lucerne and the Aargau to the great fairs of Champagne and Flanders. Altogether, the Habsburgs owned several dozen toll stations which milked this trade, which was at this time mostly in wool, cloth, metals, and fish. The table land of the Aargau was also agriculturally lush, and the peasants who worked its fields paid the Habsburgs rents, in cash and kind, as well as dues for rights to forage, milling, and pasture. Hence, from one early fourteenth-century register for a village close by Castle Habsburg, 'The two crofters at Windisch shall give annually as rent two pecks of rye each, making a bushel, two pigs, one of which shall be worth eight shillings and the other seven shillings, two lambs, each worth eighteen pennies, four hens and forty eggs.' (Twelve pennies make one shilling, and one bushel is sixty-five pints or thirty-five litres).[10]

Elsewhere on the Habsburg estates in the Aargau, the obligations of the peasants included a payment of three shillings to the lord 'for the wife's first night.' Nationalist historians need villains, and in Swiss accounts the Habsburgs have traditionally played the role. So much was later made of the three shillings by Swiss historians, who saw it as a demeaning tax levied upon them by their former Habsburg masters in lieu of a degrading sexual right. The *droit de seigneur* is, however, the prurient invention of later generations. The three shillings were simply a payment given upon marriage and no different from the Lenten gift that marked the end of Carnival. It was common enough elsewhere in the Swiss lands. In fact, Habsburg charges on the peasantry were seldom pursued with much vigour, and many lapsed over time. The crofters of Windisch were hardly burdened.[11]

By the thirteenth century, the bulk of Habsburg income derived from tolls, particularly those raised on the bridges at Baden and Brugg. Further income came from the administration of justice. In the register of properties and incomes drawn up at the start of the fourteenth century for the Habsburg estates, this was the right that was usually first enumerated—'to fine and compel, and to judge theft and violence.' Since fines and confiscations often went to the lord, this was an important source of revenue. With their wealth, the Habsburgs attracted other landowners into their service. In return for serving as vassals, they were given or allowed to build castles, which they held on behalf of their Habsburg overlords. By the fourteenth century, the Habsburgs had about thirty castles stretching from Lake Constance to the left bank of the Rhine and Alsace, to each of which were attached villages, manors, and farms. The Habsburgs were emphatically not the 'poor counts' of some historians' imagination.[12]

To begin with, the Habsburgs were just one of many lordly families in the Swiss Aargau. Historians usually attribute their rise to politics. In the twelfth century, they backed Emperor Lothar III (1125–1137) against his Staufen rivals, on account of which Lothar gave them a bundle of new properties in Upper Alsace as well as the prestigious title of landgrave. Then, in the middle of the century, the Habsburgs swung round to supporting the Staufen. Werner II, the grandson of the first Werner, died near Rome in 1167 while fighting for the Staufen emperor, Frederick I Barbarossa. His son, Albert the Rich, and his grandson, Rudolf the Old (also the Kind or Good, died 1232), supported respectively the claims of the Staufen heirs, Philip of Swabia and Frederick of Staufen. Rudolf later bankrolled Frederick's military campaign that resulted in Frederick taking power in the Holy Roman Empire in 1211, subsequently becoming Emperor Frederick II. Rewards followed—marriage into the Staufen line, Frederick II's gracious decision to stand as godfather to Rudolf the Old's grandson, and further swathes of territory in the south-west of the Holy Roman Empire.

The rise of the Habsburgs owed more, however, to what may be called 'the Fortinbras effect.' In the final scene of Shakespeare's *Hamlet*, all the protagonists lie dead, at which point Prince Fortinbras of Norway arrives to claim the vacant throne, to which he recalls 'some rights of memory.' Like Fortinbras, the Habsburgs swept up after everyone else had perished. During the twelfth and thirteenth centuries, they intermarried with the neighbouring lordly families in what is now Switzerland and south-western Germany. When their lines faltered, the Habsburgs claimed their own rights of memory, obtaining either fully or in part the vacant estates of the Lenzburg, Pfullendorf, and Homburg families. Although to begin with the Habsburgs took over only a part of the Lenzburg inheritance, the land obtained in the 1170s brought with it the title of count. Hitherto, the Habsburgs had only held the title honorifically.[13]

But the most significant addition to the Habsburg properties in the south-western part of the Holy Roman Empire came with the extinction of the Zähringen and the Kiburg lines in 1218 and 1264 respectively. The Zähringen were old foes of the Staufen, and their possessions were extensive, reaching from the Black Forest to Savoy. On the death without heir of the last duke, Berthold V, the Zähringen property was divided up. Much of it went to the Kiburgs by virtue of the previous marriage of Berthold's sister to a Kiburg. But in 1264, the Kiburgs also died out in the male line. Since his mother was a Kiburg, Count Rudolf of Habsburg (1218–1291), who was the grandson of Rudolf the Old, took the bulk of their patrimony, which lay between Zurich and Constance. With the Kiburg estates came the Zähringen lands and that part of the Lenzburg inheritance that the Habsburgs had missed out on a century before.

The territorial foundations of Habsburg power were weaker than a list of their acquisitions suggests. The family's properties and possessions were not contiguous but intersected by church lands and other lordly estates and by cities and free villages. Some Habsburg estates were pawned, while others were given over to servants and officials in place of an income. Rents and other dues had also been sold or farmed out in return for a lump sum. The complexities and changes in even small parts of the Habsburg lands make it hard to conceive of a uniform and unified lordship, for each fragment stood in a separate relationship to its Habsburg master. Even so, by the mid-thirteenth century the Habsburgs were the most powerful family in the duchy of Swabia. Their estates reached from Strasbourg to Lake Constance and from the Aare River to the wooded valleys of the Alps, so from what is now eastern France to Austria's western border, taking in a chunk of northern Switzerland. It was from this broad band of territory that Rudolf the Old's grandson, Count Rudolf, would launch the Habsburgs' most ambitious enterprise yet: to capture the Holy Roman Empire itself.[14]

The Habsburgs were lucky to have their heartland straddling the roadways and toll places that led from northern Italy to France. They were fortunate too in their political alliances. Yet behind the early growth of Habsburg power lay their genealogical endurance. As the diligent student of Franz Ferdinand's ancestry learned, the Habsburgs were survivors. Generation after generation, they produced heirs; if sons were missing, then cousins and nephews were always at hand. With longevity came the opportunity to take the wealth of the less-enduring families into which they had married. Over the centuries that followed, the Habsburgs would have equal biological good fortune and other Fortinbras moments of opportunity. 'Who talks of victories when to survive is all?' asked the Austrian poet Rainer Maria Rilke (1875–1926). In the case of the Habsburgs, it was their survival that brought their earliest victories.

2

THE HOLY ROMAN EMPIRE
AND THE GOLDEN KING

In 1184, Emperor Frederick I Barbarossa (ruled 1155–1190) built a toll tower at Kaiserswerth for the purpose of taxing more intensively the river traffic on the Rhine. He dedicated it with the inscription, 'Emperor Frederick built this splendour of the Empire to enlarge justice and bring peace to all.' A tax demand bearing such lofty sentiments would today be scorned, but Frederick's words tell us much about the way the Holy Roman Empire was understood at the time. It was not seen as a unified kingdom at all, but as an association of increasingly independent territories and cities, each of which had its own 'rights and freedoms.' The purpose of the empire was to provide the mechanisms and context whereby these rights and freedoms were protected so that, in accordance with the contemporary understanding of justice, 'to each be rendered his due.' Tolls justly levied by a just ruler amplified the good order that he was expected to promote. They were to be celebrated, in the same way as illegal tolls gathered by unscrupulous lords were to be deplored.[1]

The problem was that the Holy Roman Empire had no government with which to maintain each in their rights and freedoms. There was no central administration, no regular revenue, no capital city, and no hierarchy of courts dispensing a delegated justice on behalf of the ruler. Power rested instead with the great lords and princes, and it was they who elected the monarch as 'king of the Romans'—only when crowned by the pope did he become emperor. The lords, churchmen, and representatives of cities, who intermittently gathered in what were known as 'court assemblies' or 'court diets', found consensus difficult. They still looked to the ruler for leadership, but he lacked the capacity to coerce. To persuade, he often had to concede, making compromises that nibbled away at what little influence he had left. In one vivid description from the late thirteenth century, the emperor was shown no longer as the eagle that he bore on his coat of arms, but as just a woodpecker on a rotten tree.[2]

The solution was for the ruler to build up his private wealth in order to wield public power. Historians continue to criticize this policy, accusing successive emperors of establishing their own personal power bases and of ignoring the larger need. It was, however, precisely because they developed such extensive properties in Swabia that the Staufen rulers, of which Frederick Barbarossa was the first to become emperor, were able to exert influence. But the Staufen line of emperors also looked to make their mark in Italy and to establish a territorial base there. This brought them into conflict with the popes and with other contenders for Italy's riches. In his last dozen years as emperor, Frederick Barbarossa's grandson, Frederick II, was first excommunicated and then deposed by the pope. In the two decades following Frederick II's death in 1250, his son, bastard heir, and eldest grandson all perished in Italy—the last on the executioner's block in the square of Naples.

In the Great Interregnum that lasted from 1250 to 1273, all semblance of government evaporated. Since there was no agreement on who should succeed Frederick II, unlikely outsiders forced an entry. For reasons that even his latest biographer cannot fully explain, the Spanish Alfonso X of Castile put himself forward as ruler, but he never bothered to visit the empire. The rival Richard of Cornwall, younger son of England's King John, had the broad support of the three archbishops and of the dozen or so lay lords that chose him as their king in 1257. But his interest was to outmanoeuvre the last of the Staufens to make good the fantastical English claim to Sicily. Richard was effective on those four occasions on which he visited the empire, but he stayed too briefly to leave any lasting mark.[3]

The death of Frederick II in 1250 was followed by the wholesale destruction of the Staufen lands, offices, and revenues in Swabia. The Staufen possessions were invaded, and even the imperial lands that the Staufen rulers had held as emperors and not as family estates were seized. What was not taken was often given away by Frederick II's hard-pressed heirs. Plundering soon gave way to feuding as quarrels arose over the spoils. In the general free-for-all, properties that had never been part of the Staufen patrimony were grabbed, illegal tolls collected, and many minor landowners dispossessed. 'The days of evil approach, and the evil is growing,' wrote one chronicler about 1270. Across the pillaged countryside, processions of penitents moved, whipping themselves to appease God's wrath and rehearsing older heresies.[4]

Foremost among the beneficiaries of the collapse of the Staufens was Count Rudolf of Habsburg (lived 1218–1291). The grandson of Rudolf the Old, Count Rudolf inherited the main body of the Habsburg lands upon the death of his father, Albert the Wise, in 1239. Much he obtained with the semblance of legality, convincing Frederick II's heirs to assign him lands, revenues, and rights. Even so, he took advantage of the breakdown in authority to rob the widow of the last of the Kiburgs of her dowry. His greed earned him enemies, on which account Rudolf fought no fewer than eight feuds with his rivals. Although feuds were supposed to be conducted according to an etiquette, with days off and due concern shown for the vulnerable, Rudolf was, by his own admission, an insatiable warrior. The contemporary *Annals of Basle* give us a glimpse of him: in 1269, he slew some knights in Strasbourg; in 1270, he besieged Basle for three days; in 1271, he levied unprecedented taxes, burnt down a monastery, and seized villages; in 1272, he destroyed Tiefenstein Castle and marched on Freiburg, killing and burning the crops on the way; in 1273, he razed the village of Klingen, and so on.[5]

The death of Richard of Cornwall in 1272 gave the electors an opportunity to reconvene and begin at least to consider the restoration of order. Notwithstanding the crowded circumstances of Richard's election in 1257, it was generally held that there should be seven electors, but quite who they were was uncertain. Under intense pressure from Pope Gregory X, the leading lords of the empire agreed in advance that the vote should be unanimous, for a split threatened to throw the country into civil war. The problem was that there was no obvious candidate for the throne.

The most powerful prince in the Holy Roman Empire was the king of Bohemia, Ottokar II. He sought to become ruler of the Holy Roman Empire and considered that, since Bohemia was a part of the empire, he should have a vote for the next king of the Romans. But Ottokar was widely distrusted, and his Slavonic ancestry was invoked as a disqualification, on which account the duke of Bavaria took his place as an elector. Among the other great lords, there was not much interest in the office. For more than two centuries, the office of sovereign had been caught up with the politics of Swabia and the neighbouring duchy of Franconia, to such an extent that these two duchies were now considered synonymous with imperial affairs. Brandenburg and the Saxon duchies were remote from this heartland, and their rulers preoccupied with their own affairs and with expansion eastwards. The Wittelsbach dukes of Bavaria and the Palatinate were brothers, who were sufficiently at odds to sabotage each other's interests.[6]

There was no-one, therefore, among the electors with either the interest or support to muster a unanimous vote. Rudolf of Habsburg seized the opportunity. His interest was precisely the one that dissuaded others: the connection between the imperial office and the south-western part of the Holy Roman Empire, into which the Habsburgs were already expanding. But there was more to his ambition than just territorial politics. As the godson of Emperor Frederick II, Rudolf considered himself next in line to the throne, now that all of Frederick's natural heirs had died. He was, moreover, the greatest lord in Swabia, which was the home of the Staufen rulers, and thus uniquely qualified to pursue the succession. In this respect, he stood not as an outsider but as the 'continuity candidate.'[7]

As far as the electors were concerned, Rudolf was a good choice. He was already fifty-five years old and so an improbable threat in the long term. Having pilfered from the Staufen lands, Rudolf was unlikely to demand that the lands that the other great lords had seized be returned. Cynical considerations aside, Rudolf looked the part. He was tall—one account gives his height at seven feet, at a time when the German *Fuss* was slightly longer than today's British foot (30.48 cm)—and his appearance was distinctive. As one jibe put it, his nose was long enough to obstruct the traffic. Moreover, at a time when most princes only talked about going on crusade, Rudolf had actually taken the cross, fighting during the 1250s in the fastnesses along the Baltic shore against the pagan Prussians (albeit as penance for having burnt down a nunnery). Rudolf was elected in Aachen on 29 September 1273 and crowned the next month with the royal diadem.[8]

Contemporaries recorded several scores of anecdotes about Rudolf, pointing to his wit, courage, piety, and wisdom. Doubtless, many of these emanated from Rudolf's propaganda, but they hint at a man of exuberant character, who was the very reverse of how his tame clerks chose to depict him—'as moderate in his eating and drinking and in all things.' The most important lesson he had learned from a lifetime of soldiering and rapine, however, was patience and strategy, in which respect it may be no accident that he also played chess. The speech he gave immediately after his coronation in Aachen was a masterpiece of contrived modesty: 'Today, I forgive all those wrongs that have been done to me, release the prisoners suffering in my gaols, and I promise from now on to be a defender of peace in the land, just as I was before a rapacious man of war.'[9]

Rudolf was so far only a king. To become emperor, he needed to be crowned by the pope in Rome. Even so, Rudolf spoke in elevated terms of 'We and the Empire', and he added to his title the phrase that would remain a part of the ruler's style until the nineteenth century—'forever an enlarger of the Empire.' Rudolf also stuck pretty much true to his coronation address. He settled his feuds, albeit on terms advantageous to himself, and joined with the cities of the Rhineland to eliminate the brigands' nests in the Rhine valley. The ruins of Sooneck Castle, near Rüdesheim, although partly rebuilt in the neo-Gothic style of the nineteenth century, still bear witness to the order he brought; likewise the legend of how Rudolf hanged the robber knights of nearby Reichenstein, with the wood from their gallows being recycled to build a chapel, where masses were said for their souls.[10]

No less significant was Rudolf's reorganization of the administration in the service of order. Many rulers had previously proclaimed a 'peace of the land', prohibiting all violence, and had ordained harsh penalties for any violation. Few, however, had established adequate mechanisms to police it, with the result that feuding and the 'law of the fist' had soon returned. Rudolf, however, linked the peace of the land to the appointment of 'protectors of the land' or *Landvogts*, who were charged with maintaining order by military means. In order to provide the cash for them, Rudolf ordered in 1274 a general tax on all the cities of the empire, which he repeated eight years later. The division of the empire into regions, each of which was responsible for maintaining a local peace, prefigured what became after 1500 the system of 'imperial circles' and of an institution of law enforcement that would last until the nineteenth century.[11]

The *Landvogts* were not only charged with the maintenance of order but with the recovery of all imperial lands that had been given away after 1245.

The policy, backed up by force, was implemented with moderate success in Swabia and neighbouring Franconia. The properties so recovered went straight to Rudolf, since he, as king, was considered their rightful owner. Rudolf, however, neither relinquished the imperial lands that he had merged into his own private domain nor surrendered the other territories that he had seized illegally. Nor did he think it worthwhile to inflame relations with the Wittelsbach dukes of Bavaria and the Palatinate by obliging them to disgorge the properties that they had seized.[12]

The programme of recovering the lost imperial lands extended to legal rights and entitlements. None had infringed upon these more than King Ottokar of Bohemia (lived circa 1232–1278). While still heir apparent to the Bohemian throne, Ottokar had occupied the duchy of Austria, which had fallen vacant upon the death in 1246 of the last of the Babenberg line, Duke Frederick II. Ottokar had rested his claim upon the invitation of the Austrian nobility, and it does seem that he had a good measure of support in the duchy. To cement his rule, Ottokar married Duke Frederick's sister, Margaret. Margaret had form. She had previously been married to the son of Emperor Frederick II, the leper Henry, and upon widowhood had become a nun, but she had relinquished the cloister to argue her own claim to the dukedom of Austria. Nearly fifty, she was almost thirty years older than Ottokar. Besides the obvious problem that no heir could come of their union, Ottokar had a further difficulty. As an imperial fief, Austria should have reverted to the crown upon the expiry of the Babenberg line and been apportioned to whomever the ruler chose. Notwithstanding the decision of the Austrian nobles and his own marriage, the duchy did not belong to Ottokar.

In the decades that followed, Ottokar extended his rule to Styria, which had previously been occupied by the Hungarian king, and to the neighbouring duchies of Carinthia and Carniola, both of which he claimed by a dubious right of inheritance. He also became king of Bohemia in 1253 upon the death of his father. The issue of the Babenberg inheritance remained, however, unresolved. Richard of Cornwall had in 1262 recognized Ottokar as the rightful heir, but Richard's rule was contested, and what little influence remained to him vanished after his final departure for England in 1269. Moreover, Ottokar had after a few years of marriage repudiated Margaret and taken instead as his wife a sixteen-year-old Hungarian princess. The toothsome Kunigunda gave Ottokar the heir he wanted but was of no value in prosecuting Ottokar's rights to Austria.

Ottokar was not only a usurper but also dangerous. In terms of territory, he was foremost in the empire, ruling a bloc of lands that reached across its eastern flank. His wealth was prodigious, being mostly derived from his Bohemian mines and from the lucrative mints he owned. His treasure lay, according to a contemporary account, piled up in four strong castles, and amounted to no less than two hundred thousand silver marks and eight hundred golden marks, held in coin, plate, and jewel-encrusted goblets. Ottokar's annual income from Bohemia is further estimated at around a hundred thousand silver marks, to which may be added an equivalent sum from his Austrian possessions. To put these figures in context, the entire income of the archbishop of Cologne amounted at this time to fifty thousand silver marks and of the duke of Bavaria to twenty thousand of the same. The imperial revenues consisted then of just seven thousand silver marks. Rudolf's celebrated remark that he had no need to employ an imperial treasurer because all he had was five shillings in bad coin was not entirely fanciful, nor the contemporary description of Ottokar as 'the Golden King.'[13]

Like Rudolf, Ottokar had also taken the cross—not once but twice— and the crusading Teutonic Knights of the north had named in his honour the city he helped found on the Baltic shore, Königsberg (literally 'King's Mountain', now Kaliningrad in Russia). For Ottokar, Rudolf was a nobody who was unworthy of the royal title—and Ottokar did not hesitate to tell the pope so. Ottokar had opposed Rudolf's election and continued to claim that it was illegal, since he had been denied a vote. Publicly, Ottokar flaunted his ambition, imitating in the style of his correspondence the forms of imperial charters and using the imperial eagle as one of his own devices. Although Bohemia was, like Austria, a fief of the empire, Ottokar ignored this, proclaiming that he held power not of the ruler but 'by the grace of God, by whom kings reign and princes rule.'[14]

Rudolf outmanoeuvred Ottokar. He reconciled himself with his enemies, binding them to him by marriages to his daughters, of whom he had no fewer than six to spare. He also presented Ottokar's actions as a slight not against him but against the dignity of the Holy Roman Empire. Shortly after his election as king, Rudolf persuaded a court diet to condemn Ottokar's retention of land that belonged by right to the empire. When Ottokar refused to submit to the diet's decision, he was put under a ban of outlawry, which in the contemporary description reduced him to the status of a wild bird (*Vogelfrei*)—to be cared for by nobody, forced to dwell in the woods, and even killed at will. To press home the point, the archbishop of Mainz excommunicated Ottokar, absolved his subjects of their oaths of allegiance to him, and forbade the celebration of the sacraments in Bohemia. Throughout Ottokar's kingdom, religious life came to a halt.[15]

Rudolf bided his time, enlarging the number of his allies and fomenting rumours—that the pope had also excommunicated the Golden King; that Ottokar had banished his ten-year-old daughter to a nunnery to prevent her marrying one of Rudolf's sons; that a hermit had dreamt of a sphinx, which had prophesied Ottokar's imminent defeat, and so on. Finally, in the late summer of 1276, Rudolf struck, attacking down the Danube and not into Bohemia, as Ottokar had expected. Faced with rebellions at home and with his enemies already in Vienna, Ottokar capitulated. A contemporary chronicle describes how Ottokar, resplendent in his finery, submitted to Rudolf. Rudolf received the Golden King dressed only in the cheapest clothing, saying, 'Often has he mocked my grey mantle, let him mock it now!' Ottokar prostrated himself before Rudolf, who sat on a stool, and received back from him the Bohemian kingdom as a fief, but he did not recover his Austrian lands, which Rudolf instead conferred on himself.[16]

The image of the overmighty and overjewelled king humbling himself before his meanly dressed adversary is a medieval trope intended to show Rudolf's humility. Plainly, though, Ottokar had no intention of keeping faith with Rudolf. Once returned to Bohemia, he used his wealth to suborn Rudolf's former allies and to foment discontent with Habsburg rule in Austria. Warfare recommenced in the summer of 1278, with Rudolf relying extensively on troops obtained from Hungary. The two armies met at Dürnkrut, forty kilometres (twenty-five miles) north-east of Vienna. With about ten thousand troops Rudolf's army was numerically the larger, but most of his forces were light cavalry and infantry. So Rudolf resorted to subterfuge. Breaking the conventions of chivalry, which saw ruses on the battlefield as shameful, Rudolf hid his reserve of several hundred armoured knights. At a critical moment, they flung themselves on the enemy's flank, routing Ottokar's army and slaying the Bohemian king. Rudolf's troops violated the dead king's body, hacking at it as they stripped off the costly armour.

To ensure that no pretenders emerged claiming to be Ottokar, Rudolf had the Bohemian king's remains eviscerated to delay putrefaction and put them on public display in Vienna for more than six months. The next year, in 1279, the corpse was carried to Bohemia, eventually to be interred in

Prague's St Vitus's Cathedral, where it remains to this day. It is housed beneath a fourteenth-century effigy of the king that has been described in the secret language of German art historians as *dumpf-erregt*, which might just about be translated as 'lumpishly animated.' Rudolf, however, did not take possession of the Bohemian kingdom, reckoning it a hopeless entanglement, but instead married his last unwed daughter to Ottokar's son and heir, the habitually dissolute Wenceslas II.[17]

The remainder of Rudolf's reign up until his death in 1291 was marked by failure. He did not manage to have himself crowned emperor by the pope but had to make do with the title of king. Like all his predecessors, he also failed to establish a hereditary monarchy in the Holy Roman Empire. Instead, he had to make do with packing the number of electors with princes whose loyalty he thought he had secured by marriage into his own family. Rudolf's attempt to reestablish the duchy of Swabia for his heirs likewise came unstuck, not least because all but one of his four sons predeceased him.[18]

In Dante's *Purgatory*, written in the early fourteenth century, Rudolf and Ottokar are spotted together in 'the valley of negligent princes', which is reserved for monarchs who in return for worldly glory have disregarded their souls. Ottokar comforts Rudolf there. The epic clash between Rudolf and the Golden King determined more, however, than just their individual fates. The capture of the Austrian lands made Rudolf master of a large chunk of Central Europe and transformed the fortunes of the Habsburgs. With a solid body of territory in the east to add to the family's Swabian lands, the Habsburgs looked ready to refashion the Holy Roman Empire, converting their private resources into public power and giving government. But it was a false dawn, both for the Holy Roman Empire and for the Habsburgs.[19]

3

LOSING PLACE AND FORGING A PAST

*T*he fourteenth century should have belonged to the Habsburgs. Across Central Europe, the lines of kings and princes faltered. In 1301, the Hungarian Árpád line came to an end; five years later, the Bohemian Přemyslids expired, to whose house Ottokar II had belonged. Then, in 1320, the last of the Ascanian margraves of Brandenburg died. But the Habsburgs did not benefit from the biological misfortune of others. Instead, over the fourteenth century they themselves were squeezed out of office and eminence in the Holy Roman Empire. For the time being at least, the future seemed to belong to the Wittelsbach rulers of Bavaria and the new Luxembourg kings of Bohemia.

On his death in 1291, Rudolf was buried in the crypt of Speyer Cathedral beside the tombs of previous emperors of the imperial Staufen dynasty. But the electors were determined that the Habsburgs should not take the Staufens' place and treat the Holy Roman Empire as if it was a family possession. So they initially conspired to prevent Rudolf's son and heir, Albert (1255–1308), from succeeding. Nonetheless, Albert skilfully ensured the election by a handful of princes of a puppet candidate, Conrad of Teck. Within forty-eight hours of his election, Conrad was dead, his skull cleft open by a nameless assassin. Conrad's and Albert's rival, Adolf of Nassau, now became king. The majority of electors backed Adolf precisely because he had no lands of his own and so was no threat, but once in office Adolf sought to grab what he could. The electors turned to Albert for help, who defeated and killed Adolf. In return, they elected Albert king in 1298.[1]

King Albert I has been badly treated by historians, who have too readily embraced the propaganda of his enemies—that he was 'a boorish man, with only one eye and a look that made you sick . . . a miser who kept his money to himself and gave nothing to the empire except for children, of which he had many.' Certainly, Albert lacked an eye. In 1295, his physicians had mistaken an illness for poisoning and to expel the imagined fluid they had suspended him upside-down from the ceiling. The consequent compression to the skull had robbed him of an eyeball. Albert was a prolific father too, siring no less than twenty-one children, of whom eleven made it past childhood. Their consequent marriages into the royal and princely houses of France, Aragon, Hungary, Poland, Bohemia, Savoy, and Lorraine indicate the prestige that now attached to Albert and to the family of which he was head.[2]

Like his father, Albert endeavoured to be crowned emperor in Rome. Pope Boniface VIII received Albert's embassy haughtily, declaring the imperial title to be his to give or withhold. Seated on the throne of St Peter, his head weighed down by the massive papal tiara of St Sylvester, with its 220 precious jewels set in gold, Pope Boniface boasted, 'I am the King of the Romans, I am Emperor.' But it was not the pope but instead a family dispute that brought Albert down. King Rudolf had promised his younger son, Rudolf, an inheritance equal to Albert's, but had not made good his vow. The younger Rudolf's heir, John, smarted under the jibe of 'Duke Lackland' and pressed to be given a share of the Habsburg patrimony, but Albert preferred to bestow titles and wealth upon his own children. On May Day 1308, John, along with several knights, ambushed Albert and slew him. The murder was a pointless act that brought John lifelong incarceration in a monastery in Pisa and the label of 'the Parricide.'[3]

Upon Albert's death, the electors chose Henry of Luxembourg for the same reason that they had a decade before elected Adolf of Nassau—to forestall a Habsburg succession by choosing a ruler who was insufficiently powerful to threaten their own interests. But like Adolf, Henry immediately set about constructing his own power base, in this case by taking the Bohemian crown. In 1312, Henry even travelled to Rome, to be crowned emperor there by the pope, which was the first time in almost a century that a king had done so. He died the next year from malaria contracted on the journey. By this time, German chroniclers were so used to having their rulers killed that they reported Henry to have been murdered at the pope's instruction with poisoned communion wine.[4]

Gathering at Frankfurt in 1314, the electors feared to appoint Henry's son, the startlingly courageous John of Luxembourg. Instead, the electors split their vote between Albert's son, Frederick the Fair of Habsburg (lived 1289–1330), and the Wittelsbach Duke Louis of Bavaria. For ten years the two men were at war, each claiming the royal title. Frederick the Fair's fate was impoverishment, defeat, imprisonment, a disadvantageous settlement, and an early death in 1330 in the lonely fastness of Burg Gutenstein, west of Wiener Neustadt. Frederick's two brothers hurried to make peace with Louis, acknowledging him as the lawful king. By this time, the decline of the Habsburgs was palpable. Whereas a generation before, they had married into the royal houses of Europe, they were now reduced to seeking spouses from a humbler stock of obscure Polish dukes and minor French nobles.

Emblematic too of the Habsburgs' declining fortunes was their defeat by the Swiss. The Swiss forest cantons of Uri, Schwyz, and Unterwalden had united in 1291 to form a defensive alliance, but it had rapidly become an offensive one, aimed against the Habsburgs. This was mostly due to Habsburg expansion into the Alpine valleys, where the family had taken over territories, toll stations, and rights of lordship following their acquisition of the Kiburg lands. As part of his struggle with Frederick the Fair, King Louis brought the cantons onto his side. At the end of 1315, when Frederick's brother Leopold marched into the valleys to assert his rights, he was ambushed and defeated by the men of Uri and Schwyz. The battle of Morgarten was the first major engagement in which the Swiss deployed the lethal pole-and-axe halberd against cavalrymen, using its hooked blade to drag the enemy's knights from their mounts and its spiked tip to skewer them. The halberd remains the ceremonial weapon of choice for today's Pontifical Swiss Guard in the Vatican.

The final blow to Habsburg prestige came in 1356. In that year King Louis's successor, Charles IV of Luxembourg, who had just been crowned emperor in Rome, published his so-called Golden Bull (named on account of its hanging gold seal or *bulla*). The Golden Bull contained a new scheme for the election of the ruler, which fastened down the identity of the seven electors—the three archbishops of the Rhineland and four secular lords, who held the office henceforth by right of inheritance. Even though they had participated on several occasions in electing kings, the Habsburgs were omitted from the new college of electors, thus writing them out of the most important constitutional document in the history of the Holy Roman Empire. In the seating plan that he separately drew up for future meetings of the diet, Charles made clear their diminished status, placing the Habsburgs in the second row, behind the electors, senior clergy, and high dignitaries of the empire. The Habsburg response was ideologically devastating and would change forever the way they thought about themselves and their historical role. To counter Charles IV's insult, they jettisoned their Swabian past and became instead Austrians and Romans.[5]

For the first fifty years of their rule as dukes of Austria, the Habsburgs had regarded the duchy as secondary in importance to their traditional heartland in Swabia. They had milked Austria to fund the defence of their other territories, and they had used it as a starting place for campaigns into Bohemia, which they regarded as the greater prize. It was only after 1330, when Frederick the Fair's brother, the arthritic Albert the Lame (lived 1298–1358), assumed headship of the family, that the Habsburgs showed any sustained interest in Austria. Since the Swiss continued to press against the Habsburg lands and strongholds in the Aargau, Albert moved his court to Vienna's Old Fort, in the heart of what has become the Hofburg Palace. Albert also began the construction of a family mausoleum at Gaming in Lower Austria, and he repossessed Carinthia and Carniola, which his grandfather had pawned. Albert's prolonged stays in Austria earned the Habsburgs the description from one chronicler of 'the Austrians', the first time the term was used in this way. Whereas in the past, the Habsburgs had administered Austria through regents, it was now their Swabian possessions that had governors appointed to them.[6]

The Habsburgs may not at first have known what to do with Austria, but Austria knew what to do with the Habsburgs. Originally a borderland called the 'eastern realm' (*Ostarrîchi*—the name first appears in 996), its earliest rulers belonged to the Babenberg family. The Babenbergs aspired to greatness, marrying into the lines of both Holy Roman and Byzantine emperors, on which account they thought of themselves as trustees of the inheritance of Rome. Their conspicuous dedication to the faith was marked by the founding of a dense network of monasteries, in return for which generations of monks wrote their praises. The reputation of the Babenbergs is shown in the soubriquets by which they were recalled—the Illustrious, the Devout, the Glorious, the Strong, and the Holy. Only the last of the Babenberg line, Frederick II (died 1246), had the unhappier nickname of 'the Quarrelsome.'[7]

Genealogies of the Babenbergs sometimes included quaint descriptions of the countryside and its cities. Little by little, however, a belief in the exceptionalism of the ruling family fused with the conviction that the land and its people were special. A literary tradition arose, which saw the Austrians as descendants of the Goths of classical antiquity, or which proposed an even more illustrious descent from Greek and Roman heroes. The old Roman name for Austria, Noricum, invited the possibility that Austria was founded by Norix, the son of Hercules, who, coming from the lands about Armenia, had invested his heirs with Austria and Bavaria respectively. The Babenberg lands were also home to the *Nibelunglied* epic, which in its early versions coupled stories taken from Germanic mythology with episodes in the ruling dynasty's history.[8]

The Habsburgs consumed all of this, adding to the Babenbergs' religious foundations at Heiligenkreuz and Tulln and enlisting chroniclers and poets to proclaim their own piety. Gradually, the history of the Babenbergs and Habsburgs merged into one, so that the Babenbergs became ancestors to the Habsburgs, in token of which the Habsburgs frequently adopted the Babenberg baptismal name of Leopold. This was important since it harked back to the Babenberg Leopold III, who although not yet a saint had posthumously performed enough miracles to qualify as one. At a time when saintliness added lustre to a family, the Habsburgs were otherwise short of suitable forebears.

The Habsburgs were also swift to discover Roman credentials of their own, promoting their supposed descent from the allegedly senatorial family of Colonna. Chroniclers added to the story, describing how two brothers exiled from ancient Rome had gone north of the Alps, one of whom went on to found Castle Habsburg. Even more imaginatively, the author of the Königsfelden Chronicle interwove his account of the Habsburgs with a Roman inheritance, saintliness, and prophecy. Having enumerated the line of Roman emperors from Augustus to Frederick II, he went on to tell the life of King Rudolf of Habsburg. He then related the biography of Rudolf's granddaughter Agnes, who after a short time as queen of Hungary had forsaken the world to live next to Königsfelden Abbey, near Brugg. First of all, however, the chronicler rehearsed an old tale of the discovery in Spain of a huge book concealed in a stone, with pages of wood on which was written in Latin, Greek, and Hebrew the entire history of the world, including the time to come and the Last Judgement. The implication was clear—made holy by the devotions of Agnes, the Habsburgs were both destined and foretold to rule as Roman emperors.[9]

Exceptionalism was in the 1350s transformed into a political programme. Offended and diminished by Charles IV's Golden Bull, Rudolf of Habsburg (lived 1339–1365) was intent upon both restoring his family's prestige and welding together a territorial state which outstripped its rivals. He did so with an energy, pace, and imagination that belied his youth and confounded his rivals. Within a few months of the death of his father, Albert the Lame, in 1358, the young Rudolf instructed his scribes to confect five fraudulent charters. Their purpose was to establish the Habsburgs as leading princes in the Holy Roman Empire by melding the Habsburg inheritance with Austria and Rome. Rudolf's was the most ambitious work of forgery in medieval Europe since the eighth-century Donation of Constantine, which had appointed the pope as the ultimate ruler of Christendom. It was also rather better done.[10]

Of the five charters, three were confirmations of the others, thus textually interlocking the whole deception. The substance of the forgery lay with the first two charters, which are known as the 'Pseudo-Henry' and the 'Greater Privilege.' The author of the Pseudo-Henry, who was probably Rudolf's chancellor, pretended that it was a charter issued by Emperor Henry IV in 1054, drawn up to record the contents of two letters in the keeping of Duke Ernest of Babenberg. The first letter was supposedly addressed by Julius Caesar to the people of the 'eastern land', by which was plainly meant Austria. Julius Caesar ordered the easterners or Austrians to accept his uncle as their ruler, who was given an absolute power over them as their 'feudal lord.' The fake letter also admitted Julius Caesar's uncle to the innermost counsels of the Roman Empire, 'so that henceforth no weighty matter or suit be resolved without his knowledge.' In the other letter contained in the Pseudo-Henry, the emperor Nero similarly addressed the people of the east. Nero declared that because they outstripped in splendour all other peoples of the Roman Empire, he had upon the advice of the senate released them from paying all imperial taxes and awarded them freedom for ever more.

In contrast to the Pseudo-Henry, the Greater Privilege was at least partly authentic, being based upon the text of the charter given by Frederick

I Barbarossa in 1156, which had elevated Austria to a duchy. Much, however, was added to the original text. Austria was now acknowledged as the 'shield and heart' of the Holy Roman Empire, by virtue of which its duke had full rights within the duchy. The duke was given the title of 'palatine archduke', which brought with it a special crown and sceptre and the right to sit at the emperor's right hand, equal in precedence to the imperial electors. To strengthen the duke's dominion, he was permitted to pass on the duchy intact to his eldest son and, in the absence of sons, to a daughter. The concocted version was known to posterity as the 'Greater Privilege' to distinguish it from the genuine privilege of 1156, which was subsequently called the 'Lesser Privilege.'

The other three charters which confirmed the Pseudo-Henry and the Greater Privilege added some more points. In formal processions, the archduke, as he had become, and his retinue were always to have first place, and it was permitted that the archducal crown include the fillet or headband of majesty, normally worn by kings beneath their crown. The archbishop of Salzburg and the bishop of Passau, both of whom had jurisdiction over Austria in church matters, were made subject to the archduke. Like the charters that they confirmed, these secondary instruments indicate that Rudolf was not, as is often alleged, moved only by resentment of Charles IV's Golden Bull of 1356 and so primarily bent on scoring points. With its stress on the archduke's complete power in Austria, the subordination of the church to him, and the complete inheritability of his office, the forgeries were as much intended to advance the power of the archduke in his own lands as to influence etiquette in the imperial court and the archduke's own headwear.

The Pseudo-Henry with its letters of Julius Caesar and Nero was almost immediately denounced. The Italian scholar Petrarch wrote to Emperor Charles IV in 1361, highlighting anachronisms in the text and dismissing it as 'vacuous, bombastic, devoid of truth, conceived by someone unknown but beyond doubt not a man of letters . . . not only risible but stomach-churning.' The Greater Privilege, however, fared rather better. Invoked to justify the succession of Maria Theresa to Austria on the death of her father Charles VI in 1740, it was proved to be a forgery only in the mid-nineteenth century. The Donation of Constantine, by contrast, was exposed as fraudulent in the fifteenth century.[11]

In 1360, Rudolf presented the five false charters to Emperor Charles IV for confirmation, interspersing them with seven genuine documents.

Charles quibbled over some details, but grudgingly confirmed the whole package, 'insofar as its provisions be lawful.' He did not, however, alter the composition of the college of electors or seating arrangements at the diet to accommodate Rudolf's pretensions. Nevertheless, Rudolf now used the title of archduke and sported the archducal crown he had devised. After some hesitation, both the crown and, more slowly, the title became the style of his successors and, by no later than the mid-fifteenth century, of all senior members of the Habsburg family.[12]

The duchy of Austria, along with the neighbouring duchies of Styria, Carinthia, and Carniola, constituted not so much a defined territory as a bundle of rights. Some properties belonged to the archduke, but others were held independently of him as lands bestowed separately by the monarch. The Greater Privilege had proclaimed the archduke's absolute authority within Austria, and Rudolf now sought to make good his claims. All lands held of the monarch were transformed into lands that belonged to him, which he alone had the right to distribute. One of the largest holders of imperial lands in Carinthia was the patriarch of Aquileia, whose grand title was a relic of the sixth century, hardly matching the patriarchate's now puny power. When the patriarch proved obdurate, Rudolf invaded his lands and forced his submission. Even though Alsace had nothing to do with the Greater Privilege, Rudolf extended the same principle there, declaring that his rank meant that he was not the subject but rather 'the master of all rights and freedoms.'[13]

The archbishop of Salzburg and the bishop of Passau proved harder nuts to crack, for neither was ready to shrink his diocese by giving way to Rudolf's plan for an Austrian bishopric based in Vienna. Rudolf proceeded, nonetheless, to rebuild St Stephen's in Vienna as if it were a cathedral rather than just a parish church, replacing the Romanesque nave with a massive Gothic one and planning the construction of two towers (only one was ever built). He gave the church its own chapter of canons, to which it was not entitled since it had no bishop, and he decked the canons out as cardinals, giving them scarlet birettas and gold pectoral crosses. The refashioned church was also intended to celebrate the Habsburg family, so Rudolf placed statues of himself and his forebears around the nave and made the crypt into a mausoleum for his descendants. Beside the church, Rudolf set up a university, which was intended to rival Charles IV's foundation in Prague. By virtue of his rebuilding of St Stephen's, Rudolf is known to posterity as 'the Founder.'

He chose the soubriquet himself and had it carved in magic runes upon his sarcophagus in the north choir of the church.[14]

In the art of deception, Rudolf found an equal. The county of the Tyrol was wealthy from its gold and silver mines and from the tolls of the roads that linked Italy to the German cities on the other side of the Brenner Pass. The Tyrol was held in the early 1360s by the widow Margaret, whose nickname of *Maultasch* ('Big Mouth') is the kindest in a long list of epithets. Previously married to a Luxembourg and then to a Wittelsbach prince, she lost her only surviving son at the beginning of 1363. Tyrol was there for the taking, and there was no lack of contenders. But Margaret was not easy prey. She had physically kicked out her first husband, not bothered with a divorce before marrying her second, put up with excommunication, and tyrannized both her new spouse and her recently deceased son.

Margaret did a deal with Rudolf. In return for allowing her to keep the county during her lifetime, she promised to assign the Tyrol to him in advance. But her ministers, who were also the county's principal landowners, forced her in January 1363 to agree that all treaties with foreign princes required their consent. Margaret attempted to win them round with gifts of land and other inducements, but without success. Even Rudolf's personal appearance in the Tyrolean capital of Innsbruck made no difference. To convince the ministers, Margaret and Rudolf concocted together a fake charter. The forgery showed that four years previously Margaret had promised to assign the Tyrol to Rudolf in a solemn deed that could not be retracted. Even though the forged charter used the wrong seal, it was believed. With the January agreement ostensibly voided, Margaret's ministers gave way, recording their consent in a letter to which they appended their own fourteen seals. By the end of the year, Rudolf had convinced Margaret to abdicate, offering her a wealthy retirement in Vienna. The Tyrol was now his. On the back of the Tyrol later came the county of Gorizia (Görz-Gradisca) on the Adriatic, which belonged to a distant line of Margaret's family that eventually expired in 1500.[15]

Rudolf died in 1368, at the age of just twenty-five. Since it was high summer and his corpse was decomposing fast, it was boiled to remove the flesh. But his bones were put in the crypt of St Stephen's and not, as he had planned, in the sarcophagus in the choir. The empty tomb with its runes and life-size effigy of Rudolf wearing the archducal crown stands in some ways as a metaphor for his reign—bombastic and self-promoting, but also hollow. In his lifetime, Rudolf failed to obtain the reputation for himself and the eminence for Austria that he worked and forged for. He won neither the bishopric he wanted nor recognition as the equivalent to an elector. His university, still today named in his honour, comprised just several rooms in a school. It would be his brother who recruited the professors and gave the university proper accommodation. Obtained through subterfuge, the Tyrol was his principal acquisition.[16]

Rudolf's achievement was, however, a more subtle one. By giving the Habsburgs a historical consciousness and set of beliefs about themselves, Rudolf made them more than just a group of blood relatives. The imagined Roman and Austrian past, with the invented archducal crown and title, inspired a sense of solidarity and purpose among his successors that became more embedded with the passage of each generation. Others might hold the rank of elector by virtue of a modern emperor's gift, but the Habsburgs owed their eminence to Julius Caesar and to privileges confirmed by successive emperors over the centuries. Even in death, the family was united in the new mausoleum built in St Stephen's crypt. In the making of the Habsburgs as a dynasty, Rudolf was indeed, as the cryptic message on his empty tomb proclaimed, 'the founder.'

Habsburg redoubt at Baden reduced to its present ruin by Swiss cannons. Castle Habsburg also fell at this time to the Swiss confederates. The remaining rump of Habsburg lands in Swabia was reorganized as Further Austria and administered from Innsbruck.

Habsburg fortunes turned with the rise of Duke Albert (lived 1397–1439), who took over the governance of the duchy of Austria in 1411. Albert was pious, an energetic reformer of the church, a capable administrator, formidable in battle, and, by all accounts, an agreeable companion. He was also illiterate and cruel. In 1420, he gave up the Habsburg tradition of protecting Austria's Jews and subjected them to a persecution of such intensity that even the latest pope complained. His interest was purely to loot Jewish money, which he used to support King Sigismund in his war against the Hussite heretics in Bohemia. Having been given command of Moravia, Albert renewed his Jew-baiting there. Albert's support for Sigismund, who was crowned emperor in 1433, won him the hand of Sigismund's daughter, Elizabeth. Sigismund, who had no sons of his own, further nominated Albert as his successor in Bohemia and Hungary.

Albert succeeded effortlessly to the throne of Hungary upon Sigismund's death in 1437, and he also managed to be chosen as king by the Bohemian diet. By this point, the electors of the Holy Roman Empire had realized the error of appointing a weak ruler. As they explained, the current circumstances were simply too grave—the institutions of the church were in disarray, with several popes competing for recognition; in Bohemia heresy prevailed, while the Turks were pressing westwards and from their fastnesses in Bosnia even now raiding the empire's borders. Accordingly, in March 1438 the electors unanimously chose Albert as Sigismund's successor, even though he had not announced his candidacy. The Holy Roman Empire, the duchy of Austria, and the kingdoms of Bohemia and Hungary were thus united under the rule of one man. Eighteen months later, Albert died of dysentery, leaving no male heir but only a pregnant wife. Seers and midwives confidently predicted a daughter. Elizabeth confounded them with a boy.[3]

The most senior surviving Habsburg was Frederick, duke of Styria, Carinthia, and Carniola (lived 1415–1493), who was Albert's second cousin (they shared a common great-grandfather in Albert the Lame). He was duly elected as King (later Emperor) Frederick III in 1440. Frederick looked like a ruler, having inherited the physique of his mother, the Polish Cymburga, who was renowned both for her beauty and for her ability to drive nails into oak planks with her bare fists. Tall and spare, with long blond hair, Frederick had all the qualifications for greatness. He had visited the Holy Sepulchre in Jerusalem, where he had been dubbed a knight, and he was a member of all the right chivalric societies. Moreover, he was called Frederick. At this time, a wave of prophecy told how a mighty emperor named Frederick would unite the world under the true faith, travel to Jerusalem, and, by abdicating there, usher in the Day of Judgement. There were many variations on this theme, which built on occult texts and imaginative readings of the Bible (the books of Daniel and Revelation were plundered for secret meanings). Frederick did nothing to dissuade a credulous audience that he was the Frederick foretold in prophetic utterance. Indeed, Styria was a major hub for the dissemination of apocalyptic texts.[4]

Such expectations meant that Frederick could not fail both to be elected sovereign and to disappoint. Over the years to come, his long hair became lank and grey and his body obese. He contracted diabetes, sucking on melons to slake his persistent thirst. Eventually, in his seventies, a foot became gangrenous from a blood clot and required amputation under an opiate anaesthetic. A full account survives of the operation, which was performed in public in Linz by barber surgeons working under the direction of Frederick's physicians. The operation was by all accounts a resounding success. When the patient died ten weeks later, the melons were blamed.[5]

It was not so much Frederick's physical decline that dismayed contemporaries as his slothful demeanour. For more than twenty-five years (1444–1471), Frederick never ventured beyond Styria and Austria to visit the rest of the Holy Roman Empire. The French ambassador struggled to find the best word for a ruler whose manner he described as 'indolent, morose, brooding, sulky, melancholy, miserly, frugal, and troubled.' Enea Silvio Piccolomini, the future Pope Pius II and a confidant and advisor to Frederick, disparaged his master as the Holy Roman Empire's 'Arch-Sleepyhead', while the bishop of Pécs in Hungary attributed Frederick's character to the wrong star:

> *Rome once was saved by Fabius' delaying,*
> *But your delays, Frederick, have brought it to breaking.*
> *You're always consulting and never quite doing.*
> *Couldn't you act for once and stop all this chewing?*
> *You harken to Saturn, the most frozen of stars;*
> *Far better if emperors were guided by Mars.*[6]

The contrast between icy Saturn and rubicund Mars was a familiar literary trope. Certainly, Frederick was introspective, moody, and penny-pinching, even to the extent of travelling with hen coops to save on the cost of buying eggs. He was, however, far from indolent. First, he stuck to Austria and Styria because these territories were threatened and his rule there was incomplete. He took seriously the guardianship of his great nephew Ladislas, the posthumously born son of King Albert II, and he promoted the boy's claims to both Bohemia and Hungary, which required him remaining close by. Even before Ladislas's death in 1457, Frederick's younger brother, Albert, had openly challenged Frederick's rule in Austria, claiming that his guardianship was illegal and with it Frederick's right to govern the duchy. The division of Austria into two halves along the River Enns did not appease Albert's ambition. Frederick's confirmation of the Greater Privilege, which stressed the exclusive rights of the eldest Habsburg, was equally ineffective.

Second, Frederick was not supine. Certainly, there were whole years when he did not stray from Linz or Wiener Neustadt, but he did travel twice to Italy—in 1452 to marry a Portuguese bride and to be crowned emperor by the pope in Rome, and again in 1468–1469 to revisit the Holy See. He used the occasion of his second journey to Rome to convince the pope to give St Stephen's in Vienna a bishop, thus fulfilling his great-uncle Rudolf's ambition. Indeed, he went further. Having previously obtained papal consent to make Ljubljana in Carniola a bishopric, he now persuaded the pope to raise Wiener Neustadt and three other cities to the status of bishoprics and, a dozen years later, to canonize Leopold the Good of Babenberg, who was by now regarded as a Habsburg forebear.[7]

Even when not travelling, Frederick was active, but as a man of Saturn and not of Mars. He attended meetings of his council on a daily basis, even though its deliberations might go on from the late afternoon to midnight. Altogether in a reign of just over fifty years, Frederick's chancellery issued some fifty thousand letters and charters, of which many bore a mark indicating that they had been composed on Frederick's personal instruction. To make up for the administrative deficit in the Holy Roman Empire, Frederick appointed commissioners, whom he charged with following up on complaints of injustice and with enforcing his decisions. Many of Frederick's interventions either on paper or through his commissioners concerned the regions 'near to the ruler'—Swabia, the Rhineland, and the leaderless duchy of Franconia to their east. But his agents were also active further afield, intervening to resolve disputes in Saxony, along the Baltic shore, and as far north as the outpost of Livonia (now Latvia and Estonia), even though it had only the most tenuous relationship to the Holy Roman Empire.[8]

Frederick was also a builder. It was during his reign that stone vaulting was put into the nave of St Stephen's in Vienna and work begun on raising a second spire to match the first, which at 137 metres (450 feet) was the tallest then in continental Europe. (Old St Paul's in London and Lincoln Cathedral were both taller at respectively 150 metres / 490 feet and 160 metres / 524 feet). Frederick was, however, driven out of Vienna in 1462 by his brother, the permanently dissatisfied Albert. He retreated to Wiener Neustadt, 60 kilometres (40 miles) south of Vienna, and it was there that he ordered the construction of his most celebrated monument. On the west facade of the chapel of St George, next to the ducal castle, craftsmen sculpted a 16-metre (50-foot) relief made up of more than a hundred coats of arms. At the base stood a youthful Frederick, with long hair and wearing the archducal crown. An angel on his right bore a shield, on which was written the letters AEIOU.

AEIOU was Frederick's personal device and probably in origin a code for his birthday, but like all such acrostics, it was capable of multiple meanings. First recorded in 1437 in one of Frederick's notebooks, the letters are thought to conceal several hundred different readings. Of these, the most commonly cited is 'Austria is ruler of the whole world', a formulation that worked in both Latin and German (see the Introduction, p. 4). But there were other interpretations that played on equally grand themes—hence, by reference to the imperial device, 'The chosen eagle rightly conquers all' (*Aquila Electa Iuste Omnia Uincat*), or 'The best emperor encourages all the arts' (*Artes Extollitur Imperator Optimus Universas*), and so on.

What did Frederick mean by these ruminations? The answer partly lies with the relief on the west wall of St George's. Of the 107 coats of arms, only nineteen relate to lands that were at the time of the composition in Habsburg possession. The remainder were the imagined armorial bearings of all the rulers of Austria back to the time before Christ. In devising these, the architect borrowed from the most celebrated chronicle circulating in the Habsburg lands, the 'Chronicle of the Ninety-Five Lords', from which we know Frederick took inspiration. Originally composed at the end of the fourteenth century, the chronicle began with the foundation of Austria by the Jewish knight Abraham of Temonaria (a nonsense place), who came from the fabled Land of Admiration some 810 years after the Flood, which is by biblical reckoning about 1500 BCE. It concluded with the ninety-fifth lord, who was Frederick III's great-uncle. In between, the course of government meandered through a host of imagined Jewish patriarchs, the Babenberg rulers of Austria, and onto the Habsburgs, with long digressions on papal history. The armorial bearings of each lord were inventively described. In between, the author listed the Roman emperors, the line of which then merged with the history of the Habsburg rulers.[9]

Genealogical romances were a late medieval literary genre, which sought to link aristocratic and royal lineages to contemporary place names and to a mythic past populated with mermaids, Amazons, giants, and dragons. The 'Chronicle of the Ninety-Five Lords' is, nevertheless, exceptional in its blending of biblical, imperial, and Austrian history and in its combination of the fantastic with heraldry and biography. Fifty manuscript versions survive from the fifteenth century, attesting to its popularity, and its content was amplified by subsequent writers. They interwove the chronicle's text with the story of Austria's foundation by Norix, the son of Hercules, wrote that Julius Caesar had founded Vienna (he was said to have stayed there two years, a biennium, whence the city's name), and included the fraudulent letters of Caesar and Nero. Others inserted what they could into ambitious 'world chronicles', which brought together the history of the four empires (the Assyrian, Persian, Greek-Macedonian, and Roman), onto which they tagged the lives of the most prominent Habsburg rulers.

The AEIOU acronym, the coats of arms on the west wall of St George's, and the burgeoning chronicle literature spoke, however, to the same theme. Austria was not just a location. It was also a land whose rulers were preordained for greatness and government. Indeed, Austria was not really a land at all, but a learned construction that brought together the themes of empire, mission, inheritance, and destiny. Other rulers might call themselves after their principal territory—the House of Brandenburg, the House of Saxony, and so on. But Austria was different, for it signalled a set of beliefs about the ruling house that stood apart from geography. Later Habsburg princes who went off to Burgundy or moved to take on the Spanish crown still referred to themselves, therefore, as members of the House of Austria even though their physical relationship to the duchy of Austria was remote. When the Habsburgs spoke of Austria, they were signalling as much an idea as a space.

The conviction that Austria and its rulers had a vocation to fulfil was also a theme hammered out by Enea Silvio Piccolomini, who besides being a counsellor to Frederick was also the most influential historian of his day. In a fictional conversation, written in the early 1440s for Frederick's edification, Piccolomini stressed the obligations incumbent upon the rulers of Austria: to defend and promote the imperial power, to bring order to Italy, to expand the bounds of Christendom, and to magnify the happiness of subjects. In an address delivered a few years later to the Church Council meeting at Basle, Piccolomini further extolled Austria as directed in all its affairs by the divine will, in evidence of which he pointed to the way it had produced kings and emperors. He also borrowed freely from the Chronicle of the Ninety-Five Lords, adding scholarly approval to the fabulous descents it wove and exalting the Habsburg mythology of greatness foretold.[10]

Frederick long defied the expectations that others invested in him. He was, however, a firm believer in prognostication. Frederick welcomed astrologers to his court, and he scrutinized mouse droppings in the way later generations would examine tea leaves. Whether moved by the appearance of a comet (two were separately observed, in 1468 and 1471) or by a change of disposition, around 1470 Frederick discarded the frozen robe of Saturn and took up the mantle of Mars. In 1468, he proclaimed a peace of the land in his territories, declared its infringement to be a treasonable offence, and locked up a Styrian mercenary captain who had insolently taken up arms against him on account of an unpaid debt. He also imposed Habsburg rule on Trieste, converting its previous nominal submission to a real one and giving his territories access to the Adriatic. Three years later, in 1471, Frederick journeyed to Regensburg to a gathering of 'Christian princes', where he sought to coordinate policy against the growing Turkish challenge in the east—in vain as it turned out. The output of his correspondence and his appointment of commissioners intensified, while the composition of Frederick's court became more reflective of the broader ambit of his power. He now recruited almost a half of his councillors from outside the Habsburg lands.[11]

From the 1470s onwards, Frederick was in close diplomatic contact with the Burgundian duke, Charles the Bold. Both needed one another. Charles hankered after a royal title that would give his sprawling possessions unity and advance his personal status. In return for granting Charles the title of king, Frederick hoped to obtain security for his remaining possessions in the south-west, which he now planned to weld together into a separate duchy. But Frederick had no title to give that was commensurate with Charles's ambition, on which account their relations soured. It did not help that, when the two men met in 1473, Charles offended etiquette with his lavish gifts and ostentatious dress (one outfit included several thousand pearls and rubies). Discussion gave way to warfare and then once more to negotiation. Eventually, Frederick and Charles agreed to an alliance between the houses of Austria and Burgundy, which was to be cemented by the marriage of Frederick's son, Maximilian (1459–1519), and Charles's daughter, Mary.[12]

Charles's possessions as duke of Burgundy comprised two parts, both of which straddled the border between France and the Holy Roman Empire. The southern part consisted of the duchy and county of Burgundy and Charolais, centred on Dijon and Besançon respectively. The northern part included Luxembourg and the Low Countries (now Belgium and the Netherlands) and also a chunk of France running south of Calais. In order to join the two parts together, Charles invaded Lorraine in 1475 and then turned his attention to the Swiss Vaud, at which point his enemies joined forces against him. Two years later, Charles was slain in battle by a Swiss halberdier.[13]

Since Charles had died without a male heir, Frederick claimed his lands as properties that had reverted to imperial ownership. Eight months after Charles's death, Maximilian married his daughter, Mary, thus making the Burgundian lands Habsburg family possessions. Maximilian had to ward off the claims of the French king, Louis XI, who had meanwhile occupied the duchy of Burgundy, but he nevertheless retained the bulk of Charles the Bold's lands, including the Low Countries, the county of Burgundy (Franche-Comté), and Charolais. Meanwhile, Frederick was engaged in the east against the king of Hungary, Matthias Corvinus, who invaded Austria and installed himself in Vienna. But Matthias died in 1490, after which Frederick ousted the Hungarians from his territory.

Frederick owed much to his longevity. He outlived both his relatives and his adversaries and was thus able to reconstitute the divided Habsburg patrimony as a single unit. His brother, Albert, predeceased him in 1463, without heir, after which Frederick retook possession of Upper Austria, while his cousin, Sigismund, who ruled the Tyrolean part of the Habsburg lands, abdicated in 1490 in favour of Maximilian. Lower Austria fell to Frederick by virtue of the death, again without heir, of his great-nephew, Ladislas, in 1457. Of his rivals, both Matthias Corvinus and Charles the Bold died before Frederick, the one of a stroke and the other in battle. Moreover, Frederick had assured the succession, for in 1486 he had prevailed upon the electors to crown Maximilian as king of the Romans, which was the first time in almost three centuries that the electors had agreed to appoint a son as king during his father's lifetime.

Frederick III was buried in a colossal sarcophagus in the south-east corner of St Stephen's cathedral in Vienna. Nine tons of marble were used in its construction, for the transporting of which the bridges along the route to Vienna had to be reinforced. The sarcophagus bears both Frederick's effigy and the letters AEIOU. But, unlike the tomb of his great-uncle Rudolf, it is not a metaphor for a hollow reign, for Frederick lies within, and his accomplishments in the service of both Saturn and Mars were the greater. At the start of the fifteenth century, the Habsburgs had seemed unlikely contenders for the imperial throne. By the time of Frederick's death in 1493, they looked imperial, having already been in place as rulers of the Holy Roman Empire for fifty-five years. They had history on their side, but they also had an aspiration to greatness that was now part of the tradition and mythology of the Habsburg House of Austria. Back in 1437, Frederick's AEIOU with its pretension to world domination looked not only vainglorious but also foolish. By the 1490s, it was both credible and on the edge of being realized.

5

MAXIMILIAN AND THE
COLOUR-CODED KINGS

*F*rederick's son, Maximilian, was elected king in 1486 and moved smoothly into power upon his father's death seven years later. The itinerary of his travels marks him out as quite different from Frederick III, for he was always on the move, scarcely staying more than a few weeks in any one place. Yet, like all his predecessor kings and emperors, his route stuck to the region that was traditionally close to the ruler—Swabia, Franconia, and the Rhineland, to which were now added the newly acquired provinces in the Low Countries. He never visited Saxony, Brunswick, Brandenburg, and the principalities along the southern Baltic shore. German historians ponder why their country did not develop into a unified national state like France or Spain. Any number of reasons may be proposed, but one is surely that large chunks of the Holy Roman Empire were never integrated into the sovereign's journeys. It was only in 1712 that an emperor visited Pomerania in the German north-east, and he was the emperor of Russia.

Maximilian's style of rule depended on personality and presence, in the absence of which his image had to suffice. Several thousand surviving portraits attest to Maximilian's determination to make his face the best known in Europe. Artists were enlisted to communicate his image and achievements in yet more dramatic ways. Albrecht Dürer, Albrecht Altdorfer, and a team of less well-known engravers designed for him the two massive woodcut series, *The Triumphal Procession* and *The Triumphal Arch*, which advertised Maximilian's ancestry and deeds. Made up of interlocking printed sheets, they were intended to be pasted up as wallpaper in the palaces and council chambers of the several hundred lords and cities to which they were sent.

Maximilian also spread his renown by commissioning poems in his honour. He won over the Renaissance scholar Conrad Celtis by crowning him a poet laureate and installing him as master of a new College of Poets and Mathematicians in Vienna's university. Celtis returned the honour by penning panegyrics that extolled Maximilian as a great huntsman and warrior, comparing him to heroes of classical antiquity and German history. Besides Celtis, Maximilian crowned almost forty poets with laurels, all of whom churned out verse celebrating his reign. Maximilian not only instructed that the verses be printed but also protected them with some of the earliest privileges, giving copyright. Even so, Celtis's edition of Tacitus's first-century *Germania*, to which he added digressions on Maximilian's achievements, was widely reproduced by others, thus further broadcasting the ruler's reputation.[1]

Maximilian was also active in his own fashioning. He oversaw the composition of three allegorical autobiographies in which he depicted himself as the most chivalric and accomplished of knights. In the *Theuerdank*, Maximilian related an entirely fictional account of how the eponymous hero, literally Noble Thought, ventured abroad to marry the Lady Ehrenreich ('Rich in Honour'), who represents Maximilian's wife, Mary of Burgundy. On the way to her, Theuerdank undergoes all sorts of tribulations brought about by his adversaries—broken staircases, avalanches, poisoned food, and so on. Having won the lady's hand, Theuerdank departs to go on crusade. In reality, Maximilian's journey from Vienna to his marriage in Ghent took three months on account of the grand receptions and feasting to which he was treated, but he was indeed wed in a suit of silver armour.[2]

The *Theuerdank* was lavishly illustrated with 118 woodcuts, and the text used the black-letter typeface that later became the basis of German Gothic script or *Fraktur*. Maximilian published the *Theuerdank* for private distribution in 1517, and two years later it went on general sale. The accompanying volume, *Freydal* ('Fair and Courteous'), did not, however, make it to the printer but remains, except for five illustrations, only in manuscript form. The *Freydal* recorded Maximilian's accomplishments in jousting and combat with more than two hundred alleged adversaries, often in front of admiring audiences and celebrated with masked balls.[3]

The best known of Maximilian's autobiographical romances is the *Weisskunig* ('White King'). Published posthumously, it described Maximilian's upbringing and many of his military campaigns under the allegorical name of the White King. The story rehearses the White King's education—his immediate grasp as a child of the seven liberal arts (grammar, rhetoric, logic, arithmetic, geometry, music, and astronomy) and progression to the study of genealogy, the science of mining, minstrelsy, painting, and, indeed, almost everything else, including the comprehension of birdsong. In truth, Maximilian was a poor student and until the age of nine an 'elective mute.' Even so, Maximilian's alter ego, the White King, effortlessly acquires new languages, speaking seven fluently. He even delves into the black arts, but never so deeply as to imperil his soul.[4]

As a ruler, the White King desires only peace, but he is constantly beset by the traitorous cunning of others. They are duly listed by colour or device—the Green King (of Hungary), the Blue King (of France), the Red and White King (England), the King of Fish (Doge of Venice), the King of Crowns (the pope), the Black King (Aragon), the King of Molten Iron (Burgundy), and so on. In his enthusiasm, Maximilian sometimes muddled the colours, with several kings confusingly changing hue. When not fighting the Coloured Kings, the White King engages in war with armies raised by the cities of the Low Countries, where his rule was long contested—the Brown, Grey, and Apple-Grey Companies, against which he musters the White Company, whose members comprised in reality thuggish mercenaries. In a few places, Maximilian forgets colour and device, so the Swiss are simply 'peasant boors', the White King's son (and Maximilian's too), Philip, is 'the Beautiful King', and the French dauphin who vies in vain for Mary of Burgundy's hand is 'Pugface.'

A selection of chapter headings for the year 1509 indicates the rather monochrome character of the text:

How the White King made an alliance against the King of Fish.

How the King of Crowns and the Blue King made war on the King of Fish.

How the Blue King attacked the King of Fish and prevailed upon him in battle.

How the White King campaigned against the King of Fish and captured many cities and much land.[5]

There is nothing original in the colour-coding of champions and adversaries. The contemporary *Le Morte d'Arthur* of Sir Thomas Malory has an ample selection of Blue, Red, Green, Black, and Yellow Knights, while the most accomplished chivalric romance of the late fifteenth century, the Valencian *Tirant lo Blanc*, is also named after a white knight. But the *Weisskunig* lacks the moral ambiguities, tainted enchantments, and bleak destinies of *Morte d'Arthur*, and it has none of *Tirant lo Blanc*'s narrative complexity and élan. It is an uncomplicated piece of vanity publishing, redeemed only by the 250 woodcuts that adorn the text.

Maximilian intended the three autobiographical allegories to be the starting point of a vast publishing enterprise, which would distil separate branches of knowledge into what amounted to a multivolume encyclopaedia. Each part would contain a summation of all that pertained to cooking, horsemanship, falconry, horticulture, artillery, fencing, morality, castles and cities, magic (including black), the art of love, and so on. Of the list of more than 130 titles planned, only two were ever completed. Their contents, which enumerate the best places for hunting and fishing in the Tyrol and Gorizia, depict Maximilian casting nets, inspecting river banks, and conversing with huntsmen, and they suggest the motif that drew together the vast project: Maximilian himself. All aspects of the encyclopaedic enterprise were intended as celebrations of his rule, accomplishments, and virtuosity, which united in his person all human experience.[6]

The same self-promoting bricolage attended Maximilian's forays into history and genealogy. At a time when most rulers were content to trace their descent from the Trojans, Maximilian worked even further back, to Noah, and he bullied the theology faculty of Vienna University to confirm his Old Testament ancestry. The professors prevaricated, and it was left to a later scholar to 'prove' the descent. Maximilian also built outwards, linking his family tree by marriage and kinship to Old Testament prophets, Greek and Egyptian deities, one hundred popes, almost two hundred saints (123 canonized and 47 beatified), and all the ruling houses of Europe. Effigies of some of these were placed around Maximilian's black marble tomb, work on which began in 1502. Originally intended for the palace chapel in Wiener Neustadt, the mausoleum became so large that it had to be moved during construction to the court church in Innsbruck. Surrounding the monument are twenty-eight oversize bronze figures sculpted by leading artists, including Albrecht Dürer and Veit Stoss. They comprise not only Maximilian's Habsburg forebears, but also Frankish kings, the first king of Jerusalem, and the English King Arthur. A further dozen bronzes, thirty-four busts of Roman emperors, and a hundred statues of saints were planned but never executed.[7]

The woodcut assembly known as *The Triumphal Arch* brought these genealogical fancies together in a medley of competing allusions. At the top of the arch, in the so-called tabernacle, sits Maximilian, adorned with hieroglyphic symbols that point to his descent from the Egyptian Osiris. Below are three matrons, symbolizing the Habsburg inheritance of Troy, of the early kingdom of France, and of Sicambria, meaning the lands of Austria and Hungary that were supposedly settled by the Trojan Hector. On adjacent towers rest the imperial and archducal crowns, which recollect the gifts to Austria of Caesar and Nero. Panels at the side are devoted to real and imagined ancestors and to Maximilian's exploits as a ruler, combined with poems that explain his achievements and name his forebears. Two knights in antique armour bear aloft emblems of an eagle and a dragon, signifying the battle standards of ancient Rome and of the line of emperors, of whom Maximilian was the latest and—as an inscription next to the arch explained—most suited to dwell in the company of his imperial predecessors.[8]

The Triumphal Arch wove together motifs of empire and of dynasty, blending together the Habsburg inheritance and the legacy of ancient Rome. Its accompanying composite of woodcuts, *The Triumphal Procession*, added to these conceits a territorial conception that was entirely new. *The Triumphal Procession* was made from more than 130 separate woodcut blocks and, when assembled, reached 54 metres (180 feet) in length. To this should be added Albrecht Dürer's *Triumphal Carriage* (2.4 metres or 8 feet in length), which was printed separately but originally intended to form part of the collage. The illustrations depict an imaginary scene based on a Roman triumph, with the procession led by drummers, jesters, and knights. They are followed by carriages bearing the standards of Maximilian's lands, depicting his conquests, and conveying his ancestors.

Each of these tableaux is predictable, but what follows at the end of the procession is unexpected. Preceded by an elephant, several groups of people follow in the baggage train, dressed either in quasi-Asian garb with turbans or as Native Americans with feathered bonnets. An inscription tells us that these are the 'distant Calicuttish folk' from southern India, newly brought beneath the sway of Maximilian's empire. The artist of the relevant panel, Hans Burgkmair, had never visited the New World or the Indian Ocean, and so his depiction is a pastiche of previous artists' impressions. Even so, Maximilian's empire did not include any distant peoples or possessions. But for Maximilian, who closely supervised the artists working on *The Triumphal Procession*, this was an irrelevance. In his imagination, his empire was not only Roman and Habsburg, but also unlimited geographically, encompassing the globe. Maximilian thus translated the allegorical AEIOU of his father's ruminations into a vision of world domination, in which even far-off peoples were numbered among his subjects.[9]

Maximilian's vision was fantastic and implausible. Throughout his reign, he was unable to match income to ambition. At a time when the kings of France could count on an annual revenue of several million ducats, Maximilian could muster from his Central European possessions only around six hundred thousand. In the Low Countries, the provincial assemblies and cities resisted his demands for taxes, forcing him to rely on the profits made by minting coin, which amounted in the 1480s (admittedly a bad decade) to only about two hundred thousand ducats. The Holy Roman Empire contributed on average just twenty thousand ducats a year. At his death, Maximilian left debts amounting to almost five million ducats.[10]

Maximilian strove hard to repair his finances. He introduced to Austria, Styria, and the Tyrol methods of state finance and government pioneered in the Low Countries. His division of the administration in each of the lands into separate branches—government (*Regiment*), treasury (*Kammer*), and chancellery (*Kanzlei*)—provided the institutional basis of Habsburg rule until the eighteenth century. His attempts, however, to free the treasury apparatus of the influence of the diets were less successful. Since the diets voted on taxes and were responsible for their collection, their representatives demanded to be members of the councils administering the provincial treasuries. Nevertheless, Maximilian was able to force through a reform that made all the local treasuries subordinate and answerable to an Austrian treasury based at Innsbruck in the Tyrol.

Maximilian's choice of Innsbruck for the treasury is telling. Close to the gold and silver mines of the Tyrol, the central treasury was best placed to mortgage the future profits of mining against the ready cash provided by the Fugger and Welser bankers of Augsburg, whose high-interest loans kept Maximilian financially afloat. In token of the new importance attaching to Innsbruck, Maximilian rebuilt the palace there. On one side, he threw up a 'heraldic tower' on which were emblazoned the coats of arms of his assorted lands. On the other, he built a loggia overlooking Innsbruck's main square, from which he could watch tournaments and displays of horsemanship. The loggia's 'Golden Roof' (Goldenes Dachl), the copper tiles of which were fired using an amalgam of gold, still dominates Innsbruck's main square.

During the 1480s, Maximilian was principally involved in stamping his authority on the Low Countries. Following Mary of Burgundy's death in 1482, several of the cities and the province of Flanders in the Low Countries rebelled against Maximilian, claiming that his authority had ceased upon his wife's death. In 1488, the citizens of Ghent seized Maximilian and held him captive for several months, until his father intervened with an army to secure his release and suppress the revolt. Several years later, a popular uprising broke out in Holland. Under a banner depicting bread and cheese, villagers and townsfolk violently protested Maximilian's taxation. The rebellion was put down by German mercenaries, who marched under their own flags sporting beer mugs.

To maintain Habsburg authority in the Low Countries, Maximilian was obliged in 1494 to hand power over to his son, Philip (1478–1506), whose descent from the last Burgundian duchess made him more palatable to the cities and noblemen of the Low Countries. Even so, Philip was obliged to rule in concert with a council, consisting of the principal aristocrats. But Philip died in 1506, at which point Maximilian assumed the regency on behalf of Philip's infant son, Charles of Ghent. To blunt the opposition, Maximilian gave the regency to his daughter, Margaret, although he continued to claim an income as the boy's guardian.

No sooner was peace obtained in the Netherlands than a new front opened in northern Italy. In 1494, the French king, Charles VIII, invaded the peninsula and briefly captured the kingdom of Naples. He was soon expelled by a coalition that included Maximilian, but Charles's adventure had disclosed just how ready for plucking the city-states of Italy were. Over the following decades, the resources of Italy were plundered from both without and within, as individual cities made war on their rivals and enlisted foreign aid. In 1498, therefore, Maximilian invaded northern Italy at the invitation of Ludovico Sforza of Milan, with the aim of crushing the pro-French city of Florence. Ten years later, he joined the League of Cambrai and in alliance with the pope and Louis XII of France made war on Venice. Then, just a few years later, Maximilian switched to supporting Venice and in alliance with the pope turned on the French king.

This manoeuvring provided a good part of the plot for the *Weisskunig*, but it availed Maximilian not a jot. In 1508, Maximilian had married Bianca Sforza, but he was unable to restore his wife's uncle to power in Milan. Instead, northern Italy was effectively divided between the French king, who made himself duke of Milan, and Venice, which recaptured Padua after a brief occupation by Maximilian's troops. Meanwhile, Ferdinand of Aragon took possession of the kingdom of Naples, joining it to Sicily, which was already united to the Aragonese kingdom.

By his own reckoning, Maximilian undertook seventeen military campaigns, each of which was celebrated with banners in *The Triumphal Procession*. To fund his wars, Maximilian also looked for support to the untapped resources of the Holy Roman Empire. For more than half a century, reformers had contemplated the reorganization of its structures. None, however, thought in the manner described by some historians— of state evolution, of federalization, or even of reconciling 'non-statehood' with 'non-non-statehood', with a vector towards the second. Instead, the majority looked back to a mythical past and envisaged the reestablishment of a divinely ordained state of affairs where justice prevailed under the joint leadership of ruler and princes. Maximilian, by contrast, was interested in coordination from the point of view of raising troops and cash, and he was reluctant to share power in the way reformers envisaged.[11]

Maximilian failed in making the Holy Roman Empire pay for what at the time were understood to be 'his wars.' But in his attempts to extract money, reformers led by the archbishop of Mainz forced him briefly to share power with a council made up of the electors and other princes. He also had to consent to the establishment of a central court of justice, known as the Imperial Chamber Court, which was intended to prosecute breaches of the peace, but the members of which were mainly appointed by the lords and princes of the empire. Accordingly, Maximilian established his own separate court in Vienna, the jurisdiction of which trespassed upon the Imperial

Chamber Court at Frankfurt, thus effectively establishing two rival judicial structures. To buttress the ruler's authority, Maximilian obtained in 1508 the pope's permission for kings of the Holy Roman Empire to call themselves 'elected emperors' and to use the imperial title even though they had not been crowned in Rome. From this point onwards, the title of king was used for the 'emperor in waiting', who had been elected and crowned in his predecessor's lifetime with a view to ensuring his succession.

Some order came to the empire's affairs with the inauguration in 1500 of 'imperial circles', which were groups of territories that were bound together with the aim of contributing troops for the enforcement of court decisions. The circles were the institutional descendants of the *Landvogts* established by King Rudolf of Habsburg back in the thirteenth century, except that they were administered not by the ruler's appointees but by committees of local lords and princes. Reformers were successful, too, in building up the imperial diet, transforming it from an informal event into an institution that made binding laws. Even so, Maximilian made sure that he still had overall charge of business. He was needed to open the diet, and he put forward its agenda and retained a right of veto. To become laws, decisions needed the emperor's approval as well as the support of the diet's three separate 'colleges' of electors, princes, and cities. Despite sessions that lasted from four AM to midnight, diets often broke up without agreement.

Maximilian and the princes effectively blocked one another. Neither side wanted a powerful government at the centre, lest it diminish their own influence. The Holy Roman Empire thus remained at best a policing institution that existed to curb excesses of violence. As before, day-to-day power was exercised by the great lords and princes in their territories, which included the Habsburgs in their far-flung possessions. The Holy Roman Empire, which sat above princes and territories, fulfilled therefore only the most basic of functions, operating as a security organization of last resort in the manner of what nineteenth-century German theorists called a 'night-watchman state.'

Maximilian was forever embracing initiatives which either were impossible or fizzled out through neglect. He regularly announced that he was going on crusade and in 1494 established a new chivalric order, the Knights of St George, to coordinate the recapture of Jerusalem, but in the end he never went. His dealings with Austria's Jews were equally inconsistent. On the one hand, he ordered their expulsion from Styria in 1495 but then offered them a refuge in Lower Austria. He pondered the mystical Jewish Kabbalah for secret meanings, then declared all Jewish writings banned, but reversed his decree almost at once. In 1511, after the death of his second wife, he thought to make himself pope. Maximilian's plans were sufficiently advanced for him to have worked out the cost of bribing the cardinals, and he convinced the Fugger bankers to bankroll his candidacy. In a letter to his daughter, Margaret, he promised celibacy, 'never again to pursue naked women', and signed himself, 'Maxi, your good father, future pope.' Nothing came of this, or of his plan a few years later to make the Burgundian lands into a kingdom with the antique Frankish name of Austrasia.[12]

Maximilian's marriage policy was similarly ambitious and, but for luck, might easily have unscrambled and brought ruin to his heirs. In 1496 and 1497, he wed both his children to the Spanish royal line—his son, Philip, married Juana (later called 'the Mad'), the melancholic daughter of Ferdinand of Aragon and Isabella of Castile, while his daughter, Margaret, married Ferdinand and Isabella's only son, Juan. These were high-stakes unions, for should the marriage of Juan and Margaret have yielded a son, then he, a Spanish prince, would have had a claim to at least a part of Maximilian's possessions. As it happened, it was Juan who died first—so worn out, we are told, by the sexual demands of his bride that his fate became an advertisement for self-restraint. By contrast, the union of Philip and Juana prospered, notwithstanding her periodic bouts of depression. She bore six children before Philip's early death in 1506 from sunstroke. The elder of their sons, Charles of Ghent, went on to inherit Maximilian's titles as well as the entire kingdom of Spain. Even so, this was not a foregone conclusion. Marrying for a second time in 1505, Ferdinand of Aragon intended to leave his kingdom to any son he had by his new wife, Germaine of Foix. But the son she eventually bore him in 1509 only lived a few hours.[13]

Both Frederick III and Maximilian had long sought to bring Hungary into the Habsburg orbit, but their negotiations for a marriage alliance with King Matthias Corvinus of Hungary (ruled 1458–1490) had been thwarted by Matthias's inability to sire a legitimate heir. Discussions with Matthias's successor, Wladislas Jagiello, who was also king of Bohemia, proved more successful and resulted in the double betrothal of 1515, whereby Maximilian's grandchildren, Mary and Ferdinand, were pledged respectively to Wladislas's son and daughter, Louis and Anne. The two couples were formally married in separate ceremonies in 1521–1522. Once more, the double marriage risked Austria being taken over by the House of Jagiello. As it turned out, it would be the other way round, with the Habsburgs swallowing up Hungary and Bohemia.[14]

The two double marriages arranged by Maximilian into the house of Spain and into the Jagiello line were both gambles. As Charles of Ghent, by this time Emperor Charles V, later advised, marital diplomacy was uncertain and dangerous, for outcomes could never be assured. As it turned out, however, Maximilian's wagers both paid off, making his heirs the masters not only of Europe but also of the globe. As a later, seventeenth-century tag put it, 'While others wage war, you Happy Austria get married.'[15]

We may laugh at Maximilian's extravagant delusions, his pretentious displays, and his dilettantism. But by his scheming, he succeeded in converting the allegory of the White King into a political reality for the Habsburgs, rendering his heirs masters of a large chunk of Europe and, through the Spanish connection, of a large part of the New World. Within just a few decades of Maximilian's death, even the 'distant Calicuttish folk' of *The Triumphal Procession* had become Habsburg subjects. Given the humiliations, divisions, and defeats that the Habsburgs had experienced over the previous two centuries, Maximilian's accomplishments look all the greater and his self-aggrandizing imaginings not entirely fantastic. By luck, marriage, and war, he transformed the Habsburgs from a middle-rank Central European dynasty to the premier power in Europe next to France. Under his successor as emperor, Maximilian's grandson Charles V, the Habsburgs would go one step further and become a world power.

6

CHARLES V: RULER OF THE WORLD

aximilian died in 1519. We are not sure of what since the physicians in attendance listed him as afflicted with every type of ailment—jaundice, colitis or peritonitis, gall stones, pleurisy, dysentery, and so on. (In fact, he most probably died of syphilis.) Maximilian was buried, however, not in the extravagant tomb he had ordered in Innsbruck but instead in St George's Chapel in Wiener Neustadt in a plain block of marble that also served as an altar. He was laid there as a penitent, and according to the protocol he had previously devised, his corpse was before interment scourged, his hair shorn off, and his teeth broken. Even in death, Maximilian had not lost his touch for the grand gesture.[1]

A few years before his death, Maximilian instructed the artist Bernhard Strigel to paint a family portrait, showing him with his first wife, son, and grandchildren. The composition is the most famous of its type in the history of the Habsburgs, but the setting is entirely fictional. Maximilian is depicted in healthy middle age, but he was at the time of painting so beset with illness that he travelled with his coffin prepared. He was, furthermore, no longer clean shaven but wore a thin grey beard. His wife and son, depicted as standing beside him, were both long departed from this life—indeed, Mary of Burgundy's gaze is lifted to the heavens precisely because she is dead. Moreover, the three children in the picture had never actually met, since

Ferdinand, who is shown cuddling his grandfather's arm, had been brought up in Spain, and Charles of Ghent, in the centre, in the Low Countries. The third child, with the long blond locks, is, in fact, not a Habsburg at all, but the Jagiello king, Louis of Hungary, now linked to the Habsburgs by virtue of the double betrothal conducted in 1515. Left an orphan the next year by the death of his father, Wladislas, Louis had agreed to Maximilian becoming one of his guardians—hence his incorporation in the picture.

Strigel's portrait of Charles of Ghent, the future Emperor Charles V, is generous, since at the time of composition Charles's jaw was so misshapen that its upper and lower parts did not mesh, while a carriage accident had already robbed him of his front teeth. (Presumably, he wore false teeth thereafter, just as he later relied on spectacles.) Enlarged adenoids also meant that his mouth permanently gaped. An insensitive Spanish courtier later advised Charles that he should take care lest flies settle in his throat, since the blue-bottles of Castile were notoriously insolent. Historians have been no less cutting, describing Charles as mediocre, talentless, and a relic from the Middle Ages. 'Not very interesting' was the stark verdict on Charles V of the eighteenth-century Scottish philosopher David Hume. Since depression is seldom treated with much sympathy, Charles's mental collapse in the mid-1550s, followed by his abdication, has become a metaphor for failure.[2]

The young man entered upon his Spanish inheritance in 1516 following the death of his maternal grandfather, Ferdinand of Aragon. Charles's Spanish possessions included Sicily and southern Italy and Sardinia, augmented between 1510 and 1520 by enclaves on the North African coast, which are still partly Spanish today, and later by Tunis. It was also during Charles's reign as king of Spain that much of the New World became Spanish—Mexico after 1519; the former Inca Empire, centred upon Peru, after 1529; and what would become Chile in the late 1530s. Further afield, the Philippines were claimed for Spain by the explorer Magellan in 1521, later being named in honour of Charles's son, Philip. The vast spread of Charles's possessions rendered him in the opinion of contemporaries 'Lord of the World' or, as Hernando Cortés, the conqueror of Mexico, put it, 'king of kings' and 'monarch of the universe.' For Charles's new Mexican subjects, he was also 'Lord of Earthquakes', for his power was thought to extend to the giant subterranean armadillos, whose burrowing caused the earth to move.[3]

Shortly after Charles's first visit to Spain in 1517, there was a revolt against his rule, provoked mainly by the avarice of his overdressed Flemish courtiers, who had started to pillage Spanish revenues. The rebellion was put down, but Charles learned from it. Hereafter, his preferred method of rule, both in Spain and elsewhere, was to work in collaboration with the existing power holders and elites, deferring to their privileges and seeking to achieve consensus. Although he did not generally entrust Spanish aristocratic grandees with a share in the practical work of government, he gave them military commands and viceroyalties abroad. He also admitted them to the Order of the Golden Fleece, an originally Burgundian chivalric society whose members were at its meetings able to treat with the monarch on equal terms. On these occasions, Charles listened to complaints from the assembled knights about his procrastination, overattention to detail, and indebtedness, and vainly promised to mend his ways.[4]

Charles's preference for negotiation was most apparent in his dealings with the Castilian and Aragonese parliaments. He met with the Castilian parliament, the Cortes, roughly every three years, and with its Aragonese equivalent, the Corts General, about every five. Charles never submitted to the principle that Spain's parliaments should only grant the ruler new taxes in return for him agreeing to their demands. Nevertheless, by hearing petitions of the Cortes and Corts General, and often enacting them as law, Charles reinforced the idea that there was a contract between monarch and subjects and that the royal power was not unlimited but to some degree constitutionally constrained.

Charles made a political virtue out of financial exigency. He needed money. In Castile he had the right as monarch to collect a range of taxes without the consent of the Cortes. These were always the first revenues to be allocated to support his ventures or to be offered up as collateral on loans. After that, he depended on special votes of money by the Cortes, which meant that it had to be summoned. By the 1530s the Cortes of Castile was protesting that the wealth of the kingdom was exhausted and too much misspent abroad, and it resisted Charles's demand for additional taxes. By this time, however, Charles had access to fresh funds, in the form of the revenues of the New World, to which were soon added the profits of the Bolivian silver mines. Even so, the sums obtained from Spain and the New World were insufficient, and Charles was obliged to borrow from German and Italian bankers, often at ruinous rates of interest that reached 100 per cent in the early 1550s. Although comparisons can be misleading, in respect of his principal adversaries Charles obtained from Spain and its overseas possessions a little under half the revenues available to the French king and less than a quarter of the Ottoman sultan's income.[5]

Impecuniousness did not restrict Charles's ambition. For half of his forty-year reign, Charles was at war with France, fighting in Italy, the Pyrenees, and along the western frontier of the Holy Roman Empire. He engaged the Ottomans on the Danube, led fleets against their North African allies, and campaigned in the Holy Roman Empire. In terms of battles lost and won, the balance sheet is mixed. Charles did not recover the Burgundian lands lost to France in 1477, but he made good his claims in Italy, driving his rival, Francis I of France, out of the peninsula. In the Holy Roman Empire, he failed, being unable to carry forward the fight against the enemies of the church. He took Tunis in North Africa in 1535, and its Kasbah would for forty years be a Spanish garrison, but in 1541 his fleet was wrecked before Algiers.

On his abdication, Charles listed his travels to an audience in Brussels:

> I have been nine times to Germany, six times to Spain, and seven to Italy; I have come here to Flanders ten times and have been four times to France in war and peace, twice to England, and twice to Africa . . . without mentioning other lesser journeys. I have made eight voyages in the Mediterranean and three in the seas of Spain.[6]

(Charles had visited England in 1520 and 1522 to negotiate an alliance with Henry VIII. He was the only reigning Habsburg emperor to cross the Channel.) The device that Charles bore as his personal emblem, the Pillars of Hercules with the motto *Plus Ultra* ('Still Further'), also spoke to a reign spent mostly either on horseback or, on account of piles and gout, on a litter. The Pillars of Hercules subsequently became a favourite symbol of the Habsburgs, signifying the global reach of their dominions. Together with *Plus Ultra*, they continue to feature on the Spanish flag.[7]

Cervantes partly modelled the wandering Don Quixote on Charles V, but Charles's activity shows that he was not a throwback to a bygone age. In Spain, Charles pursued a programme of institutional reform, building on the work of his predecessors, but also borrowing Burgundian financial practices. Councils and committees, staffed by lawyers and skilled secretaries who were often drawn from the lower nobility and from cities, oversaw the business of government, preparing summaries of discussions and making recommendations to him. Government was still small. In the localities and cities its writ barely ran, and in the turbulent kingdom of Aragon the royal will was frequently thwarted. As for the New World, the sea journey to and from Cadiz took on average four to five months, which meant that royal instructions, when they came at all, had been invariably overtaken by events. 'If death came from Spain, we would be immortal' soon became the adage of colonial government.[8]

In 1519, Charles was elected in his absence Holy Roman Emperor and successor to his grandfather, Maximilian. The outcome was not a foregone conclusion, for the French king, Francis I, was also a serious candidate (and Henry VIII of England a less plausible one). But Charles had the support of the South German bankers. Their bribes to the electors, delivered as post-dated cheques redeemable only in the event of Charles's election, proved decisive. Hastening to Germany, Charles was crowned king of the Romans in Aachen. Shortly afterwards, he presided over the meeting of the imperial diet at Worms. It was there that he met Martin Luther, who had already been excommunicated by the pope on account of his theology. Luther re-stated his beliefs before the diet, and Charles confirmed them as heretical, because of which he forbade Luther's teachings and condemned him as an outlaw.

Yet even at this critical moment, the young Charles showed willingness to compromise. Luther was not only a monk but also a professor at the University of Wittenberg, which had been founded by the current elector of Saxony, Frederick the Wise. Frederick was a devout Catholic, whose collection of relics amounted to some twenty thousand holy bones and other items; it was calculated at the time that penitents who viewed them contritely were entitled to 1,902,202 years and 270 days remission from the pains of Purgatory. Even so, Frederick loyally supported his professor, and Charles knew not to take Frederick on. Accordingly, Charles did not pass on to Frederick the edict banning Luther, thereby signalling to him that he might shield the reformer from punishment and persecution, which Frederick duly did.[9]

Following the diet, Charles returned to Spain. He appointed his brother, Ferdinand, as his regent in the Holy Roman Empire and assigned to him the Habsburg lands in Austria. Ferdinand was unable, however, to halt the spread of the Protestant Reformation which Luther had inspired. Although it would be several decades before most of the empire's princes and great lords sided definitively with the Reformation, many adopted a tolerant position, not wishing to offend their vassals or inflame relations with the cities, where the new teaching established early footholds. More extreme varieties of the new faith also prospered. Often combining with apocalyptic teaching, they fed ideas of social revolution and contributed to the massive popular uprising in Germany in 1525 known as the Peasants' War. In the meantime, the Ottoman Turks tested the Holy Roman Empire's defences, even to the extent of briefly besieging Vienna in the autumn of 1529. For almost a decade Ferdinand was left to face these challenges alone.

Charles had in the meantime married the frail but beautiful Isabella of Portugal. It was in origin a match made of diplomatic expediency, and the couple met for the first time only on the day of their wedding. But Charles soon fell in love with Isabella, and he trusted her sufficiently to appoint her his regent in Spain during his absences abroad. Isabella died in 1539, following a miscarriage, having already born Charles five children. Charles recovered sufficiently from her death to take on mistresses. But he never ceased to lament Isabella's passing, commissioning Titian to paint her posthumous portrait and often instructing his musicians to play in her memory the mournful French chanson 'A Thousand Regrets' (*Mille Regretz*).

Charles left Spain and Isabella in 1529, travelling from Barcelona to the Holy Roman Empire via Genoa. Only two years before, his troops had defeated a coalition of the French king and the pope and had sacked Rome. Charles lamented the brutality of his soldiers but took political advantage of it, since with Pope Clement VII his effective prisoner, he could compel him to agree to Charles's coronation as emperor. Pressed by Ferdinand, however, Charles cut his journey short and was crowned by the pope not in Rome but instead in Bologna in February 1530. The coronation was accompanied by festivities and processions through triumphal arches, crafted of wood and plaster but made to look of marble and stone. These portrayed the full repertoire of Roman emperors, along with globes of both the earth and the heavens. Charles was feted as a new Augustus, whose rule would usher in the Golden Age, foretold by Virgil in the *Aeneid*, while an image of Neptune, shown with tritons, sirens, and seahorses, drew attention to his expanding overseas possessions and to his lordship over the ocean.[10]

Charles's predecessors had all heaped images of imperial destiny together, indiscriminately mixing classical allusions with genealogical fancy and personal accomplishments. Charles's advisors added to these conceits, rehearsing ideas that they borrowed from Erasmus and Dante of peace among Christians in a united Christian commonwealth and of a world led by a single monarch. As one of Charles's closest confidants, the Spanish humanist Alfonso de Valdés, enthusiastically wrote, 'The whole orb will be put under this very Christian prince and will receive Our Faith. So will be fulfilled the words of Our Redeemer, *Let there be one flock and one shepherd.*' He went on to advise Charles to cultivate learning and take on the mantle of a philosopher-king so that he might become a new Solomon.[11]

Others recommended that Charles as 'lord of the world' look towards Jerusalem to restore there the holy places, cultivating a destiny 'established by God, predicted by the prophets, preached by the Apostles, and approved by the Lord Himself in being born, living, and dying.' Blending together medieval prophecy, New Testament theology, and Italian legal theory, Charles's chancellor, Mercurino di Gattinara, envisaged Charles as a 'world ruler' practising a mild hegemony, under whose beneficent sway local princes, privileges, and customs continued to prosper. He dressed up his account with elaborate allegories, predicting 'nests of donkeys', 'gigantic priests', and a king of the bees, with 'snake-like limbs', against whom Charles would rage as 'a new David, come to repair the altar of Zion.' The humanist Erasmus specifically recommended Charles to institute a 'theory of government according to the example of Eternal Power.'[12]

Charles had been taught in his youth by the distinguished humanist Adrian of Utrecht, the future Pope Adrian VI. But he had been a poor student who preferred reading courtly romances to composing elegant Latin prose. In manhood, Charles was disdainful of lofty cogitations, allegorical conceits, and theories of government. Notwithstanding his advisors' ruminations, the conception he had of his imperial role was overwhelmingly practical. He recognized that his ancestry and descent imposed obligations, foremost among which was to promote the Catholic faith and bring God's grace to this world. Probably the first pronouncement that Charles wrote himself (in French) was his condemnation of Luther at the diet of Worms in 1521. In it, he recalled his German, Austrian, Spanish, and Burgundian predecessors, all of whom, he averred, 'were, their whole life long, faithful sons of the Roman Church . . . defenders at all times of the Catholic Faith, its sacred ceremonies, decrees, and ordinances, and its holy rites. . . . They were at all times concerned for the propagation of the faith and the salvation of souls.' As the 'true follower of these our ancestors', Charles had, he explained, no alternative but to proceed harshly against heresy.[13]

Descent conveyed responsibilities, but so too did the global reach of Charles's rule. Charles accepted the idea that a great Christian leader should work for 'peace among Christians', but he saw this again in practical terms. His idea was to have rulers cooperate by linking them through marriage. So he had his sister marry King Francis of France; his son, Philip, first wed a Portuguese princess and then an English queen, and another sister subsequently cemented the union with Portugal. He sent a succession of nieces to marry Italian dukes in the hope of locking the peninsula more closely to the Habsburg side. By the end of his reign, the skein of Habsburg marriage alliances reached from Poland and Scandinavia, via England and Bavaria, to the Mediterranean. This was a dynastic policy that aimed at the 're-ordering of the world' in the interests of peace and not a wager on the biological survival of others, like his grandfather's. When it failed to deliver the peace he hoped for with France, Charles adopted an even more straightforward approach, but the French king turned down his challenge to a personal duel.[14]

'Peace among Christians' was not the same as world peace. Cooperation was to be only the prelude to a war of religion aimed at destroying the Ottoman Empire and liberating both Constantinople and Jerusalem, which had been 'put in infidel hands as a punishment for our sins' (Alfonso de Valdés). This was a struggle which meshed in Charles's imagination with the chivalric romances he read and with the idea of crusade, which had long informed the policies of his Spanish forebears as well as his grandfather Maximilian's rhetoric. It was in this spirit that in 1535 Charles launched his successful assault on Tunis, which had been recently taken from a Spanish tributary by the Turkish admiral Barbarossa. The action drew on Spanish, Portuguese, Genoese, and Maltese forces, as well as on Charles's Italian possessions, and was blessed by the pope as a crusade, participation in which merited remission of sins.

In token of his victory, Charles commissioned the largest ever set of tapestries for a Habsburg ruler. Twelve enormous panels, occupying altogether 600 square metres (6,500 square feet), recorded the campaign, beginning with Charles reviewing the troops at Barcelona and concluding with their re-embarkation after the capture of Tunis. For Charles, the Tunis campaign embodied the realizable imperial ambition of bringing Christian princes together, in peaceful union under his leadership, in order to wage war against the infidel. The tapestries moved between the main audience chambers in

Brussels and Madrid, with replica sets going to Charles's sister, Mary, and to the royal court in Lisbon.[15]

In order to obtain peaceful relations with Christian princes, Charles was ready to negotiate and compromise. It was in this spirit that he sought a theological formula that would bridge the differences between Catholicism and Protestantism. When this failed, he pushed successive popes to undertake a reform of the church, by which he hoped both to reinvigorate Catholicism and to remedy the sort of abuses of which Protestants complained. Charles believed a council of the church the best vehicle for undertaking this reform, but the popes were wary, lest a council usurp their prerogatives. It was only in 1545 that the Church Council assembled at Trent, and it promptly affirmed Catholic doctrines, which were inimical to most Protestants.

In anticipation of a military showdown in the empire, in 1545 Charles prepared detailed 'painted maps' showing in one contemporary description 'the location of towns as well as the distances between them, and rivers and mountains.' Although now lost, these constituted the first comprehensive maps ever made of the German lands. Charles also prepared the political ground. Instead of proclaiming a religious war, he moved against the leading Protestant princes with the excuse that they had occupied territories to which they were not entitled. This divided the enemy and so prepared the way for Charles's stunning triumph over the leading Protestant princes at the Battle of Mühlberg in 1547.[16]

Even in victory, however, Charles showed moderation. Instead of seeking to impose Catholicism by force, he imposed an interim religious agreement that permitted some elements of Protestant worship in return for recognition of papal supremacy and was applicable to both Protestants and Catholics alike. In effect, he established a separate scheme of faith for the Holy Roman Empire, albeit still under the nominal leadership of Rome. But neither side was willing to give ground, and both had misgivings about the power that victory had placed in Charles's hands. Consequently, the interim agreement was accepted only in those territories which Charles had occupied militarily. In 1552, a Protestant league for 'liberty and freedom', but backed by the Catholic French king, put Charles to flight. Outmanoeuvred by his adversaries and deserted by his Catholic allies, Charles fled in a litter to the safety of distant Carinthia.

Charles handed over to his brother Ferdinand the negotiation of a peace in the empire, which following discussions at Augsburg in 1555 gave its princes and lords the right to choose between Catholicism and Lutheranism. By this time, Charles had reached the end of his physical and mental strength. Alternating between vacancy and weeping, he spent his final years as emperor taking clocks apart and having his servants make them tick in unison. From 1555, he abdicated his realms in stages and retired to live beside the monastery of Yuste in Castile. He did not live there as a monk, as is sometimes said, but instead with a household of fifty staff, and he divided his time between expatiating on politics, religious devotion, and gorging on oysters, eels, and anchovies, downed with copious draughts of beer. According to Charles's doctors, it was overeating that caused his death in 1558, although a more plausible explanation is malarial fever.[17]

Throughout his reign, Charles was alert to the new discoveries made abroad in his name. He corresponded with the conquistadors of Mexico, exhibited the trophies that they sent home, and tracked their explorations on maps. He also followed the progress of the first Habsburg to settle in the New World. This was Brother Peter of Ghent (Fray Pedro de Gante), who besides being the bastard son of Maximilian founded over a hundred Franciscan schools and churches in Mexico. Charles saw his first Native American in 1520 in Brussels—he was shivering, so Charles ordered him to be given a cloak. Thereafter, Charles maintained a diligent concern for the indigenous population, commanding that they be fairly treated, not rounded up as servile labour, and brought by kindly example to knowledge of the faith.[18]

Charles's interest in the New World was emphatically not conditioned by the loot it brought to the Old World. The 'distant Calicuttish folk' were part of Charles's world empire and thus, as he explained to his son Philip, also his responsibility, 'for the honour of God and for the sake of justice.' Yet even as Charles's possessions reached further across the ocean to include the Pacific, the universal monarchy was split in half by confessional division. For all his hopes of bringing peace among Christians, Charles could no longer count on the religion of Christians being the same as his own. The Peace of Augsburg now permitted the Holy Roman Empire's division into territories ruled mostly by princes who adhered to a Lutheran scheme of worship and belief and by a minority which stayed committed to the old faith.[19]

In the abdication speech he gave in Brussels in 1555, Charles had tearfully apologized to a crowd of courtiers. He had done, he explained, all that he could, and he was sorry not to have done better. Even as he spoke, his vast dominions were being divided. His brother, Ferdinand, refused to

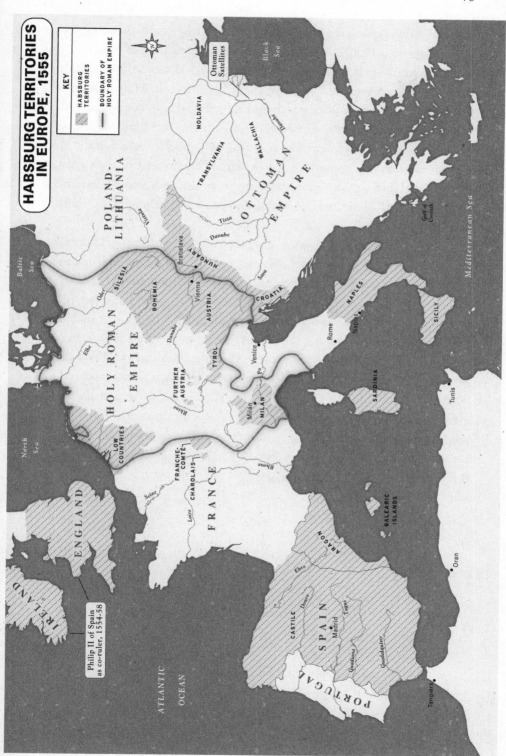

HABSBURG TERRITORIES IN EUROPE, 1555

KEY

HABSBURG TERRITORIES

BOUNDARY OF HOLY ROMAN EMPIRE

Ottoman Satellites

Philip II of Spain as co-ruler, 1554-58

POLAND-LITHUANIA

MOLDAVIA

TRANSYLVANIA

WALLACHIA

OTTOMAN EMPIRE

Black Sea

Baltic Sea

SILESIA

Bratislava

HUNGARY

HOLY ROMAN EMPIRE

BOHEMIA

Vienna

AUSTRIA

CROATIA

Save

Tisza

Danube

Vistula

Oder

Elbe

NAPLES

Rome

Naples

SICILY

Mediterranean Sea

TYROL

Venice

Po

FURTHER AUSTRIA

Rhine

Danube

SARDINIA

Tunis

MILAN

Milan

LOW COUNTRIES

North Sea

FRANCHE-COMTÉ

CHAROLAIS

FRANCE

Rhone

Seine

Loire

BALEARIC ISLANDS

ENGLAND

IRELAND

ATLANTIC OCEAN

ARAGON

Ebro

CASTILE

Madrid

Tagus

SPAIN

Guadiana

Guadalquivir

Douro

PORTUGAL

Tangiers

Oran

Gulf of Corinth

N

consider relinquishing the prospect of the imperial office by handing it over to Charles's son, Philip. Ferdinand had been elected king of the Holy Roman Empire in 1531 and had every expectation of succeeding Charles as emperor. So he resisted the idea of keeping Spain and the Holy Roman Empire united under one ruler, even though Charles held out the prospect of an alternating office, whereby Ferdinand's son, Maximilian (the later Emperor Maximilian II), would follow Philip as monarch of both Spain and the Holy Roman Empire. The consequence was that at the moment of their greatest extent the Habsburg dominions were cut in two, into a Spanish part ruled by Charles's son, Philip, and a Central European part belonging to Charles's brother, Ferdinand.[20]

Charles's achievement was, nonetheless, palpable. The Habsburgs would continue to gather mythologies, build grandiose mausoleums, and stage displays of victory in the manner of Roman triumphs, but these would no longer be empty exercises in self-promotion. They would, instead, be increasingly infused with the same purpose of which Charles had spoken at the Diet of Worms—to align the dynasty with the defence of the faith. The adjustment would take time and pulse at first more slowly in Central Europe than in Spain. Whereas Philip's zeal was boundless, Ferdinand and his heirs tended to embrace Charles's readiness to negotiate and strike deals, even to the extent of compromising their own commitment to the Catholic religion. Gradually, though, the pieces would fall into line, adding to the acronym of AEIOU Charles's vision of the Habsburg dynasty as bound to the service of the Catholic Church.

7

HUNGARY, BOHEMIA, AND THE PROTESTANT CHALLENGE

*O*n the evening of 29 August 1526, the Hungarian army was destroyed in less than two hours by the Ottoman Turks on the field of Mohács. The battle claimed about a half of the leading magnates and seven bishops and archbishops, who had led their contingents personally into battle. The young Louis, king of Hungary and Bohemia, whom we previously saw as a child in Strigel's portrait, perished in the rout. He was just twenty years old. Louis's death opened the way to the acquisition by the Habsburgs of the Hungarian and Bohemian kingdoms, for his successor would be the boy on the left in Strigel's picture—Maximilian's younger grandson, Ferdinand of Austria (1503–1564). This was for the Habsburgs to be the greatest 'Fortinbras moment.' On the ruins of the Jagiello monarchy of Hungary and Bohemia, Ferdinand and his successors would build the conglomeration of Central European territories that historians call the Habsburg Empire.

Louis of Jagiello was doubly linked to the Habsburgs. His sister, Anne, was married to Ferdinand, while Louis himself had in 1522 wed Ferdinand's sister, Mary. Once the Turks had withdrawn from Hungary, Mary took immediate charge of the government and, since the dead king had no immediate heir, she worked energetically to have both his Hungarian and his Bohemian kingdoms pass to her brother. Ferdinand was by this time already acting as Charles V's regent in the Holy Roman Empire, and Charles had also assigned to him the government of the Habsburg possessions in Central Europe. The boy in Strigel's picture was by now a young man of explosive temper who, having been brought up in Spain, favoured the black clothing that was fashionable there. With high cheek bones, a thin face, and spindly limbs, he resembled a spider.

Historians continue to be misled by the special pleading of Ferdinand's predecessors in Bohemia and Hungary. In order to obtain foreign troops and subsidies, both Louis and his father, Wladislas II (lived 1456–1516), had convinced foreign ambassadors that the Bohemian and Hungarian realms were impoverished and thus unable to mount an effective response to the growing Ottoman Turkish challenge. It is from the envoys' reports of financial distress that historians take most of their information. In Bohemia, the royal claim of penury was true only to the extent that the kingdom's diets routinely blocked the ruler's request for extra taxes, but the monarch still had significant private resources of his own in the form of the royal right to the profits of minting, mining, and commercial tolls. In Hungary, it was a downright falsehood. Most royal income was distributed at source and never went through the treasury's books. Even so, it may be estimated at about six hundred thousand gold florins or ducats per year, to which should be added forced loans and sundry windfalls. One bishop found to have embezzled money from the royal treasury paid four hundred thousand florins for his freedom.[1]

Not only did Louis's income from Hungary compare favourably with the revenue obtained by Archduke Ferdinand from his Austrian lands, but it also rendered the Hungarian army one of most modern and well-equipped in Europe. Had it been deployed in Italy, its pike men, harquebusier gunners, artillery, and mixed cavalry units, all operating according to an integrated battle plan, would surely have taken the peninsula. But at Mohács it faced instead the Ottoman Turks—and twenty-five thousand troops, however well commanded and furnished, will seldom triumph against an army three times the size. Even so, Sultan Suleiman's advisors considered the Hungarian army to be a formidable opponent and ranked its king among 'the great rulers of the infidels.' For this reason, Suleiman launched a 'double army' against Hungary, made up of both his Anatolian (Turkish mainland) and his Balkan contingents.[2]

There were good reasons, therefore, for Ferdinand to strive for the crowns of Bohemia and Hungary, for both were relatively wealthy kingdoms. Nevertheless, the double union contracted between the Habsburgs and the family of Bohemia and Hungary's ruler was not enough to ensure an easy transition. Both kingdoms had powerful nobilities, which claimed the right through their diets to determine policy and the royal succession. The Bohemian diet was the better organized, and its membership was augmented by representatives from around thirty cities. Meeting three or four times a year, it had by the beginning of the sixteenth century converted the kingdom's government into its own instrument, even to the extent of appointing the principal royal officers.

But the Hungarian diet was the scarier. Although usually meeting only once a year, its assemblies were often crowded, for all noblemen in the kingdom had the right to attend, which meant that up to ten thousand nobles might be there in person. The diet often met on the Rákos Plain next to Pest. Corralled in a fenced, open-air arena, the assembled nobles berated the king and his officers, who were seated on a dais before the multitude, while armed Gypsies patrolled the perimeter. The nobles not only attended the diet in battle harness but sometimes also set up an executioner's block or gallows as a warning to traitors. They were not slow to point these out. Unsurprisingly, many royal officers fled on the earliest occasion. In this charged atmosphere, the monarch first presented his proposals, to which the nobles responded with their 'grievances.' The task was then to reconcile the two positions and arrive in private negotiation at a text that both sides could agree on. Often as not, no compromise was reached, on which account the affairs of the kingdom moved into a precarious limbo.[3]

The death of King Louis at Mohács left both kingdoms ripe for the taking. Of the two, Ferdinand regarded Bohemia as the greater prize and moved swiftly to take possession of its crown. In order to further Ferdinand's suit, both his agents and the widowed queen stressed his kinship through marriage to the dead king Louis. The Czech lands comprised, however, a number of parts. Besides Bohemia, there were Moravia, Silesia, and Upper and Lower Lusatia, each of which had its own separate diets and laws. (Silesia is now mostly in Poland, and the Lusatias are divided between Poland and Germany.) These territories were willing enough to recognize Ferdinand's right of inheritance, albeit at one remove as devolving to him through his wife, the dead king's sister. The most powerful of the diets was, however, the Bohemian. It considered the crown to be elective, and it was this assembly alone that decided on the identity of the monarch.

There were besides Ferdinand at least nine other candidates for the Bohemian throne: various German princes, several ambitious Czech lords, and Francis I of France. Plainly, the French king's failure to be elected emperor seven years previously had not diminished his ambition. A committee of the Bohemian diet evaluated the merits of each and settled on Ferdinand, for only he was thought to have the resources to defend the kingdom against the Turks should they decide to march northwards from Hungary. It also helped that Ferdinand promised to pay off the debts contracted by his Jagiello predecessors to individual noblemen. Even so, to secure his election Ferdinand had to make concessions, which included recognizing the elective character of the monarchy, confirming the Bohemian nobility in their rights, and acknowledging the religious freedoms belonging to the Czech Utraquists.

The Utraquists were the followers of the Prague preacher Jan Hus, who had been burnt for heresy in 1415, and they were the largest religious denomination in Bohemia. They celebrated the mass in two kinds (*sub utraque specie*, whence their name). This meant that they distributed both the bread and the wine to communicants, including to babies, which their critics thought especially disgusting, whereas in the Catholic Church the wine was mostly reserved for the clergy. The Utraquists also had their own separate church hierarchy, at the top of which sat a committee of administrators, who served in place of the Catholic archbishop of Prague. The Utraquists disputed the authority of the pope while conceding that he was 'theologically necessary', and they still required their priests to be ordained by Catholic bishops. The Church Council meeting at Basle had in 1433 agreed to permit Utraquism, but the pope had subsequently condemned Utraquism as heretical. By acknowledging the rights of the Utraquist Church in Bohemia, Ferdinand was therefore confirming a heresy.[4]

Early in 1527, Ferdinand was crowned in St Vitus's Cathedral in Prague by the bishop of Olomouc (the see of Prague being vacant). The oath that he swore on this occasion included not only to maintain the Catholic Church but also to defend the Utraquist Church. In deference to his oath, Ferdinand never sought to curb the Utraquists, but he stood instead, albeit reluctantly, as the sworn guardian of its heretical theology and rites, including ceremonies celebrating the Czech martyr Jan Hus. It was a curious position for a Habsburg ruler to have been forced into.[5]

The royal succession in Hungary followed no clear rules but was determined both by hereditary right and by election of the diet, with the precise mix depending upon the political balance at the time. Three months after Louis's death, the diet elected John Zápolya as his successor. Zápolya was the governor or voivode of Transylvania, which constituted at the time the easternmost province of the Hungarian kingdom. Zápolya had not an ounce of royal blood in him, but he had a considerable following among the common Hungarian nobility. Zápolya was duly crowned by the bishop of Nitra in the coronation city of Székesfehérvár, which lay south-west of the capital city of Buda. On his head the bishop placed the Holy Crown of St Stephen. Named after Hungary's first Christian king, who lived at the beginning of the eleventh century, the diadem was in fact a later confection, made up of two coronets welded together, with a cross bolted onto the top. Nevertheless, until crowned with it, no ruler was considered Hungary's true monarch.[6]

Resting his right to the throne on his marriage into the dead king's family, Ferdinand marched into Hungary, distributing largesse and titles, and drove King John Zápolya eastwards. The diet duly reconvened and chose Ferdinand king. Only a month after Zápolya's coronation, Ferdinand was also raised to the throne—with the same holy crown, in the same coronation city, and by the same bishop. Meanwhile, the noble diet of the kingdom of Croatia (what is now northern Dalmatia, on the Adriatic coast), which had since the twelfth century been joined to Hungary, voted Ferdinand its king. The Croatian nobility did so unconditionally, recognizing Ferdinand's hereditary claim to the Croatian throne and acknowledging in full the rights of his heirs. By surrendering so meekly to Ferdinand, the Croatian diet ensured that it would never again choose its king but take whomever the Habsburgs offered.[7]

With two rival kings installed, both of whom had been correctly crowned with St Stephen's diadem, Hungary collapsed into civil war. Since Ferdinand had the upper hand militarily, John Zápolya reluctantly allied in 1529 with the Ottoman Turks, becoming the sultan's vassal. The deal was confirmed on the former battlefield of Mohács, amid the ruin of war and the skulls of the dead. In support of Zápolya, the sultan now invaded Ferdinand's territories and in the same year put Vienna under siege. A three-way struggle began, pitting, on one side, the uneasy alliance of Zápolya and the Turks and, on the other, Ferdinand. An attempt by Zápolya to betray the sultan by coming to terms with Ferdinand, followed by Zápolya's death in

1540, led the next year to the Turkish occupation and garrisoning of the middle portion of the Hungarian kingdom. As evidence that they were there to stay, the Turks moved the corpses of their most precious dervishes into shrines on Hungarian soil.

Bit by bit, Hungary split in three—an eastern part made up mostly of Transylvania, which belonged to Zápolya's son, the infant John II Sigismund (lived 1540–1571), and which followed its own laws and had its own diet; a crescent of land reaching from the Adriatic coast to the northeast, over which Ferdinand ruled; and a broad central corridor, which lay in Turkish hands. The capital city of Buda became the seat of a Turkish pasha or governor, while its principal church, the so-called Matthias Church, was converted into a mosque and its spire made a minaret. The Turkish occupation of central Hungary would last for more than 140 years.

Beginning in the 1520s the Reformation burst upon Central Europe, adding to its political uncertainties and divisions. In the Bohemian lands, Lutheranism radicalized Utraquism, fomenting a division between moderate and reformist wings, and inspired religious sectaries who adopted even more extreme positions: Anabaptists, who embraced both adult baptism and social revolution; Demoniacs, who raved in divine ecstasy; Adamites, who taught that nakedness and promiscuity restored the innocence of the Garden of Eden; Unitarians, who denied Christ's divinity, and so on. In Hungary, meanwhile, Lutheranism took an early hold in the royal court. Even before Mohács, Queen Mary's Protestant sympathies had been sufficiently well attested to earn her the soubriquet from the papal ambassador of 'the Lutheran lioness', while one of King Louis's main advisors, George of Brandenburg, had taken time off from his duties at court to introduce the Reformation to his estates in Silesia.[8]

Lutheranism prospered where Germans were in the majority—in the principal Hungarian cities, where they made up the commercial class, and in Transylvania, where they had settled as merchants and farmers from the twelfth century, led there in legend by the Pied Piper. But it was the sterner reformed faith of John Calvin that from the late 1530s onwards won over the Hungarian countryside. Calvinism's stress on divine providence suited Hungarians as it provided an explanation for their country's occupation by the Turks and Habsburgs. Calvinist preachers taught how the tribulations of the Hungarians were akin to those suffered by the Israelites in the Old Testament, on which account they too constituted a Chosen People.

Calvinism and, unusually, Unitarianism also flourished in Transylvania under the care of austere but 'godly' noblemen and urban patricians. For a century and a half, the main church in Cluj in Transylvania, the massive St Michael's, was a Unitarian place of worship.[9]

Unlike Catholics and Lutherans, Calvinists and Unitarians denied that Christ was physically or substantially present in the bread and the wine of the communion, which made them targets of persecution. Even so, the new faith prospered under the protection of local landowners, while in the eastern, Transylvanian part of the kingdom, the diet gave Calvinism and Unitarianism the status of official religions. In the Turkish-occupied area, there were no controls on religious observance whatsoever. The pasha in Buda categorically affirmed in 1548 that 'all Hungarians and Slavs should be able to hear and receive the Word of God without any danger.' By the end of the century, if not before, three-quarters of parishes in the three divided parts of the Hungarian kingdom had in one shape or form become Protestant.[10]

Ferdinand's response to the spread of heresy was to declare in 1527 that the ban on Luther's teaching pronounced at the Diet of Worms applied under pain of death to all his lands and kingdoms. By this time, however, Lutheranism had also captured Austria. An inspection or 'visitation' of parishes and religious houses undertaken the next year revealed a condition of profound decay. The Scottish Monastery (Schottenkloster, founded by Irish monks) in the heart of Vienna had only seven monks left, while at the university the number of students had fallen to barely thirty. Other reports spoke of nuns forsaking their vocation and either wandering the land or taking husbands. At Admont in Styria, the nuns were found not only to keep Protestant books but also to have plundered the convent's treasures.[11]

Ferdinand might indeed lament 'with a heavy heart and sighing breast the evil and shocking mass of errors and the divisions within the Holy Christian Religion', but he was powerless to make good his threats. By the 1530s, Protestants were a majority in the diets of Upper and Lower Austria. Digging deep in their pockets, the provincial nobility was by the end of Ferdinand's reign capable of raising upon request up to several million ducats in taxes. Had Ferdinand used force against the Lutherans, he would have not only brought about a civil war that he could not win but also jeopardised vital revenues in the war against the Turks. Moreover, so many noblemen and others had embraced Protestantism that there were insufficient Catholics left to staff Ferdinand's administration and household. Ferdinand relied on Protestants to work the machinery of government, even including them in his Privy Council. Most extraordinarily, Ferdinand's main advisor on religious policy was a married priest.[12]

Similar circumstances prevailed in Hungary, where Ferdinand also relied on Protestant advisors and power brokers. His principal ally and, from 1554, his chief minister or palatine was Thomas Nádasdy, whose private press in Sárvár in western Hungary churned out Protestant literature, including the first printed Hungarian translation of the New Testament. In Bohemia the more extreme variety of Hussitism embraced by the Unity of Czech Brethren, which stood theologically midway between Lutheranism and Calvinism (with pacifism mixed in), experienced only sporadic persecution. Even so, where he could Ferdinand advanced Catholics to political prominence. In the wake of a fire that burnt down the royal archive in Prague in 1541, destroying the deeds of many noblemen and others, Ferdinand confirmed the rights of Catholic sympathisers but disavowed the privileges previously granted to Protestants. A foiled uprising in Prague in 1547 gave Ferdinand a further opportunity to reward Catholic nobles at the expense of Protestant rebels.

The relative tolerance that prevailed during Ferdinand's reign was not only the consequence of expediency. Ferdinand believed that a middle course was possible in matters of religion and that reconciliation might be obtained between Catholics and Protestants. In this respect, he came close to Erasmus's conviction that the best solution would be a negotiated compromise between the rival confessions. Accordingly, he shied away from confrontation and put pressure instead on the pope to permit clerical marriage and communion in both kinds as a means of reconciliation. His initiatives on behalf of the Catholic faith were similarly gentle and largely uncontroversial—refounding the archbishopric of Prague, establishing the Catholic Clementinum College in Prague to rival the Utraquist Charles University, sponsoring the educational work of the new Catholic missionary order known as the Jesuits, and promoting the appointment of worthy bishops to the beleaguered diocese of Vienna.

Ferdinand's territories embraced a wide swathe of Central Europe. On top of this, Ferdinand was also regent on behalf of his brother in the Holy Roman Empire, finally succeeding him as emperor in 1558. Because of his frequent absences, he gave over the government of Hungary and Bohemia to regency councils. Much of their time was taken up by hearing appeals from lower courts and attending to petitions. Coordination of policy was achieved by one institution only: the Privy Council. Founded in 1527, the Privy Council comprised no more than a dozen advisors who accompanied Ferdinand on his travels.

Political complexity and local interests stood in the way of joined-up government. The imperial treasury, also founded in 1527, looked after the private estates of the ruler in the Austrian lands and occasionally administered the allocation of tax revenues. Nevertheless, most income either went directly to the separate treasury office in Innsbruck or was withheld by the Bohemian treasury in Prague. The Hungarian treasury office constituted the only functioning administrative institution in Hungary and so performed most of the work of government there. The Imperial War Council, founded in 1556, was responsible primarily for provisioning the border with the Turks and with military strategy, but its authority in the Austrian lands was restricted by competing military councils. To save time, Ferdinand also suggested that the diets of his Central European territories should meet together, but his proposals were blocked by the nobilities of each.[13]

Ferdinand was unable to impose a uniform government any more than he could enforce religious conformity. The lands and kingdoms over which he held sway were possessed of powerful nobilities, obstructive diets, and noisy Protestant majorities. Ferdinand was accordingly obliged to proceed piecemeal, making gains where he could and compromises where he must, even to the extent of permitting Lutheranism's advance and swearing to defend the Utraquist heresy. Ferdinand's legacy was a patchwork of offices of shifting competences and a web of local concessions. For all its shortcomings, it amounted to a workable solution, but one which could only be temporary.

8

PHILIP II: THE NEW WORLD, RELIGIOUS DISSENT, AND ROYAL INCEST

Upon Charles V's abdication in 1555, his son Philip succeeded to the Spanish throne. Along with Spain came the Spanish possessions in the New World, the Low Countries, the Franche-Comté (the county of Burgundy), Naples, Sicily, Milan, the Balearic Islands, and Sardinia. But Philip II inherited something more. From his father, he took the conviction that Habsburg rulers should defend and promote the Catholic faith and that this was the dynasty's primary obligation. It was in this spirit that Philip built the Escorial Palace outside Madrid. Intended originally in remembrance of his father, the Escorial symbolized the fusion of dynasty with religious mission. A subterranean vault was set aside there for Charles V and Isabella of Portugal, which was later expanded into a mausoleum to hold the bodies of other family members. Philip transferred there the remains of his aunt, Mary of Hungary, along with three of his four wives (his second wife, Mary Tudor, is buried in Westminster Abbey). To emphasize the Escorial's link to the dynasty, the corners of the square wall enclosing the complex were each crowned with towers, recalling the design of the Habsburg Old Fort in Vienna. Even more ambitiously, the layout within the walls was intended both to replicate Solomon's Temple and to imitate the gridiron on which the Escorial's patron saint, the third-century St Lawrence, was roasted to death.[1]

The Escorial was not just a royal residence and burial site. Made up of four thousand rooms set around sixteen courtyards and linked by 160 kilometres (100 miles) of corridors, only a quarter of the building constituted royal apartments. The rest comprised a basilica, a monastery with fifty monks, and a small school. Its sacredness was amplified by Philip's museum of relics, which amounted to 7,422 items. Besides fragments of the True Cross and Christ's Crown of Thorns, the collection included twelve whole bodies of saints, 144 heads, and the miscellaneous body parts of no fewer than 3,500 martyrs. From an internal window in his bedroom, Philip could see the altar in the basilica where masses were performed in almost continuous sequence for the souls of his deceased relatives. Above all else, the Escorial was a prayer factory for the Spanish branch of the Habsburgs.[2]

The Escorial overlooked gardens and an imported forest of twelve thousand pine trees. Beyond these stretched a bare landscape, parched for most of the year against a cloudless sky. The starkness of aspect had its counterpart in Philip's uncompromising manner. Historians have recently drawn attention to the lighter side of the king's personality—his love of dancing, tournaments, bullfights, and womanizing and the pleasure he took in the company of jesters and dwarves. But Philip is better judged by the explanation he gave several times for his conduct: 'Rather than suffer the least injury to religion and the service of God, I would lose all my states and a hundred lives if I had them, for I do not intend to rule over heretics.' His personal motto, 'The World Is Not Enough', spoke to the same theme—that earthly dominion counted for less than heavenly glory.[3]

Philip was convinced that his own policy conformed to the divine will. On several occasions, he explained to his ministers that they were acting in his service and the Lord's, 'which is the same thing.' When faced with insurmountable obstacles, he was convinced that a miraculous intervention would dispel them, for the 'Christian certitude and confidence that we must justly have in the cause of God will remove them and inspire and strengthen us to overcome them.' In his dealings with successive popes, he entertained no doubt that his apprehension of God's will was superior to theirs, even to the extent of accusing one pope of disseminating Protestant ideas. Indeed, his genealogical investigations not only proved Maximilian's fabulous descents but also demonstrated his ancestry in Melchizedek and the priest-kings of the Old Testament.[4]

Philip's absolute conviction that he was fulfilling a divine plan not only led him to unrealistic decisions but also freed him from scruples. Since his choices corresponded to Christ's own, all things were permitted to him. His conscience spared of doubt, Philip persecuted all whose allegiance to Catholicism, and thus to himself, might be suspected. During his brief spell as king of England (1554–1558) and consort of Queen Mary Tudor, Philip was complicit in the judicial murder of almost three hundred Protestants, thus overseeing one of the most intense religious persecutions in sixteenth-century Europe. Upon his return to Spain, he rooted out Protestant communities in Valladolid and Seville, with about 100 people burnt, and sent an expedition to destroy a French Protestant or Huguenot colony on the Florida coast, which was preaching to the Native people there—143 settlers were duly butchered.[5]

But it was not only the Lutheran heresy that agitated Philip. Spain had a population of around half a million Muslims (out of a total population of seven million), who were the legacy of the centuries when most of the Iberian Peninsula had been under Islamic rule. These had been continuously hounded by Spain's Catholic rulers, who had forced them to convert and become so-called New Christians. In many cases, their conversion was skin-deep, and they still practised their older beliefs in secret. Philip continued to oppress them, not only as apostates but also as potential fifth columnists. His fears were not unwarranted, for some of Spain's 'crypto-Muslims' plotted rebellion in collaboration with allies of the Turks in North Africa. Philip's measures to outlaw the distinctive dress, diet, Arabic language, and bath houses of Spanish Muslims led to a major rebellion in southern Spain in 1568–1569 and, upon its suppression, to the expulsion and dispersal of about half of the Muslim population.[6]

Spain also had about three hundred thousand Jews, who had been similarly forced to embrace Catholicism. Most of these were by the mid-sixteenth century well on the way to acculturation, their older religious practices reduced to obscure rituals performed in private. Having lost their visibility, however, Jewish New Christians became the object of fear, since their numbers and activity were no longer obvious. Suspicion was fuelled early on in Philip's reign by the 'discovery' of secret correspondence, allegedly between Jewish elders in Spain and rabbis in Constantinople. The Protocols of the Elders of Zion, forged by the Tsarist secret police in the late nineteenth century to justify the hounding of Russian Jews, were anticipated in this equally clumsy fake. In it, the rabbis of Constantinople responded to the complaints of Spanish Jews by recommending the infiltration and overthrow of Catholic society: 'In connection with what you have said about them murdering you, then turn your sons into doctors and apothecaries, so that they may murder them. . . . Turn your sons into clergymen and theologians so that they may destroy their churches.' The letter went on to recommend that Jews also enter the law and administration in order to subvert the government and judiciary.[7]

But since Jews were now so hard to detect, new methods had to be found to determine their concealed Jewish identity. During the sixteenth century, therefore, it became increasingly common for guilds, religious orders, and chivalric societies to demand proof of descent as a precondition for membership. Philip II championed this practice by upholding the rights of corporations to undertake investigations and to exclude those whose bloodline had been supposedly contaminated by either Jewish or Muslim ancestry. In order to establish 'purity of blood' (*limpieza de sangre*), genealogy became an obsession throughout Spanish society and the production of false documents a new industry.

Spain's possessions in the New World expanded during Philip's reign as adventurers made new conquests on his behalf and missionaries consolidated their religious hold on the population. Beneath the viceroys of New Spain and Peru, based respectively in Mexico City and Lima, stretched a hierarchy of governorships, captaincies, and mayoralties, all of which were overseen by visiting judges and courts, and ultimately by the Council of the Indies in Madrid. In reality, Spanish control was weak. The Council of the Indies had little grasp of conditions overseas, on which account Philip ordered in 1569 a statistical survey of Spain's New World possessions, based on a questionnaire sent to all mid-level officials working there. The results yielded a trove of remarkable information and, as is the fault with all such inventories, the illusion of order. Large parts of the Latin American countryside were still wholly mysterious, while others had already been lost to bands of renegade soldiers and black slaves, who had escaped from the plantations and set up their own 'maroon states.' The vital land route across the Isthmus of Panama was regularly rendered impassable by maroon bandits, who preyed on the off-loaded cargoes.[8]

From the 1560s onwards, the Spanish New World was a Pacific as well as an Atlantic phenomenon. Silver mined in Bolivia now went westwards via Acapulco to the Spanish port of Manila in the Philippines, founded in 1571,

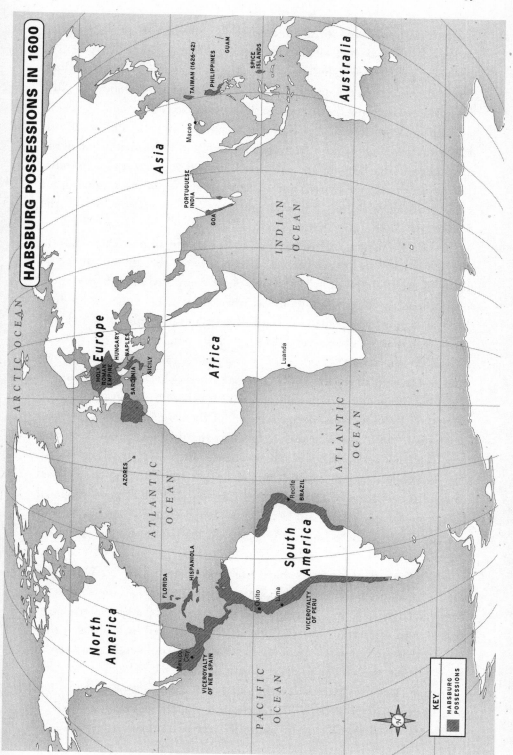

HABSBURG POSSESSIONS IN 1600

ARCTIC OCEAN

North America

FLORIDA

AZORES

ATLANTIC OCEAN

HISPANIOLA

MEXICO City

VICEROYALTY OF NEW SPAIN

PACIFIC OCEAN

Quito

Lima

South America

Recife
BRAZIL

VICEROYALTY OF PERU

ATLANTIC OCEAN

Europe

HOLY ROMAN EMPIRE

HUNGARY

NAPLES

SARDINIA

SICILY

Africa

Luanda

INDIAN OCEAN

Asia

Macao

PORTUGUESE INDIA

GOA

TAIWAN (1626-42)

PHILIPPINES

GUAM

SPICE ISLANDS

Australia

KEY

HABSBURG POSSESSIONS

where it was exchanged for silk and porcelain. Silver pieces of eight minted in Peru and Mexico had within a few decades become a globally recognized currency. To the trade in bullion, the Manila galleons added deerskin, which was highly prized in the manufacture of Japanese samurai armour. In 1580, King Henry of Portugal died, necessarily without heirs since he was a cardinal and so sworn to celibacy. Through his mother, Isabella, Philip claimed the throne, driving his rivals from the kingdom. Philip II's acquisition of the Portuguese crown brought not only Brazil but also outposts at Goa in India, Macao on the Chinese coast, and (briefly) Nagasaki on the southernmost coast of Japan. Habsburg Spain was now the foremost power in both the Pacific and the Atlantic Oceans.[9]

Even so, Spanish rule in the Pacific was spread thinly. There were in the 1580s no more than seven hundred Spaniards throughout all the islands of the Philippines, while Manila itself comprised only eighty Spanish households. Philip's ambition was whetted by officials there who drew his attention to the opportunities available on the mainland of China and south-eastern Asia. Over several decades, Philip pondered 'the enterprise of China' (*la empresa de China*), which was a project to invade the coastal region and then to advance into the interior, gathering local support along the way. Since Hernando Cortés had captured Mexico with just several hundred troops, six thousand were deemed ample for the conquest of China. As an alternative, Philip considered overthrowing the rulers of Sarawak in Borneo, Thailand, and Cambodia and advancing northwards to roll up China. The loot obtained from Sarawak might, he was advised, even be deployed to fund the invasion of England. As it turned out, Philip's plans of global conquest were not tested, still less realized, while the great invasion fleet or armada that he launched against England in 1588 foundered uselessly in the North Sea.[10]

New Christians were prohibited from travelling to the New World, but they went anyway, seeking both opportunity and refuge. As one chronicler complained, Mexico was 'too much filled and settled by a people, base, corrupted, and untrustworthy. And since it is not allowed in Spain that they do come into these parts, I know not what cause could suffice to keep us from ejecting them.' The principal instrument for the persecution of New Christians was the Spanish Inquisition, which Philip introduced to Lima and Mexico City in 1570–1571. Although originally founded in Castile at the end of the fifteenth century as an office of government under a royally appointed inquisitor-general, the Spanish Inquisition operated largely free of royal control and was staffed by priests trained in the law. Originally introduced to combat religious backsliding or apostasy, the Inquisition soon expanded its remit to heresy, blasphemy, bigamy, and sexual crimes. It was also empowered to exact the full range of punishments. Those condemned to death were often publicly burnt at the stake in religious ceremonies known as autos-da-fé ('statements of faith'), but not before they had been preached at and paraded in humiliating vestments.[11]

Beside this, the Inquisition was empowered to censor books and to restrict the flow of students to foreign universities, where they might pick up unwelcome ideas. It thus sought to put both Spain and the New World in an intellectual quarantine. In this respect, it mostly succeeded, eliminating all literature that was not strictly orthodox. A visiting ambassador to Spain noted the void in the imagination caused by censorship. As he complained, Spanish nobles spoke in the manner of blind men describing colours, for their intellectual experiences were so narrow. In the New World, the Inquisition tightly controlled the printing presses in Mexico City and Lima, limiting their output in the sixteenth century to fewer than two hundred titles, mostly teaching materials of the dullest content. Its censorship extended not only to the printed word but also to tattoos and branding irons.[12]

In the New World, the Inquisition very much returned to its original role of hunting down Jewish apostates. Between 1589 and 1596, two hundred people were tried for this crime by the Inquisition in Mexico City, of whom nine were executed. This effectively destroyed the Jewish community in New Spain. It was subsequently reconstituted by immigrants from Portugal, but ruined once more in the 1640s, when more than thirty Jews were sent to the stake and a further hundred burnt in effigy (having either died in prison or escaped). In Lima, persecution beginning in the 1570s had by the next century eliminated most Jews.[13]

Only a very few of those brought before the Inquisition suffered the death penalty—somewhere between 1 and 2 per cent overall. But death was not the only way to destroy lives. The Jews of New Spain and Peru were broken by the confiscation of their property, while the Inquisition routinely deployed torture and harsh physical punishment. Figures from Spanish Sicily in the middle decades of the sixteenth century indicate that while only 22 of 660 people convicted of crimes by the Inquisition were executed, 274 were either sent as slaves to the galleys or tortured by water-boarding, by the strappado pulley that dislocated the shoulders, or by the rack that tore apart its victims' ligaments. Moreover, the spectacle of the auto-da-fé, which was often attended by several tens of thousands, was intended to impress conformity. As one Spanish jurist explained, the purpose of public execution was 'not to save the souls of the accused but to procure the public good and instil fear and modesty in the people.'[14]

In the New World, Philip had to put up with overmighty subjects who had carved out by the sword vast territories of their own. Indeed, the 130,000 square kilometres belonging in the later sixteenth century to Martin Cortés, son of the conquistador Hernando Cortés, probably made him the world's richest private individual. Philip also confronted a bureaucracy there that was not only understaffed but also frequently uncooperative—'I obey but do not comply' was the watchword of many a colonial administrator. Philip did not, however, have to contend in the New World with ancient liberties that constrained the royal power, with noblemen and grandees who badgered for a role in government, and with parliaments that claimed a share of sovereignty. His rule over the New World was in this respect more complete. Even Martin Cortés was not above arrest and exile.[15]

The difference between Spain's New and Old Worlds was that one was a colonial enterprise, uniformly administered from Madrid, while the other was a composite monarchy—an assemblage of lands and kingdoms that had been brought together under a single Habsburg ruler but whose parts still retained their separate privileges, institutions, and representative bodies. Charles V had always recommended the maintenance of these, since 'it is important to rule each land according to the practices to which it is long accustomed.' Philip had no reason to ignore his father's advice. On the occasion of his accession or of his first visit, he duly promised to maintain the particular rights of each of his dominions. Thus, for the provinces of Hainaut and Brabant, he swore to uphold 'all statutes, privileges, letters, exemptions and immunities, all judicial and manorial rights, all town laws, land laws, water laws and all customs of the province, old and new.' Likewise in 1581, when crowned king of Portugal (the only coronation he went through, since elsewhere a proclamation sufficed), he solemnly promised to uphold his new kingdom's traditional freedoms.[16]

For the most part, Philip stood by his commitments. Providing the parts contributed enough money through taxation to keep the whole in motion and stayed free of heresy, he was content to allow government to take its course and for the local nobilities to enjoy their freedoms. In Sicily and Naples, therefore, a largely aristocratic regime was maintained, which did nothing to alleviate the condition of endemic corruption and banditry. A viceroy appointed from among the local nobility and the extensive powers permitted the parliament at Dole were similarly enough to win the loyalty of the Franche-Comté. Elsewhere, assassination, denunciation, and threats were usually sufficient to compel obedience.

When persistently thwarted, however, Philip inclined to force, albeit reluctantly. Aragon in north-eastern Spain had in the 1580s become restive, with its corts or parliament increasingly resentful of what it considered to be illicit interventions by Madrid in the kingdom's affairs. It was probably around this time that members of the corts elaborated on the basis of older texts their famous 'oath of loyalty' to the monarch—'We, who are as good as you, swear to you, who are no better than us, to accept you as our king and sovereign, provided you observe all our liberties and laws, and if not, not.' When in 1591 the city of Zaragoza rose in support of an Aragonese court that had refused to give up a fugitive from Castile to the Inquisition, Philip sent in an army. The ringleaders of the rebellion were rounded up and the powers of the corts duly trimmed.[17]

The Low Countries proved to be a harder nut. In the early 1560s, Philip proposed reforms that threatened the rights of the leading aristocrats to both a share in government and the choicest church offices. When they resisted his plans, he excluded them from government. When in 1566 they made common cause with the small but vociferous minority of Protestants and demanded religious toleration, he refused concessions. But when disaffection spilled over into rebellion and the destruction of Catholic churches, Philip dithered, allowing resistance to spread, and he only sent in an army in the autumn of 1567. His general, the Duke of Alva, imposed a regime that executed over a thousand heretics and rebels, including the most disaffected aristocrats. Philip's cousin, Archduke Charles of Styria, who was no friend to Protestants, urged the king to win over his subjects by 'kindness and compassion', but Philip preferred the type of rule where, as Alva put it, 'every individual has the feeling that one fine night or morning the house will fall in on him.'[18]

With insufficient cash to fund the army from other sources, Philip taxed the cities of the Low Countries. But the cities refused to collect the levy, deeming it illegal since it had not been agreed by the local parliaments. Left unpaid, Philip's troops mutinied, ravaging the land and, in 1576, sacking Antwerp. Although by negotiating a deal with the aristocratic leaders in the southern provinces (roughly, the area of modern Belgium and Luxembourg) Philip was able to hold onto a part of the Low Countries, the rest was permanently lost. The seven northern provinces of the Low Countries accordingly formed after 1581 an independent Protestant republic, the United Provinces of the Netherlands. Over several decades, Philip fought in vain to break the republic, deploying mercenary armies of ever-increasing size. But the cost of the war in the Low Countries ruined the Spanish treasury. Notwithstanding the flow of New World bullion, Philip was forced on four occasions to cancel his debts, converting them into state bonds on which only the interest was ever paid.

Had Philip visited the Low Countries personally in 1568, as he originally intended, then he might have been able to dampen passions. But he was held up in Spain both by the Muslim revolt in that year and by family tragedy. Not only had Philip's son and heir, Prince Carlos, been born physically disabled but he was also mentally ill and delusional. Attempts to cure him by having him share his bed with a mummified saint brought little relief, and the young man became increasingly violent. Eventually in 1568, Philip was obliged to imprison him. By all accounts, Carlos seems to have starved himself to death, although Philip's adversaries were swift to accuse the king of poisoning him.[19]

The madness of Don Carlos was almost certainly due to inbreeding, since on account of intermarriage he had only half the requisite number of great-grandparents. Indeed, Juana the Mad of Castile was the mother of two of his four grandparents, while his own mother, Maria Manuela of Portugal, was also his second cousin. As the Reformation took its toll of eligible families, incestuous unions became even more common among the Habsburgs, with both Spanish and Central European branches exchanging spouses every generation. Altogether, out of seventy-three marriages contracted by the two branches between 1450 and 1750, there were four uncle-niece marriages, eleven marriages between first cousins, four marriages between first cousins-once-removed, eight between second cousins, and many other marriages with more remote kinship. Each of these, being forbidden according to church law, required special papal dispensation.[20]

Marriage had once served the Habsburgs well. Now because of consanguinity it brought both misshapenness and mental incapacity. The jutting jaw and drooping lower lip, which had already made Charles V conspicuous, became enlarged to the point of deformity, earning one Habsburg ruler the name of Fotzenpoidl (which might be generously translated as 'twit face'). In others, it brought about mental illness and epilepsy, stillborn babies, and sickly infants. Of the thirty-four children born to the Spanish royal line between 1527 and 1661, ten did not survive their first year, and a further seventeen died before the age of ten, yielding an infant mortality rate of 80 per cent, which was four times the average for this time.[21]

By the end of the sixteenth century, foreign propagandists had woven together the Inquisition and its tortures, the maltreatment of populations, and the depredations of Spain's armies into a literary genre that would later be known as the 'Black Legend' (actually a twentieth-century term). Philip's own lingering death in 1598 and the physical torment he suffered in his final days fitted into this scheme by showing God's retribution for the monarch's crimes. To these descriptions of cruelty were now added tales of depraved couplings in the royal house between fathers and daughters and of monstrous births, which stood as metaphors of decay and moral dissolution.[22]

For Protestant publicists (and also Jews), Philip II's reign stood as a warning that monarchy too easily led to tyranny and religious persecution. Indeed, some of the rhetoric used against Charles I of England at his trial in 1649 was borrowed from charges first levelled at Philip II. For Spanish writers and dramatists, however, the spread of Philip's dominions and his resolute commitment to the Catholic religion marked Spain out as vested with a mission to uphold the faith and with an imperial destiny that was as great or even exceeded that of the Roman Empire. In a new genre of 'sacramental festivals', performed in villages and town squares as well as royal palaces, the identification of Spain with the spread of Catholicism was played out in eucharistic devotions that joined symbols of the Host with representations of Spain and of its ruling dynasty. As one celebrated author put it, addressing his countrymen, 'God chose you to be his special people. He chose you, O Spain! Because he honours you to be universal, Catholic and perfect, protecting and defending the Holy, Catholic, and Apostolic Roman Church, to enlarge it throughout the world, honouring Christ, Our Lord.' The ambition of world empire in service of the faith was now firmly planted in Spain.[23]

9

DON JOHN AND THE
GALLEYS OF LEPANTO

n the autumn of 1559, a twelve-year-old boy called Jerome was
taken by his guardian to a Cistercian monastery set in the woodland some twenty miles from Valladolid. King Philip was staying
close by to hunt; seeing him approach, the lad knelt. No sooner had he done
so than the king raised him to his feet and asked him if he knew who his
father was. Shamefacedly, Jerome explained that he did not, at which point
Philip embraced him. They had the same father, the king said, which meant
that they were brothers, for although born of different mothers they were
both sons of the late Emperor Charles V.

The story of a prince's concealed identity is typical of Spanish Golden
Age drama, but it seems in this case to be true, at least in its essentials. The
boy was born in 1547 of Charles V's dalliance with Barbara Blomberg of
Regensburg. Barbara was not a singer, as is usually alleged, but a scullion
at an inn where the emperor once stayed. The child was whisked away in
infancy from his mother, to be fostered first in the Low Countries and then
in Spain. Charles tracked both son and mother, endeavouring to see the boy
and marrying off the woman to one of his officers in Brussels. At the very
end of his reign, Charles formally conceded his paternity, which was when

Philip first learned that he had a half brother. Charles also instructed that the boy be found a suitable position in the church and that his name be changed from Jerome to John or Juan, in honour of Charles's mother, Juana. It was as Don John, therefore, that the boy was subsequently known. He should not be confused with the libidinous Don Juan of English and continental drama and verse.[1]

To begin with, Philip abided by his father's instructions, sending Don John to the University of Alcalá near Madrid. The university specialized in training for the priesthood, but Philip soon found that he needed his half brother as a political player. The nobility of the Low Countries expected to be ruled by a member of the ruling house. Charles's first governor there had been his aunt, Margaret, and then after her death in 1530 his sister, Mary of Hungary, but Philip lacked a cohort of suitable close kinsfolk. So he pressed Mary to stay in office even after her retirement in 1555. When she refused, Philip turned to his half-sister, Margaret of Parma, to replace her.

Like Don John, Margaret was another illegitimate child of Charles V, born this time of a Flemish serving wench, and deployed in her youth as a serial bride in Italy. As governor of the Low Countries, Margaret cultivated a trimmed moustache to give her an air of authority, and she ordered medals to be struck that showed her as an Amazon. Still, she was out of her depth in the vicious politics of the Low Countries, and Philip sought her replacement. Don John was one choice but on account of his youth a still distant one. Even so, Philip prepared the young man for greatness, admitting him in 1566 to the Order of the Golden Fleece. Although the knights of the order no longer met in company with the ruler, for Philip disliked criticism of his policies, the Golden Fleece still counted as Europe's most illustrious chivalric society.[2]

Don John was ambitious. He thought to marry Elizabeth I of England and to lead her subjects back to the faith of Rome, but he also schemed to free the Scottish queen, Mary, from Elizabeth's captivity and, ogling her portrait, to make her his wife too. Although Philip appointed him to leading offices in Spain, he judged Don John too headstrong to be entrusted with sole responsibility for any enterprise. So, although he intended to appoint him to eventual command of the Low Countries, he had him work in collaboration with the more experienced politician and soldier Luis de Requesens. It was in combination with Requesens that Don John suppressed the Muslim rebellion of 1568–1569 and in 1571 engaged in the campaign that made his reputation. This was the war in the Mediterranean with the Ottoman Turks that culminated in the Christian victory at Lepanto.

The history of the Ottoman Empire is frequently written in terms of a rapid rise under the first ten sultans, culminating in the reign of Suleiman the Magnificent (ruled 1520–1566), followed by more than four centuries of decline under the rule of the next twenty-six sultans. In fact, the astonishing territorial growth of the Ottoman Empire in the Later Middle Ages owed much to the weakness of its neighbours. Even during Suleiman's reign, the Ottoman Empire was grinding to the limits of expansion. Its way to the east was blocked by the Persian Safavid Empire and by the advance of Muscovy from the north. On its western border, a line of defensive works built across Hungary by Ferdinand I impeded further movement into Christian Europe. And in the Indian Ocean the Portuguese had seized control of the spice trade that fed the European markets, diverting a part of it via the Cape of Good Hope.

There was in Istanbul considerable interest in the discovery of the New World. One of Columbus's earliest maps survives in a copy of a copy made by Ottoman navigators, versions of which were at the request of Suleiman's first minister or grand vizier presented personally to the sultan. But any interest the Ottoman court might have entertained in the Americas was thwarted by a lack of suitable shipping and by the Saadi rulers of Morocco, who by opposing Turkish expansion into north-western Africa closed off the Atlantic to Ottoman ships. Nevertheless, much thought was given in Istanbul to how to break the empire's encirclement. Plans were vainly laid to build a canal not only at Suez but also between the Don and Volga Rivers to open the way to Central Asia, and much effort was spent on building Ottoman power in the Indian Ocean. Even so, the despatch in the 1560s of a flotilla to Aceh in Sumatra, bearing cannons and foundry workers to help the local sultan fight the Portuguese, proved inconsequential. The sultan put greater trust in his six hundred war elephants, and he left the cannons to rust.[3]

Europe's Christian rulers were, however, convinced that it was the Ottoman Empire which encircled them. Seafarers mistook the Muslims whom they encountered in the Indian Ocean and Pacific as servants of the Ottoman sultan, even though they acknowledged 'the Great King of the West' only in passing in Friday prayers. Some of these Muslims spoke Spanish, for they were in origin Spanish Muslims. As early as 1521, Ferdinand Magellan had encountered exiles from Spain in the Philippines. But they were not agents of Istanbul, still less conspiring with Muslims on the other side of the world. They were simply the sad flotsam of persecution, driven by circumstance 12,000 kilometres (7,500 miles) eastwards.[4]

Throughout the sixteenth century there had been a tug-of-war between Turks and Spaniards in North Africa. Spanish garrisons were established at strategic points along the Mediterranean coast, mostly for the purpose of combating the local corsairs, who often worked in concert with the Ottoman navy. The reach of the Muslim corsairs was formidable. Not only did they imperil the sea routes between Spain and its possessions in southern Italy, but they also ventured out into the Atlantic, disrupting the flow of trade to the New World. The corsairs were not, however, discriminating, raiding the English coast, Ireland, and Iceland in their search for slaves. Their depredations fed the Ottoman slave trade, which at its peak was consuming a hundred thousand European slaves a year.[5]

During the middle decades of the sixteenth century, Sultan Suleiman the Magnificent consolidated his hold on North Africa, picking off the Spanish garrisons and assigning the captured forts either to his own officers or, more usually, to puppet princes. By the 1560s, little more than Oran and the neighbouring port of Mers-el-Kébir remained in Christian hands, and the Spanish coastline was dangerously exposed. It was, however, to the Mediterranean islands of Cyprus and Malta that Suleiman and his successor, Selim II (1566–1574), aspired. Both were nests of corsairs, who preyed not only on shipping but also on pilgrims taking the maritime route to the holy places. In 1564, the Knights of Malta captured several merchant vessels belonging to the chief eunuch in Istanbul and seized the costly cargoes of silk destined for the sultan's harem. In retribution, Suleiman besieged Malta the next year but was unable to dislodge the knights.

In 1570 the Turkish ambassador to Venice delivered his master's ultimatum demanding the cession of Cyprus. When this was refused, Sultan Selim ordered his navy to convey a seaborne army of as many as seventy thousand men to take the island. The scale of the Ottoman assault brought together the Catholic Mediterranean powers, which were spurred on by a vigorous Venetian diplomacy that also included overtures to Muscovy. But the heart of the gathering coalition rested on an alliance between Philip II and Pope Pius V (1566–1572), who for the time being laid aside their quarrel over the extent to which Rome might interfere in Spanish affairs. Pope Pius's promotion of the venture meant that the alliance of Spain, Venice, Genoa, and Malta could name itself the Holy League. But it was Philip II who provided the bulk of the finance for the fleet and one quarter of its vessels, so he presumed the right to name the commander in chief.[6]

Although Philip chose Don John for the role of commander, he required him in his letter of appointment to defer to Requesens and to take the advice of the more experienced Venetian and Genoese captains. But he also impressed upon Don John the political importance of his role, for the fleet once gathered might be used to shore up the western Mediterranean and limit further Ottoman advances there. So, even though the last Venetian stronghold on Cyprus capitulated in the summer of 1571, its captain being flayed alive by the victorious Turks, there was no halt in the league's preparations. In the middle of September, the Christian fleet in the Sicilian port of Messina weighed anchor to hunt down the Ottoman navy and its seaborne troops as the preliminary to an assault on Cyprus.

Both fleets comprised galleys, which in the light Mediterranean winds depended on oarsmen. Although the Turkish galleys sat lower in the water, at 40 metres by 6 (130 by 20 feet) the vessels on both sides were mostly comparable in size. A single deck of oarsmen, with three men to each oar, sat on several dozen benches that ran along each side of the ship. The majority were slaves, although the stroke setters at the end of each bench were often experienced freemen. Because there were no sanitary arrangements and waste fell into the bilge, a galley half a kilometre distant could be detected by its stench. There were, however, many variations in the size of the galleys, not least the galleass, which was in origin a large merchant vessel, often with five men to each oar and thirty or so benches. Once adapted for military use, the height of the galleass meant that it could accommodate cannons on its sides as well as in the bow. Otherwise, the principal fire power of the galley was one large cannon on the prow, which for loading powder and shot moved back and forth on rails.[7]

The two fleets, made up of roughly two hundred vessels apiece, met near Nafpaktos or Lepanto at the mouth of the Gulf of Corinth in the Ionian Sea. How much the deployment of the Christian fleet owed to Don John is impossible to say. He relied for advice on the Genoese admiral Giovanni Andrea Doria, with whom he had a close friendship (the prince confided in Doria details of his love life and various illnesses), and it is likely that Doria inspired the battle plan. Knowing that the Ottoman fleet would try to outflank him, Don John arranged his ships in a long line, with the left wing nestling up against the land. In front of the line, he stationed six galleasses, which puzzled the Turks, for they took them to be supply boats. At about eleven in the morning of 7 October, the Turkish admiral fired a blank shot to signal his readiness. Don John, now dressed in dazzling polished armour, returned the challenge, but he did so with an iron cannon ball. Its splash enabled his artillery men to calibrate their weapon sights.

As the Ottoman fleet closed, the galleasses revealed their purpose, training broadside fire onto the approaching enemy. After each volley, they spun round so that the other side of the ship might fire while the first reloaded. As the Turkish ships passed between the galleasses, they suffered the onslaught of the galleasses' bow cannons, while from the higher decks of the galleasses harquebusiers fired shot onto the exposed oarsmen and crew. Even before it had engaged with the enemy, one third of the Ottoman fleet was either sunk or disabled. It was, as one Italian wrote in celebration of the battle, 'an incredible thing' to witness the destructive power of the pirouetting galleass.[8]

For reasons that remain unclear, the right wing of the Christian fleet became detached, briefly allowing some Turkish ships to break through the gap. But the Christian left flank and centre held firm, engaging with the enemy at close quarters. The Holy League had the advantage here. Whereas the Turkish troops swung on ropes Hollywood-style onto the opposing galleys, the Spanish ships were equipped with nets and matting, which allowed their soldiers to board en masse. Once on the enemy deck, the Spanish troops advanced with pikes in square formation, pushing their opponents back and providing support for the harquebusiers. Slaves who had been unfettered so that they would not go down with their vessels now joined in, fighting their masters. By early evening, the Christian victory was so complete that the foes gave up fighting, playfully exchanging volleys of oranges and lemons. More than a hundred Turkish galleys had been captured and a further fifty or more sunk. The number of Turkish dead was put at the time at 35,000 (almost certainly an exaggeration) as against 7,500 for the Holy League.[9]

News of the Christian triumph at Lepanto was greeted throughout Europe with rejoicing. In Rome, Pope Pius V was reported to have lauded Don John by quoting from the Gospel—'There was a man sent by God, whose name was John'—and he ordered that 7 October be henceforth kept as the Feast of Our Lady of Victories (now Our Lady of the Rosary). But the triumph otherwise yielded little of permanence. The Ottoman fleet was rapidly rebuilt, while the Christian allies bickered over the division of ships and slaves. Contrary instructions from Philip II left Don John uncertain whether he should keep to the league's purpose and press on to Cyprus and beyond or withdraw the Spanish vessels westwards. Resting up in Messina, the prince went into a deep depression. Meanwhile, the Venetians made peace with the sultan in exchange for guarantees for Crete, Corfu, and Venice's remaining Adriatic possessions.

In 1573, Philip II appointed Requesens as governor of the Low Countries, with the intention that he prepare the way there for Don John. Requesens was a skilled diplomat and peace maker, but he was limited by Philip's instruction that he make no concessions in matters of religion. Don John, meanwhile, led the Spanish fleet to Tunis, which capitulated immediately upon his arrival. The prince pleaded with King Philip to give him the title of King of Tunis, but Philip instead ordered him to return with the fleet to Italy, with the result that the city immediately returned to Ottoman rule. It was only with the death of Requesens in 1576 that Don John received the governorship of the Low Countries for which he had all along been intended. But like his predecessors, he could make no headway for as long as King Philip insisted that the rebels return to the Catholic faith.

Don John cursed his thwarted destiny and lamented that he was 'the most neglected knight in the world.' Consistently outmanoeuvred both diplomatically and in battle by the rebel leaders, he also lost the support of the moderate Catholic aristocracy in the Low Countries, who invited the Austrian archduke Matthias to replace him as governor. Broken physically and mentally (possibly as the consequence of syphilis), Don John succumbed to a fever and died in October 1578. It is a comment on Spain's military weakness in northern Europe that it was judged unsafe to repatriate Don John's corpse by sea lest it be seized by rebel Dutch or English vessels. Instead, it was cut into four, packed in saddle bags, and sent secretly overland through France to Madrid, where it was reassembled for burial in the Escorial.[10]

Don John's interment in the Escorial was an honour never bestowed on any other illegitimate Habsburg and was entirely due to the reputation he had earned at Lepanto. Contemporaries were convinced that Lepanto constituted some sort of divine test, which Christianity had passed, but they struggled to locate its larger significance, since the naval and military power of the Ottoman Turks was soon shown to be undiminished. In their quest, commentators turned not only to the Bible but also to classical texts, and few were pored over more diligently than the prophecy of the Cumaean sibyl or seer given in Virgil's *Eclogues*, written around 40 BCE:

> *Now the age of Cumae's prophecy has come;*
> *The great succession of centuries is born afresh.*
> *Now too returns the Virgin; Saturn's rule returns;*
> *A new begetting now descends from heaven's height.*
> *O chaste Lucina, look with blessing on the boy*
> *Whose birth will end the iron race at last and raise*
> *A golden through the world . . .*[11]

(Saturn is here the god of plenty; Lucina is the goddess of childbirth.)

With its explicit reference to a virgin and apparent foretelling of Christ's birth, this short verse was seized upon by Philip II's publicists to demonstrate how the blessings of the Virgin Mary and service to the faith would yield a comprehensive and gilded reordering of the world. In the fulfilment of this scheme, Lepanto was an episode, but it was also an allegory into which artistic and literary representations of the dynasty might be pressed. As a sea battle, it evoked the conceits that surrounded the Habsburg emblem of the Golden Fleece, recalling the treasure seized by the sea-faring Jason of mythology. (It helped that Don John's flagship at Lepanto had been named *The Argo*, after Jason's own.) The Christian emblem unfurled in the battle, the monogram IHS, standing for the Cross and *In Hoc Signo*, 'In This Sign', similarly harked back to the triumphal device of the first Christian emperor of Rome, Constantine the Great (312–324 CE). In Titian's *Allegory of Lepanto* (1573–1575), Philip elevates to God his newly born son, Ferdinand (he would later die in infancy), as if he were the consecrated Host, thus interlocking the battle, which is being played out in the background, with the dynasty's commitment to eucharistic observance.[12]

These representations were all commissioned by Philip and his entourage, but foreign and popular depictions of the battle conveyed an equally fulgent symbolism. French writers spoke of Lepanto as a new battle of Actium and of Philip II as a new Augustus (Octavian, later named Augustus, had won the naval battle of Actium in 31 BCE against Mark Anthony and Cleopatra). Like their Spanish counterparts, they joined the Spanish fight against the Ottoman Turks with the Catholic struggle against heresy and made a new cult of warrior saints. In 1585, James VI of Scotland composed in Lowlands Scots an epic poem on Lepanto, which passed rapidly into Latin, French, Dutch, and German translations. Even salt cellars and ink wells might be embossed with reliefs of the battle, while in the Church of St Mary of Pazzalino in Locarno in what is now Switzerland, a local artist painted a fresco showing the Virgin instructing the infant Christ to throw cannon balls at Turkish warships.[13]

Ferdinand's son and successor, Emperor Maximilian II (ruled 1564–1576), played no part in the events leading up to Lepanto, shunning overtures from both Pius V and Philip II to join the Holy League. As Maximilian explained, the Protestant German princes would not support a league headed by the pope. But behind this also lay Maximilian's preference for negotiating differences, which he had inherited from his father, and his own lukewarm commitment to the Catholic religion, which arose from his own personal doubts and spiritual introspection. An enthusiastic reader of the Italian theologian Acontius (c. 1520–1566), Maximilian seems to have embraced the idea that there was a true religion hidden behind superficial differences, and that Turks and even Jews might have a role in recalling Christians to duty. He did not embark on persecution, concluded a peace with Sultan Selim in 1568, and thereafter confined his military endeavours to a clockwork warship or *nef* with which he entertained his dinner guests.[14]

In the last decade of his life, the artist Titian (c. 1488–1576) composed two paintings on the theme of the 'Succour of Religion.' One went to Philip II and the other to Maximilian II. Maximilian's has been lost but may be reconstructed from an engraving to show religion as a distressed damsel, threatened by coiled snakes. But a female warrior in a tiara and gossamer tunic comes to her aid, bearing aloft the imperial standard. Strewn around her feet lie discarded weapons. In the picture sent to Philip II, the characters have been subtly changed. Religion's succourer is now clad in armour, and she bears a spear, sword, and shield, emblazoned with the arms of Spain. In the background a turbaned Turk poses as Neptune, but his sea-chariot is sinking beneath him. In two almost identical paintings, Titian laid out starkly the different approaches adopted by the two branches of the Habsburgs to the Catholic faith: the one bringing the gift of peace and compromise, and the other the sword of militant Spain, fresh from its victory at Lepanto.[15]

10

RUDOLF II AND THE
ALCHEMISTS OF PRAGUE

*F*rom the fifteenth to the seventeenth centuries, most rulers dabbled in alchemy and magic. Even Philip II's Escorial housed several laboratories where the king supervised the distillation of essences and experiments in the transmutation of metals. Alchemy and the occult were not seen, however, as diversions from rulership. They were central to it, for the realms of magic and of hidden truth were thought to hold the solution to how the world might be brought into conformity with the cosmic order. They also inspired other activities of kingship, from the way royal collections were organized to the commissioning of works of art. Occult knowledge was a self-enclosed intellectual system, which was tantalizingly opaque and yet logically built up, albeit from dubious first principles. It caught Maximilian II's son, Rudolf II (ruled 1576–1612), in its snares and may have driven him to the episodes of depression and self-imposed isolation that beset his reign.

The content of the occult world, as it was imagined in early modern Europe, is best broached through *The Emerald Tablet* (*Tabula Smaragdina*). Translated from Latin to Czech in Rudolf's court, it starts as follows in English, in Sir Isaac Newton's translation:

'Tis true without lying, certain and most true.
That which is below is like that which is above and that which is above
is like that which is below to do the miracles of one only thing.
And as all things have been and arose from one by the mediation of one:
so all things have their birth from this one thing by adaptation.
The Sun is its father, the moon its mother, the wind hath
carried it in its belly, the earth is its nurse.
The father of all perfection in the whole world is here.
Its force or power is entire if it be converted into earth.
Separate thou the earth from the fire, the subtle from
the gross sweetly with great industry.
It ascends from the earth to the heaven and again it descends to the
earth and receives the force of things superior and inferior.
By this means you shall have the glory of the whole world
and thereby all obscurity shall fly from you.[1]

The text of *The Emerald Tablet* was believed to have been originally carved on a slab of jade that Alexander the Great found in the crypt of the magician Hermes Trismegistus (the Thrice Great). In fact, it was probably first composed in the Syriac language in the eighth century before being translated into Arabic and then into Latin. By the mid-thirteenth century it was circulating widely in Christian Europe, often being communicated with other passages of equal obscurity.

In the 1460s, a bundle of fourteen letters written in Greek arrived in Italy from Istanbul, which purported to be of similar origin to *The Emerald Tablet* and to have been composed by the same Hermes Trismegistus. By now, scholars were convinced that Hermes was a real person (it helped that St Augustine had discussed him at length) and that he either was a contemporary of Moses or had even lived before the Flood, possibly being identical with the Egyptian god Thoth. These letters, and a further three that subsequently came to light, were in fact composed in Egypt in the second century CE and combined Egyptian mythology and magic with a reworking of Plato's philosophy. The letters were rapidly translated from Greek to Latin, and they created a sensation, for they amplified *The Emerald Tablet*, coming from much the same intellectual milieu.

The Hermetic Corpus, as these letters are known, contains spells and invocations as well as discussions of amulets and charms and their magic powers, while the lengthy dialogues into which the text is divided presume the existence of angels and demons and that matter may be transmuted into gold in the way alchemists imagined. A constant theme in the letters is the idea that heaven, the macrocosm, is united with the microcosm of this earth and, indeed, with all smaller microcosmic units, down to individual rocks and plants. Everything is energized with the spirit of the universe and thus driven to fuse with it, for 'the plenitude of all things is one and in one' or, as *The Emerald Tablet* put it, 'That which is below is like that which is above.'[2]

The teachings of Hermes presented a universe that was in harmony because everything, both in the heavens and upon earth, was infused and directed by one spirit. They also stressed the singleness of all phenomena and the idea that behind outward differences lay a single substance or essence, which may be called 'prime matter' (sometimes identified with the Philosopher's Stone, although the term was a catchall for many phenomena). But the writings of Hermes also embraced trends in second-century Greek Gnosticism, which taught that a higher spiritual state obtained through prayer and secret rituals of initiation was a precondition of knowledge. Understanding the universe and its hidden harmonies required dedication and, as *The Emerald Tablet* hints, some type of process before glory may be won and obscurity banished.

Hermetic thought underpinned alchemical practice, confirming the principle that all matter was actually the same, on account of which the prime matter out of which everything was made might be transformed into gold. It also drove scholars to seek out symbols or 'monads' which might mystically convey the universe's unity and to find ways by which studying the stars gave new insights into the world below. Like Rudolf II, princes across Europe assembled collections of the weird and the marvellous, often displaying them randomly in Wonder Chambers (*Wunderkammer, Kunstkammer*). By contemplation of the unrelated, the unity of all things might be apprehended, and so pangolins and pinecones were often placed together. Artists and musicians also endeavoured to have their works convey or conform to the teachings of Hermes, while physicians strove to find the universal 'quintessence' that would heal all afflictions. All branches of knowledge thus began to converge on *The Emerald Tablet* and Hermetic Corpus.[3]

So too did the politics of religion. Difference of belief was antithetical to the teachings of Hermes, which presupposed a harmonious ordering of the universe, where everything existed in orderly concordance. By this measure, the arguments of theologians were superficial, overlooking the larger, anterior truth which they held in common. Hermetic teaching thus reinforced the humanist position that Christians should set aside their quarrels and search for a middle way between contending faiths. It was surely to this philosophical principle that Emperor Maximilian II came through his reading of Acontius. When challenged as to whether he was a Catholic or a Protestant, he answered simply that he was a Christian. For Maximilian, the differences between the two confessions mattered less than the truth embedded in the Christian message.[4]

Emperors Maximilian II and Rudolf II were never less than ambiguous in their religious convictions. Many were convinced that Maximilian's slipperiness in matters of religion hid a secret adherence to Protestantism. Philip II of Spain used the courtier Adam von Dietrichstein to spy on Maximilian's religious observance but was disappointed by what he learned. Dietrichstein reported in 1571 that even a heart attack had not brought the emperor to take the sacraments—on the contrary, he had just recruited to his court a married Lutheran pastor. Maximilian went to his deathbed refusing the Mass.[5]

Rudolf's beliefs were equally mysterious. Although he experienced bouts of Catholic fervour, there were long periods when he too refused to take Mass. Nobody accused the emperor, however, of Protestantism. Instead, many imagined something far worse. As his nephews reported in 1606— 'His Majesty has now reached the stage of abandoning God entirely; he will neither hear nor speak of Him, nor suffer any sign of Him. . . . He strives all the time to eliminate God completely so that he may in future serve a different master.' Rudolf also died without confessing.[6]

Rudolf spent his teenage years in Spain, since after the death of Philip II's son, Don Carlos, he counted for a time as Philip's closest male relative. Following his return to Vienna in 1571, Rudolf preferred to speak Spanish and to dress in the fashion of the Spanish court, wearing a broad white ruff around the neck, set off by a doublet and hose of intense black, coloured with a Mexican dye called 'raven's wing', and studded with gold. But Rudolf's manner also changed. Aping Spanish etiquette, he became stiff and formal. Elizabeth of England's envoy, Sir Philip Sidney, who met Rudolf in 1577, reported that he was 'few of words, sullen of disposition, very secret and resolute, having nothing the manner his father had in winning men in his behaviour . . . extremely Spaniolated.'[7]

It was, however, Rudolf's depressive moods that alarmed observers. For long periods, Rudolf would withdraw from the rituals of court and the affairs of state, secluding himself in the royal castle in Prague, to where he moved the seat of government from Vienna in the early 1580s. For more than two years, even the Spanish ambassador was unable to have an audience with him. As one observer commented, 'Disturbed in his mind by some ailment of melancholy, he has begun to love solitude and shut himself off in his palace as if behind the bars of a prison.' By the time this report was penned, towards the end of Rudolf's reign, others were diagnosing madness and even diabolic possession.[8]

The claim of insanity is plausible only to the extent that it lacks diagnostic precision. Rudolf never married but contented himself with a long-term mistress and concubines whom he changed monthly. Altogether they bore him at least six children. Of these the eldest, Don Julio, who was the product of a fleeting liaison with an unnamed *baronessa*, was clearly deranged. In a life dedicated to cruelty, Don Julio's final excess was to murder his girlfriend, mutilate her dead body, and nail up the corpse in a chest, after which he took his own life. To extrapolate the mental incapacity of the father from the actions of the son is, however, not only bad medicine but also overlooks the ordinariness of Rudolf's other five children, none of whom made any mark, violent or otherwise.[9]

It is, however, entirely possible that Rudolf's depressive demeanour was a pose. Depression is in many respects the invention of the late fifteenth century, for it had previously been an affliction that was thought to be mostly confined to monastic communities. Melancholy, as it was then known, was not considered a good thing, for it led directly to the sins of sloth and listlessness. Paradoxically though, after around 1500 depression was also cast as a sign not only of intellectual endeavour but, following the classical tradition, even of genius. Philosophers were considered the most inclined to fall into the condition, since it was regarded as a stage in the ascent to knowledge. Albrecht Dürer's androgynous angel in his woodcut *Melencolia I* thus darkly broods, contemplating the forms of geometrical and mathematical knowledge—a stone polyhedron and sphere and a square of numbers, the sum of which make 34 in 1,232 different combinations. Cosmic events play out in the distance over an inland sea, while at the angel's feet lie discarded the human tools of understanding. More prosaically, a bat warns of the perils of working late into the night.[10]

The angel is, however, not only a geometrician but also an alchemist. Behind the angel, flames lick around a crucible, and there is a ladder of seven rungs, symbolizing the seven prime and secondary elements. The keys and purse hanging from the angel's dress hint at the alchemist's fabled wealth and power. The emaciated dog symbolizes Saturn, standing on this occasion as the bringer of melancholy and guardian of sacred writing, while the cherub, busy writing, may show that melancholy does not always lead to inactivity. The polyhedron is also more than just a geometric form for it stands for universal matter—the prime material out of which the alchemist sought to make gold. Its irregular shape indicates that it has yet to go through the adaptive process that will bring it to perfection.[11]

Dürer was not alone in recognizing the link between melancholy and alchemy, for it was a familiar trope. Like the philosopher, the alchemist would, so it was believed, encounter depression and despair as a necessary first step in his spiritual ascent. Beyond this, however, the alchemist's journey was considered analogous to the craft he practised. Like the substances with which he worked, the alchemist also had to be purged of impurity and to be spiritually reconstituted, since in one contemporary description, 'gold is not procured except by melancholy and the contemplation of Saturn.' Only after the combustion of melancholy, which was at the time defined as dry and arid, might the alchemist 'either by natural heat or by movements of his enkindled mind become reddened, hot and luminous', empowered with the capacity to transmute matter.[12]

Now it may well be that Rudolf genuinely had depression, or as one of his courtiers suspected, feigned it simply to avoid making hard political choices. What is incontestable is that Rudolf's Prague became Europe's leading centre of alchemical practice and Hermetic magic, accommodating as many as two hundred alchemists. They were so numerous that they spilled out of the palace walls into the gardens, setting up their forges among the flowerbeds. Rudolf himself practised alchemy, on one occasion singeing his beard when an experiment went wrong. He did not, however, wear a black cloak adorned with a pentagram—this idea only comes from a recently fabricated source (the so-called Diary of Damiano).[13]

The alchemists and magicians who thronged Rudolf's court constituted a broad spectrum. At one end were charlatans looking to win patronage. Among these we may count the drunken medium Edward Kelley, who by the time he arrived in Prague had already had his ears cropped for the crime of counterfeiting. At the other end were genuine practitioners whose rigour in observation and experimental method provided the foundation of modern science. These included Tycho Brahe, who during his short stay in Prague (1599–1601) built an observatory to plot the movement of the stars, and Johannes Kepler, who worked as Rudolf's principal astrologer between 1600 and 1612. Kepler's observations yielded the earliest insights into how the planets moved within the sun's gravitational field, and with his improved telescope he detected that Jupiter also had its own moons.

Others added their own arcane knowledge to the mysteries of Hermetic magic. The English wizard John Dee, who had previously dedicated his treatise on the celestial symbol of the monad to Maximilian II, sought Rudolf's favour in the 1580s, but Rudolf confessed that he did not understand Dee's work. Dee then tried to stimulate Rudolf's interest with his angel summoning, whereby he caught angels in a mirror or crystal ball and convinced them to foretell the future. He even composed a special language, called Enochian, in which to communicate with them. But the angels could only be seen and heard by Edward Kelley, which cast doubts on Dee's credibility. The angels became troublesome, demanding that Dee give over his wife to Kelley's pleasure, which he did, and prophesying the imminent destruction of the Catholic priesthood, which the two men incautiously reported to the pope's envoy. Accused of conjuring up the dead, Dee fled Prague in 1586. Kelley stayed on, eventually dying in gaol.[14]

Rudolf's younger brothers complained that the emperor collected around him 'wizards, alchemists, cabbalists and the like.' The list of those associated at one time or other with his court includes, however, many of the foremost philosophers of the late sixteenth century—the polymath Giordano Bruno; the Jewish mystic and Kabbalist Rabbi Judah Loew, who would later be credited (wrongly) with making from clay a golem or humanlike monster; the Polish metallurgist Sendivogius (Michał Sędziwój), and so on. But Rudolf also collected objects, which he installed in galleries built along a wing of the castle in Prague. Here were displayed works by some of the greatest artists of the sixteenth century, including Dürer, Brueghel, Raphael, Titian, and Correggio, sculptures and busts, clockwork automata powered by the recent invention of the tempered steel coil, and perpetual-motion machines (they worked by harnessing changes in atmospheric pressure). These were shown together with curiosities obtained during overseas exploration—unusual stones, fossils, and illustrations drawn from the natural world.[15]

Rudolf's Wonder Chamber was designed to impress, and it was here that he received visiting envoys. Yet the chamber functioned also as a microcosm of the universe, bringing together nature and art in what was known at the time as a 'theatre of the world.' The objects themselves frequently drew on Hermetic and alchemical imagery. The portraits of Arcimboldo, which constructed faces out of natural objects, were not intended as jokes, as some contemporaries believed. Commissioned by both Maximilian and Rudolf, they were intended to show how the variety of macrocosmic nature might be distilled into the human microcosm. Rudolf himself received the supreme accolade: a portrait rendered out of fruit and vegetables, which cast him as Vertumnus, the god of seasons and abundance and the brother of Hermes.[16]

A later catalogue divided Rudolf's collection into 'natural' and 'man-made' objects, but the emperor favoured items which by transgressing boundaries disclosed the principles of unity and harmony which governed the workings of the universe. Clockwork figures, including a tiny representation of himself on board a ship (now in the British Museum), blurred the distinction between categories—likewise a goblet wrought of a rhinoceros's horn and of the tusks of a warthog. Rudolf's artistic commissions were also extraordinary in their contraventions. In the paintings of Rudolf's court artist, Bartholomeus Spranger, lascivious old men dally with young girls, while women are frequently depicted with a taut male physique or even cross-dressing.

Historians and others have invoked this disturbed sexual imagery as symptomatic of Rudolf's agitated mind or of a homosexual inclination (for which there is no evidence). But sexual symbolism pervaded alchemy, with the furnace cast as a womb, matter being 'impregnated' by noble metal, and the elements, being either male or female, combining in a 'chemical marriage.' Within this construction, the male stood for fixed matter and the female for the volatile. Illustrating their harmonious union was rendered the more complete by emphasizing the superficial disharmonies of age, with the man as aged Neptune or Vulcan and the woman as Venus or the dainty earth goddess Maia. The product of their union was the most perfect of forms: the hermaphrodite, the child of Hermes and Aphrodite, who brought together the two genders in a single being. The tight haunches of Spranger's women and the angel in Dürer's *Melencolia I* illustrate both the hermaphrodite's perfection and, more prosaically, the chemical fusion of mercury with sulphur.

In his final years Rudolf was, like Prospero in Shakespeare's *The Tempest*, so 'transported and rapt in secret studies' as seldom to leave his castle in Prague. But notwithstanding his reclusiveness, Rudolf was in one way also the most universal of Habsburg rulers, for he aimed at nothing less than complete knowledge of the cosmos. In his Wonder Chamber and through Hermetic magic and alchemical symbolism, Rudolf sought the philosopher's 'Triple Crown of Enlightenment: Omniscience, Omnipotence, and Joy of Eternal Love.'

'The glory of the whole world', as told in *The Emerald Tablet*, would not, however, be Rudolf's. Sharing Prospero's fate, Rudolf would instead confront political ruin and the loss of all his kingdoms. Alchemy and occult magic were not a durable basis upon which to construct a vision of Habsburg power. The tide of events was already changing in Europe and the showdown between Catholicism and Protestantism could not long be delayed. There were only two possibilities: either a Central European solution resting on religious compromise and accommodation or a Spanish one that looked towards intolerance and exclusivity. Dallying between the two poles, Rudolf conjured a politics as sterile as the hermaphrodite of his alchemical imagination.

11

THE TRIUMPH OF THE HERETICS

*B*y the last decades of the sixteenth century, Protestantism seemed to have won in much of Europe. In England and Scotland, Catholic worship was banned, and Protestant governments ruled over the provinces of the Netherlands. The Scandinavian kingdoms and Baltic Livonia had embraced Lutheranism, and even the Saami people (or Lapps) in the Arctic north were making their slow transition from shamanism and bear worship to Protestantism. In Poland and France, large Protestant minorities challenged Catholic hegemony. Religious freedom yielded the solution to religious division in Poland, but in France, where compromise proved elusive, a long war broke out in the 1560s. It was, however, Moldavia (now split between Romania and Moldova) that produced continental Europe's first officially Protestant monarch, the Greek-born Jacob Heraclides (1561–1563), who governed the principality with the title of despot.

Protestantism had by the second half of the century made similar gains in the Holy Roman Empire. Of the larger principalities there, only Lorraine and Bavaria kept loyal to the Catholic religion. Although some forty Catholic bishops and archbishops remained in place, along with a further eighty abbots and priors, these often had to contend with hostile populations that disrupted services and processions, seized church vessels and property, and distracted monks and nuns from their vocations. As early as the 1550s, a visiting Italian cardinal regarded the Catholic Church in the Holy Roman Empire as lost—better to let it fall, he recommended, and hope that something good might emerge from the ruin. The bishop of Hildesheim put it more starkly: 'My Church and I are destroyed.'[1]

Austria and the neighbouring Habsburg duchies were part of Catholicism's larger ruin. By the middle years of the sixteenth century, almost all the cities and most of the nobility—between 80 and 90 per cent—had gone over to Protestantism, and they now took over parish churches and organized their own schools. There was pressure from below too, with country folk demanding that the Mass be distributed in both kinds and the liturgy performed in German. Where priests refused, they either were driven out or saw their congregations running off to attend services elsewhere. Among the Slovene-speaking peasantry of Styria and Carniola, who remained largely impervious to the 'German religion' of Protestantism, a lack of pastoral control meant that older, pagan observances crept back. Ecstatic writhing and wild dancing, led by 'leapers and hurlers' (*Springer, Werfer*), consumed several woodland communities.[2]

The institutions of the Catholic Church withered. Even in the Catholic heartland of the Tyrol, monasteries and nunneries fell empty. The great Cistercian abbey of Stams was by 1574 left with only two elderly monks. Elsewhere in the Tyrol discipline collapsed, with the nuns of Sonnenburg drinking and dining in the local taverns and riding out at night to the homes of noblemen. Even so, the Sonnenburg convent was rated by visiting clergy at the time as 'not as bad as others.' Monastic finances buckled from the number of concubines, illegitimate children, and hangers-on living with the monks, all of whom had to be provided for. The priesthood was little different. An inspection in 1571 of the cathedral chapter at Brixen found only five canons in attendance, all of whom immediately relinquished their vows upon being called to discipline.[3]

Religious toleration was partly a philosophical choice. It chimed with Hermeticism and the belief that all phenomena were the expression of a single idea. It also fitted with the humanist search for a 'middle way' between extremes and, in the later decades of the sixteenth century, with the increasingly popular intellectual stance of Neo-Stoicism that taught moderation and the avoidance of extreme conduct. But toleration was a political choice too. In view of the spread of Protestantism, only tough measures were likely to bring about a restoration of Catholicism. The example of other countries where dogmatic policies had been pursued was, however, salutary—the carnage caused by the Spanish occupation of the Low Countries in the late 1560s; the Massacre of St Bartholomew's Day in France in 1572, when tens of thousands of Protestants had been killed; the destruction of Antwerp by a Spanish army in 1576, and the many assassinations of kings and other political leaders that were motivated either wholly or in part by religious zeal.[4]

Accommodation, by contrast, yielded obvious gains. In return for granting religious freedom to the nobles of Upper and Lower Austria after 1568, Maximilian II obtained a vote from their provincial diets of 2.5 million ducats. The extension of toleration to the 'Inner Austrian' duchies of Styria, Carinthia, and Carniola by Maximilian's brother, Archduke Charles, yielded in 1578 a further 1.7 million ducats and the continuing financial commitment of their diets to buttress the defence of Croatia. Moreover, by staying aloof from Rome, Maximilian II and Rudolf II were able to help themselves to the incomes of religious houses through the newly instituted Monastic Council (*Klosterrat*), even though Maximilian had set this up with the ostensible purpose of remedying abuses.[5]

By the terms of the 1555 Peace of Augsburg, the reigning prince determined the religion in his principality. So it was up to the Habsburg rulers of Austria and its neighbouring duchies to define what their subjects should believe. Maximilian II, however, had insufficient confidence to express what his own religion was, let alone what the religion of his subjects should be. Rudolf II evinced a stronger commitment to the Catholic faith, but there were long periods when he eschewed religious observance. A fracas in Vienna in 1578, when a religious procession led by Rudolf was set upon near the cathedral (the so-called Milk War, since jugs of milk were thrown) seems to have plunged him into despair and convinced him to move for good to Prague.[6]

In the aftermath of Rudolf's withdrawal, the religious initiative passed to his uncles, Ferdinand of the Tyrol (1529–1595) and Charles of Styria (1540–1590). Ferdinand was not a man to be trifled with. Able to cast an infantryman's pike in the manner of a javelin, he had defied convention by marrying a commoner, Philippine Welser, whom he had met *inconnu* at a masked ball. The daughter of an Augsburg banker, Philippine was also heiress to Venezuela through the pledge on a debt owed by Emperor Charles V to her uncle. The debt was written off only shortly before her marriage, so the Tyrol never became a colonial power. Ferdinand was the founder of the great Wonder Chamber which still exists in Castle Ambras near Innsbruck and builder of the Star Palace (Hvežda) outside Prague, which was designed on alchemical principles, with its base forming a hexagram.

Ferdinand's brother, Charles, was remarkable for his parsimoniousness, keeping a court in Graz that scarcely amounted to thirty servants and officers. He had good reason to be frugal, since Styria bore the financial cost of maintaining the Croatian border against the Turks. Nevertheless, it was Charles who founded the stud near Trieste at Lipica (now in Slovenia), where he crossbred horses from Andalusia in Spain to make the famous white Lipizzaner breed. These were then trained in the high-knees action of the 'Spanish walk' and exhibited in a makeshift arena constructed by Maximilian II next to the Hofburg Palace in Vienna. The successor to the wooden Rossturnplatz is today's Spanish or Winter Riding School, built in the 1730s.[7]

Despite these distractions, the brothers were unfaltering in their Catholicism and zeal. Together with Duke William of Bavaria, Charles and Ferdinand met in 1579 at Munich, where they worked out a scheme for the reconversion of the Tyrol and the Inner Austrian duchies. The minutes of their meeting survive, and they are as spine-chilling to read today as the plan they disclose was masterful. The privileges given to the nobility in respect of religious freedom 'should be revoked at the earliest opportunity', but it would be opportune, they agreed, to withdraw them gradually and piecemeal. No concessions had been formally made to the cities, so they might be subject to compulsion in religious matters—a strategy which would serve to divide them from their noble co-religionists. If challenged, the archdukes could always claim that they were abiding by the terms of the Peace of Augsburg. They should also deliberately confuse compliance in matters of religion with allegiance to themselves, in furtherance of which they would now only promote Catholic noblemen to high position.[8]

The scheme drafted in 1579 is one of the strongest statements in the much larger process called 'confessionalization', whereby uniformity of belief and religious practice was not only insisted upon but also identified with political loyalty to the ruler and with due subservience to the instruments of his authority. As Archduke Charles explained to the Carniolan diet, reviling the sacraments and engaging in blasphemous acts brought disorder and so diminished the ruler. Accordingly, he observed, the imposition of Catholic discipline was 'no longer a matter of religion alone, but of sovereign supremacy and the preservation of due obedience.' The future bishop of Vienna, Melchior Khlesl, put it even more bluntly: 'It is in the nature of false belief to be disloyal.' Around this time, a new word entered Catholic political discourse: 'herebel' (*Retzer*), which fused together the words 'heretic' and 'rebel.'[9]

The next few years saw the Munich programme of 1579 unleashed. Preachers were driven out of the cities of the Tyrol and Inner Austrian duchies, and magistrates were compelled to sign up to a Catholic 'statement of faith.' In 1585, Ferdinand of the Tyrol ordered an inspection of all religious materials in the Tyrol, ranging from hymnals to schoolbooks, and he affirmed that only those who subscribed to the Catholic faith might expect preferment. In Styria, meanwhile, a religious test was applied to the burghers of cities and towns. Those who failed it were deprived of citizenship and often the right of residence. As the 1579 programme had anticipated, the nobles complained but took no action in support of their co-religionists.[10]

Opposition mainly came from below. In Graz in 1590, Protestants rioted, threatening 'a bloody Parisian wedding'—a reference to the St Bartholomew's Day massacre in France some twenty years before. They were dispersed by a thunderstorm. In the countryside, meanwhile, Protestants left their villages to find a more congenial environment, with the consequence that the mining industry in Styria and the Tyrol collapsed. Those that stayed moved their services into the forests and fields. Place names, still in use today, bear witness to their continued commitment to Protestantism: 'Church in the Wood', 'Chapel Meadow', and 'Preaching Stone' (Waldkirche, Tempelwiese, Predigerstein).[11]

Despite this resistance, the Munich programme was also adopted in Upper and Lower Austria by its governors. Once again, the first targets were the cities, and during the 1580s the Lower Austrian cities of Vienna, Krems, and Stein were duly cleansed. Upper Austria proved harder to crack, partly because the diet was spurred to action by the dashing Calvinist nobleman George Tschernembl. But a peasant uprising in 1596 yielded the excuse for tough measures. Under the direction of Melchior Khlesl, bishop of Wiener Neustadt and soon to be bishop of Vienna, a far-reaching programme of conversion was set in train. Despite all the evidence that the rebellion had been motivated by economic grievances, Khlesl maintained that it was due to ignorance and heresy, which the local lords had failed to confront. A thorough disciplining of the clergy had to be instituted, through a reformed

Monastic Council, and the common folk forced to embrace the true faith. Khlesl's recommendation was terrorism: the introduction of troops taken exclusively from the Catholic regiments employed on Spain's side in the Low Countries, 'for they were braver, and more experienced in robbing, looting, and fighting.'[12]

The success of Khlesl's policy may be judged by the increased reliance after this time on militarized Reform Commissions, which coerced the countryside into compliance even to the extent of throwing folk into rivers as a means of speedy baptism. It may also be shown by the spread of onion domes, placed on churches as a sign of their reconversion to Catholic worship. More, however, was owed to the patient work of Catholic ministry: the establishment of schools and universities, notably the Jesuit foundations in Graz, the gentle preaching of Capuchin friars, and new forms of religious participation through processions, local pilgrimages, and collective acts of devotion. 'Confessionalization' was as much a cultural and social phenomenon as a top-down exercise in building a disciplined community of subjects.

In 1593, the Ottoman Turks launched a war in Hungary that would go on for thirteen years. It was primarily a war of sieges, marches, and pillage, with only one battle of note, fought at Mezőkeresztes in 1596, which the Habsburg army decisively lost. During this war, Rudolf was briefly reconciled with the Catholic God, on which account he began to press forward with a plan to reconvert Hungary. He was encouraged both by the so-called Spanish faction in Prague, which urged him to assume a less cautious approach in religious matters, and by a period of chaos in Transylvania, which permitted him in 1601 to occupy the principality militarily. Thereafter, he turned his army on the main religious strongholds in northern Hungary. When in 1604 the Hungarian diet complained, Rudolf had his secretary draw up a decree that masqueraded as an act of the diet, in which all Protestant worship was banned.

On top of this, Rudolf commenced the indiscriminate prosecution of Hungarian noblemen on suspicion of treason. Since the Hungarian law of treason was vague in its definition of the offence, Rudolf's agents were able to bring within its purview a medley of crimes, ranging from questioning the king's rights of jurisdiction to incest and assault. Conviction for treason automatically resulted in the seizure of property, which as the Hungarian leaders complained, Rudolf had, like some new Babylonian king or Nebuchadnezzar, squandered on commissioning a new crown for himself. (It eventually became in 1804 the imperial crown of the Austrian Empire.) So fearful were the leading magnates of the penalty of confiscation of property that they concealed the crimes of Elizabeth Báthory, the infamous murderer of her serving girls, lest Rudolf go off with her estates too.[13]

The result was predictable: a Protestant rebellion in both Hungary and Transylvania. Led by Stephen Bocskai, a Catholic landowner now conveniently turned Calvinist, the uprising drew on Turkish support and the cattle drovers and cowboys of the Hungarian plain, who were inspired to martial fervour by an apocalyptic reading of the Bible. In 1605 the diets of Transylvania and Hungary elected Bocskai as prince, thereby repudiating Rudolf's rule. By this time Habsburg authority in both the kingdom and the principality had collapsed almost entirely, being confined to just a handful of counties in the westernmost part of Hungary. In token of Bocskai's victory, the sultan sent him a spare crown from his treasury. Although pressed to do so, Bocskai never assumed the title of king, but he kept the crown anyway.[14]

Rudolf's inability to control events forced a showdown with his family. In the spring of 1605, his brother, Matthias, and three of Rudolf's nephews demanded that the emperor hand over conduct of Hungarian affairs, which he reluctantly did, appointing Matthias as his viceroy in Hungary. Advised by Bishop Khlesl that he might need 'to bite into a sour apple in matters of religion', Matthias concluded the Peace of Vienna with the Hungarians in 1606, giving them complete freedom of worship. At Bocskai's request, the terms of the peace were guaranteed by the diets of Bohemia, Moravia, Styria, and Upper and Lower Austria, which meant that they might lawfully take up arms in defence of the settlement. At the same time, Matthias negotiated a treaty with the Turks at Zsitvatörök that recognized their continued possession of several of Hungary's most important fortresses.[15]

Franz Grillparzer's play *The Brothers' Quarrel* (*Ein Bruderzwist in Habsburg*), first performed in 1848, portrayed Matthias as a scheming bungler whose dark purpose was to deprive his well-intentioned but absentminded brother of his crowns. Certainly, Matthias's Spanish cousins never forgave his naïve intervention in the Low Countries, where in the interests of reaching a settlement he had in the late 1570s briefly acted as a tool of the rebels. In fact, Matthias was considerate, open, and friendly (the English envoy, Sir Philip Sidney, found him the most amiable of Maximilian's five sons), and it was the unpredictability of his brother that compelled him to play the usurper's part. Since Rudolf refused to sign the Zsitvatörök treaty, the Turks threatened to recommence the war. Matthias implored Rudolf to commit to the treaty but received only the response that the emperor 'should not be bothered.' Nor did Rudolf summon the Hungarian diet, even though this was a condition of the Peace of Vienna.[16]

Hungary stood once more at the brink of rebellion. Matthias accordingly had no alternative but to call the Hungarian diet himself and to use its envoys to explain to the sultan that no breach of the peace terms was intended. Matthias's nephews had previously backed Matthias against his brother, but they now stood aside, leaving Matthias dependent on the Austrian, Bohemian, and Moravian diets that had guaranteed the Hungarian settlement. The diets now formed a compact to support Matthias in his endeavours to bring peace to Hungary but added in clauses of mutual defence. Effectively, therefore, Matthias was bound to the diets, and they followed a largely pro-Protestant political agenda which aimed to roll back recent Catholic gains.

The reckoning came fast. Upper and Lower Austria had laboured for a decade under a harsh regime that was bent on the forcible conversion of their populations to Catholicism. The diets of the two duchies now jointly pressed for complete religious freedom, with the Upper Austrian proclaiming at Linz that 'the three estates of Lords, Knights and Cities are of one mind and will that religious life be restored in the cities and towns with churches and schools, and be achieved with one estate helping the other.' When, to force his hand, the diets threatened to withhold allegiance from him, Matthias buckled entirely. 'My God, what am I to do?' he exclaimed. 'If I withhold this concession, I shall lose domain and subjects; if I grant it, I am damned.' He chose to forfeit his soul, finally conceding in 1609 a general religious freedom in Upper and Lower Austria. In Hungary, meanwhile, Matthias's negotiations for the crown, which he finally received in 1608, were made dependent not only upon his confirmation of the Treaty of Vienna but also upon the expulsion of the Jesuits from Hungary and the closure of their schools.[17]

In all this, Rudolf was hardly blameless. To outmanoeuvre Matthias, he had begun negotiations of his own not only with the Protestant leaders in Upper and Lower Austria but also with Calvinist princes in the Holy Roman Empire, thus emboldening demands for religious freedom. His own meddling in Hungarian affairs on the eve of Matthias's coronation had, moreover, obliged Matthias to concede more in matters of religion than he would have wished. Now, in a vain attempt to keep hold of Bohemia, Rudolf sought to enlist the Protestants there to his side. In 1609, he capitulated entirely to their demands and published the so-called Letter of Majesty.

The Letter of Majesty rested on a statement of faith drawn up by Lutherans and Utraquists in Bohemia in 1575, the purpose of which had been to define a common position in their theology, for the approval of Emperor Maximilian II. But Maximilian had only given a verbal assurance that those who adhered to the 'Bohemian Confession' would not be troubled in their belief. Now this document was given full legal recognition, and all those who adhered to its broad scheme of faith could practise their religion freely, 'without let or hindrance from any person, spiritual or temporal.' The settlement was to be policed, moreover, by twenty-four 'Defenders' appointed by the diet. With indeterminate and therefore expandable powers, the Defenders effectively constituted a shadow government.

The terms of the Letter of Majesty were subsequently extended to the other lands of the Bohemian crown—Moravia, Silesia, and the Lusatias—but they did not save Rudolf's throne. When Rudolf attempted to backtrack on his concessions and threatened to bring in troops mustered on the border by the bishop of Passau, the Bohemian diet called on Matthias for assistance. Matthias entered Prague with an army, browbeat Rudolf into abdicating as king of Bohemia, and in March 1611 was duly elected and crowned in his place. Matthias was subsequently joined in Prague by his new wife, his cousin Anna of the Tyrol. A kindly woman of exceptional girth ('*monstreux de voir*'), Anna's skill at the clavichord was matched only by her dedication to penitential self-flagellation. It was she, however, who remained by Rudolf's corpse when the ageing emperor died of heart failure in Prague at the beginning of 1612. As predicted by his astrologers, Rudolf's passing coincided with the death in the castle zoo of his favourite lion.[18]

Matthias succeeded Rudolf as emperor, being elected king of the Romans and crowned in Frankfurt in June 1612. Yet his personal victory had come at the cost of the triumph of heresy. Except for the Tyrol and the Inner Austrian duchies of Styria, Carinthia, and Carniola, Protestantism was not only on the ascendant in the Habsburg lands but now formally recognized as legal. From Linz in Upper Austria to Wrocław in Silesia, Lutheran worship was conducted openly, while in Hungary Calvinist preaching went mostly unhindered. In Transylvania, which Rudolf and Matthias never succeeded in recapturing, Lutheran, Calvinist, and Unitarian services continued as before. But it was a false dawn, for waiting in the wings was the Habsburg who would change history and bring Protestantism to its knees in Central Europe: Rudolf and Matthias's cousin, Ferdinand of Styria.

12

FERDINAND II, THE HOLY HOUSE, AND BOHEMIA

erdinand of Styria (born in 1578) was the son of Archduke Charles and cousin of the two emperors Rudolf II and Matthias. His parents sent him at the age of eleven to the Jesuit boarding school at Ingolstadt in Bavaria. Several years later he progressed to the nearby university as the first ever Habsburg to read for a degree (in the *trivium*, or liberal arts). He did not live in Ingolstadt as an ordinary schoolboy or student but lodged with a household of his own in the town's gaunt Herzogskasten Castle and hunted between classes. His father died shortly after his arrival in Ingolstadt, and his mother, Maria Anna, visited him only once. Even so, Ferdinand corresponded lengthily with his mother and would continue to do so until her death in 1608. In the making of the young Ferdinand's limitless devotion to the Catholic Church, Maria Anna was probably more influential than his Jesuit tutors.[1]

In 1596, at the age of eighteen, Ferdinand came of age as ruler of Inner Austria. Soon after, he journeyed on a pilgrimage to Rome. On the way there he stopped off at Loreto to visit the Holy House, the place of Christ's childhood which angels had miraculously transported from Nazareth to the Italian coast in the thirteenth century. Within the stonework of the Holy

House was a niche, in which was set a small statue of the Virgin carved out of Lebanese cedar. Kneeling before the shrine, Ferdinand is said to have made a solemn vow to continue his father's work and rid his possessions of all heretics.[2]

The story of Ferdinand's vow may be no truer than the legend of the Holy House. Nevertheless, upon his return to Styria, Ferdinand recommenced the programme of persecution that his father had initiated. First, he moved against the towns, chasing out Lutheran preachers and shutting down their schools, and then he closed in on the nobles, who claimed that their right to practise the Protestant religion was entrenched in the 1578 privilege that Ferdinand's father had granted them. Ferdinand ignored their complaints and sent in Reform Commissions backed up by troops. Maria Anna urged her son on, declaring that he was not bound by his father's concession and that he should 'show his teeth.'[3]

Ferdinand had another weapon. Roman law is, as its name suggests, of considerable antiquity, going back to the period of the Roman Republic and Empire. From the late fifteenth century onwards, it started to exert a strong pull on legal developments in the Holy Roman Empire and Central Europe. The Roman law texts followed there derived from the codification made in the sixth century by the Byzantine emperor Justinian. This not only aimed at completeness and communicated categories into which the law might be arranged, but it also extolled the authority of the ruler. 'What pleases the prince has the force of the law' was how one Roman law text put it. Other passages emphasized the right of the ruler to do as he wished 'on his own volition' (*proprio suo motu*), irrespective of legal constraints.

It was to the Roman law that Ferdinand turned in his dealings with the querulous diets of Inner Austria. He explained to them that he enjoyed a complete authority by virtue of the sovereign power with which he had been invested. It was his wish that Protestantism be rooted out, and he acted in this respect 'on his own volition.' Moreover, he explained, he was doing the heretics a kindness, recalling them from their false ways so that they might enjoy eternal life. Many years later, his confessor recollected Ferdinand's words: 'Non-Catholics think me unfeeling for banning heresy. But I love them rather than hate them. If I didn't love them, I would freely leave them in their errors.'[4]

Ferdinand was devout, kneeling in prayer seven times a day and attending Mass twice. But he was also extravagant and unconcerned with details. He was an 'ideas man', who could not be bothered with processes and balance sheets. Even more dangerously, he believed that he had a special channel of his own to the Almighty. God performed miracles on his behalf, and in times of danger God even spoke to him from the crucifix before which he prayed. (The crucifix was moved after his death to the high altar of the Hofburg Chapel, where it continued to perform wonders.) In one of his last letters to his mother, Ferdinand explained his commitment to the faith in words that echo Philip II: he 'would prefer to lose land and people rather than bring harm to religion.'[5]

Ferdinand generally held aloof from the struggle between Rudolf and Matthias, not committing himself completely to either brother. He did, however, make overtures to Duke Maximilian of Bavaria. The Bavarian Wittelsbachs provided after Spain a second reservoir of Catholic spouses for the Habsburgs. Ferdinand's mother, Maria Anna, was a Bavarian, as was Ferdinand's first wife, his cousin, who was also called Maria Anna (they married in 1600). But Bavaria traditionally jostled for leadership with the Habsburgs in the southern part of the empire. Maximilian of Bavaria was as committed to Catholicism as Ferdinand. Indeed, he went one step further than his brother-in-law, signing a vow of personal dedication to the Virgin in his own blood. Religious partisanship drew Maximilian and Ferdinand politically closer. In 1609, Ferdinand joined the Catholic League that Maximilian had founded in defence of Catholicism, as a counterweight to the Protestant Evangelical Union, which had also proclaimed a defensive purpose.[6]

Matthias succeeded his brother as emperor in 1612 but proved almost as helpless as Rudolf, for he was routinely incapacitated by ill health. Nor was there much prospect that he might sire a son from his increasingly stout wife. Matthias had no great affection for Ferdinand, for he distrusted his religious zeal. But Matthias's brothers were either dead or dying, and none had left an heir, on which account Matthias's only obvious successor was his cousin, Ferdinand. It also helped that by 1614 Ferdinand had two sons of his own, thus ensuring the Habsburg line. Matthias duly prepared for Ferdinand to succeed to his thrones.

Negotiations began with the Hungarian diet in 1616. Ferdinand was distrusted in Hungary on account of his Catholic fervour, but the newly appointed cardinal primate, Peter Pázmány, worked hard on Ferdinand's behalf. Pázmány explained to one group of Hungarian noblemen that the kingdom had two options: to submit to the Turks or to 'rest under the wings of the neighbouring Christian prince' and recognize the Habsburgs as 'the bastion of our country.' Pázmány also convinced Ferdinand to make explicit assurances that he would uphold religious freedom in Hungary, as guaranteed in the 1606 Treaty of Vienna. In return for his election and coronation as king, Ferdinand duly published a contract drawn up by the diet, in which he committed himself to adhere to seventy-seven articles, including 'that no one shall be troubled in the practice or exercise of his religion.' This was then published in 1619 as the first law of Ferdinand's reign.[7]

Ferdinand never backtracked on the commitments he made in Hungary at the time he was crowned. Sworn during the sacred act of coronation, at which the new king took Mass, they constituted solemn undertakings that might not be countermanded even on Ferdinand's 'own volition.' Indeed, at the diet held in 1622 at Sopron, Ferdinand even took as his first minister, or palatine, the leading Protestant nobleman, Stanislas Thurzó, thus deferring to the diet rather than (as his predecessors had done) suspending the office until the diet chose someone more to his liking. It seems probable that Ferdinand would have also maintained the concessions granted to Bohemia in the Letter of Majesty had not the Bohemians rebelled against him.[8]

Ferdinand was elected king of Bohemia by the Bohemian diet in 1617. Matthias proved on this occasion skilful in his politicking, convincing the nobles one by one in private that Ferdinand's succession was a done deal and that it was in their interest to back his candidacy. But the Bohemians were also mindful of the Moravian nobles, who contested the Bohemian diet's exclusive right to elect the ruler and thus the primacy of Bohemia within the complex of the Bohemian crown lands. By not upsetting the tradition of Habsburg succession, the Bohemian nobility hoped to maintain the political status quo and thus their preeminence. As part of his negotiations for the crown, Ferdinand committed himself to uphold the Letter of Majesty, the terms of which he swore to uphold at his coronation.[9]

Many of the terms of the Letter of Majesty were vague. A row over Protestant churches built on land belonging to a local abbot and the archbishop of Prague had festered over years, with Matthias largely ignoring the problem. Eventually, after several protests at the demolition of the churches, the Protestant Defenders, appointed under the terms of the Letter of Majesty, summoned in 1618 an assembly in Prague to put pressure on Matthias. He had not yet formally relinquished the government of Bohemia to Ferdinand but had placed it in the hands of an interim regency council. Matthias now sent from Vienna a sharp note to the Defenders, instructing them never again to trespass upon his authority.

The Defenders were not used to Matthias taking a firm line, and they suspected that the letter had been written on his behalf by the regency council. In May 1618, a confrontation in Prague Castle between regents and Defenders turned unexpectedly ugly, and the two officials thought to be behind the letter were ejected from a high window, along with a secretary. They fell twenty metres (sixty-five feet) but survived—they either landed on a pile of rubbish or, as some contemporary accounts tell, had their descent slowed by the intervention of angels. Either way, the three men survived both the defenestration and the cowardly gunshots that followed as they ran off. Ferdinand soon afterwards ennobled the secretary for the blameless attack upon him, granting him the title of 'von Hohenfall' (of the High Fall).

Not only had the Defenders thrown Matthias's officials out of a window, but by doing so they had also overthrown his government. Although this was still a local quarrel, Ferdinand was taking no chances. He watched with alarm as the rebels in Prague established their own government, recruited troops, and began negotiating with the other Bohemian provinces to form a confederation in which the monarch would be powerless. As a first step, he arrested Melchior Khlesl, reckoning him too ready to make compromises, on which account the pope promptly excommunicated Ferdinand, for Khlesl was a cardinal. But Ferdinand answered to a higher authority than the pope, and he correctly reckoned that he would soon enough receive absolution.

Meanwhile, the rebels had enlisted to their side the more radical nobles of Upper and Lower Austria, who saw the opportunity to form a united front for the defence of Protestantism. The death of Matthias, in March 1619, gave them the chance to contest Ferdinand's succession to his cousin's titles and force concessions from him. A noisy band of Lower Austrian nobles duly presented Ferdinand in Vienna with a petition to confirm their religious freedom and recognize their right to make an alliance with Bohemia. Outside the city a Bohemian army mustered threateningly. Only the chance arrival of troops loyal to Ferdinand saved the day, for otherwise he had no support in Vienna except for the small garrison and a band of students, mustered under the improbable command of their professors.[10]

Despite having almost lost his capital city, Ferdinand succeeded in August in obtaining his election as emperor in Frankfurt. He had the backing there of the three archbishop-electors and of the duke of Saxony, who although a Protestant favoured a cautious policy of 'containment.' Ferdinand also had his own vote as king of Bohemia, which he cast for himself, not wanting, as he explained, to do himself an injustice. Seeing themselves outnumbered, the Protestant electors of Brandenburg and the Palatinate concurred, rendering Ferdinand's election unanimous. Early the next month he was crowned with Charlemagne's diadem in Frankfurt cathedral.[11]

Over the course of 1618–1619, two decisions were made that widened and, indeed, 'internationalized' the revolt, but neither of them was Ferdinand's doing. Philip III of Spain (1598–1621) had watched with alarm the progress of the Bohemian Revolt. His immediate thought was to send a fleet against the rebels, for like Shakespeare he imagined Bohemia to have a coast, but he prudently left it to his Council of State to recommend policy. The council met in July 1618 and was divided. One group, backed by the duke of Lerma, advocated caution and the concentration of Spanish resources on the Mediterranean. The other, led by the duke of Zúñiga, invoked broader strategic concerns, including the damage that would be done both to supply lines and to morale were the Central European branch of the Habsburgs to be abandoned.

It was then that Zúñiga delivered the bombshell. He reported that, without reference to Madrid, the Spanish ambassador to Vienna had already committed troops serving in Italy to support the crushing of the revolt. As Zúñiga now explained, 'To dismiss the regiment while it is actually on active service would be to ruin the emperor's position absolutely, for such a withdrawal of Your Majesty's protection would deprive him of all reputation.' The die was thus cast, and the king of Spain was already a combatant. Faced with this ambassadorial coup, Philip III sent immediate funds to support his Austrian relatives. By April 1619, the first contingent of seven thousand troops had arrived in the empire; more than thirty thousand would follow in the next two years.[12]

The second decision was made by the rebels in Prague. In August 1619, the Bohemian diet deposed Ferdinand on the grounds that he had been improperly elected. Having sought in vain for a responsible adult to take Ferdinand's place, the diet settled on the callow Calvinist prince Frederick V of the Palatinate (lived 1596–1632). Frederick was a political madman, convinced that he was destined to overthrow Catholic tyranny and restore an illusionary lost freedom to the Germans. In masked balls, Frederick provocatively dressed up as the German Arminius, who back in the first century had defeated the Roman legions, and as the mythological Jason, who had stolen the Golden Fleece (a Habsburg symbol). By opening the Bible in random places and fastening on individual passages, Calvinist preachers and publicists discerned that he was the Roaring or Midnight Lion foretold in the Old Testament Book of Ezra, whose reign would culminate in the destruction of the Antichrist. Confident that his election was due to 'the special providence and predestination of God', Frederick accepted with little demur the Bohemian crown.[13]

Almost all the lords and princes of the Holy Roman Empire, Catholic and Protestant alike, considered Frederick's taking of the crown to be an unacceptable assault on the principle of monarchy. Frederick was now abandoned, even by his father-in-law James I of England (VI of Scotland). The Calvinist ruler of Transylvania, Gabriel Bethlen, also proved an unreliable ally, abandoning Frederick when Ferdinand's agents recruited Polish Cossacks to devastate his principality. To buttress his ailing cause, Frederick was obliged to open implausible negotiations with the sultan, requesting support in return for an annual tribute. Although a Turkish envoy eventually turned up in Prague, his main interest was to see the famous window from which the regents had been pushed.[14]

Until his deposition, Ferdinand had been ready to make terms with the Bohemian rebels. Now, however, they had torn up all hope of a deal and brought in a leading prince of the empire as their champion. Ferdinand was thus obliged to look for military allies of his own. Maximilian of Bavaria was an obvious choice, and he on Ferdinand's behalf readied the Catholic League. Ferdinand did, however, have to promise to repay Maximilian's expenses, on which account he pledged Upper Austria to him. The Lower Austrian nobility also proved pliant, but to win their support Ferdinand confirmed the religious freedoms earlier conceded by Matthias. Upon consulting the pope as to the rectitude of this concession, Ferdinand was advised that a 'blind eye' would be shown. As it turned out, Ferdinand would after a few years go back on this commitment, claiming that he only intended to spare Protestant consciences not churches. Nevertheless, by his posture of tolerance, Ferdinand won over John George of Saxony, but only after he had guaranteed his expenses as well, giving the Lusatias in pledge. Meanwhile, Spanish troops poured into the Low Countries in readiness.

The outcome was predictable: a victory for the Virgin Mary, to whom Ferdinand had given nominal command of his forces. A thirty-thousand-strong army, led by the Bavarian commander Tilly, crushed in November 1620 its numerically and organizationally inferior foe in less than two hours at the Battle of the White Mountain outside Prague (now the site of Prague airport). Frederick V, the so-called Winter King, whose Bohemian rule had not lasted fifteen months, fled Prague Castle, leaving behind his entire correspondence. This was subsequently published at Maximilian of Bavaria's instruction, but edited to cast Frederick in the worst possible light—as one of a band of 'shameful, ungodly people who for long strove for the crown and to destroy the House of Austria and seize Catholic churches.'[15]

With Bohemia vanquished, Tilly swung westwards to invade the Palatinate and to join up with Spanish forces from the Low Countries. These crushed the few Protestant allies that remained to Frederick, after which his fairytale palace at Heidelberg and seven-sided fortress at Mannheim were bombarded and seized. Frederick sought safety in The Hague in Holland. The final humiliation came in 1623. Not only Frederick's lands but also his electoral title were conferred upon Maximilian in a solemn ceremony that rehearsed Frederick's crimes. For good measure, Ferdinand's charter recording the investiture placed Frederick and his heirs under ban of outlawry.[16]

Bohemia was now crushed. Forty-eight ringleaders of the rebellion were condemned to death, although one was dramatically reprieved on the scaffold. The 'theatre of blood', which took place in June 1622 on Prague's Old Town Square, was accompanied by a band of drummers whose task it was to drown out the final speeches of the victims. In Bohemia and Moravia (but not in Silesia or the Lusatias, which were now occupied by John George of Saxony), a far-reaching programme of reconversion was put in train. Rebels were fined or had their lands confiscated. On top of this, all who refused to convert to Catholicism were forced into exile, again with loss of land, prompting the flight of about 150,000 persons. A new generation of Habsburg loyalists was duly installed in their place. The university, formerly a hotbed of religious radicalism, was merged with the Jesuit Clementinum College and, in the countryside, the usual Reform Commissions sent out.

Ferdinand had twice committed himself to uphold the Letter of Majesty, including at his coronation. In justifying his repudiation of its terms, Ferdinand turned once more to the Roman law, his reliance upon which is nowhere clearer demonstrated than in the Renewed Constitution (*Vernewerte Landesordnung*) that he gave Bohemia in 1627. Despite its name, this amounted to the comprehensive reordering of the public law in the kingdom and the destruction of its historic institutions—the crown was now to be hereditary, the role of the diets confined to approving the ruler's instructions, especially in regard to taxation (which might not be 'made conditional or delayed by improper conditions . . . as has happened in the past'), and the new constitution itself made subject to alteration by the monarch 'on his own volition.'[17]

In explaining the grounds on which he overturned Bohemia's historic constitution, Ferdinand made the presumption that all authority rested with him. The nobility and the diet did not possess rights of their own, except those that had been ceded to them by the monarch. This was pure Roman law, for otherwise the traditional or customary law presupposed that ruler and diet had equal, autonomous, and separately generated rights. Since the Bohemians had risen against him, Ferdinand went on to explain, he was entitled to revoke the privileges that he and his predecessors had given them, for they had forfeited any right to enjoy them. Henceforth, Ferdinand reserved to himself and his heirs 'the power to enact laws and decrees, and everything devolving from the legislative power [ius legis ferendae—another Romanism] which belongs to Us, as the King, alone.'

But, of course, not all Bohemians were rebels, which led to Ferdinand's second Roman law solution. The revolt, he explained, had taken place 'in a collective manner' (in forma universitatis), and so each was bound by the corporate or group decision. Consequently, all might be punished irrespective of their personal guilt, and most duly were. Although the contention that Bohemia now entered upon three centuries of 'Darkness' is the overstated claim of Czech nationalist historians, the historic kingdom effectively became an annex of the Austrian lands. In token of its subjection, even the Bohemian chancellery, which undertook much of the routine work of government there, was in 1624 moved from Prague to Vienna.[18]

In 1627, in the same year as the Renewed Constitution was proclaimed, Ferdinand's second wife, Eleonora Gonzaga of Mantua (they had married in 1622), dedicated a new chapel in the Augustinian Church in Vienna. It was modelled exactly on the dimensions of the Holy House in Loreto and made of the same roughly hewn stone. The Loreto Chapel became Ferdinand's place of prayer. He adorned its walls with the banners of his defeated foes, and it was there that he rededicated himself to the Virgin. We do not know for sure whether, thirty years earlier, Ferdinand had vowed at the Holy House to extirpate heresy in his lands. Had he done so, then in his prayers in the new Loreto chapel, he must surely have recalled the promise, which he was now on the way to fulfilling.

The Loreto Chapel stands for more, however, than a task near completion. It became the dynastic chapel of the Habsburgs, in which they made their vows of marriage and prayed for the reward of children. A small cupboard (subsequently enlarged) was also cut into its wall to house urns containing the hearts of Habsburg rulers, archdukes, and archduchesses. Divided three ways on death, their bodies now went with the heart removed to the crypt of Vienna's Capuchin Church, and their surgically removed intestines to the crypt in St Stephen's that Rudolf the Founder had intended for the complete remains of his descendants, but which had since been neglected in favour of Wiener Neustadt and Prague.

Following Burgundian custom, it had been usual in the sixteenth century for Habsburg rulers and princes in Central Europe (but not in Spain) to be divided two ways at death, with their hearts and corpses separately interred. The practice of three-way burial began with the tripartition of Matthias's corpse in 1619, although the interment of all his parts had to be delayed until the Loreto Chapel and the Capuchin Crypt were completed in the 1630s. The postmortem dissection of Habsburg bodies into three parts was not designed as a macabre death cult but had an intensely religious purpose. The three-way housing of the corpse in separate churches increased the 'treasury of merits' belonging to the dead person. In each church, Masses were recited for the deceased, and their efficacy was enhanced by the physical proximity of his or her remains, speeding the soul heavenward at thrice the pace of ordinary sinners.[19]

The dissection of the corpse on death symbolized the intimacy of the dynasty's connection to the Host, which was displayed whenever priests performed a Mass beside a body part. Ferdinand had not only embraced the militant spiritual mission borne by his Spanish cousins and in-laws, but he had also invested his branch of the dynasty with a sacred purpose, which he demonstrated by his dedication to the Virgin and to the celebration of the eucharist's power, even in death. His descendants were no less devoted, leading processions, founding chapels in conspicuous commemoration of the Host, and cultivating remembrance of King Rudolf and of his respect for the priest bearing the communion. To AEIOU, Ferdinand II's heirs added a new acrostic in token of their commitment to the Catholic religion: EUCHARISTIA, which may be unravelled to disclose HIC EST AUSTRIA: 'This is Austria.'[20]

13

THE THIRTY YEARS 'WORLD WAR'

T he Bohemian Revolt marked the opening phase in the Thirty Years War (1618–1648). Although often presented as a religious war, the Thirty Years War defies easy categorization. Like most great contests, the Thirty Years War comprised separate struggles with their own discrete causes. Each phase, however, bore within it the seeds of future conflict, to such an extent that contemporaries considered the fighting to be a single prolonged period of warfare. Much of the contest took place in the Holy Roman Empire, but it spilled over to draw in the Low Countries, Britain, Denmark, France, Spain, Portugal, Hungary, Transylvania, northern Italy, Sweden, and Poland, and, via Poland and Sweden, even distant Russia.

Although British diplomacy almost succeeded in recruiting the sultan to the Protestant cause, the Ottoman Empire remained aloof from the contest. With this exception, the Thirty Years War was the first war to involve the entirety of the European continent. But it was a global struggle too, for the combatants also fought in Africa, the Indian and Pacific Oceans, and the West Indies. German historians complain that the Thirty Years War was unnecessarily intensified and prolonged by foreign intervention, becoming 'an international war fought out on German soil.' But the Thirty Years War can also be seen the other way around too—as a German conflict that drew in most of Europe and eventually spilled across the world.[1]

The struggle between Habsburg Spain and the Dutch United Provinces was the lightning rod that made the Thirty Years War a worldwide
contest. The war in the Low Countries that had begun in the 1560s during
the reign of Philip II became part of the Thirty Years War. But while the
fighting in the Low Countries consisted primarily of sieges and stalemates,
the seaborne contest between Spain and the United Provinces was fought
on several wide fronts. Spanish overseas possessions were targets for the
Dutch. So too were the colonies of Portugal, the crown of which had passed
in 1580 to Philip II and his heirs. As much as plunder, the Dutch purpose
was to cut Spain off from its wealth and so, in the words of one informed
observer, 'to divert the king of Spain's arms from our throats and sever
the sinews with which he sustains the wars in Europe.' For the Habsburgs,
however, Dutch activities not only imperilled their trade routes but also
threatened dynastic catastrophe. According to a favourite theory in the
Spanish court, the Habsburg possessions were so enmeshed that defeat in
any one place could bring down the whole edifice. The global interlocking
of Habsburg power made the Thirty Years War a global contest.[2]

The Dutch were after 1625 assisted by their British allies and by enter-
prisers or privateers who pursued their own material interests while sailing
under the British flag (or, indeed, any flag save the red or black standard
of the pirate). The British were unreliable allies and soon abandoned the
Dutch in favour of peaceful relations with Habsburg Spain. Even so, they
managed to establish a foothold on the island of St Kitts in the West Indies,
from which they went on to seize the Leeward Islands. The islands provided
a base for English privateers, who in the 1640s ravaged Spanish possessions
in the Caribbean, seizing most of Jamaica in 1643. It would be more than
three centuries before the British left.

Dutch ambitions were larger. The Dutch government and States General or parliament in The Hague outsourced the task of fighting the Spanish
and Portuguese overseas to two merchant companies, the East India Company (founded 1602) and the West India Company (founded 1621). Both
could sell stock to build war fleets, to seize and administer colonies abroad,
and, indeed, to found their own commercial empires. Shortly after its establishment, the 'Nineteen Gentlemen' who managed the West India Company drew up a 'grand plan' (*Groot Desseyn*), which proposed an attack on
the Portuguese colony of Brazil and the capture of both the Brazilian sugar
plantations and the Central African slave trade.

Habsburg Spanish and Portuguese possessions in the New World rapidly fell victim to the West India Company. In 1628, the entire Spanish treasure fleet was captured off Cuba; shortly afterwards, about half of Brazil was overrun by the Dutch, who established their own New Holland colony. But the Dutch settlers were never able to win the loyalty of the Portuguese plantation owners, who rebelled against them in 1645. Inadequately funded by the West India Company, whose shareholders expected a profit, the New Holland colony was recovered by Portugal in 1654. The Dutch had during their administration permitted a relative freedom of worship, so New Holland had a large Jewish population. Possibly, as much as a half of the non-native population of New Holland was Jewish, and the capital of Mauritsstad (now Recife) was the first place in all the Americas to have a synagogue. The return of Brazil to Portuguese rule saw this inheritance squandered by religious persecution.[3]

The Spanish Habsburgs had additionally acquired through Portugal a small coastal settlement in modern-day Angola, based on Luanda. The kingdom of Kongo to its north also lay within the Portuguese cultural orbit and influence. Kongo held in the seventeenth century the region around the mouth of the Congo River, extending southwards into Angola, with its capital at São Salvador (modern-day Mbanza Kongo). Despite its location, Kongo was a culturally complex state, governed by a literate elite which had not only embraced Catholicism but also assumed Portuguese names, ranks, and coats of arms.[4]

During the 1620s, however, the Portuguese governors of Luanda targeted Kongo. Having subdued the neighbouring Ndongo kingdom, they now thought to convert Portuguese cultural supremacy in Kongo into political hegemony. To their side, they enlisted the terrifying Imbangala. The 'Spartans' of south-western Africa, the Imbangala practised cannibalism and infanticide, recruiting to their war bands only children born to outsiders, who were then made pliant by elaborate rituals of initiation. Faced with the ruin of his kingdom, Pedro II of Kongo appealed to the Dutch for help, offering in return gold, silver, ivory, and slaves. The kingdom of Kongo was thus drawn onto the Protestant side in the Thirty Years War.[5]

In response to Pedro's plea, a Dutch flotilla bombarded Luanda in 1624, but the king's early death put a halt to further military ventures. In 1641, however, King Garcia II of Kongo renewed Pedro's diplomacy, since, as he complained to an agent of the West India Company, he continued to 'suffer much' from Portuguese political meddling and military incursions. Accordingly, a West India Company fleet seized Luanda, ejected the Portuguese, and briefly began the construction of a Dutch colony. In the fighting that followed the capture of Luanda, both the Dutch and the Portuguese recruited local tribes, fielding armies of up to thirty thousand troops supported by artillery, with hundreds of villages destroyed. No mere sideshow, the war in Kongo also fed Habsburg global aspirations to restore the African inheritance of the Roman general and alleged Habsburg ancestor Scipio Africanus (236–183 BCE), the conqueror of Carthage and mythic source of Spanish imperial power.[6]

Meanwhile, Habsburg possessions in the Indian and Pacific Oceans were threatened by the Dutch East India Company. From footholds on the Molucca Islands and on the Indian coast, Dutch vessels disrupted the Spanish and Portuguese trade in spices. In the Pacific Ocean, the Dutch East India Company occupied a part of modern-day Indonesia, founding Batavia, now Jakarta. From there, its vessels blockaded Manila and raided Spanish shipping. The main contest was, however, fought out in Taiwan (Formosa), which was almost simultaneously occupied by Spanish and Dutch forces in the 1620s. At San Domingo (now in New Taipei), the Spanish governor built a fort, which counted as the first stone building in Taiwan. The brick arches of its solid red facade were supported by the twin columns that symbolized the Pillars of Hercules and Habsburg power.[7]

The Spanish aim was to use Taiwan to tranship goods to China and to protect Manila from Dutch attacks. But both the Spanish and the Dutch also competed for souls, for commercial opportunities with Japan, and for workers from the Chinese mainland to work Taiwan's sugar plantations. The influx of Han Chinese dramatically altered the ethnic composition of Taiwan, where head-hunting aboriginals had previously been in the majority. The Spanish colony was finally abandoned in 1642, following a Dutch artillery assault on the fort of San Domingo. Even so, the decades in which the fate of Taiwan was intertwined with the Thirty Years War contributed to demographics that remain to this day a source of political contention.[8]

The Thirty Years War in Europe was fought in a more geographically concentrated space and was accordingly less momentous in its global consequences. But it was altogether bloodier. In the Holy Roman Empire alone, about 5 million people, amounting to 20 per cent of the population, were killed or died as an immediate consequence of the war. Lower Austria was particularly badly hit. Its population of 600,000 people in 1600 had fallen fifty years later by 25 per cent, to 450,000. Of the lives lost during the war, civilians suffered disproportionately, as invading armies plundered and terrorized the populations through which they moved, contaminated water supplies, and indiscriminately shelled cities, sometimes with shells of poison gas extracted from arsenic and henbane.[9]

The greatest atrocity took place on 20 May 1631, when an imperial army stormed the independent Lutheran stronghold of Magdeburg in Saxony. Death by fire and slaughter accounted for possibly as many as thirty thousand people. One survivor reported how the imperial troops 'drove small children into the fire like sheep, sticking them with spears; God knows Turks and barbarians would not have done otherwise.' The victorious commander, von Pappenheim, drily noted: 'I believe that over twenty thousand souls were lost. It is certain that no more terrible work and divine punishment has been seen since the destruction of Jerusalem. All of our soldiers became rich.' With the fall of Magdeburg, a new word entered the German vocabulary—*Magdeburgisierung*, 'to make like Magdeburg.'[10]

The Sack of Magdeburg was reported in the most graphic terms in hundreds of pamphlets, broadsheets, and pulpit sermons. Catholics described the Sack in terms of divine vengeance and pointed out (correctly) that it was Magdeburg's own citizens who had started the fire which ravaged the city. Even so, Ferdinand II's reputation was diminished, for he too was now tarnished with the 'Black Legend' of Habsburg oppression and savagery. As one of Ferdinand's commanders explained, after Magdeburg the Catholic cause was politically isolated and stuck in a 'labyrinth' of its own making. Coming on top of a series of blunders, the Sack of Magdeburg almost cost the Habsburgs the Thirty Years War.[11]

The first decade of the war, following the defeat of the Bohemian rebels, had gone well for Ferdinand II. The Protestant supporters of the Winter King, Frederick of the Palatinate, were routed and a Danish intervention halted by the forces of the Catholic League. In order to free himself of his political dependence on the Bavarian-led league, Ferdinand turned to the Bohemian nobleman Albrecht Václav Eusebius z Valdštejna. Even though his first language was Czech, z Valdštejna is better known as Wallenstein, the German form of his name. Wallenstein was of humble origin, but he had made money fast by marrying a wealthy widow, currency speculation, and buying up cheaply the land of exiled Protestants. He had his horoscope cast several times by Kepler, but Kepler made several miscalculations so his lucubrations on Wallenstein's character (agile, active, merciless, and so forth) may be safely disregarded. More revealing of the man is the garden of the palace he built in Prague. The geometric and symmetrical arrangement of the flower beds contrasts there with an enormous dripstone wall, made up of faux stalactites and leering faces, beside which Wallenstein kept his collection of owls.[12]

In 1625, Wallenstein offered Ferdinand not a regiment, as was a common enough gesture for noblemen, but a whole army. The army would be provisioned by requisitioning and its other costs borne by loans, which were to be securitized and sold on as bonds. Munitions would come in part from Wallenstein's own foundries and factories. Having won Ferdinand's approval, Wallenstein fitted out an army of (eventually) a hundred thousand men, which he used to force the Danes out of the Thirty Years War and to put distant Stralsund in Pomerania under siege. Ferdinand awarded Wallenstein the title of admiral of the North and Baltic Seas, thus hinting at further conquests. To reimburse Wallenstein's costs, Ferdinand also gave him in 1628 the duchy of Mecklenburg in the north of the Holy Roman Empire, which Ferdinand had seized from its rulers on account of their support for the Danes.

Mecklenburg was the second duchy that Ferdinand gave away; the first had been the Palatinate, which Ferdinand had taken from Frederick of the Palatinate and handed over to Maximilian of Bavaria. To justify these confiscations, Ferdinand appealed not to the Roman law but to feudal law. The dukes of Mecklenburg were, like Frederick of the Palatinate, 'notorious rebels', on which account, Ferdinand explained, he might dispossess them entirely of their lands. But this was not true. Lands confiscated should have been given over to close kinsmen, which Wallenstein was not. Moreover, the lands confiscated in both duchies were a medley of fiefs and ancient estates, which was held in full title and so inalienable. By treating these properties as all the same Ferdinand demonstrated that he was no stickler for legality.[13]

Now, on top of this legal sleight of hand, Ferdinand revisited the Peace of Augsburg of 1555. Interpreting its terms to his own advantage, he demanded that all ecclesiastical properties occupied by Protestants since 1552 (the operative date in the original peace treaty) be returned to the Catholic Church. The Edict of Restitution of 1629, which demanded the restoration to the Catholic Church of its lost properties, threatened to ruin many

Protestant rulers in the empire who over the preceding decades had seized no fewer than two archbishoprics, thirteen bishoprics, and some five hundred monasteries and convents. When Ferdinand refused to back down, the Protestant rulers led by the duke of Saxony began mustering 'for defensive purposes.' Then, in 1630, the Swedish Lutheran king, Gustavus Adolphus, landed in Pomerania. Gustavus's purpose at this stage was probably only to secure parts of the Baltic coast, for he had brought no maps of the interior with him. Lauded, however, as the great Protestant avenger and the new Midnight Lion of the North, Gustavus Adolphus cloaked himself in the mantle offered.[14]

By the Edict of Restitution, Ferdinand sought the comprehensive restoration of the Catholic Church in the Holy Roman Empire, but he lost his advantage, for on top of the Edict came the Sack of Magdeburg. The Protestant leaders could no longer remain neutral in the face of the atrocity and the imminent seizure of their lands. The dukes of Brandenburg, Saxony, and Mecklenburg, which Gustavus had returned to its rightful rulers, swung round to support the Swedish king. After several stunning victories that took the allies into Bohemia, Silesia, and Bavaria, Wallenstein saved the day. Having been previously forced into retirement by Ferdinand, who resented his successes, Wallenstein was reinstated, and he rolled the Protestant forces back. At the Battle of Lützen in 1632 Gustavus Adolphus was killed, immediately provoking a political crisis in Sweden, for his heir was a girl of six. But the Swedish chancellor and regent Oxenstierna had no intention of giving up, and he used the crisis instead as a way of putting pressure on the Protestant rulers and France to fund the Swedish army.

In view of Oxenstierna's continued commitment to the struggle, Wallenstein realized that a demonstration of armed might had to be matched by a diplomatic offensive, and so he opened talks with the enemy. On discovering Wallenstein's dealings, Ferdinand declared Wallenstein a 'notorious rebel', and in February 1634 he ordered his death. A week later, Wallenstein was murdered on Ferdinand's instruction. Ferdinand's tame propagandists excused his actions with a pamphlet entitled *The Havoc of Treason and the Hell of an Ungrateful Soul*, but the verdict of Louis XIII of France's chief minister, Cardinal Richelieu, was the more accurate: 'Wallenstein's death remains a monstrous example . . . of the cruelty of his master.'[15]

Ferdinand subsequently appointed his son, Ferdinand (later Emperor Ferdinand III), as Wallenstein's successor as commander of the imperial forces. The young Ferdinand was to prove an astute tactician, able commander, and skilled diplomat. But the emperor soon realized that Wallenstein had been right. The war could not be ended without negotiation. Even the deployment of a Spanish army in the heart of the empire failed to change Habsburg fortunes, notwithstanding the combined victory of the young Ferdinand and the Cardinal-Infante Ferdinand of Spain at Nördlingen in 1634. In the Peace of Prague of 1635, Ferdinand II duly made terms with the German princes, effectively withdrawing the Edict of Restitution. The text of the treaty underlined its purpose: 'that the bloodletting be ended once and for all, and the beloved fatherland, the most noble German Nation, be rescued from final ruin.'[16]

Ferdinand II died from a stroke in 1637. His heart went straightaway into the cupboard in the Loreto Chapel and his body to Graz, where a mausoleum had for more than two decades been under construction to receive his corpse. The young Ferdinand, who had already been elected king of the Romans, succeeded him, and he maintained his father's search for a solution that would end the war. In the aftermath of the Peace of Prague, French forces took the lead in maintaining the fight against the Habsburgs, in alliance with the Swedes. The war thus largely lost its religious character, becoming instead a political contest between France and the Habsburgs. In this phase of the struggle, the French supported the revolt of Catalonia against Philip IV of Spain and the secession of Portugal in 1640, thus fatally weakening Spanish Habsburg power.

Paradoxically, the opening of peace negotiations in the late 1630s intensified the conflict as the belligerents sought fast gains to preempt the decisions of the conference table. As one envoy to the talks put it, 'In winter we negotiate, in summer we fight.' The last year of the war saw a Swedish army occupy Prague Castle—the site of the defenestration that had begun the conflict three decades before. The Swedes packed up what remained of Rudolf II's Wonder Chamber, ransacked Prague's monastic libraries for valuable books, and sent the lot to Stockholm. But they searched in vain for Rudolf's fabled 'Nebuchadnezzar crown', since it had been previously moved to Vienna.[17]

By 1648 the Habsburgs were militarily exhausted. Not only had Prague fallen, but Vienna was also threatened by a Swedish army. Ferdinand III hastily erected in the city a marble column to the Virgin, who duly drew the Swedes off in another direction. Bavaria had by 1648 been overrun twice by the French. It was reckoned, meanwhile, that four-fifths of strongholds and fortified garrison towns in the Holy Roman Empire were in enemy hands. But the enemy was divided, with the governments in Stockholm and Paris frequently at odds over strategy and distrustful of each other's motives. By promising to let the French king, Louis XIV, have a free hand in Spain and to maintain neutrality in the war on the Pyrenees, Ferdinand was able to convince his principal adversary to negotiate. A hefty promise of cash brought the Swedes round.[18]

The Peace of Westphalia, which ended the Thirty Years War in 1648, was mostly concerned with nuts and bolts—what borders should be

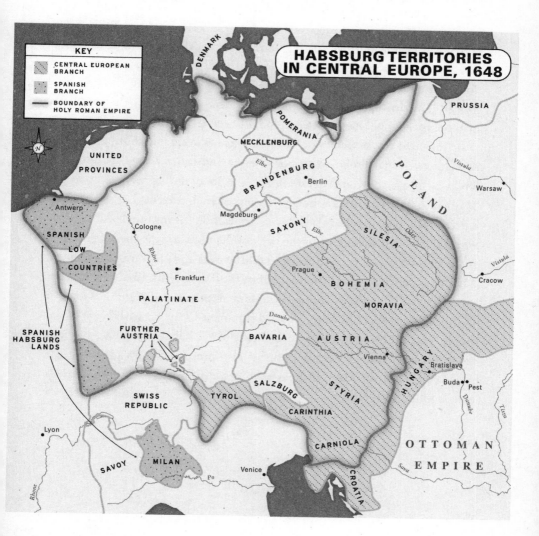

changed, whose rights to territory affirmed, and whether the dukes of Bavaria should be allowed to keep the title of elector, originally conveyed upon them by a grateful Ferdinand II in 1623. It affirmed, however, that the princes of the Holy Roman Empire might choose their own religion and admitted Calvinism as one option, but it allowed their subjects the right to practise their own beliefs too (within certain limits). In future, disputes over church property and the extent of freedom of conscience were to be a matter for the courts to decide—and the central court of the empire was specifically renewed to this end, with equal numbers of Protestant and Catholic judges appointed. An important exemption was won, however, by Ferdinand III, which meant that he was not obliged to permit freedom of worship in his territories. The labour of reconversion to Catholicism that had been undertaken in Bohemia and the Austrian lands was not, therefore, to be reversed.

The Peace of Westphalia aimed to achieve 'a general peace in Christendom', on which account it has been celebrated as providing the first 'European constitution' and as marking a crucial moment in the evolution of modern Europe. But it was a global peace treaty, too, since its provisions included the settlement of all conflicts between Habsburg Spain and the Dutch United Provinces, 'upon the sea and other waters, as upon the land . . . in the East and West Indies, and in Brazil, as well as upon the coasts of Asia, Africa and America.' Conquests achieved to date were recognized, and the Dutch were now given preferential terms in respect of trade with the Spanish colonies. On the back of the peace treaty, the Dutch West India Company rapidly succeeded in taking over and enlarging the Central African slave trade. In the half century after Westphalia, about fifty thousand African slaves went through the Dutch 'processing plant' at Curaçao in the southern Caribbean for onward shipment to the Spanish New World and its Pacific Ocean territories. The Peace of Westphalia may have brought an end to the Thirty Years War, but it also promoted the violence of the worldwide traffic in African slaves that would ultimately claim more than twelve million lives.[19]

THE ABNORMAL EMPIRE AND THE BATTLE FOR VIENNA

he Peace of Westphalia of 1648 had left it unclear what the Holy Roman Empire was. Thanks to the work of the French philosopher Jean Bodin (1530–1596) political power was now understood in terms of an indivisible sovereignty exercised over a defined territory. But where sovereignty lay in the empire was uncertain, and one author (Johann Jacob Moser) wrote no fewer than seventy volumes trying to unravel the conundrum. For some, the empire remained as it always had been: a hierarchical structure at the apex of which was the emperor, with an authority that was in theory complete. For others, however, it was a confederation of equals under the collective presidency of emperor and princes, in which sovereignty was shared. Generations of public lawyers puzzled over the Holy Roman Empire and whether it constituted a monarchy, an aristocracy, a common body made up of sovereign parts, or indeed something that altogether defied categorization, being in the words of one influential commentator 'abnormal and freakish.'[1]

The first diet after the Peace of Westphalia met at Regensburg in 1653. The arguments of lawyers were immediately translated into disputes over protocol and courtly etiquette. The duke of Württemberg was convinced that he was possessed of a sovereignty as complete as any other prince, and so he rode into Regensburg accompanied by trumpeters and a soldier with a bass drum—hitherto a prerogative of the electors. But Emperor Ferdinand III (1637–1657) held to the opposite, believing the Holy Roman Empire to retain a strictly hierarchical and monarchical form. So he refused to consider the envoys of the princes as the equivalent to royal ambassadors, and he took offence when princes acted as if they were his equals. As one historian has recently explained, two 'grammars of ceremony' were now in competition— one monarchical and the other aristocratic, each reflecting a different conception of what the Holy Roman Empire should be.[2]

Ferdinand could have retreated politically into Austria and the neighbouring kingdoms of Bohemia and Hungary. The expansion of French influence into the Rhineland, where many princes had allied with Louis XIV, invited a Habsburg withdrawal from imperial politics. But Ferdinand chose otherwise. His arrival in Regensburg was carefully choreographed to emphasize his majesty, and he entered the city through triumphal arches that extolled his achievements. Ferdinand was the centre of spectacle in pageants and processions, but he was the architect of spectacle too, building a wooden opera house in the city and presiding over a demonstration of *Magdeburger Halbkugeln*—two conjoined copper hemispheres from which the air had been expelled and which teams of horses could not pull apart. In lavish ceremonies held during the diet, both his son Ferdinand IV and his wife were crowned king of the Romans and empress respectively, but their coronations were marred by princely bickering over the order of precedence. (Ferdinand IV died in 1654, before becoming emperor, but is always given the number IV.)

Even so, ceremony and performance only achieved so much. As one of the leading exponents of the aristocratic interpretation put it, protocol relied on impressions or simulacra of power. These were, however, only 'empty signs and shadowy conceits' unless they were buttressed by the reality of power. The conversion of the symbols of authority into their substance was precisely what Ferdinand III and his son and eventual successor, Leopold I (1658–1705), managed to achieve. In the half century after Westphalia the emperor resumed a leading role in the Holy Roman Empire, notwithstanding its princes' claim to an equal and competing sovereignty. By sheer hard work, Ferdinand III made himself a political necessity—championing the smaller principalities in the south-west of the empire against the mightier and arbitrating between the different factions at the diet. He personally presided for eighteen months over sessions of the diet that convened in 1653. Typically, he refused to give up working even when beset by a fatal stomach condition and 'looking like the grave.' As he made his last confession in April 1657, he boasted that he still had years left to him.[3]

Leopold's achievement would be a military one—the defence of the Holy Roman Empire and Christendom against the Turks and the French. Leopold was an unlikely champion. Intended for the church, Leopold was thrust as a teenager into the imperial office because of his elder brother Ferdinand's death. Slight and frail in appearance, Leopold was a ditherer who confused activity with purpose, keeping an obsessively detailed diary which itemized every despatch sent and every penny lost at cards. He was, like his father, an accomplished musician and, despite an abnormally protruding lower lip, a virtuoso flautist. Many rulers are extolled for their talents in musical composition. Leopold retains the distinction of still having his works performed today.

Leopold's sensibilities did not, however, extend to Protestants or to Jews, whom he respectively persecuted and robbed. His second wife, who was also his niece (she referred to him throughout their marriage as 'Uncle'), is the sweet blonde child portrayed in Diego Velázquez's portrait of *Las Meninas* (*The Ladies-in-Waiting*). But brought up in Spain, Margaret Theresa had inherited the prejudices of the peninsula. It was at her instigation that Leopold evicted all Jews first from Vienna and then, in 1671, from Lower Austria, seizing their wealth. Since the imperial treasury depended on the loans of Jewish bankers, the consequence was the near ruination of Leopold's finances. It was a catastrophic misjudgement, from which Leopold failed to learn. Eventually readmitting several of the wealthiest Jewish families back to Vienna, he proceeded after a few years to plunder them again. For long periods, Leopold had to live off Dutch and British subsidies.[4]

Two enemies loomed. The first was France, now recovered from the intrigue and civil war that marked the period of the Frondes (1648–1653)—so called from the sling shots that the Parisian mob directed at the homes of the king's ministers. Louis XIV had resumed the French policy of expansion, seeking to roll up the cities and duchies on the left side of the Rhine, thus proving the *bon mot* that he was as free with other rulers' territories as he was with other men's wives. Louis was ruthless in the pursuit of his goals, intimidating the princes along the Rhine into compliance and distracting others with subventions of cash. Leopold coordinated resistance to him, forging alliances abroad and convincing the imperial diet to fund the struggle against the French invaders. He thus stood, in his own words, in defence of 'the Holy Roman Empire, the liberty of the German nation, and the interest and welfare of its individual members.'[5]

The second enemy was the Ottoman Turks. In the century after the battle of Lepanto in 1571, the Ottoman Empire had been in retreat. Although historians are wary about using the term 'decline', this was precisely how officials and commentators in Istanbul defined the condition of Turkish power. Their remedy was to return to the past, with an invigorated centre that cracked down on corruption and renewed the expansionist policies of Suleiman the Magnificent. A new dynasty of Ottoman first ministers or grand viziers put this programme into effect. In the half century after 1656, the Köprülü family dominated the office of vizier, holding power for thirty-four years in all. The Köprülüs' mission was to transform the rhetoric that surrounded the sultan—'emperor of the world', 'God's shadow on Earth', and so on—into political reality by going to war against the Habsburgs in Europe.[6]

Leopold I's advisers were divided on how to deal with the double challenge posed by France and the Turks, with some asserting the priority of combating Louis XIV and others pressing for a war against the Ottoman Empire, which still occupied the central part of Hungary. In fact, the two theatres were linked. Louis XIV gave financial support to rebellions against Habsburg rule launched from Transylvania, which was for much of the time a Turkish vassal state, and he took advantage of the Habsburg armies being occupied in the east to renew pressure in the west, both on the Rhine and against the Habsburgs in Spain, capturing the Spanish-ruled county of Burgundy (the Franche-Comté) and Charolais in 1674. At critical moments Leopold had to abandon campaigns against the Ottomans, redeploying his resources from east to west, not only to defend the Rhine but also to shore up Spain's frontier in the event of a tussle over the succession.

During the 1660s, it looked likely that Transylvania's subordination to Istanbul would soon be complete. Having driven out Transylvania's independently minded prince, the sultan replaced him with a puppet and garrisoned the principality, thus provoking a war. It is a measure of the political influence of the emperor in the Holy Roman Empire that in taking up arms against the Turks Leopold was supported not only by the imperial diet, which promised twenty thousand troops, but also by the armies of several of the greater princes. Even so, he was unable to build on the victory over the Turks achieved by the combined armies at Szentgotthárd (St Gotthard) in Hungary in 1664 for fear that Louis XIV was about to invade Spain. Only a few weeks later, Leopold concluded with the sultan the Treaty of Vasvár, which restored the territorial status quo.

Disappointed with the poor terms of the Treaty of Vasvár, some of the leading Hungarian aristocrats plotted to depose Leopold with the help of Louis XIV and the sultan. The 'magnates' conspiracy' was comprehensively bungled. Its architects were incapable of secrecy, openly receiving ambassadors, distributing printed propaganda, and in the case of one of the plotters entrusting his wife's lover with politically compromising letters. Their overtures to the sultan were, moreover, promptly reported to Leopold by the Ottoman dragoman (an office midway between official interpreter and foreign minister), who had been educated in Vienna. After giving several warnings, which went unheeded, Leopold sent his armies into Hungary in the spring of 1670. He had the principal conspirators arrested, occupied their castles, and sent them to the block. A heavy-handed investigation yielded a further two thousand suspects. Many of these were proceeded against by special courts that made up the rules as they went along and automatically equated Protestantism with treason.[7]

Leopold now sought to repeat in Hungary what his grandfather, Ferdinand II, had done to Bohemia. In this, he had the support of his councillors. As they advised, 'Your Imperial Majesty has conquered Hungary by force of arms, and so you may set up a government according to your liking.' Raimondo Montecuccoli, the victorious commander of Leopold's forces at Szentgotthárd, put it more bluntly: the Hungarians were akin to ravenous animals, he explained, who crept from holes in the ground to plunder and destroy. They would only respect an iron rod. Leopold followed their advice, establishing a regime led by the grand master of the Teutonic Order, Johann Ampringen, with the instruction that it restore order. At the suggestion principally of Montecuccoli, for whom Protestantism and rebellion were bed mates, Leopold agreed that the new government should also reimpose Catholicism on the country.[8]

The Ampringen government was inaugurated in 1672 in a drunken ceremony from which its German members never seem to have recovered. But the Hungarians in the government, led by the primate of Hungary,

Archbishop Szelepcsényi, pressed hard for a religious cleansing. It was at their initiative that Protestant magistrates were driven out of towns, churches closed, and school buildings occupied. Most notoriously, they clamped down on Protestant preaching in Hungary, and when the Lutheran and Calvinist clergy ignored the prohibition, they instructed the arrest in 1674 of several hundred preachers. Of these, forty were condemned the next year to be sent to the dockyards of Naples as galley slaves.

The enthusiasm of Archbishop Szelepcsényi could not have come at a worse time for Leopold. Across Protestant Europe, the suffering of the preachers on their journey to Naples became the subject of angry pamphlets, printed updates, and public collections for their ransom. Yet Leopold depended on the support of the Protestant United Provinces, Saxony, and Brandenburg in the war with France that had broken out in 1672. Leopold's advisors urged him to put an end to the diplomatic disaster, but he procrastinated and only ordered the release of the captives in March 1676, by which time several of the preachers had died of their privations. Upon their arrival the next month in Naples, the survivors were brought before the Spanish viceroy of Naples, who promptly handed them over to the safety of a Dutch flotilla. The damage to Leopold's reputation had, however, been done, and he was now publicly reviled in Protestant Europe as the author of 'cruelties much worse and more intolerable than the severest tortures of the Diocletian persecution.' (Diocletian was a third-century Roman emperor and notorious persecutor of Christians.)[9]

In the wake of the drama of the preachers' progress, Leopold abandoned the Ampringen government, recommitting himself in 1681 to toleration in Hungary. By this time, however, persecution was pointless. The energy of the Catholic clergy was making dramatic inroads in Hungary, to the extent that most of the aristocracy had forsaken Protestantism. The gilded magnificence of the restored Catholic churches, many of which were now rebuilt in the style of the Baroque, and education through plays, processions, and preaching in the vernacular did much to win over the countryside. Tellingly, the most prominent of the galley slaves, Ferenc Fóris Otrokócsi, subsequently converted to Catholicism, abandoning his refuge in Oxford to teach at the Catholic university of Trnava in Hungary.[10]

Ottoman policy thrived on Leopold's blundering. The Turkish pasha in Buda provided a shelter in Ottoman-occupied Hungary for religious malcontents, who launched increasingly bold attacks on Habsburg positions.

The 'crusaders' (*kurucok*), as they called themselves, were savage in their methods, using impalement to intimidate the local population. Their ranks were augmented by Cossacks recruited from the steppe land north of the Black Sea and by Turkish irregulars, and stiffened with French officers sent by Louis XIV. A report survives from one Turkish-occupied town on the Hungarian Plain, dated 2 January 1678: 'Crusaders and French were in Kecskemét, 1180 in all. They forced many people to join them, drank a lot of wine, and did much damage.' The same account noted the passage of Ottoman troops through the town, making their way to raid across the border.[11]

Despite the treaties of Nijmegen (1678–1679), which concluded the war launched in the west by Louis XIV in 1672, French forces continued to press towards the Rhine, occupying Strasbourg in 1681. By this time, however, the Ottoman threat in the east was manifest. Not only did the new Köprülü vizier, Kara Mustafa, reject Leopold's offer to extend the Treaty of Vasvár, but he also promoted the swashbuckling leader of the crusaders, Imre Thököly, to the title of King of Hungary. Thököly was subsequently crowned by the pasha of Buda with a diadem taken from the sultan's treasury in Istanbul. His coronation was attended by Prince Michael I Apafi of Transylvania, who committed the principality's forces to support the Turks and crusaders in their war with the Habsburgs. By the end of 1682, the crusaders had taken most of northern Hungary (now Slovakia) and were raiding Silesia and Moravia.[12]

Leopold responded accordingly, working together with the pope to construct a 'holy alliance' that brought to his aid Bavaria and Protestant Saxony as well as a huge slice of church wealth. One-third of ecclesiastical property in the Austrian lands was sold off to fund the allies. Importantly also, Leopold won over the king of Poland, John III Sobieski—it had been his Cossacks who had previously supported the crusaders. As it turned out, Sobieski's army of forty thousand men would prove vital. Although the imperial diet had voted to support Leopold with sixty thousand troops, it left it to the individual princes to decide on the numbers they would field. Anxious not to offend Louis XIV, and seduced by his subsidies, the electors of the Palatinate and Brandenburg and the archbishops of Mainz and Cologne stood aside.

At the beginning of April 1683, the Ottoman army began the march from its muster point at Edirne, just west of Istanbul. Its progress overland to Belgrade was watched by Leopold's envoys, who described in awe the lines of wagons pulled by buffaloes, the supply train with sixteen thousand head of cattle, the thousands of red-coated infantrymen all bearing heavy muskets, and the passage of falcons, leopards, and a company of eunuchs. The army took a whole morning to pass them by. Early on in June, it reached the frontier with Habsburg Hungary, by which time reinforcements had swollen the Ottoman army to over a hundred thousand men.[13]

The imperial commander, Charles of Lorraine, was an experienced soldier who had fought with Montecuccoli at Szentgotthárd, but he was entrusted with the defence of Hungary with insufficient troops and without any maps. By July, he was in full retreat. Rather than allow his troops to be surrounded, he pulled most of them west of Vienna towards Linz, where he waited for reinforcements. Leopold, meanwhile, took refuge in Passau, since even Linz was dangerously exposed to raiders. Vienna was thus left unprotected and dependent on its garrison. With no force standing in its way, the Ottoman army put Vienna under siege in July 1683, encircling the city. Its fall seemed inevitable. Not only was the garrison outnumbered by a ratio of ten to one, but the city's walls and bastions had also been long neglected. The vizier Kara Mustafa, who had accompanied the army, seemed on the edge of seizing the 'Golden Apple', which was both a Turkish name for Vienna and, as one Turkish legend told, a massive ball of gold hidden in St Stephen's Cathedral until such a time as its spire became a minaret.[14]

The siege lasted for two months, and its decisive actions were fought in the maze of trenches both sides built in front of the city walls and underground by companies of sappers laying mines and counter-mines. Dysentery and starvation took their toll of the garrison and of those citizens who had not fled. Donkeys and cats were soon in short supply. In the first few days of September, Turkish mines blew up sections of the wall, opening a breach that could not be repaired. Realizing the end was close, the defenders fired distress rockets from the top of St Stephen's. On the night of 7–8 September, they were answered by flares from the direction of the Kahlenberg Mountain, on the Vienna side of the Danube. In his habitual dress of a mildewed wig and scuffed boots, Charles of Lorraine had returned, but this time he had brought with him the armies of Saxony, Bavaria, and Poland.

King John Sobieski's pride would not let him serve as anyone's second, so it was under his command that the allies smashed the Ottoman army beneath the Kahlenberg Mountain on 12 September 1683. Sobieski's journey from Warsaw had been laborious. Not only did he, too, lack a map, but he also had no idea of the terrain in which he would fight. 'What mountains are there? Is there open ground? What rivers are there, and where are the passes?' he asked in one of his letters to Charles of Lorraine. But as evening approached without a decisive conclusion to the fighting, it was Sobieski who led what is thought to be the largest cavalry charge in history. At the head of eighteen thousand horsemen rode Sobieski's Polish lancers, from whose armour projected wings made of eagle and ostrich feathers that keened in the wind.[15]

Now it was the turn of the Turks to experience the humiliation of the slave market, with captive soldiers and their female camp followers sold at auction in Vienna. Although still formidable militarily, the Ottomans never recovered from their defeat outside Vienna. Nor indeed did the vizier, for Kara Mustafa was strangled on the sultan's orders because of his failure. Three years later, Leopold's generals captured Buda, and supported by Saxon, Brandenburger, Hanoverian, Bavarian, and Swedish troops, they went on to liberate most of Hungary. Thereafter, Habsburg armies pushed south into the Balkans, briefly occupying Skopje, which is now the capital of North Macedonia and only 200 kilometres (120 miles) from the Aegean coast.[16]

Once again, however, warfare in the west obliged Leopold to withdraw his troops and abandon the Balkans south of Belgrade. After a little resistance, however, Transylvania capitulated to Leopold in return for guarantees of religious freedom. But Transylvania was not conjoined to Hungary. Instead, it continued to constitute a separate country with a government appointed by the emperor and a chancellery in Vienna to oversee its affairs. Imre Thököly, whose troops had supported the Ottoman army in the campaign of 1683, continued fruitlessly to oppose the Habsburg takeover of Transylvania as an ally of the Turks until his lonely death in 1705 on the shore of the Sea of Marmara, near Istanbul.

Leopold used his victory over the Turks to force a cowed Hungarian diet to recognize the Habsburgs as hereditary monarchs of Hungary. Hungary, however, followed customary law, which meant that decisions and laws of the diet were not persuasive until confirmed by practice. Even so, Leopold's achievement in liberating Hungary was the more remarkable because of the support he received from the princes and diet of the Holy Roman Empire in what might have been considered a private, dynastic war. Protestant princes, like the elector of Brandenburg, who had previously suspected Leopold of trying to restore Catholicism by stealth in the empire, now rallied to his side. So too did the Bavarian ruler, despite his family's traditional rivalry with the Habsburgs. The imperial diet provided cash and urged the supply of troops to support Leopold, and from 1663 it moved into perpetual session, meaning that it could make decisions faster. On this foundation, Leopold built the next round of the conflict with France.

In 1688, Louis XIV took advantage of Leopold's campaigning in the Balkans to begin an assault on the Rhine Valley that soon swallowed up most of the Palatinate. Leopold and the Dutch leader William of Orange (who became that year William III of England) took the lead in forging a coalition which soon gathered together most of the princes of the Holy Roman Empire as well as of Savoy and Spain. As in the Thirty Years War, the fighting spilled over to include Spanish Habsburg possessions overseas, with French naval attacks in the Spanish Caribbean and on treasure fleets. The Treaty of Ryswick in 1697 brought a truce between the belligerents, but not peace. Following the death of the heirless Charles II of Spain in 1700, the conflict was renewed. Both Leopold and Louis XIV vied for the dead king's inheritance, and the European powers looked aghast at the prospect of the French king swallowing up Spain and its overseas territories.

In the War of the Spanish Succession (1701–1714), Louis XIV succeeded in winning over Bavaria and fomenting an uprising in Transylvania that soon spread to Hungary. Leopold, however, renewed his earlier alliance with Britain and the Dutch. In 1704, the British commander, the duke of Marlborough, and the head of the Imperial War Council, Eugene of Savoy, decisively defeated a joint French and Bavarian army on the Danube at Blindheim. The battle is better known by the anglicized name of Blenheim and feted as a British victory. In fact, the army that Marlborough led was not the 'scarlet caterpillar' of red-coated British troops that crept across Europe to victory, as described by Sir Winston Churchill: only nine thousand troops out of its total complement of forty thousand wore the British uniform. Like Eugene of Savoy's army, the bulk of Marlborough's forces comprised troops supplied either by the Dutch or by the princes of the Holy Roman Empire.

Blenheim was also the triumph of Leopold. It demonstrated once more that the emperor—whether by diplomacy or war—might still exert an influence and leadership that gave meaning to the imperial office. Plays and engravings extolled Leopold's martial achievements. For his vanquishing of the Turks, he was already the Austrian Hercules who had crushed the Asiatic hordes. Now, because of his resistance to Louis XIV, Leopold was also portrayed as a German Achilles or as a Ulysses to the Holy Roman Empire's Penelope (Ulysses' wife). But these images conveyed a profounder reality. Notwithstanding the quibbling of lawyers and competing ceremonial grammars, the Habsburg emperor was back as leader of the Holy Roman Empire. By perseverance and the work of his generals, Leopold had renewed the connection between the Habsburgs and the imperial office that sustained the dynasty's claim to greatness.[17]

15

SPAIN'S INVISIBLE SOVEREIGNS AND THE DEATH OF THE BEWITCHED KING

*T*he only Habsburg ever to visit the Habsburg New World was the Franciscan missionary and illegitimate son of Emperor Maximilian I, Brother Peter of Ghent (Fray Pedro de Gante, c. 1480–1572). Peter's care for the spiritual and material welfare of Mexicans is commemorated by a statue of him on the base of the Columbus monument in the centre of Mexico City. When it was made in the 1870s, the sculptor, Charles Cordier, had no idea what Peter looked like. So he modelled his head on a bust of the Greek philosopher Socrates, while also giving Peter a tonsure (which Franciscans do not wear).[1]

At least the statue placed in Brother Peter's honour commemorates a presence in Mexico that had once been real. In the overseas territories of the Habsburgs, where no ruling Habsburg ever went, image substituted for reality, with representation replacing the tangible through the simulation of the royal presence. The real and the imagined blurred there in simulacra of a kingly ideal and in an iconography that spoke to the majesty and immanence of an absent sovereign. But the images conveyed did not only stand for the missing king. They also masked his absence by substituting the figurative for object and matter, while simultaneously appealing to the same idea of kingship that invested kings with their identity.[2]

The pattern of representation was established with the death of Charles V in 1558. Throughout his realms, mock funerals were organized, with processions, black-draped buildings, and tiered catafalques set up in cathedrals, each variously decorated with images of the emperor and of his realms and victories. A portrait, crown, or urn at the centre of the catafalque symbolized Charles's body, already interred in the monastery at Yuste (whence it would later be removed to the Escorial Palace). The catafalques were brightly lit with banks of candles, which in the darkness of a cathedral nave gave the impression of a 'room of light.' Printed funeral books recorded for posterity the arrangement of the catafalque, the organization of the festivities, and the moral worth of the dead emperor.[3]

The catafalques were temporary structures, made of wood, canvas, and plaster. They were mostly discarded at the end of the commemoration, although the proximity of so many candles caused several to catch fire. The funeral books provided, however, a guide to future commemorations, illustrating the way the catafalques should be built, the emblems and panegyrics that were the most suitable for adornment, and the order in which the accompanying processions and *tableaux vivantes* should be conducted. They also invited competition. Throughout Habsburg Spain, cities vied to construct the most elaborate multitiered catafalques, often more than thirty metres (one hundred feet) in height. Onto these were piled tapestries, portraits, heraldic devices, and macabre death figures.

The catafalques erected in the New World were no less splendid than their European counterparts. The one erected for Charles V in 1559 in the chapel of San José de los Naturales in Mexico City stood fifteen metres (fifty feet) high and comprised a cruciform building in which a symbolic crown was placed and, above it, a large lantern bearing the imperial double-headed eagle and Charles's motto *Plus Ultra*. The catafalque was smaller than its counterpart in Lima but more richly decorated, with pictures illustrating Charles's victories, classical heroes, and the Spanish conquest of Mexico. Its decoration was largely the work of native artists, organized by Brother Peter of Ghent. Their sensibilities were accommodated in the staircase of nine steps leading to the catafalque, which recalled the nine terraces used in the construction of Aztec and Maya pyramids. Conceivably, too, the so-called Chaldean letters that reportedly adorned the structure were Aztec hieroglyphs.[4]

Equally intense ceremonies inaugurated the dead monarch's successor in the New World. After several months of mourning, the proclamation announcing the new king was read out and a portrait or banner placed beneath a golden canopy. The delay in celebrating the new king was entirely artificial, since news of the royal death and the proclamation of his successor usually arrived on the same ship. Brightly coloured silks and brocades now hung in the streets, and there was a festival atmosphere, with stalls selling ice cream, chocolate, and marzipan. Similar excitement prevailed whenever the New World received good tidings from the Old—of a royal marriage, birth, or baptism or on the monarch's saint's day or some other auspicious event.[5]

There was a living simulacrum of the sovereign too. Viceroys in the New World were elevated to a status that fell only a little way short of the monarch in whose place they stood. As one churchman recorded in Peru, 'We may appropriately say that the viceroy is not different from the royal person, since the king lives in him by transmission.' A new viceroy was greeted as if a king, progressing beneath a canopy through triumphal arches that bore both classical and Aztec or Inca motifs, some of which were curiously combined—hence Ulysses bearing a parrot on his shoulder. Their inauguration provided the occasion for a weeklong fiesta, which assumed the character of a carnival, with released prisoners, prostitutes, and buffoons heading the celebrations. In Manila, where a governor acted in the capacity of viceroy, fireworks attended his arrival, along with what one programme of events billed as 'Official Festivities and Spontaneous Entertainments.'[6]

As 'the representative and living image of His Majesty', the viceroy was expected to maintain a kingly deportment—to be slow of walk and grave in demeanour and not displaying extravagances such as a feather in his hat. As the monarch's surrogate, however, he was intended to be seen. The vice regal palaces in Mexico City and Lima thus fronted the main square, which was where in full public view the viceroys performed their most important ceremonial tasks: presiding over autos-da-fé, taking their annual oath of office, and receiving felicitations on their birthdays. Both palaces had tall windows on their upper floor, from which the viceroy was expected to show himself to the crowds below on the plaza major. The palace in Mexico City had for this purpose no fewer than twelve balconies.[7]

Paradoxically, however, the very visibility of the viceroy disclosed his incompleteness as a simulacrum of the king. During the sixteenth century, monarchs throughout Europe became increasingly hidden and confined from public view. This partly arose from the adoption of the high etiquette pioneered at the Burgundian court, which was necessarily imposed to give rulers relief from their importunate subjects. Instead of invading the king's bedroom and (as one French king complained) borrowing his clothes, courtiers and others were now spatially distanced from the ruler and their access to him restricted. Henceforth, proximity to the king's person depended on status and was converted into a mark of esteem. So for a plate of food to reach the ruler, it might have to go through as many as twenty-four separate pairs of hands, with each succeeding bearer being entitled to approach the sovereign just a little more closely than the one before. As Eugene of Savoy drily observed, the physical distancing of the ruler had at least the merit of keeping waitresses beyond the royal grasp.[8]

But the distancing of the monarch also arose from the idea that his office was divinely ordained and that he should assume a corresponding remoteness. In imitation of God, he was in one contemporary description 'perfect . . . unchanging in majesty . . . omnipresent, and so incomprehensible that none can reach his secrets.' From the 1580s, the Habsburg kings of Spain were conventionally addressed as *Señor* or 'Lord', which was precisely how one addressed the Almighty in prayer. The monarch was, moreover, not only godlike but also an embodiment of the sun, and it was as the Sun King that Philip IV (ruled 1621–1665) was known, well before Louis XIV appropriated the title. The Spanish king's court and palace were accordingly arranged like the universe on principles of celestial harmony and mechanical predictability, with each minor sphere revolving according to its ordained place in the heavenly hierarchy. Within this scheme, the king's activities were also measured and predetermined, so much so that he moved according to one visiting French nobleman 'with such regularity that, day by day, he knows exactly what he will do for the whole of his life.'[9]

Burgundian court ceremony has been described as combining 'sacralization, distance and discipline', but it was more complex. The fifteenth-century Burgundian dukes valued remoteness and yet had no wish to be cut off completely from their subjects. For this reason, the last of the Burgundian dukes, Charles the Bold, reserved three evenings a week to the hearing of petitions of poor people, much to the irritation of his attending courtiers. The formal adoption of Burgundian court practices in Spain, which took place in 1548 and was preceded by several weeks of retraining for household staff, saw this principle carried over into Spanish protocol. Even in the seventeenth century, the kings of Spain dedicated several days a week to the hearing of petitions, with the instruction given to the palace doorkeepers that no supplicant be refused entry.[10]

.   Bullfights, displays of horsemanship, and religious processions gave further opportunities for the king to be seen. But his appearances on these occasions were crafted so that no glimpse was given of the human being beneath the cloak of majesty. The king's movements were stiff and mannered, his face was fixed in austere solemnity, and he proceeded in silence. Even with his ministers and while at ease in the palace, Philip IV was notoriously unyielding. He admonished his wife for laughing at a buffoon's tricks and was both unmoved and unmoving when a minister collapsed with a stroke before him at a council meeting. As one Spanish counsellor shrewdly pointed out, court etiquette had also rendered the sovereign 'but a ceremony.'[11]

Monarchs became increasingly remote from government too. Philip II had been what is now called a micromanager, doing so much poring over and directing of details that administrators felt rudderless in his absence. At the time, Philip's obsessive attention was thought a mark of his dedication to Spain and of his commitment to just government. Philip's son, Philip III (ruled 1598–1621), started off by trying to emulate his father, busying himself with committees and drawing up plans for the invasion of Ireland and Africa. But when his grandiose plans came unstuck, he became lazy and diffident, entrusting his affairs to his advisors and, increasingly, to his *valido* or confidant, the duke of Lerma. The *valido*, halfway between a royal favourite and a prime minister, took care of most royal business and, in the case of Lerma, usurped his position to make a personal fortune. Even so, a *valido* was useful to the ruler and not only as a work horse. When policies failed, he could be blamed.[12]

Valimiento or 'government by *valido*' continued into the reign of Philip IV, being discharged by the Count-Duke of Olivares and, from the mid-1640s, by Don Luis de Haro. Their mastery of government left Philip IV free to undertake the ceremonial functions of kingship, commission great works of art, and perform what he did best, which was to father illegitimate children, of whom he had no fewer than thirty. In between his dalliances, Philip maintained a voluminous correspondence with the levitating abbess and mystic Mary of Jesus of Agréda, confessing his sins of the flesh and receiving advice on the conduct of policy. She urged him to take up the reins of government and rule personally, dispensing with favourites. Her advice was seconded by noblemen who felt they had been left without influence. King Philip bowed to the pressure, dismissing Olivares in 1643, but he soon raised Don Luis de Haro to take Olivares's place.

Opinion at the time was convinced that kings should rule and not delegate their responsibilities. As one of Philip IV's advisors observed, *valimiento* was 'the misfortune of our century', for it led to factionalism, resentment, disaffection, and bankruptcy. The king had been appointed by God and so should follow God's example by governing in his own person. This appeal to the cosmic order of the universe was typical of a broad range of monarchical literature in Spain. As one jurist explained, the monarch was 'a simulacrum of God on the Earth, whose actions he must follow and imitate.' It followed that he could not share his sovereignty with another but should discharge 'an absolute royal power' (*poderio real absoluto*).[13]

Absolutism is a term coined after the French Revolution to describe the type of monarchical rule practised in France before 1789, but the adjective 'absolute' goes back to the Middle Ages. Deriving from the Latin *absolutus* or 'absolved', it had a predominantly legal meaning, describing power that took no heed of the law's constraints. It chimed with Roman law's elevation of the royal will as the source of legislative capacity, rendering the king of Spain's 'absolute power' the fount of legal authority. Some royal officials certainly came to this conclusion—hence, from the second half of the seventeenth century, their opinion that 'the command of the prince is law', that 'His Majesty is absolute master and may order as he wish, without excuse or delay', and that the king should be obeyed 'as the absolute and despotic (*despótico*) lord of our persons and property.'[14]

But these were the pleadings of lawyers, for the royal power was constrained both in principle and in practice. First, it was widely believed that the monarch's right to make law was limited by previous statutes and inherited traditions, the setting aside of which jeopardised the established harmony within the kingdom which it was his duty to preserve. An analogy frequently made was the similarity between royal government and a harp, the strings of which should be tightened or relaxed to produce a melodious consonance among the king's subjects. Other writers compared monarchy to a clockwork engine, which the king was tasked with keeping in running order. It was not for him to innovate but instead to preserve and renew.

From this, it followed that the king might not disregard Spain's historic parliaments, the Cortes of Castile and the Corts General of Aragon. Although the Habsburg kings of Spain never accepted the principle that taxation should be made dependent upon the crown remedying the complaints of the deputies, the right of the Castilian Cortes to approve taxes was never called into question. Such, indeed, was the partnership between monarch and parliament that the king allowed the deputies to monitor royal expenditure and even to lay down precisely how it should be spent. Even in the turbulent kingdom of Aragon, government sought cooperation and not confrontation, notwithstanding the Corts General's insistence on *pactismo*—that the Aragonese obeyed the ruler only for as long as he kept to the terms that the Corts General laid down.[15]

Certainly, during the second half of the seventeenth century, both the Cortes and the Corts General of Aragon withered, seldom being summoned. Discontinuation suited Philip IV, for it spared him the financial burden of hosting these assemblies—the cost of cushions alone (for the deputies' comfort) was prohibitive. But it also appealed to the cities of Castile, which resented paying salaries to the deputies when they took bribes anyway. Nonetheless, consensus building and agreement still prevailed, with the king or his *valido* making agreements with smaller committees, deputations, and the governments of the kingdom's individual cities. The theatre may have changed, but the underlying assumption that royal rule proceeded by way of discussion and agreement had not. It helped that the ambitions of Louis XIV reminded even the obstructive Aragonese nobles that there were other methods of rule that they might find less to their liking.[16]

When established methods of consultation were set aside, as under the Count-Duke of Olivares in the 1620s and 1630s, then disharmony was considered the natural consequence. Olivares sought to increase the tax and military contribution of the non-Castilian parts of Spain, claiming they were not paying their way, but his disregard for established rights and procedures provoked in 1640 a rebellion in Catalonia and the secession of Portugal. Critics of his policies were not slow to point out that he had neglected 'the prudence and judgement of his ancestors, whom long practice and dearly-bought experience had instructed', and so mistuned 'the harp of kingdoms and commonwealths.'[17]

The fall of Olivares exposed the limits of government. The kings of Spain lacked the capacity to impose their will, for large parts of the kingdom operated outside their control. To raise cash, rulers had over generations sold offices, exemptions from taxation, and rights to property. Most of these passed into the possession of the cities and greater or 'titled' noblemen, who carved out large landed estates over which they exercised an almost complete territorial authority. The nobles protected the integrity of their estates by converting them into trusts, thereby avoiding the ruinous partition of landed wealth between heirs. By the seventeenth century, four-fifths of all land in Castile was owned by the crown, titled nobles, cities, and the church. The kingdom's free peasants were squeezed into the remainder and over time transformed into indebted, share-cropping tenants. Likewise, minor nobles or hidalgos were often pressed into the service of greater lords, becoming in effect their retainers.

Similar conditions prevailed in the New World. The viceroys and governors in America and the Pacific held an authority that was conceived as absolute and discharged a power that was considered divine. The only ostensible difference between the viceroy and his royal master was that he might not sign proclamations as 'I, the king' (*Yo, el rey*). But although the viceroys did not have to put up with parliaments, they still had to negotiate. In cities and towns, powerful municipal councils made up of largely hereditary officeholders obstructed the viceroys' commands. When in 1609 Philip III broached the idea to institute a Cortes in Lima, the viceroy advised that it could only lead to restlessness and that having to deal with city councils was bad enough.[18]

Most of the Spanish population in the New World was squeezed into the cities. In Mexico around the year 1600, almost 60 per cent of Europeans lived in eleven cities, each laid out in a gridiron fashion, with a central plaza and streets running at right angles. The countryside constituted 'the republic of the Indians', which followed its own laws, had its own native nobility, and continued to blend Aztec and Mayan traditions with Catholic Christianity and imported European conventions. As best they could, priests and friars protected the natives from abuse by 'the republic of the Spaniards', but they could not prevent the Indians from being enlisted to serve in the plantations and mines of Spanish-owned estates or *haciendas*. Where native workers were unavailable, settlers brought in African slave labour. Across large parts of the New World, *haciendas* constituted mini-kingdoms, which functioned independently of Habsburg governors and viceroys. In Paraguay and deep in the Amazon rain forest, Jesuit missionaries also carved out their own theocratic states, fielding armies and corralling the natives into concentrated villages, the better to control and convert them.[19]

Spanish colonial society was by no means homogeneous. The stress on 'purity of the blood' (*limpieza de sangre*), inherited from Spain, was amplified in the New World. Privilege was defined by race. Only first-generation

Spanish immigrants (*peninsulares*) and their unsullied descendants (*criollos*) were entitled to go to university, serve in the administration, join most guilds, and enjoy exemption from taxes. Over time, distinctions became increasingly subtle, with persons of mixed-race divided into a hierarchy of subgroups, depending on the degree of mixing and with whom, whether a native Indian or a black slave. The higher up the hierarchy, the more opportunities to make the leap by wealth or marriage into the otherwise exclusive category of *criollo*. To make sure that everyone knew their place, artists composed detailed 'casta portraits' that contrasted the sixteen mixtures thought to be possible, their different skin colours, and the impoverishment and moral decay that belonged to those whose blood was the more 'tainted.'

The Habsburg New World was no less devoted to the Catholic religion than Spain, displaying the same marks of piety. But caste and race subverted observance. The conspicuous dedication to the Host and Virgin, which Habsburg rule impressed on subjects, was performed in the New World against a backdrop of segregation in churches, parishes, and processions. Religious vocations adjusted to 'pigmentocracy' too. Since nunneries usually only accepted women of pure blood, a mark of social esteem was to display at home a portrait of a relative either in nun's habit or as she prepared to enter the novitiate, crowned with garlands of flowers. Portraits often included a coat of arms or recorded the sitter's lineage through an inscription at the bottom of the painting, signalling the racial integrity of their family and of the home in which their image hung.[20]

Images of crowned nuns were as unreal as the representation of a dead king on his catafalque. Both, however, were intended to display a divinely ordained order, at the top of which stood a racially pure elite and the sovereign ruler, discharging an unlimited authority as God's likeness on earth. But the gulf between the image of monarchy and its reality was becoming increasingly stark. On Philip IV's death in 1665, the succession passed to his infant son, Charles II (lived 1661–1700). A pitiful imbecile, Charles long surprised contemporaries by continuing to live. He left no heir, for he was plainly incapable of performing the sexual act. After ten years of marriage, his first wife, with whom he shared a pathetic intimacy, was unable to say whether she was still a virgin. His second wife was intent mainly on plundering her husband's palaces for furniture and paintings which she sent to her needy parents in the Rhineland. Contemporaries attributed the king's maladies to sorcery, on which account Charles was known as the 'Bewitched' (*El Hechizado*) and ceremonies of exorcism performed. With the king clearly incapable of government, power was exercised on his behalf by his widowed mother, his second wife, and a succession of *validos*.

Unwashed and unkempt, Charles II spent his last months wandering through woods, watching magic lantern shows of a pious content, and examining the corpses of his ancestors in the vault of the Escorial palace. The only task left to him was the assignment of a successor. The Council of State headed by Cardinal Portocarrero pressed the king to name Louis XIV's grandson, Philip of Anjou, the later Philip V of Spain. The Council's reasoning was strategic and motivated by interests of peace on the Pyrenees and of the protection of Spain's colonies abroad, but French bribes also helped. On 28 September 1700, Charles received the last rites. Three days later, he signed off on the testament Portocarrero brought him, gasping, 'Now I am nothing.' Still he defied his doctors, only expiring after an agonizing final month.

A postmortem of the dead king disclosed 'a very small heart, lungs corroded, intestines putrefactive and gangrenous, three large stones in the kidney, a single testicle, black as coal, and his head full of water.' A modern review of the medical evidence concludes 'that Charles suffered from posterior hypospadias, monorchism and an atrophic testicle. He probably had an intersexual state with ambiguous genitalia, and a congenital monokidney with stones and infections'—in other words, he had a single kidney and a single testicle, and his urethra exited on the underside of an undeveloped penis. The same account additionally proposes Fragile X syndrome, typically leading to some mental retardation and an elongated face, which may be attributed to generations of inbreeding within the Habsburg family.[21]

The tragedy of Charles became a symbol for contemporaries, embodying the decline of Spanish royal power and the decay of the kingdom. The evils of the nation were seen as one with his own, and his physical afflictions likened to the kingdom's misfortunes. A stylized lament on Charles's death in 1700 extolled the glory that the king had brought to the house of Austria and his contribution to the 'double empire of two worlds.' But with Charles's passing, Habsburg rule in the peninsula drew to a close and, along with it, Habsburg mastery of the Americas and the Pacific Ocean. From now on, the Habsburg dominions were confined to their European possessions. Their 'empire of two worlds' was at an end.[22]

16

THE THEATRE OF THE BAROQUE

The Baroque is the artistic form associated with the recovery of Catholic and Habsburg power in Central Europe and, more particularly, with the reigns of Emperor Leopold I (1658–1705) and of his two sons, Emperor Joseph I (1705–1711) and Emperor Charles VI (1711–1740). But it was also a universal idiom that the Habsburgs spread across the world. The term 'baroque' derives from *baroco*, which was the name given in the sixteenth century to an overcomplicated syllogism in Aristotelian logic—for instance, 'Every fool is stubborn; some people are not stubborn; hence some people are not fools.' One of the earliest works to describe the art and architecture of the Baroque lamented its excesses as 'the superlative of the bizarre, the excessive and the ridiculous.' Later commentators were equally dismissive. For the Italian philosopher and historian Benedetto Croce (1866–1952), the Baroque was 'a form of artistic ugliness . . . an artistic perversion, dominated by a desire for the stupefying.'[1]

The Baroque style which Croce had in mind is the bombastic, highly ornamented variety of architecture and of church design. Framed in wedding-cake stucco, cherubs and putti cavort (they look the same, but only cherubs are holy), angels lift saints heavenwards, and spangled beams of reflected light burst from altars. The Baroque employs visual tricks, with reflecting pools that double the size of buildings, and trompe l'oeils that create false interior spaces and make curtains from marble. In portraiture and art, the Baroque embraces size, with great canvases showing enormous figures looming out of a half light, often twisted into unnatural poses or with their limbs dramatically foreshortened. Unsurprisingly, the Baroque has become the 'dictator style' of choice for modern-day despots. Its lavish ornamentation and grand poses have been transported, albeit without the angels and saints, to presidential palaces as far afield as Saddam Hussein's Baghdad and General Noriega's Panama City.

The Baroque was not supposed to have ended up as the opulent backdrop for tyrants. It is vulgar, but in the older sense of the word, in that it was intended to stir the popular imagination. The Baroque developed out of the exaggerated and tense style of Renaissance mannerism. But what gave it impetus was the mid-sixteenth-century Council of the Church at Trent, which declared that art should be in the service of religion and should appeal to the emotions, even to the extent of giving 'a glimpse of heaven.' Art and architecture should overawe, yet the Virgin and saints (whose mediation the Council of Trent confirmed as efficacious) provided through their veneration the means of bridging the gap between the earthly and the divine. The Baroque was in this respect another way of affirming Christ's redemptive grace, which He has bestowed on all humankind.[2]

The Baroque speaks in code. But whereas the symbolic language of the alchemists was intended to obscure and hide, the Baroque uses a semiotics that is easily understood. At its heart lies allegory, which is often disclosed in the form of an emblem—a motif or pictogram that sums up an attitude, action, or aspect of the human condition. In Baroque art, however, the motif is often combined with verses that explain its meaning. So tennis balls may show how God manipulates kings, or they may disclose how the devil directs souls to perdition. The accompanying verse will tell us and explain the meaning. The Baroque is above all a learning tool, and there is no point instructing in a language that the audience cannot understand.[3]

Baroque church interiors are saturated with allegories and emblems. The rays of the sun projecting from the tops of altars emanate from a circle or sphere, which as the most perfect shape symbolizes God. Depictions of flames and combusting saints speak to the radiance of God's spirit and to the intensity of the Catholic Church's work of conversion. A concave mirror, by which the sun's beams could be concentrated to make fire, brings the two emblems together in a single allegorical device. A monstrance, in which the Host was displayed to the congregation, might yet be decorated with ornate silverwork that showed, in commemoration of the Battle of Lepanto, wrecked galleys, fallen sails, and torn rigging. Christ's birth also received attention, with the first allegories of the Nativity told in wooden carvings—the forerunners of today's Christmas nativity scenes. The earliest was set up in Prague in 1562. Within twenty years the custom had reached Spain.[4]

Frescoes on the ceilings of Baroque churches often created the illusion that the nave was unroofed and open both to the heavens and to sunbursts of angels, saints, and martyrs. Depiction of the celestial Jerusalem provided the opportunity for an 'apotheosis', by which a saint's soul was shown as being received into heaven, guided by angels. As they approach the Godhead, the saints each spread their arms and open their mouths in the expectation of ecstasy. It is the same act of surrender as envelops Bernini's statue of St Theresa D'Avila, although she, having been penetrated by Christ's lance, is also in rapture. Cherubs tumble around the saints, blowing trumpets or holding aloft garlands of flowers or laurel wreaths as the symbols of triumph. But the cherubs themselves are illusions—angels or spirits that have briefly assumed human form so that they may be seen by mortal eyes.[5]

Lower down, there were often reminders of human mortality—tombs inlaid with skulls, chandeliers made of rib cages, and depictions of the dance of death. During the seventeenth century, it was the fashion across Central Europe for churches and noblemen to buy 'catacomb saints', which were whole skeletons exhumed from the cellars beneath Rome that were believed to be of Christian martyrs. A dedicated office in Rome gave the skeletons fictitious names and certificates of authenticity, after which they were sold. For a further fee, a martyr might be found whose name coincided with the buyer's. Having reached their destination, the bones were reassembled and displayed in glass-fronted cabinets, close to the altar of a church. Monks and nuns dressed the skeleton in finery, putting coloured glass in the eye sockets and jewels on the finger bones, after which the martyr was usually put on his or her side in a reclining position, facing the congregation.[6]

But audiences were expected to do more than gawp and tremble. The Baroque invited participation, through processions, public penitence, and pilgrimage. In villages and towns, confraternities dedicated to special saints enjoined charitable activity as well as frequent confession and communion, while the passing landscape was made sacred with shrines, wayside chapels, and calvaries. In religious services, rosary prayers to the Virgin were included as a way of involving the congregation, while worshippers were encouraged to act out Christ's Passion as they knelt beside the stations of the cross set up within churches.[7] Commemorations of this type had previously been enacted as part of the displays in which the Habsburgs had advertised their devotion to the eucharist, Cross, and Virgin. Now their commitment as a dynasty to the marks of the Catholic faith were transformed into acts of public piety, and the populace enjoined to practise the same dedication. The piety of the ruling house became 'Austrian piety', whereby the people and land of Austria were confirmed as uniquely blessed.

Baroque Catholicism was most strikingly performed in religious drama. The Jesuit missionary and teaching order was at the forefront of making the theatre a means both of instruction and of training students in public speaking. Across the Habsburg lands, in Europe and the New World, Jesuit schools and colleges put on tens of thousands of plays, often at the end of the academic year, when parents came to collect their children. The actors were mostly older students and teachers, and the performances lasted several hours, often concluding in torch light. Many were feeble affairs, such as the succession of thirty-six actors, each representing a historical king of Hungary, who addressed Ferdinand II with wearisome declarations to mark his coronation in Bratislava in 1618.[8]

Others, however, were far grander productions that drew on classical myths and heroes, interwoven with allegories of Christian virtues and of soon-to-be-defeated moral vices. So, for instance, fortitude might be shown as Hercules in a lion skin, love as Cupid bearing arrows, avarice as a man clutching a purse, and so on (there were plenty of manuals to aid selection). A procession of allegorical figures might take up the first half of the play, compressing the main subject into just a couple of acts. Sets also became more elaborate, framed by several or more proscenium arches to create the illusion of depth. Backdrops were repeatedly changed, often several times in an act, and the stage furnished with fountains, grottoes, and triumphal carriages. Between acts, choruses sang, or there was a dumbshow. Schools and colleges increasingly had their own dedicated theatres, with seating (as in Vienna) for several thousand spectators.[9]

Court theatre developed these trends, although parts were increasingly sung, and professional dancers led in the entr'actes what were called at the time 'ballets' or 'little dances', which would eventually become a genre. Court theatre battered the senses with its opulent displays, frequent set changes, and orchestration, but its purpose was to extol the emperor and to emphasize his virtues—as the epigone of piety, hero on the battlefield, and bringer of harmony. Most of these performances were staged indoors. Vienna's earliest theatre was set up next to the Hofburg Palace in the 1650s. Built from wood that had been floated down the Danube, it soon fell victim to rot. The next was also a wooden construction, erected between the Hofburg and the city wall (Theater auf der Cortina), that could accommodate a thousand spectators. Larger productions involving pyrotechnics or sea battles had necessarily to be held out of doors.

Accompaniment was provided by a variety of instruments—flutes, oboes, trumpets, violins, and the harpsichord (gradually superseded by the organ)—thus anticipating the modern orchestra. Harmony and a continuous melody were employed to give unity to productions, with individual soloists picking up and repeating the dominant theme. Dynamic variations created contrasts between quiet sections of music and strong *forte* parts. Composers, however, often intended their music to be danced to, on which account they alternated slow and fast movements. The dancers themselves might be horses, for the horse ballet (*Rossballett*) was a courtly diversion. Several dozen trumpets and a hundred or so string instruments were needed if the composition was to be heard over a large performance area and above the noise of harness.[10]

Leopold I is often criticized for spending too much on opera and too little on architecture, but this is unfair. Vienna's openness to Turkish attack meant that most building had to take place within its walls, which limited the opportunity for construction and contributed to the cramped pattern of its streets. A few noblemen found space within the walled area to build palaces, but most were content with mansions in the countryside. Eugene of Savoy managed both, and the Belvedere with its ornate facade, elaborate gardens, and reflecting pool represents the pinnacle of the courtly Baroque style in Central Europe. Even so, Leopold extended the Hofburg by connecting the original fort to a smaller palace built for one of Rudolf II's brothers by way of the long 'Leopold Wing.' On the city's main thoroughfare, he also ordered the construction of a twenty-metre (seventy-foot) marble column as the thank-offering of the living to God for Vienna's deliverance from the great plague of 1679. Set into one side is a relief of Leopold kneeling in prayer. To the right is a plaque depicting Christ as the Lamb of God, and to the left is a map of the world.

The imagery of the Plague Column epitomizes the Baroque style. First, it is the art of the resurgent Catholic Church of the seventeenth and eighteenth centuries. Even in secular architecture, it adopts the symbolism, emblems, and styles found on religious buildings, and although we may talk of a Protestant Baroque, it is more muted in ornamentation and plainer in design than its Catholic counterpart. Second, the Baroque is global in its reach and constitutes the first transcontinental artistic and architectural style—it is, as the panel on the column's side discloses, a 'worldwide system.' Third, it is the art of the Habsburgs. It was primarily through their patronage and example that the Baroque spread across the world. In so doing, it accommodated local traditions, yielding most spectacularly the hybrid Andean or *mestizo* style of Habsburg Peru, where the guinea pig replaced the Lamb of God amidst twisted and swirling geometric designs cut into flat surfaces. Even so, the colonial architecture of Lima is unmistakably Baroque, reflecting the global reach of Habsburg power.[11]

The worldwide power of the Habsburgs ended in 1700 with Charles II's assignment of Spain and its possessions to the French Bourbon prince Philip V. But the Central European Habsburgs were bound to resist the transfer. In anticipation of Charles's death, Emperor Leopold negotiated with Great Britain and France on how to divide up the ailing monarch's possessions in such a way as to maintain international amity. Even so, Leopold envisaged the Central European branch of the Habsburgs obtaining the lion's share of Charles II's inheritance, in anticipation of which he had named his younger son Charles. His ambition was nothing less than the restoration of Charles V's monarchy, which had united Spain, the New World, and the imperial office. Leopold also claimed headship of the Order of the Golden Fleece, which had hitherto belonged to its Spanish sovereign, and began investing new knights even before Charles II's death.[12]

Despite the tragedy of Charles's passing, the vultures soon gathered. Leopold's son, the Archduke Charles, travelled by way of England and Portugal to Spain, intent upon taking the crown for which he had been named. On the way there, he addressed the Dutch states-general or parliament and played cards with Queen Anne at Windsor. Both Britain and the United Provinces of the Netherlands feared the consequence of Spain becoming an annex of France and backed Charles's claim. Charles advertised his willingness to abide by Spanish traditions, but the British troops he brought with him made him the object of suspicion. It did not help that his military commander was a French Protestant, whereas Philip V's was the impeccably

Catholic James of Berwick, the illegitimate son of James II of England (James VII of Scotland).

The first years of the War of the Spanish Succession went well for Leopold and for his elder son, Joseph, who succeeded his father as emperor in 1705. In Spain, however, victory eluded Archduke Charles. Although Aragon, Catalonia, and Valencia declared for Charles, his support elsewhere was patchy. Five friars declared for Charles in Manila, and for three weeks the Spanish island of Guam in the Pacific hosted a British pirate fleet, provisioning it with yams and coconuts. The cool response of Spain's colonies convinced Charles that the course of events was against him. On the death of his elder brother, Joseph, who fell victim to smallpox in 1711, Charles left Spain to take up the title of Holy Roman Emperor as Charles VI. The pro-Habsburg movement on the peninsula collapsed with his departure, prompting a flood of some sixteen thousand Spanish refugees to Charles's other possessions. The final peace, agreed at Rastatt in 1714, saw Charles rewarded with the Spanish Low Countries, southern Italy, and Milan, but Spain and its colonies now passed definitively to his rival, Philip V.[13]

Charles did not, however, abandon his dream of recreating the global monarchy of Charles V and of uniting Central Europe, Spain, and the New World. Upon returning to Vienna, he commenced a building programme that replicated the architecture and symbols of his lost Spanish inheritance. He enlarged the Hofburg with the Spanish Riding School and the Imperial Chancellery Wing, and he joined up existing buildings to make a unified whole. This phase of the Hofburg's reconstruction resulted in the Old Fort being almost entirely lost to view behind new facades.

Like the imperial library built in his honour, Charles's new buildings included in their design the double columns that symbolized Habsburg Spain. Charles planned to go further still, with the conversion of the abbey at Klosterneuburg outside Vienna into a replica of the Escorial Palace, but the project ran out of money. His greatest monument is instead the massive church dedicated to St Charles Borromeo (the Karlskirche), which he had built just outside Vienna's city walls. Combining a high Baroque style with a dome that recalled St Peter's Basilica in Rome, the church was fronted with two massive pillars. Although depicting in spiral reliefs the life of St Charles, both were topped with crowns and eagles as marks of Habsburg power.

Charles was, however, most active as a builder not in Vienna but in the kingdom of Hungary. Indeed, the eulogy dedicated in the 1730s to his architectural achievements devotes more space to Hungary than to any other of Charles's possessions. Between 1703 and 1711, Hungary had been in revolt. The Hungarian nobility had grievances against Leopold's heavy-handed rule, which French diplomacy and cash exploited. The Transylvanian magnate Francis Rákóczi, having been discovered in secret negotiations with Louis XIV, fomented an insurrection on the backs of the peasantry, promising to relieve their burdens. His slogans included 'The people should not be taken for plebs, but treated like bishops.' Despite Rákóczi's lofty words, his rebellion degenerated into mayhem and murder. Soon he was in headlong retreat, although it took several years to finally dislodge him from his fastnesses on the Polish border.[14]

In 1711 Charles concluded a generous peace, which promised everything to everyone. Five years later, the Habsburg commander Eugene of Savoy honoured Charles's commitment to liberate the remainder of Hungary from Ottoman rule, capturing the Turkish province of Timişoara and pushing southwards to take Belgrade, Šumadija, and much of what is now Central Serbia. In the newly liberated territory as well as in neighbouring Transylvania, Charles built roads carved into mountainsides and massive fortifications, canalized rivers, and converted swampland into pasture. He enlisted craftsmen and farmers from across his possessions to settle in the reconquered part of Hungary—principally Germans, but also Italians, Spaniards, Flemings, and even a scattering of Armenians. Known as the Banat, this area, which is about the size of Belgium and currently divided between Serbia and Romania, remains one of Europe's most ethnically diverse regions.[15]

In Transylvania, Charles promised to uphold religious freedom, while nevertheless expelling Protestants from their churches and promoting Catholic worship. St Michael's in Cluj was now made a Catholic church and its Unitarian congregation expelled, while in Sibiu a new Catholic church in the marketplace cut off the old Lutheran cathedral from the main square. In nearby Alba Iulia, Charles made a further point by ordering the construction of a massive star-shaped fortress. Occupying an area of 140 hectares (350 acres), it was intended as much to keep Transylvania down as the Ottoman Turks out.

The Jesuit church in what had formerly been the Protestant city of Cluj in Transylvania belongs to the Baroque and is typical of Charles's foundations. Although its interior is surprisingly plain, there are the usual gilded saints and cherubs. Dedicated to the Holy Trinity, it was also thorough in its veneration of the Virgin, whose image, captured in the icon of the 'Weeping Mary', was paraded in processions and advertised as miracle-working. Next to the church lay the Jesuit Academy, which was home to some of the largest drama productions in all of Central Europe, with performances featuring up to two hundred players. Dominating both the exterior face of the church and the altar within are the double pillars, pointing to Charles VI's lost Spanish inheritance and to his vain ambition to recreate the world monarchy of his Habsburg forebears. Even far-off Transylvania was a stage on which a Habsburg ruler might announce his destiny and birthright through the universal architecture of the Baroque.[16]

Although different in scale, Cluj's Jesuit church and the Church of St Charles Borromeo in Vienna are part of the last wave of the Catholic Baroque in Habsburg Central Europe. After a rococo flourish, marked by thick white and gilt stucco interiors, church design moved towards a more austere and colder classicism, exemplified by the new cathedrals built at Vác and Szombathely in Hungary. The Habsburgs after Charles VI would be no less personally devout, but as the stage changed to neoclassicism, their religious performances would be increasingly shorn of the public ceremony and display of Baroque spirituality. Their understanding of dynastic mission would change too. The myth making and elaborate allusions would still be there, but the vision would become more secular and concerned with ideas of the state and of the function of government. Even so, the underlying assumptions would be no less ambitious: to make people's lives ordered, happy, virtuous, and productive, under the guidance of beneficent Habsburg rule, administered through a dedicated bureaucracy. But first the Central European Habsburgs had to survive biologically as a dynasty. During the last decades of Charles VI's rule, it looked increasingly as if they might not and that the fate of the Spanish Habsburgs would also be theirs.

17

MARIA THERESA, AUTOMATA, AND BUREAUCRATS

aria Theresa succeeded her father, Charles VI, in 1740 and ruled the Habsburg lands until her death in 1780. Her husband, Francis Stephen, became emperor in 1745 on which account she held the title of empress. In the spring of 1770, she welcomed into her reception room in the Schönbrunn Palace outside Vienna Wolfgang von Kempelen and his remarkable chess-playing automaton. The human-size figure was dressed as a Turk, with a turban and flowing robes, and he was seated before a cabinet on which lay a chess board. Kempelen slowly opened the doors of the cabinet and parted the Turk's dress to demonstrate the interior gearings and clockwork as well as to prove that no human being was hidden away. Then he ostentatiously wound up the automaton with a key. The energized Turk surveyed the chessboard, puffing on a long pipe, and courtiers were invited to test their skill at chess against him. An end game of random pieces was set out on the board, and the first match commenced. The concentration of the players and audience was broken only by Kempelen's rewinding of the Turk. But after just a few moves, the Turk had checkmated his adversary.

The hoax was a clever one. Within the cabinet sat a little person on a revolving chair. As the doors of the cabinet were individually opened and closed, the chair spun round to conceal him or her, substituting a bank of impressive-looking cogs and pulleys. All the rest was done with mirrors, magnets, and a hidden vent to let out the smoke from the candle by whose light the person inside worked. The trick was guessed but never proved, and Kempelen's Turk continued for almost a century to confound observers. Evidently, the nameless people inside the apparatus were virtuosos—one even caught Napoleon cheating and checkmated him. The success of the ruse owed as much to the person within as to Kempelen's technical ingenuity.[1]

Automata had been playthings for several hundred years, but by the middle decades of the eighteenth century they had become more than toys. The machine symbolized humanity's capture of nature and yet, by the regularity of its movements, its conformity to the laws of a repetitious universe as disclosed by Isaac Newton. The human form might thus be explained in mechanical terms—as, in one contemporary description, 'a machine which winds itself up, a living picture of perpetual motion.' One by one, philosophers (Kant, Herder, Rousseau, Bentham) succumbed to the illusion that human beings might themselves be organized as if they were clockwork and, moreover, that there was no sphere in which mechanical solutions might not be applied—the drilling of soldiers, the organization of hospitals, prison and workshop management, and so on. 'Effort', 'power', 'force', and 'machinery' became part of the vocabulary of eighteenth- and early-nineteenth-century philosophy.[2]

Increasingly too, philosophers and others began to conceive of society as an object to be arranged, as if it were a piece of clockwork. The cogs and levers that manipulated the population belonged to government and suggested one understanding of what the state was: an apparatus of control and surveillance, administered top-down, under the overall control of the ruler and his agents. As one of the leading exponents of the 'clockwork state' explained, 'A properly constituted state must be exactly analogous to a machine, in which all the wheels and gears are precisely adjusted to one another; and the ruler must be the foreman, the mainspring, or the soul . . . which sets everything in motion.'[3]

Maria Theresa, who governed the Habsburg territories in Central Europe from 1740 to 1780, subscribed to this principle. So, too, did her son, Joseph II, who was emperor and co-ruler after 1765 and sole Habsburg monarch from 1780 to 1790. Order, regularity, observation, accountability, and management from above marked their approach to government; likewise, their contempt for institutions that sought to constrain the foreman. Their achievements were breathtaking: a thorough military and fiscal reform, and the establishment of institutions that communicated the ruler's will through newly appointed local governments and districts. A start was even made on converting the peasants from servile tenants into yeoman farmers, obliging their children to attend school, and curbing the privileges of the nobility. But to function properly, the clockwork state required the comprehensive reorganization of society into just so many cogs and springs.

Kempelen's automaton is a metaphor for his age, but his decision to cast the chess player as a Turk is also telling. Back in the seventeenth century, the Turk had stood for brutality and violence. Now, in the wake of his defeat, he was seen as exotic and almost fashionable. Noblemen in Vienna dressed their servants in kaftans and turbans, drank coffee, and were conveyed in sedan chairs carried by Turks. Conceivably, the audience chamber in which Maria Theresa received Kempelen was the (subsequently named) Millions Room, which was itself decked out with Islamic motifs and designs. After several centuries of warfare, the Ottoman Empire had ceased to be a threat, and combat with it was comfortingly reduced to the scraping of chessmen on a board or, as we will see, mock jousts in tournaments. In place of the Ottoman Turks, a new and unexpected foe had arisen. This was the master clockmaker, Frederick II 'the Great' of Prussia—in Michel Foucault's words, 'the meticulous king of small machines, well-trained regiments and long exercises.' It was he who would bring the Habsburgs to their knees.[4]

Until the end of the seventeenth century the Habsburgs had been biologically lucky, with generation after generation producing male heirs. When these had been lacking, there had always been cousins and nephews available. The genetic good fortune of the Habsburgs had captured Burgundy, Spain, Hungary, Bohemia, and in 1580 the kingdom of Portugal. But the line withered, as it was bound to do statistically. Successive intermarriages also led to infertility and infant deaths. The same fate as had befallen the Spanish Habsburgs in 1700 now threatened the Central European branch, for Charles VI only had daughters, which made them ineligible as his successors, and none of his kinsmen had a son. The Habsburgs faced extinction.

Charles VI had taken care to ensure before his marriage in 1708 that his bride, the astonishingly beautiful Elizabeth Christine of Brunswick, was

fertile, making her submit before the wedding to a humiliating gynaeco-
logical examination. Thereafter, he had plied her with copious quantities
of red wine as an aid to conception. But nothing happened for almost a
decade, after which Elizabeth Christine quickly produced three daughters.
Then, once more, pregnancy eluded her. Contemporaries blamed Elizabeth
Christine's insincere conversion to Catholicism (she had been brought up as
a Lutheran), but the wine she consumed to aid fertility was the more likely
cause, for it had rendered the once dazzling 'Lily White' (*Weisse Liesl*) an
obese alcoholic.

Even before the birth of his daughters, Charles VI had taken precau-
tions lest he should have only female heirs. In 1713, he drew up a scheme of
inheritance that allowed any daughter he should sire to become his successor, circulating it to his ministers. With the arrival four years later of his first
daughter, Maria Theresa, Charles made the arrangement public, and he re-
quested that the provincial diets give their approval to it. All duly concurred
with the terms of the document, which was known by the grand name of the
Pragmatic Sanction, meaning a fundamental law. But the Pragmatic Sanction was more than just a document regulating the succession. It welded
together the Habsburg possessions in Central Europe by giving them their
first shared instrument of public law, joining together in a single scheme
of inheritance the Austrian duchies, Bohemia, Hungary, Croatia, and the
Habsburg possessions in Italy. 'Inseparable and indivisible', a formula originally penned by Ferdinand II back in 1621, now became the watchword of
the lands and kingdoms gathered together in an unbreakable constitutional
bond under the umbrella of the Pragmatic Sanction. It was not, however,
until 1915 that a suitable coat of arms was devised to give visual expression
to this unity.[5]

Charles VI knew from the example of Spain and his own experiences
there that a contested succession might open the way to international intervention, so he also sought to bind the European states to the Pragmatic
Sanction, but most only gave a grudging consent in exchange for territorial and commercial concessions. As part of his negotiations with France,
Charles agreed to the cession of Lorraine, held by Duke Francis Stephen, the
fiancé and, after 1736, husband of Maria Theresa. Even so, Charles managed to squander these limited gains by intervening in the War of the Polish Succession (1733–1738), which left him diplomatically isolated and cost
him the recently acquired Sicily and Naples. His only real ally was Russia,
on which account he joined the Empress Anna in a fruitless Balkan war that

saw him lose Serbia and Belgrade and forced him into a humiliating separate peace with the Turks.

With Charles's unexpected death in October 1740, the Habsburg dynasty came to an end in the male line at the very moment when it was militarily most exposed. Charles Albert of Bavaria immediately put forward a claim to the dead ruler's inheritance based on rights supposedly belonging to his wife, Maria Amalia, who was Charles VI's niece. While Charles Albert had enough backing to be eventually elected emperor, he was unable to dislodge Maria Theresa from her Habsburg possessions. But the young king of Prussia and elector of Brandenburg, Frederick II, was anxious to test out his army and his daring. Less than two months after Charles VI's death, Frederick invaded Silesia.

Frederick had no claim on Silesia. When his foreign office produced a historical justification based on a treaty concluded two centuries before, he congratulated the authors for having composed 'the work of a good charlatan.' But Frederick's cynical intervention rallied the pack, with France, Saxony, Bavaria, and Bourbon Spain hastening to join the kill. Bohemia, Upper Austria, and Tuscany, which had been given to Duke Francis Stephen in recompense for Lorraine, were all overrun, and elaborate designs were drawn up to partition the young queen's inheritance, leaving her with only Hungary and Transylvania, neither of which anyone wanted.[6]

But it was from Hungary that succour came. Shortly after her coronation there as queen in June 1741, Maria Theresa met the Hungarian diet at Bratislava. It is true that she wept beneath her crown, that she clutched to her bosom her three-month-old son, Joseph (later Joseph II), that the Hungarian noblemen in attendance promised her 'their life and blood', and that in their confusion over constitutional proprieties they addressed her as 'their king' (or possibly 'their prince'). It is also true that the diet contributed much less than it promised and did so slowly, but the queen's reception lifted her spirits and boosted the morale of her generals. Relinquishing Silesia to Frederick, the queen moved against the Bavarians, recovering Bohemia in 1742 and, a few months later, seizing Charles Albert's capital of Munich. To punish the Czechs for dallying with Frederick, she slapped down in the centre of the Moravian city of Olomouc a massive arsenal, which took the place of the market square.[7]

In Bratislava in 1741, Maria Theresa had played the damsel in distress. Now, in the aftermath of her victory, she embraced the role of the Amazon warrior. In January 1743, she treated her court to the spectacle of the Ladies'

Carousel. Sixteen women of the imperial court, headed by the queen in a tricorn hat, rode through Vienna on horseback or in carriages, firing shots into the air. In the Spanish Riding School, they held a mock tournament, which culminated in Maria Theresa jousting with the Countess Nostitz and then spearing with her lance some clay heads dressed in Turkish turbans. The women astonished the audience by riding 'in the masculine fashion.' The queen, however, rode sidesaddle and necessarily so. Although only twenty-five, she was already pregnant with her sixth child—she would eventually give birth to sixteen in just under twenty years.

Maria Theresa's 'womanly' qualities of motherhood and vulnerability together with her 'manly' resilience and courage made her the most celebrated monarch in Europe. In Britain, pub signs displayed her portrait so as to drum up business. As one English wag recalled of the struggle over the Habsburg inheritance, 'the queen of Hungary's head was to be seen in almost every street, and we fought and drank under her banner at our own expense during the whole war.' Had she known of it, the young Maria Theresa would have doubtless repaid the compliment—despite her pregnancies, she gave over many nights to drinking, dancing, and winning at cards. It was only in her thirties, by around the gestation of her eleventh child, that Maria Theresa routinely retired to bed at ten o'clock.[8]

The War of the Austrian Succession continued until 1748. Although Maria Theresa cursed the terms of the peace, the victory was hers. True, she resigned almost all Silesia to Frederick, but everywhere else she saw off her enemies and recovered territories lost in battle. By skilful negotiation she ensured, moreover, that on the death in 1745 of the luckless Charles Albert (Emperor Charles VII) the imperial title passed to her husband, Francis Stephen of Lorraine. The election was unanimous, with even Frederick II of Prussia casting his vote for Francis Stephen. Alleging grounds of cost, however, Maria Theresa refused to be crowned alongside Francis Stephen as empress, and she watched the coronation procession in Frankfurt from the balcony of a private house. Even so, she afterwards used the title of empress. In portraits of the imperial couple, she also always assumed the premier position. Nor was the dynasty renamed after the house of Lorraine, but Francis Stephen's style was tacked onto his wife's to make the House of Austria-Lorraine (later called Habsburg-Lorraine).

The Treaty of Aachen, which concluded the War of the Austrian Succession in 1748, was an armistice rather than a peace. Maria Theresa immediately began building new alliances in a vain attempt to compel Frederick II to disgorge Silesia. Hitherto, France had always been the Habsburgs' principal foe. But the empress now realized that 'whatever one might think of France, the king of Prussia is a far more dangerous hereditary enemy to the Arch-House.' She thus backed Count (later Prince) Kaunitz, her principal negotiator at Aachen and later first minister, when he recommended in 1749 that she abandon her maritime allies, Britain and the Dutch United Provinces, and seek terms instead with Louis XV. The French king was suitably suspicious, but the intervention of his mistress, Madame de Pompadour, and the outbreak of fighting between France and Britain in North America won Louis round to the 'diplomatic revolution.'[9]

Typically, however, it was Frederick who broke the peace first. Mistakenly believing that its ruler had joined the coalition against him, Frederick invaded Saxony in 1756. In the Seven Years War (1756–1763) that followed, the Habsburgs should have won. Besides France, Maria Theresa could count on Sweden, Russia, and most of the princes of the Holy Roman Empire, and the allied armies amounted to half a million men—twice the number of troops that Frederick II could muster. But opportunities, including the brief capture of Berlin by Hungarian hussars in 1757, were wasted, for the empress's generals had been schooled in defensive warfare and held back from carrying the war home to the enemy. So Berlin was abandoned in exchange for a ransom that included two dozen pairs of gloves for the empress. Louis XV, meanwhile, was distracted by British successes in North America and India and pulled resources from the European theatre to fight overseas. But it was the defection in 1762 of her ally, Russia, that forced Maria Theresa to sue for peace and to accept once more Silesia's loss.[10]

Kaunitz's 'diplomatic revolution' unintentionally established Britain as the leading global power and confirmed the declining value of French arms, but it brought no benefit to Maria Theresa. Ironically, it was in collaboration with Frederick II that Maria Theresa obtained her most substantial territorial gains. In 1770, she took with Frederick's agreement the Polish border region of Spiš and then, two years later, she joined with Prussia and Russia in the first partition of Poland-Lithuania. (Two more partitions would follow in 1793 and 1795, erasing Poland-Lithuania from the map.) The empress recognized her actions as 'immoral', and Kaunitz thought them 'disreputable', but as Frederick himself observed of her, 'She wept as she took, and the more she wept, the more she took.' Indeed, Maria Theresa did better out of the partition than either Frederick II or the Russian empress, Catherine the Great, adding to her realms 2.6 million people and an area of eighty-three thousand square kilometres (thirty-two thousand square miles). By the end of the empress's reign, the population of her Central European lands had reached almost 20 million people.[11]

Maria Theresa was at war for almost half her reign. Financial reform and the proper husbanding of resources were vital to her military survival. Advised by the remarkably capable Count Haugwitz ('a man truly sent me by Providence'), she upped the tax burden, binding the diets to ten-year agreements so that she no longer needed to bargain annually with them, and she abolished many of the financial functions previously belonging to the diets. When the diets complained, the empress was tough. To the querulous diet of Carniola, she wrote about taxation, 'the Crown expressly commands you to grant these sums voluntarily.' Similarly, in the constitution she gave in 1775 to the part of Poland-Lithuania she had annexed, now grandly called the Kingdom of Galicia and Lodomeria, she denied the diet any voice in matters of taxation. When money was demanded of them, she explained, the diet's members were not expected to ask 'whether?' but only to consider 'how?'[12]

Across Maria Theresa's territories, the diets withered. Either they were converted into ceremonial institutions, meeting for just a few hours a year, or they became agencies of central government, discharging petty administrative duties, checking up on conditions in the countryside, and responding to the plethora of decrees, circulars, and notices that came from the centre. Even the Hungarian diet languished after 1765, being called neither by Maria Theresa nor by her son and successor, Joseph II. Politics there moved down a rung, to the local county administrations. Although they could be uncooperative, county officials and magistrates generally did what they were told, knowing that too much obstruction could result in the deployment of troops and commissars against them. Hungary may have been the only Habsburg territory where nobles as opposed to civil servants still ruled, but they did so with a nervous glance over their shoulders.[13]

On the top of the administrative edifice lay an increasingly expansive central bureaucracy, headed by a 'super-ministry' that brought together many of the offices that had hitherto operated in a confusion of rival competences. The edifice, first constructed by Haugwitz in 1749 for the Bohemian and Austrian lands, was known as the Directorate of Administration and Finance. But administration and finance were then separated, with the latter returning to the imperial treasury, and the structure was renamed the United Bohemian-Austrian Court Chancellery. Below it lay a second layer of administration, the provincial governments or gubernia, and a third comprising district offices. Supposedly holding the pieces together was a Council of State, instituted by Kaunitz in 1760, whose seven members were expected to advise the monarch on policy more broadly and address the 'general good.' Hungary and Transylvania continued to have their own chancelleries. Moved to Vienna in the 1690s, they shared premises above one of the city's taverns.[14]

Government was still rudimentary, with offices scattered throughout the capital. Until the 1770s most officials kept irregular hours and frequently worked from home (thereafter, it was on paper an eight AM to seven PM regime, with a three-hour lunchbreak at noon and weekend working). Under Joseph's influence, procedures and practices were increasingly routinized. Joseph demanded much of the civil servants—that they dedicate their lives to administrative service, strive for the common welfare, eschew bribes and other inducements, and have annual appraisals. In return, they received a small but regular salary, a pension upon retirement, medals, and a uniform of dark green with gold or silver frogging. In fact, the reality of work was often quite different to what Joseph intended. A few decades later, the civil servant and dramatist Franz Grillparzer (1791–1872) summed up one of his days: 'Into the office at noon. Found nothing to do. Read Thucydides.'[15]

The civil service was still small, amounting to about a thousand officials in the capital. But these drilled increasingly deep into Habsburg society. Maria Theresa's wars required a threefold increase in the size of the army. Hitherto, armies had been raised by a mix of voluntary recruitment and coercion by the provincial authorities. There had been the usual idiocies, with stories of limping travellers press-ganged and of Prussian prisoners-of-war being made to switch uniform. From 1760, a new system of 'canton recruitment' was used, modelled on Prussian arrangements. Newly instituted military districts now fed the Habsburg army, in which commissions of recruitment officers and civilian bureaucrats kept lists of manpower. They identified the least economically valuable male inhabitants, who might be duly made to serve, and they sent out the gangs that drafted men into the ranks.

The new system required a census of the complete population, which extended to draught animals that might be used in wartime. Kaunitz found the entire exercise appalling, since it amounted to the militarization of society, 'which is the greatest slavery and atrocity, and makes the Prussian regime so repulsive', but he was unable to halt the process. Within a few years, the census takers had extended their interest to house numbering, since there is no point knowing whom you wish to recruit unless you know where to find them. The style of numbering was laid down: black digits, put beside or above the main door, three inches in height. Officials countered complaints of intrusion by pointing out that the numbering extended to imperial palaces. Nevertheless, the implication of both the census and the house numbering was clear. A new bureaucratic regime had been instituted, in which, as one of its Prussian exponents boasted, 'every citizen is a part and cog in the machine of the state.'[16]

18

MERCHANTS, BOTANISTS, AND FREEMASONS

The Schönbrunn Palace was built in the first decades of Maria Theresa's reign. It was from the very first intended to rival Versailles. The differences were, however, several. The Schönbrunn was not given over to a tame nobility as a place of residence. Nor, unlike Versailles, was the palace open to the public. The Schönbrunn remained instead a summer retreat for the use of the imperial family, and much more of its space was given over to private quarters than at Versailles. At its heart was the marital bedroom that Maria Theresa shared with Francis Stephen. This was never the site of crowded morning levées but a 'working bedroom', in which the couple exchanged intimacies and (occasionally) quarrelled. Visitors were channelled through reception rooms and audience chambers that were intended to impress. But, as today, much of the palace's space was off limits.

The gardens were established at the same time as the palace and aimed to show 'an ensemble of nature and art', with flower beds arranged in matching geometrical patterns, interspersed with sculptures and fountains. On a hill beyond the main garden still stands the Gloriette, designed as a focal point in the form of a temple and surmounted by an eagle. At its foot, facing the palace, is the Neptune Fountain, with twice life-size statues in marble of Neptune, half-fish Tritons, sea horses, and nereids. They recall the sea winds by which Neptune sped Aeneas to Italy, and so the origins in Roman antiquity of both the Habsburgs and the imperial idea. In case the allusion was missed, close beside were heaped broken statues and fallen columns—the 'Ruins of Carthage' on which the greatness of Rome was built.[1]

But Neptune, the sea god, was by the mid-eighteenth century no longer a symbol of Habsburg power and of a maritime inheritance. The realms of Maria Theresa were largely landlocked, and the acquisition of Polish Galicia had advanced the empress's continental and not overseas dominion. The Habsburgs had lost the great colonial empire they had acquired through Spain and, along with it, any pretensions to global dominion. Their physical world had shrunk to just a corner of Europe and one, moreover, where their leadership was newly challenged by the emergence of Prussia. Spatially, the Habsburgs were in retreat.

In 1775, the Anglo-German-Dutch adventurer Willem Bolst, better known as William Bolts, arrived in Vienna. As untrustworthy in business as he was inept, Bolts had been previously drummed out of the British East India Company as 'a very unprofitable and unworthy servant', whose misdeeds included the betrayal of commercial secrets. Now he presented himself before Joseph II with a scheme for an Austrian East India Company. Elected Holy Roman Emperor in 1764, Joseph had automatically succeeded his father the next year, while also officiating as co-ruler with his mother of Austria, Bohemia, Hungary, and Polish Galicia. Bolts proposed to Joseph that he let him sail ships under the imperial flag for commerce in the eastern oceans, where he would sell metals and weapons supplied to him on credit by the government and bring back tea. Prince Kaunitz recommended the deal to Joseph, which he was later to regret, and the Austrian East India Company was duly incorporated.[2]

The company's expedition departed in 1776 from Livorno in Tuscany in the *Joseph und Theresa*. Originally *The Earl of Lincoln Indiaman*, the ship was a recently decommissioned three-master of five hundred tons (and so considerably larger than both Captain Cook's *Discovery* and Captain Bligh's *Bounty*). Buying other vessels on the way, Bolts established depots on the Mozambique coast and on the Nicobar Islands north-west of Sumatra, planting on both the imperial flag. Neither venture lasted long, being

overcome by the Portuguese and Danish respectively. But among the Nicobar Islands there is one still called Teressa, in honour of the empress.

Success was equally short-lived on the Indian coast, since the British
East India Company made business difficult, not least because Bolts owed
the company money. The *Joseph and Theresa* and three other ships eventually
returned to Livorno in 1779 with an unexciting load, together with a fifth
vessel, the *Prince Kaunitz*, which brought silk, tea, and curios from Guang-
zhou (Canton). The ships and cargoes were promptly seized by Bolts's creditors, which now included the government in Vienna, since it had provided
the original export consignment. An attempt by the creditors to reconstitute
the Austrian East India Company as the Imperial Company of Trieste and
Antwerp proved equally ill starred, bringing down the Pietro Proli bank in
Antwerp in one of the most spectacular bankruptcies of the eighteenth century. Joseph himself lost fifty thousand ducats.[3]

Undeterred by failure, Bolts made in 1782 a second proposal to Joseph.
Having read unofficial reports of Captain James Cook's final voyage in
the Pacific, Bolts now suggested they establish a commercial settlement at
Nootka Sound on what is now Vancouver Island with the aim of buying
pelts and furs from the Native Americans, which would then be exchanged
in Japan and China for porcelain, tea, and silk. But Joseph was uninterested.
Two years before, an accident in the glass houses of the Schönbrunn had
destroyed the collection of rare tropical plants housed there, while a fresh
stock intended for replenishment had arrived dead. What Joseph wanted
was a scientific and botanical expedition, not a commercial one, although
(as he agreed) the two purposes could be combined to yield a compromise,
whereby Bolts would make money and Joseph have his plants.

It was an extraordinary moment. The Habsburg emperor surrendered
the benefits of a global commercial and colonial venture in return for the re-
stocking of his glass houses with the botanical fruits of the world. Nevertheless, it comported with the outlook of his grandfather, as communicated in
the furnishing of the imperial library, and with Charles VI's self-fashioning
as a Hercules of the Muses. The Habsburgs' imperial vision was built of
many strands, and it was never just territorial. Classical, religious, and historical themes coalesced to promote aspirations that looked beyond material
and spatial enlargement. The multiple meanings of the AEIOU acrostic that
rested in the angel's lap on the ceiling of the imperial library embodied a

philosophy of greatness built of several layers. Botanical specimens were as much a part of the Habsburg imperial idea as peoples and territories.

Joseph's interview with Bolts was just the most dramatic episode in a longer cultural process that had already put the Habsburgs at the centre of collecting and disseminating knowledge. This was a type of knowledge quite different to the alchemists', for it was intended to be broadcast and not kept secret. Nor did it have much relation to the contemporary fashion for zoos, of which the menagerie in the Schönbrunn grounds, founded in 1752, constituted the greatest in Europe. Zoos were primarily for entertainment, as well as in the case of the Schönbrunn a place where the imperial family might take breakfast. The Schönbrunn zoo was opened to the public in 1778, although it was a requirement that visitors came properly dressed. Thankfully, it never functioned in the manner of Louis XIV's collection at Versailles, where tigers fought elephants for the king's amusement.

Botany, by contrast, was on account of its association with medicine subject to a rigorous methodology, where stress was laid on observation, faithful pictorial representation, and classification. Clusius (Charles de l'Écluse, 1526–1609), director of Maximilian II's imperial medical garden in Vienna, had set the standard here in respect of his detailed descriptions and engravings of specimens, which included such imports from the Ottoman Empire as the tulip and horse chestnut. Three hundred years later, Clusius's illustrations were still in circulation among scholars. New varieties of plant continued to be introduced and itemized throughout the seventeenth century not only from Asia but increasingly also from the New World—the ornamental mountain ash, the Virginia creeper, and the red cedar.[4]

The flood of new specimens from the Americas in particular burst old certainties. No longer was 'encyclopedism' and the collection of everything possible, for the world evidently comprised more than the '20,000 noteworthy facts', arrangeable in thirty books, as imagined by Pliny the Elder back in the first century. One late-sixteenth-century collection alone took up four hundred catalogue volumes, all penned by the same curator. The idea, moreover, that the sophisticated scholar, versed in hermetic learning, might see beyond the superficial differences between objects to perceive their hidden resemblances also foundered on the sheer multiplication of unusual items. New categories and a new taxonomy were required, by which phenomena might be ordered, managed, and explained. The botanical world was among the first to be so arranged, with 'phytosophical tables' providing a scheme for the classification of plants that were otherwise randomly assembled in miscellanies.[5]

But knowledge itself also needed a new framework beyond the standard divisions of the 'natural', the 'crafted', and the 'miraculous' (*naturalia, artificialia, mirabilia*). Some of the earliest classifications were, indeed, fantastic, as for instance one mid-seventeenth-century scheme that placed phenomena into categories as diverse as magnetism, mummies, universal and artificial languages, astronomy, optics, and so on. Even so, the divisions favoured by collectors and the categories they adopted for practical purposes guided the organization of the first museums, with separate cabinets being given over, for instance, to coins, medals of great men, geological specimens, butterflies, and monstrous births (Joseph II donated a collection of the last of these to the university's medical faculty in Vienna).[6]

Before the eighteenth century, Habsburg rulers only systematically collected animals, which were kept in various menageries until finally united in the Schönbrunn zoo. Charles VI, however, made a speciality of accumulating coins and medals, which amounted to several tens of thousands of items by the time of his death. They included the celebrated 'Alchemists' Medal', struck in 1677 to commemorate the first allegedly successful transmutation of base metal into gold. For lack of space, Charles's collection was housed in the billiards room of the Leopold Wing of the Hofburg. Charles kept his most precious treasures with him, however, in a *Nummothek* or travelling cabinet, that had been crafted in the form of a book to display coins and medals.[7]

But it was Charles's son-in-law and Maria Theresa's husband, Francis Stephen, who expanded the art of collecting to create what became Vienna's Natural History Museum. Historians quibble over the identity of Europe's earliest modern museum, but the importance of Francis Stephen's natural history collection or 'cabinet' lay in its arrangement, which over time provided a model for other museums. The divisions that we are used to in the study of natural history and science—geology, palaeontology, vertebrates, invertebrates, insects, prehistoric humans, and so on—originate in a scheme of classification first worked out in Vienna. The practice of demonstrating human development by exhibiting the stuffed bodies of people thought to be more primitive, which was not uncommon in European museums even in the last century, was also pioneered in the 1790s by Viennese curators.[8]

At the heart of Francis Stephen's natural history collection were thirty thousand mineral samples, sea creatures, corals, and snail shells that he bought in 1748 from an Italian nobleman of Franco-Dutch descent, Jean de Baillou. But Francis Stephen did not just buy Baillou's store chests, he bought the man too, appointing him director of the imperial natural history cabinet in the Hofburg Palace. Baillou and Nikolaus Jacquin, later professor of botany at Vienna University, went on to expand Linnaeus's classification scheme to include American flora, using his system of binary nomenclature, which identifies plants by giving them two names, usually both in Latin. The cabinet was supplemented by the fruits of expeditions headed by Jacquin to Western Europe, the Caribbean, and Venezuela, and accommodated in several rooms situated in the wing of the Hofburg that also housed the imperial library.[9]

Of the rooms beyond the natural history cabinet, two were given over to astronomical instruments, and another five to Francis Stephen's coin collection, sculpted gemstones, and Egyptian and Asiatic antiquities. The separate coin collections of Francis Stephen and Charles VI were eventually merged and catalogued. Further expansion followed, including birds and mammals acquired in the expedition that Joseph II had discussed with Bolts, which had eventually been undertaken in America without the adventurer's participation. In 1795 a comprehensive reorganization followed, after which the museum was known as the Imperial and Royal Exact Sciences and Astronomy, Inventions, and Nature and Zoology Cabinet (k.k. Physikalisches und astronomisches Kunst- und Natur-Tier-Cabinet).

The Natural History Museum (to give it a less unwieldy name) was Francis Stephen's achievement. It was he who dedicated the resources and invested his own time in the project. He even undertook his own experiments there, in one of which he inadvertently (and expensively) demonstrated that a diamond subjected to intense heat would carbonize. More importantly, he brought together the scholars who would be the museum's first directors and developed an international network of contacts and correspondents to support the museum's work. Of course, it helped that he was the emperor, but what may have been of even greater assistance in building connections was that Francis Stephen was also a freemason.[10]

Francis Stephen was admitted to the masonic degrees of entered apprentice and fellow craft in The Hague in 1731 at a meeting presided over by the British ambassador, the Earl of Chesterfield. The same year, he was made a master mason in a London lodge and attended a lodge meeting in Houghton Hall in Norfolk, which was the home of the British prime minister, Sir

Robert Walpole. Francis Stephen's masonic credentials were, therefore, impeccable. In Vienna, he was linked to the first lodge to be established there, The Three Canons, founded in 1742. Freemasonry had already been condemned by the Catholic Church, and the next year the lodge was raided by troops, with Francis Stephen apparently escaping through a back entrance. Francis Stephen's subsequent involvement with freemasonry is unclear, but his continued association was suspected, and his portrait was even accompanied by freemasonic symbols.[11]

Originating in seventeenth-century England, freemasonry was by no means united, either organizationally or intellectually. At its most basic, it stood for a universal brotherhood and, as one freemason later put it, 'a temple for the benefit of all mankind, a union that brings together fine people from all classes, peoples, and parts of the world.' Regardless of race, therefore, Angelo Soliman from West Africa was accepted into the True Harmony lodge in Vienna, where he officiated in ceremonies of initiation (and so presumably had reached the degree of master mason). But the tolerance of other lodges was thin. In Croatia and Trieste, relations between German and Italian speakers were unfriendly, with the result that separate lodges were founded. Freemasonry remained, moreover, a largely elite phenomenon, drawing its membership from noblemen, officeholders, and men of independent means. The cost of regalia, subscriptions, and charitable donations was enough to dissuade the lower orders from joining.[12]

Critics were later to accuse the lodges of fomenting revolutionary ideas on the back of brotherly egalitarianism. But most lodges remained aloof from controversial practices, devoting their time to rituals, the writing of constitutions, and lectures on such harmless topics as whether Christ was a freemason. Links with the secretive Bavarian Illuminati lodges encouraged political Utopianism, but the interest of members lay more in uncovering the identity of the 'unknown masters' at the top of the Illuminati hierarchy than in engaging in subversive activity. In Hungary, lodges that followed the so-called Drašković rite often debated controversial issues such as the condition of the peasantry, the privileges of the nobility, and the reform of the laws. Nevertheless, they still made ostentatious displays of patriotism and of loyalty towards Hungary's Habsburg monarch.[13]

The connection between freemasonry and scientific endeavour was close, even to the extent that the two overlapped. Individual lodges sponsored lectures on steam engines, pile driving, and electricity, and founded libraries for scientific research. The True Harmony lodge in Vienna published its own periodical for the 'observation of the workings of nature, to determine her laws and to work for the improvement of society.' Unsurprisingly, many of the leading scholars of natural science were drawn to freemasonry, including directors of the collections in Vienna's Natural History Museum. The first grand master of the True Harmony lodge was thus the court surgeon, Ignaz Fischer, and the second the geologist and museum director Ignaz von Born. The lodge's members possibly included Gerhard van Swieten, who besides being Maria Theresa's personal physician was head of the imperial library and instrumental in founding the museum.[14]

The True Harmony lodge was the most illustrious of the sixty or so lodges in Habsburg Central Europe, and it maintained a correspondence and exchanges across Europe, from London to St Petersburg. Ignaz von Born even contemplated the True Harmony's transformation into an academy for the promotion of scientific knowledge, in the manner of the Royal Society in London (which also had roots in freemasonry). But it was by no means unique. Prague's Three Crowned Stars and Three Eagles lodges also promoted natural science, particularly geological research, while in Sibiu in Transylvania the lodge of the Three Water Lilies had the governor of the province, the polymath Samuel von Brukenthal, as its grand master. As the patron of natural scientists, Brukenthal obtained lodge membership for his personal physician and numismatist, Samuel Hahnemann, the founder of the homeopathic movement.

By admittance to fellowship, a freemason was, in the words of the oath sworn in one Innsbruck lodge, taken not only into a temple but also 'into the society of citizens' (in der bürgerlichen Gesellschaft). In respect of a 'public sphere', in the sense of an arena where citizens might gather, debate, and influence policy, the lodges in Habsburg Central Europe were almost the only civic associations in existence. The reading clubs, patriotic societies, reform circles, and literary movements which pushed and promoted an agenda for change in Britain and France were until the 1780s as missing in Central Europe as the coffee houses stuffed with newspapers and lined with political cartoons. The 'little platoons', as Edmund Burke called them in England, which provided the bedrock of an independent and stable social order, were instead absorbed by the lodges. What was left of the 'public space' in Habsburg Central Europe was largely confined to non-elite venues—beer halls and the popular theatre, where the harlequin

Jack Sausage (Hans Wurst) extemporized ribald social satires. Whether the lodges impaired the emergence of civil society in Central Europe or whether they expanded in the absence of one must, however, remain uncertain.[15]

Yet freemasonry in Habsburg Central Europe could never act as the counterweight to government and the state, or as the foundation for a civil society and public sphere that might challenge the established order. The educated classes on which freemasonry drew for its membership were overwhelmingly employees of government. So too were the scientists and scholars who gave learned lectures and performed experiments at lodge meetings. Freemasonry thus reinforced the bureaucratic, top-down management of society, adding to the conviction that change was best introduced from above, by the masonic men of virtue and science who were charged with executing the sovereign's will. At first sight, freemasonry in Habsburg Central Europe may resemble what one historian has called 'a school of civic responsibility', and its lodges seem like 'microscopic civil polities.' On closer examination, they were mirrors of government, rehearsing the prejudices and convictions of the burgeoning state bureaucracy. They were a 'closed circuit', within which there was no space to look for other avenues for reform than from government itself.[16]

For more than a century after Francis Stephen, no senior Habsburg was a freemason. Perhaps Joseph II's nephew, the Archduke John, was one, for he was instrumental in founding one of the pseudo-chivalric societies that substituted for lodges in the period after 1793, when freemasonry was banned. Joseph II's hunch-backed sister, Maria Anna, was certainly sympathetic to freemasonry. Lay abbess of a convent in Klagenfurt, she sheltered a lodge beside her Carinthian palace, had her own collection of minerals and insects, and undertook experiments in the company of Ignaz von Born. A Klagenfurt lodge was named in her honour, but we do not know if the archduchess ever became a freemason in one of the female 'adoptive lodges.'[17]

Such, however, matters little. Although they may like Joseph II have rejected freemasonry as 'charlatanry' (*Gaukelei*), successive Habsburg rulers were surrounded in court and in government by freemasons. The gardens of the Schönbrunn bear eloquent testimony to their influence. At the foot of the hill on which the Gloriette stands and east of the Neptune Fountain, there is the Obelisk, designed to resemble an Egyptian column. It records the triumphs of the Habsburgs in faux hieroglyphs, for at the time of its erection these had not yet been made intelligible. But near its base the Obelisk bears a string of freemasonic symbols—a chisel, hammer, compasses, and set square (triangular plate)—put there by the architect, Johann Hetzendorf von Hohenberg, who was a freemason. Like the Obelisk's inscriptions, the elitist assumptions of Central European freemasonry had also been etched into the fabric of the Habsburg idea, reinforcing the principle that all change must come from above and be implemented through the apparatus of a virtuous elite.[18]

19

VAMPIRISM, ENLIGHTENMENT, AND THE REVOLUTION FROM ABOVE

*D*uring the first half of the eighteenth century, vampires became a media sensation. Official reports documenting the popular belief in vampires in the part of Serbia recently occupied by the Habsburgs were leaked to news sheets and medical journals. The stories they told of the undead feasting on the living, of exhumed bodies oozing with the blood of victims, and of stakings and beheadings, were luridly reproduced and combined with older tales of shape-shifting and shroud-eating corpses. Voltaire in Paris later noted how 'between 1730 and 1735 nothing was spoken of more than vampires—how they were hunted down, their hearts torn out, and their bodies burnt. They were like the martyrs of old; the more of them that were burnt, the more they found.'[1]

Reports of contagion spread from Serbia to Hungary and Transylvania. Unusual deaths or sightings, outbreaks of plague, and the discovery that a corpse had mummified rather than decomposed prompted copycat explanations and exhumations. There were plenty of educated authors who investigated the phenomena and found the evidence for vampirism to be lacking, but they often dressed up their otherwise measured accounts with sensationalist descriptions. Michael Ranft, whose sober treatise on whether corpses munched through their shrouds was first published in 1725, reworked his account a decade later to include a graphic account of the Serbian vampires, which he published in his compendious *Treatise on the Chewing and Gnawing of the Dead in Their Graves, in Which Is Revealed the True Nature of the Hungarian Vampires and Bloodsuckers* (Ranft thought Serbia to be in Hungary).[2]

Vampirism was reported in Moravia too. In 1755, with the agreement of the church authorities, the body of a woman was exhumed, decapitated, and burnt on the grounds that her corpse had been attacking villagers at night. This was the fourth time in three decades that the diocese of Olomouc had sanctioned exhumation, including in 1731 the disinterment of seven children, whose bodies had all been burnt. On news of this latest episode, Maria Theresa sent two doctors to investigate, but the terms of their commission left in no doubt what the empress expected of them. As she explained, it would be of 'great service to mankind' if their report could wean 'credulous people' from their misbelief.[3]

The doctors' findings were submitted to Gerhard van Swieten, who made a summary which he subsequently published as a pamphlet. Van Swieten trebled up as Maria Theresa's court librarian, personal physician, and censor. Thoroughly imbued with the spirit of rationalism, van Swieten rejected the supernatural for the same reason that he refused to wear a wig, since neither might be logically explained. Unsurprisingly, van Swieten found the Moravian case to be the product of error and rumour, akin to the conviction that black cats harboured devils or to the magical potions of conjurors. He wrote that on those occasions when corpses were found undecomposed, natural explanations might be found, most obviously that the weather was cold. Likewise, strange symptoms often proved to be the result of commonplace illnesses. Blameless people were being dug up in graveyards, van Swieten lamented, and the grief of mourners needlessly prolonged.[4]

Upon receiving van Swieten's report, Maria Theresa published in 1755 an instruction forbidding churches to permit exhumation on grounds of 'posthumous magic.' As she explained, accusations of this type were almost always the product of superstition and fraud. In future, they and all cases of hauntings, witchcraft, and diabolic possession were to be referred by churchmen to local government offices and to be investigated by medical personnel. For good measure, she also banned the prognostication of winning lottery numbers.[5]

Maria Theresa's response to rumours of vampirism is a lens through which to view the Enlightenment and the ways in which it influenced policy in Central Europe. The Enlightenment stood above all else for reason and for explanations that were rooted in the laws of nature and human conduct. The empress's appointment of doctors to lead the investigation into vampirism in Moravia, and of van Swieten to summarize their reports, and both van Swieten's and her own verdicts, are characteristic of an enlightened manner of thinking that preferred rational to supernatural explanations. Rather than attribute vampirism to diabolical forces, Maria Theresa was readier to believe that natural causes or malevolent earthly agents were responsible.

The Enlightenment was not, however, a single phenomenon but manifested itself differently according to location. In Britain and North America, the Enlightenment tended towards the extension of popular sovereignty, curbs on government, and a new 'science of freedom' aimed at securing individual liberty and the rights of the citizen. In Central Europe, the Enlightenment tended towards the reverse—towards regulation, the 'science of the state' or 'science of order', and the subjection of the individual to the common good, as the sovereign understood it to be. As one of the main exponents of the Central European Enlightenment put it: 'All duties of people and subjects may be reduced to the formula: to promote all the ways and means adopted by the ruler for their happiness, by their obedience, fidelity and diligence.'[6]

Bureaucracy and a conviction that officials knew best is manifested in the role that Maria Theresa accorded the civil service in the case of the Moravian vampires. Already, the medical profession had been regulated, and many of its members converted into government officers responsible to local boards of sanitation. These newly created officials were now entrusted with the investigation of allegedly supernatural events, even in graveyards and what had hitherto been an exclusive preserve of the church. The Central European Enlightenment was not anticlerical, but it opposed the special rights of the clergy and the separate status that the church enjoyed. Unleashing the medical profession on cemeteries was a practical manifestation of this imperative.[7]

Maria Theresa's concern was for the welfare of her subjects. Her injunctions against 'posthumous magic' are characteristic of her paternalism or even maternalism, for she willingly embraced the soubriquet of 'Mother of her People.' To that end, she cajoled her subjects and nannied them into good behaviour—forbidding them from blowing post horns at night, requiring tobacco pipes to be fitted with lids, banning candles from barns, prohibiting advertisements for arsenic, and so on. More lastingly, she banned torture and most trials for witchcraft, and she made a start on the education of the peasantry, declaring that all children attend six years of schooling. For the good of her subject's souls she also deported several thousand Protestants from the Austrian lands to Transylvania, and she briefly ejected Jews from Vienna on the grounds that she found their presence in the city objectionable. In many ways, Maria Theresa was also strikingly unenlightened.

Underpinning Maria Theresa's intrusions was her conviction that monarchs were appointed by God for the common welfare. To this were added the principles of natural law, which by the eighteenth century dominated the universities and educated discussion. Natural law theory rested on two principles, both of which fed into the Central European Enlightenment. The first was that society and sociability were implicit in the human condition. The second was that government existed for the benefit of society—kings did not only rule because God had appointed them; their dominion was for a purpose that lay in the society of their subjects.

Reason, natural law, and a generalized idea of the 'social good' provided, however, few guidelines for most of the tasks confronting government. The key to policy lay instead with what was known at the time as 'cameralism' or 'treasury science' (from the *camera* or *Kammer*, meaning a treasure chamber). This was the study of how states and institutions might maximize revenues both for their own defence and for the benefit of their citizens, as a way of enlarging the people's wealth and happiness. The measure of this intervention differed from author to author. Some believed that it was enough to create the conditions for happiness, for it was the individual's right to determine how he reacted with the external world. Most, however, assumed that individuals could not be trusted to secure an order of maximum perfection and that a benevolent government should intervene and direct, even at the expense of individual liberty.

Cameralists frequently advocated what amounted to a 'programme of total regulation.' Within this scheme, individual rights took second place to the interests of the larger society. Hence, because a burgeoning population was conceived to be good thing, abortion should be clamped down on, and people with physical disabilities removed from public places lest they shock women into miscarriages. Active minds needed to be refreshed in the open air, so universities should be provided with gardens and the students made to enjoy them. Because Shakespeare's *Romeo and Juliet* might make audiences melancholic and listless, the final scenes should be made jollier. And because servants and officials could not be trusted, rulers should build in their palaces secret corridors, passages, and loopholes so that they might listen in unobserved to private conversations.[8]

At its worst, cameralism could lead to a dull utilitarianism which sought to banish literature, philosophy, and astronomy from the university curriculum, claiming they were not 'useful.' At the other extreme, it threatened social revolution. The rights of the nobility, of their antique diets, and of the church rested on tradition, and they could hardly be justified in terms of their social benefit. They might thus be voided in the interests of the greater good. As one imperial advisor put it, 'Every tradition which has no justifiable basis should be abolished automatically.' Maria Theresa did not, however, take cameralism to its logical conclusion, for she understood the preservation of the established hierarchy to be also one of her duties. But her son did not hesitate to release a revolution from above. In so doing, he demonstrated a contempt for traditions and institutions that was matched only by his conviction that he, ultimately, was right.[9]

Joseph's short, ten-year reign (1780–1790) saw a breathtaking range of activity—reform of the church, the promotion of a new economic and social agenda, and genuine attempts to better the lot of the peoples over whom he ruled by interfering in the details of their lives. Beyond this he sought to weld together his various dominions into 'just one body, uniformly governed.' We may quibble over what constitutes a state, but uniformity of government and the recognition of subjects that they owe obedience to some sort of common authority are surely important components. Joseph certainly aimed at the first, and he probably trusted that the second would follow. At least, this was the hope of the influential cameralist and rector of Vienna University Joseph von Sonnenfels, who thought the state which secured the happiness of its subjects would automatically win their affection and loyalty. State building in the sense of constructing a homogeneous and uniform single body remained an ambition for both Joseph and his successors. The 'state patriotism' in which Sonnenfels placed his trust proved, however, elusive.[10]

Joseph II governed in the same way he had sex—energetically and with such unrestraint that he looked forward to periods of abstemiousness in the countryside, 'because there the choice was between ugly peasants and falconers' wives.' (He avoided intimacy with his second wife since, as he explained, her body was covered in boils). Promiscuous, too, in the welcome he gave to petitioners, he may during his lifetime have met as many as a million of his subjects. Catherine the Great of Russia reckoned that Joseph had 'ruined his health with his eternal audiences.' When not hearing petitions, Joseph was drafting decrees, often several daily. The bureaucracy was unable to keep up with the welter of instructions they received from him, let alone monitor their effectiveness—orders limiting the number of candles in churches and the duration of sermons, requiring reusable coffins with false bottoms to be employed in funerals (to save on wood), prohibiting the kissing of the dead (to prevent disease spreading), replacing anatomical specimens with exact wax copies, and so on.[11]

By the mid-eighteenth century, most Enlightened thinkers were agreed that no single religious creed could objectively claim an absolute monopoly of the truth and that religious toleration was accordingly basic to the new, rational society that they sought to introduce. Cameralists, too, saw the exclusion on grounds of religion of a large chunk of the population from the skilled workforce as economically harmful. As one of his earliest acts as sole ruler, Joseph suspended in 1781 his mother's edicts persecuting non-Catholics and decreed a policy of toleration. Hereafter, Lutherans, Calvinists, Orthodox Christians, and (the next year) Jews could practise their religion openly, and they were permitted to occupy positions in the bureaucracy, follow their trades, and attend university. Several years later, Joseph made marriage a civil contract, which meant that all legal cases involving legitimacy and divorce now belonged to the courts and not to church tribunals.

Joseph's own devotion to the Catholic faith meant that he held back from conceding full religious freedom. The right to build churches was accordingly limited to larger Protestant communities, and non-Catholic places of worship might not front onto public squares or main streets. Moreover, Joseph's edict of toleration excluded 'sectaries' who were neither Lutheran nor Calvinist—Unitarians, Baptists, Mennonites, and so on. This gap in the law meant that Protestants were still persecuted on the grounds that they did not fit into the prescribed categories. As late as the 1830s, four hundred Protestants were driven out of the Tyrolean Zillertal valley on grounds of sectarianism. Even so, at the time of its promulgation, Joseph's edict on toleration probably made the Habsburg lands the most generous to religious nonconformists in all of Europe.[12]

Joseph's personal commitment to Catholicism did not extend to its institutions. Along with most Enlightenment opinion, he regarded monks as an almost complete waste of time. 'They sing, they eat, they digest' was Voltaire's verdict on the monastic vocation. Meanwhile in Vienna, Ignaz von Born published his celebrated *Monachologia*, in which he classified monks according to the principles of Linnaeus. Pretending to have discovered 'a new genus, which connects man, the most perfect of mortals, with the monkey, the silliest of animals', he broke down monks into categories defined by dress and conduct—hence the Benedictine was 'omnivorous, rarely fasts . . . hoards money', the Carmelite was 'pugnacious and libidinous . . . fond of brawls and quarrels', and so on. Joseph's relaxation of censorship in 1781 saw a flood of pamphlets critical of monastic institutions and church wealth. Not a few of these were, in fact, covertly published by Joseph's ministers.[13]

Lombardy and Galicia had in the 1770s been a testing ground for Habsburg policy towards the monasteries. As co-ruler with his mother, Joseph had closed about 250 religious houses in the two provinces on the grounds that they were corrupt or fulfilled only contemplative purposes, meaning that the monks and nuns did no useful work beyond praying. In a desperate attempt to forestall the inevitable, Pope Pius VI hurried to Vienna in the spring of 1782—he was the first pope to cross the Alps in almost three centuries. Joseph accommodated Pope Pius in the Hofburg but found his company 'tiring and unpleasant.' He also scorned the papal threat of excommunication, remarking to one of his advisors that 'the secret has been discovered that you can eat and drink well despite excommunication.' Even before the pope's arrival, Joseph had instructed the first Austrian monasteries to be closed, and Pius VI's visit did nothing to slow the pace of dissolution.[14]

The targets of Joseph's policy were religious houses that performed no social purpose, neither caring for the sick nor providing schools. Of two thousand foundations, seven hundred were closed, and fourteen thousand monks and nuns discharged. The monasteries and their lands were sold off, with the profits put into a special fund, the purpose of which was to build seminaries for the education of the clergy, but most of which went to pay pensions to ex-monks and nuns. Some attempt was made to save the libraries of the dissolved monasteries, with their collections being distributed to universities, schools, and the imperial library. But librarians were instructed not to bother 'with books that have no worth, old editions from the fifteenth century, and the like', so these were lost, along with all else that was deemed too troublesome to transport. Much was either left to rot or dumped in lakes. Altogether, about two and a half million books were destroyed in Europe's greatest biblioclasm before the Third Reich.[15]

Joseph's early measures were largely uncontroversial, for they chimed with both the prevailing intellectual climate and popular prejudices. Joseph's reform of conditions on the land was, however, less consensually driven and partly motivated by his desire 'to humble and impoverish the grandees' (that is, the nobility). A development of cameralism known as physiocracy taught that the nation's wealth derived from agriculture and that it was the job of government to reduce impediments to cultivation and exchange. The burdens on producers needed to be lifted and the fiscal regime reorganized in their interest through the imposition of a standard land tax, payable by all. Plainly wrong, for it dismissed commerce as an economically 'sterile' activity that produced no real wealth, physiocracy impressed by its reliance on tables and long algebraic formulae. It won Joseph over and provided the intellectual underpinning for his assault on the privileged classes.

Beginning with Bohemia in 1781, Joseph declared serfdom abolished throughout his dominions. Typically, he plucked the term 'life ownership' (*Leibeigenschaft*) from a quite different context to describe the supposedly oppressive relationship between landlord and peasant, and he declared its abolition to correspond with 'the love of reason and humanity.' From now on, Joseph decreed, peasants might leave their plots and marry without their lord's permission. In fact, by this time most could anyway. Then he instructed that peasants be allowed to purchase outright the land they farmed and convert the services they owed to their lord into a single, one-off payment. To hasten the pace of change, thirty thousand peasants rose up in Transylvania in 1784, murdering their lords in the belief that they were furthering Joseph's programme. The leaders of the revolt were captured, tortured, and killed by having their limbs and skulls smashed while stretched over a cart wheel.[16]

Undaunted, Joseph progressed to converting all dues owed by peasants into money payments and the equal sharing of the tax burden. Noble exemptions from taxation were to be abolished and a single land tax imposed. To make the tax fair, Joseph ordered a new land survey across his dominions, which would establish who owned what and how much they should be taxed. This created an immediate crisis in Hungary. First, Hungarian nobles regarded their freedom from taxation as a historic privilege, and they

Left: Imperial Library in the Hofburg, Vienna.

Below: Emperor Charles VI as Hercules of the Muses, in the Imperial Library in the Hofburg, Vienna.

Above: Castle Habsburg in the Aargau, Switzerland.

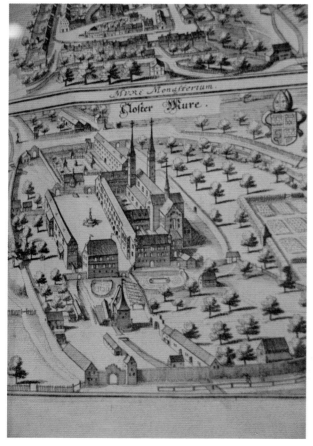

Left: Muri Abbey, circa 1650.

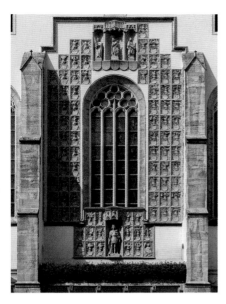

Left: Heraldic Wall of St George's Cathedral, Wiener Neustadt, with coats of arms illustrating the history of Austria and a statue of Frederick III at the base.

Below: The family of Emperor Maximilian I by Bernhard Strigel, circa 1516. The picture shows in the back row Maximilian's son, Philip the Handsome, and Maximilian's first wife, Mary of Burgundy. In the front row are the future Ferdinand I, the future Charles V, and the future Louis II of Hungary.

Above: Maximilian inspects a haul of fish, from the book on the art of fishing that he commissioned.

Right: Tomb of Emperor Maximilian I in Innsbruck. The tomb is empty, as Maximilian was buried in Wiener Neustadt.

Above: The 'People of Calicut' from Albrecht Dürer's *The Triumphal Procession of Maximilian I.*

Left: Emperor Charles V, circa 1550, after Titian.

Right: Escorial Palace, Spain, built 1563–1584.

Below: Emperor Rudolf II by Pieter Soutman.

Emperor Rudolf II as Vertumnus, the Roman god of the seasons, gardens, and orchards, by Giuseppe Arcimboldo, circa 1590–1591.

Above: *Melencolia I*, by Albrecht Dürer, 1514.

Left: Fort San Domingo, New Taipei, Taiwan. Built by the Spanish, 1637.

Left: Relief showing Leopold I on the Plague Column, Vienna, circa 1690.

Below: Eighteenth-century 'catacomb saint' with wig, named St Friedrich, Melk Abbey, Austria.

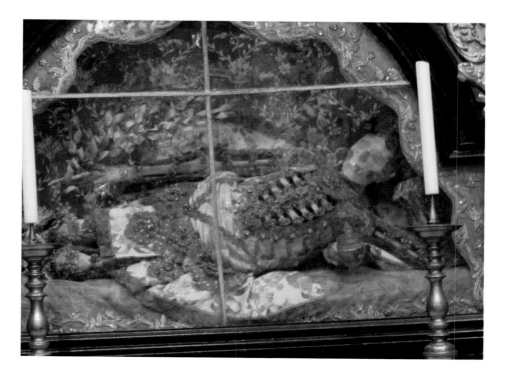

Above: An example of seventeenth-century Andean Baroque—the portal of the Basilica de Nuestra Señora de la Merced, Lima.

Below: 'Charles Church' (Karlskirche), Vienna, 1716–1737. Dedicated to St Charles Borromeo.

Left: Design for a Catafalque for Philip IV of Spain, circa 1665.

Below: Horse Ballet in the Hofburg, 1667.

Il Gran Balletto à Cauallo fattosi il dì 24 di Gennaro 1667 nel Gran Cortile del Palazzo Imperiale

Left: Maria Theresa by Martin Meytens the Younger, circa 1745.

Below: Marble tomb of Archduchess Maria Christina ('Mimi') in the Augustinian Church, Vienna, by Antonio Canova (1805).

Left: Prince Metternich in 1822, age fifty.

Below: *The Execution of Emperor Maximilian of Mexico*, 1868. Lithograph by Édouard Manet.

Above: The Looshaus in Vienna. Built in 1909 according to the design by Adolf Loos.

Right: The Hungarian explorer Count Samuel Teleki in Kenya 1887–1888.

Above: War Ministry Building in Vienna, built 1909–1913.

Below: The St Michael's Wing of the Hofburg, built 1889–1893.

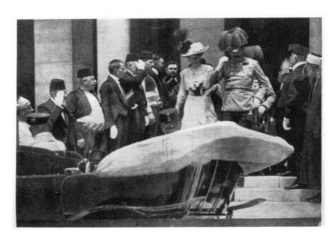

Right: Ten forty-five a.m., 28 June 1914: Franz Ferdinand and his wife leave the Sarajevo Town Hall. He is wearing a plume of green ostrich feathers. It is their wedding anniversary. Five minutes later they will be dead.

Below: Franz Joseph, circa 1885, by Carl Pietzner.

resented any diminution in their status and wealth. Second, Hungarian noblemen had over centuries gone off with properties that belonged to the crown or to their neighbours, and they had been happy to let disputes over ownership trickle unresolved through the courts. A land survey threatened to reopen dormant litigation and plunge the nobility into costly and protracted court battles.

Relations with the Hungarian nobility were already inflamed. But without Hungary's subjection and the destruction of its historic institutions, Joseph's ambition to create a common framework of government that united his possessions could not be fulfilled. So during the 1780s Joseph had made German instead of Latin the official language in Hungary and abolished the local county administration, replacing elected officers with appointed commissars, and he never summoned a diet. Most notoriously, he refused coronation as king of Hungary, since he had no wish to take the oath confirming the kingdom's liberties. Instead, he removed the Hungarian Holy Crown from Bratislava Castle and added it to his treasury in Vienna as just one bauble among many.

Joseph's behaviour prompted an upsurge in patriotic sentiment throughout Hungary. Many Hungarian noblemen now felt obliged to behave in Hungarian fashion, which they interpreted as loud swearing and ostentatious spitting. Others, misreading Rousseau's *Social Contract*, spoke of a pact between the house of Habsburg and the Hungarian nobility that Joseph's tyranny had torn up. Overtures to Prussia signalled that the Hungarian malcontents were ready to enlist foreign aid in defence of their dubious freedoms. Meanwhile, in the Austrian Low Countries, a civil war broke out, with both conservatives and progressives joining together in an uneasy coalition to overthrow Joseph's government in Brussels. West of the Tyrol, the sleepy Vorarlberg also burnt as peasants woke in defence of the Catholic Church.[17]

At this critical moment, Joseph's foreign policy unravelled. Maria Theresa had worked with the German princes in the Holy Roman Empire, enlisting them to her side both in the War of the Austrian Succession and in the Seven Years War. Despite her sex, she had retained leadership of the Holy Roman Empire, cajoling its princes to support her cause against the peril of Prussian ambition. Joseph, however, offended sentiment by meddling in the appointment of the new archbishop of Cologne and by his scheming to exchange the Austrian Low Countries for Bavaria. The deal made sense, for it swapped a distant province for one that was contiguous with the Austrian lands, but the manner of Joseph's negotiations meant that the princes of the Holy Roman Empire now saw in him the main threat to the established order. A disastrous war with the Turks, begun in 1787 in collaboration with his Russian ally, forced Joseph to turn to the Hungarians for troops. The price paid was a harsh one—the abrogation of all his reforms save the earliest, which had granted religious toleration and abolished the condition of peasant serfdom.

Joseph died of tuberculosis in February 1790 after several painful years of vomiting blood. One of his last instructions was that his coffin bear the inscription 'Here lies Joseph, who failed in everything he undertook.' Although Joseph's request was ignored, the epitaph was only partly right. True, Joseph had abandoned the great cameralist and physiocratic experiment, and he had given up on the integration of Hungary. But he had also shown what it was possible to imagine. A benevolent government, acting in the interests of the common good, might yet develop policies and goals that aimed to augment human felicity. The apparatus of rule might also be organized as a machine to that end, with bureaucrats implementing instructions from above and imposing the ruler's will on a population that was regimented, conscripted, and numbered, for its own good. Through the freemasonic connection, Habsburg bureaucrats were already convinced of their superiority as a governing elite and brotherhood of intelligence. Now, thanks to Joseph II, they had a mission—the betterment of society. It was a vision different from AEIOU and EUCHARISTIA, but with its underpinning in the new science of the state no less ambitious an enterprise.

20

ARCHDUCHESSES AND THE HABSBURG LOW COUNTRIES

*I*n the late 1760s Maria Theresa ordered that the Hall of the Giants (*Riesensaal*) in the Habsburg palace in Innsbruck in the Tyrol be entirely refurbished. She had never liked the gigantic frescoes of Hercules that adorned the walls and gave the hall its name, since 'there was far too much nakedness here and there.' Writing in her habitual mixture of French and German, she now instructed that '*il y aura der Familiensaal anstatt deren risen*'—'there should be a Family Hall in place of the giants.' The hall was accordingly remodelled, the frescoes concealed with wallpaper, and portraits hung of the empress's family, but the hall kept its original name.[1]

The refashioned Hall of the Giants celebrated Maria Theresa's fecundity. At the far end, she is depicted along with her husband, Emperor Francis Stephen, and her heir Joseph II. But along the walls are vast portraits of all fifteen of her other children, with the dead ones floating together on clouds in the company of a ghostly cherub. Above the portraits of Maria Theresa's children are twenty of her grandchildren, with spaces reserved for those yet to be born, and several of her more prestigious sons-in-law. Whereas most family galleries were made up of portraits of ancestors, the

Hall of the Giants looks to the future—to a dynasty that had survived extinction and was now replenished through the tireless childbearing of the queen-empress.

Of Maria Theresa's sixteen children, eleven were female, of whom three died young. The eight surviving women are presented in the Hall of the Giants as beautiful and wealthy, attired in the costliest damask. Several are depicted with puppies at their feet as symbols of fidelity. Even though no longer on the marriage market, they are shown as suitable spouses who add lustre to their husbands' reputations and whose own children will in time make good wives and husbands. By contrast, the males of the family assume martial poses, sometimes with battle scenes in the background.

The main function of Habsburg women was to provide male heirs. It helped if the woman was beautiful, for that made the task of the husband less onerous, especially since it was believed that the womb needed frequent lubrication to prevent it from shrivelling. Charles VI recorded in his diary his relief on finding that his bride, Elizabeth Christine (Lily White), matched expectations—'queen came . . . queen nice, beautiful, good.' Queens too were expected to show modesty and piety by taking part in pilgrimages and religious processions, bathing the (fortunately prewashed) feet of the poor, and upon widowhood retreating into seclusion in the proximity of a convent. Failure to produce the requisite son was often attributed to a spiritual failing, and so fecundity and religiosity were linked.[2]

The education of Habsburg women matched the expectations put upon them. Languages came first, since they were most likely to contract a foreign marriage. So, besides Latin, they learned Italian, French, and Spanish. Although some German was taught, Habsburg women generally spoke like their aristocratic companions in German dialect, 'as commonly as their scullion maids.' (Maria Theresa's German was thoroughly coarse.) Besides languages, girls studied music and dancing, drawing and needlework. They did not, however, receive a male education in cameral science, geography, and heraldry. Extraordinarily, although Emperor Charles knew that Maria Theresa would succeed him, he made no alterations to her education. As the empress later complained, her accession was made more difficult 'because my father had never been pleased to initiate or inform me in the conduct of either internal or foreign affairs.' Even so, she made no attempt to broaden the education of her own daughters, while recommending that they stay aloof from politics.[3]

Among the female portraits in the Hall of Giants there is one exception. It is the Archduchess Maria Anna, who was Maria Theresa's eldest surviving daughter as well as Ignaz von Born's collaborator, and subsequently a lay abbess and possible freemason. Any husband who took her on would also have to accommodate her 7,923 mineral samples, 195 varieties of preserved beetle, and 371 pinned butterflies. The portrait warns suitors off, for it shows her standing beside a writing desk on which are piled papers, books, and a globe. She points to her pen. This is a blue stocking, the artist Martin van Meytens tells us, whose interests look beyond marriage and childbearing to that other realm of Habsburg endeavour, the world of knowledge.

The example of Maria Anna indicates that women were not only seen as breeding machines and exemplars of piety. Other avenues were possible, of which the political was the most frequent. Habsburg rulers made their womenfolk regents and governors. As in much else, Maximilian I had set the pace, appointing in 1507 his widowed daughter to rule Burgundy and the Low Countries in his stead. But the Spanish connection mattered too, for in Aragon and Castile women faced few impediments, being accepted in both kingdoms as rulers and as equal heirs in the division of property. Right through to the eighteenth century, high-born Spanish women sat cross-legged on the floor, but this did not stop them from mounting the highest offices. Back in the sixteenth century, Emperor Charles V had employed his glamorous wife, Isabella of Portugal, as his regent in Spain. The last of the Habsburg Spanish line, poor Charles II, had as his regent or 'curator' his widowed mother, Mariana of Austria, whose ruthless manipulation of the young king was matched only by her political incompetence.[4]

The Low Countries were always supposed to be governed by members of the ruling house, but there were insufficient legitimate men to fulfil this role—hence the recruitment of the bastard Don John. Women stepped into the breach. For more than half the sixteenth century, the governors were female—Margaret of Austria, Mary of Hungary, and Margaret of Parma, who was both a *bâtarde* and a woman. In 1598, Philip II ceded outright the government of the Spanish Low Countries to his daughter Isabella and her husband, Albert, who was Philip's nephew several times over. Throughout her marriage, Isabella referred to Albert as 'my cousin.'

Philip intended that Albert and Isabella's descendants should rule the Low Countries as sovereign dukes, but their union was barren. On Albert's death in 1621, Isabella removed her parrots and dwarves from the palace in Brussels, cut her hair, and assumed the habit and veil of a nun. Even so, she continued to rule, but no longer as a sovereign archduchess, being now merely governor on behalf of Philip IV of Spain until her own death in 1633. Thereafter, the governorship of the Low Countries alternated between male relatives of the Spanish king and, in the absence of these, Castilian and Portuguese grandees.[5]

The Spanish Low Countries comprised ten provinces, which are roughly where Belgium and Luxembourg are today, except that they were split down the middle by the independent bishopric of Liège. Each province had its own particular 'rights, liberties, privileges, customs, and usages' that the incoming governor swore to uphold. Only in Brabant were these formally codified, which gave leeway to the governors to develop their own interpretations. Even so, the principle that taxation required the consent of representatives of the communities on which it was laid was never effaced, imposing considerable limits on the governor's power.

The Spanish Low Countries synthesized Flemish and Spanish culture. Spanish plays were frequently performed in the cities, both in the original and in translation—there were nineteen translations into Flemish of Lope de Vega's dramas alone. Spanish patrons, not least the king himself, bought the work of Flemish artists, while Albert and Isabella commissioned pieces by Rubens both for their Coudenberg Palace in Brussels and for churches in Spain. Typically, these conveyed a religious content that rehearsed the main themes of Habsburg piety: veneration for the eucharist and the cult of the Virgin Mary. More down-to-earth exchanges saw over a hundred Flemish women marry Spanish soldiers of the Antwerp garrison in the single decade 1638–1647. Even the Flemish language began to pick up a few Hispanicisms.

Religion was the cement. The dissolution of the Low Countries in the later sixteenth century into a Protestant north and a Catholic south was accompanied by massive refugee movements, with as many as 150,000 people fleeing the ten southern provinces that remained under Spanish rule. The Spanish Low Countries adopted the substance and display of Baroque Catholicism, with the densest concentration of wayside chapels, shrines, and calvaries anywhere in Europe. The religious orders and, in particular, the Jesuits not only completed the work of conversion but also instilled a deep religiosity. By the 1640s, the Jesuit 'Flemish-Belgian Province' numbered almost nine hundred Jesuit priests—eight for every 10,000 inhabitants, as opposed to five in Spain, and just one in France. Seminaries churned out clergy not only for domestic labour but also to feed Jesuit missions in Latin America, Angola, and China.[6]

The War of the Spanish Succession saw the Spanish Low Countries overrun by France and then briefly occupied by British and Dutch forces, before being assigned by treaty to Charles VI in 1713–1714. The Treaty of Rastatt obliged Charles to maintain the provinces of the now Austrian Low Countries in their liberties. The Marquis de Prié, a corrupt Sardinian in Charles's service, took the oaths on his master's behalf in grand ceremonies, for which he displayed canvases showing the emperor's victories and, in place of the usual city militias, ostentatiously mustered companies of fusiliers and grenadiers. But each inauguration was preceded by haggling with the provincial parliaments that limited the real power of Habsburg government. Even the cost of the celebratory fireworks needed negotiation. Despite Charles VI's display of military might, the Austrian Low Countries had to be run as consensually as under Spanish rule.[7]

Like their Spanish predecessors, Charles VI and Maria Theresa used their relatives, including the women, to act as governors. For thirty of the eighty years of Austrian rule, archduchesses fulfilled this role. To this, we should add the twenty years (1754–1773) in which Maria Theresa's sister-in-law, Anne Charlotte, lay abbess of St Waltraud's in Mons, held office as Madame Royale to her brother, the long-serving governor, Prince Charles Alexander of Lorraine (1744–1780). Reforming and yet sensitive to the fractious politics of the Low Countries, successive female rulers pursued largely independent policies, and they frequently blocked the plenipotentiaries appointed by Vienna to maintain imperial oversight. Neither Charles VI nor Maria Theresa wished, however, to antagonise the governors or to upset the political status quo. The Austrian Low Countries more than paid their way, also contributing to the 'secret fund' that bought the election of Maria Theresa's son, Maximilian Francis, as archbishop of Cologne.[8]

Austrian rule fostered trade and industry. By developing roads and canals to ease international commerce, customs income doubled. Supported by his abbess sister, Charles Alexander of Lorraine sponsored the newly founded Academy of Sciences, oversaw the extension of the Louvain-Dyle canal, and promoted some of the earliest research into electricity, air pressure, and thermodynamics. Like his brother, Francis Stephen of Lorraine, Charles Alexander was a freemason. He was also a profligate womanizer, who shared a mistress with Casanova. His surviving 'code of gestures' re-cords the nods and winks by which courtesans might be enticed to intimacy in the theatre—adjusting the neckpiece signifying a willingness to meet in private, taking a peck of snuff being an invitation to his box, and so forth.[9]

Despite improvements, the economy of the Austrian Low Countries remained largely agricultural, and to Joseph II's subsequent displeasure, landowning nobles continued to dominate many of the provincial estates and urban councils. In religion too, the Austrian Low Countries resembled a museum. The 'Catholic Enlightenment' sought to reconcile Catholicism with scientific enquiry, to support rulers in the business of eliminating cleri-cal abuses, and to inspire souls to godliness through personal devotion rather than collective rituals. The female rulers of the Austrian Low Countries would have nothing to do with it. The Archduchess Maria Elizabeth cracked down in the 1730s on the spread of Jansenism which taught that salvation depended entirely on God's grace and was granted only to a few, and which advocated a simpler religion shorn of ceremonial trappings. Charles VI rec-ommended that the archduchess proceed cautiously, but she allowed the ar-rest of Jansenist clergy. She also refused the emperor's request to abolish the right of asylum in churches, despite its abuse by military deserters.[10]

A particular target of the Catholic Enlightenment was the Jesuits, who were thought too dogmatic in their theology. But in the Austrian Low Countries Charles Alexander and his sister resisted calls to diminish their influence and take the training of priests out of their hands. Both also kept their Jesuit confessors. The censorship of religious materials and of Jansenist works was extended in the Austrian Low Countries, even as it was being relaxed in Vienna. The monasteries also retained their luxuries, free of Jan-senist austerity. To commemorate the passing of their abbot, the monks of St Peter's in Ghent supped as late as 1789 on a selection of meat and fish, including sturgeon, a dessert of pineapples, melons, and pears, followed by coffee and liqueurs, and finished off with oysters.[11]

Charles Alexander's saintly sister, Anne Charlotte, died in 1773, after which her brother was able to install his mistress as his consort and to con-tinue his affairs free from reproach. Like most high-born libertines, Charles Alexander was genuinely popular. Even the usually tight-fisted provincial parliaments voted a bronze statue in his honour, over the unveiling of which he presided in the dress of a Roman emperor. The prince's diary survives, which describes lazy days given over to long lunches, hunting, the popular

theatre, and losing at cards. Charles Alexander died in 1780. With his passing, the whirlwind that was Joseph II tore the sleepy Austrian Low Countries apart.[12]

Maria Christina was Empress Maria Theresa's favourite daughter, born
on her name day. The young 'Mimi' had in the early 1760s an intense relationship with Joseph II's first wife, Isabella of Parma. She may not have understood it to be sexual, but her letters to Isabella are unequivocal in respect
of their physical relations—'I love you furiously and yearn to kiss you . . . to
kiss and be kissed by you. . . . I kiss your arch-angelic little bum' (*ertzen-
glishes arscherl*), and so forth. Isabella died of smallpox in 1763, and Mimi
married the landless Albert of Saxony on the rebound. Maria Theresa loaded
the young prince with mostly empty titles, although the duchy of Cieszyn
(Teschen) in what was left of Silesia had real substance.[13]

To keep Mimi close, Maria Theresa appointed Albert her regent in
Hungary (the more suitable office of palatine depended on Maria Theresa
summoning a diet, which she wished to avoid). For fifteen years, Albert diligently ran Hungary from the capital at Bratislava, which was only two days'
ride from Vienna. Albert's affection for his wife was matched only by his
commitment to freemasonry. On Mimi's death in 1798, he would combine
his two loves in a marble tomb of dazzling eccentricity in the Augustinian Church in Vienna. Sculpted by Canova, it shows mourners descending through a gateway cut into the side of a masonic pyramid. In place of
the Eye of Providence, however, there is a roundel bearing Mimi's head in
profile. The mausoleum is the more shocking for its lack of any Christian
symbolism.

In 1780, Joseph II appointed Albert and Mimi as joint governors of the
Austrian Low Countries, but he also installed Count Belgiojoso as minister-
plenipotentiary, with the instruction that he execute Joseph's plans for the
comprehensive reform of church and government. The role of the governors
was thus reduced to the decorative. In any case, Joseph had shortly before
their arrival in the Low Countries undertaken his own tour there. He had
travelled without ceremony, staying in hotels, but had made time to hear
petitions, interrogate officials, and order the panels of Adam and Eve on van
Eyck's Ghent altarpiece to be removed because of their nudity (the offending
items were subsequently painted over). Although his visit was for less than
two months, Joseph was convinced of the wisdom of his observations, and
he had little time for Albert and Mimi's advice. As he explained pointedly

to them, ministers were chosen for their talents and suitability, but the only qualification for governors was that they were princes.[14]

Joseph pushed through the same church reforms as he had elsewhere, instructing toleration and civil marriage, closing 160 religious houses, forbidding most religious festivals, and centralizing the education of priests at a single seminary. As head of the new seminary, Joseph appointed the uncompromising Jansenist Ferdinand Stöger, whose research into early church history had led him to reject most Catholic theology. The students refused to register at the seminary, demonstrated on the streets, and hanged Stöger in effigy. They were dispersed by troops ordered in by Belgiojoso. Unperturbed, Joseph went on in 1787 to abolish the historic provinces, appoint intendants to administer the nine districts that replaced them, and eliminate as unnecessary many of the local courts of justice.

Joseph's reforms threatened virtually every institution and section of society. Rumours of tax rises and of conscription did the rest. On 30 May 1787, a mob invaded the centre of Brussels, amid reports of murder and plunder. Appearing in the middle of the night on a balcony overlooking the main square, Albert and Mimi stilled the crowd by promising to withdraw all Joseph's edicts. The rioters dispersed, church bells were rung, and the next day the two governors received a rapturous welcome as they toured the city by carriage. The chamberlain in Brussels was convinced that Mimi's clear-headedness had saved the day, but she was rightly apprehensive. 'God forfend', she wrote in her diary, 'that the affection shown to us will not become our undoing.'[15]

Joseph's ministers praised the governors' action, but Joseph roundly condemned it as an incomprehensible surrender. He made a few concessions, including the dismissal of Belgiojoso, but then resumed most of his previous measures and began mustering troops. To the general on the spot in the Austrian Low Countries, he wrote that there was 'no need to be afraid of setting an example of terror, and you should never threaten without acting, and still less should you shoot over their heads or fire blanks.' But the troops that Joseph intended to deploy had to be withdrawn to fight the Turks at the other end of Europe, leaving the Low Countries dangerously exposed.[16]

The revolution, so far a largely conservative one that aimed to restore the religious and political status quo, now became radicalized. Increasingly inspired by events across the border in France, 'democratic' politicians advanced a programme of social reform that went far beyond Joseph's imaginings. The conservative and radical revolutions fused in 1789, and their militias swept aside the Austrian army. Early the next year, representatives of the provinces proclaimed the United States of Belgium, which was the first time the name of Belgium had been used in an official way. By this time, Albert and Mimi were in exile and Joseph on his deathbed.

Joseph's last letter was to Mimi. It is brief but warm—he embraces her from a distance and bids her adieu. In fact, Joseph had never forgiven Mimi for stealing the affections of his mother and then of his first wife, Isabella, whom he loved dearly. But had he known of Isabella's private literary activity, he would have been shocked. Among Isabella's ruminations on death, philosophy, and commerce is a short text entitled 'A Treatise on Man.' It is a diatribe that vilifies men as 'useless animals' who are vain, egotistical narcissists, devoid of reason, which is the attribute of the female sex. Men's sole value is to highlight by their faults womanly virtue, and Isabella looks forward to women's enslavement one day becoming their superiority. Elsewhere, she laments the fate of a princess—unhappiness, servitude, and the toils of etiquette.[17]

Isabella's laments are understandable. She had been brought up in the stiff court of Parma, where women were expected to act as mindless but, in the words of the castrato singer Farinelli, 'eminently placid nymphs.' Even as nymphs, their silhouettes were rendered misshapen by the huge paniers attached to their hips, the purpose of which was to advertise both their fecundity and their family's wealth in damask. Although the fashions were the same, Vienna and the Habsburg courts were, however, different in attitude. In these, the space between the private world of female piety and childbearing was regularly intersected by archduchesses, wives, and widows crossing into the otherwise masculine public world. Their portraits stare down at us—women seated at desks, in confident pose, beside crowns, terrestrial globes, and sometimes paperwork.[18]

Yet there is no sense in which these female transgressions were considered at the time subversive of the established order or of the normally gendered hierarchy of power. In France, Maria Theresa's youngest daughter, Marie Antoinette (Maria Antonia), took from Vienna the assumption that women might play a role in the public sphere. Her blurring of the boundaries of gender left her open to the accusation of her French critics that she flouted constraints in general, so that all manner of crimes might plausibly be imputed to her—lesbianism, incest, and the corruption of politics by the boudoir. Her body, too, was said to sabotage conventions, being grotesquely deformed behind her capacious skirts. No such imaginings of moral and physical decay ever attached to Habsburg women. Nor was the power that some of them held, not least the empress herself, considered an unnatural inversion of norms. For Habsburg women, power and its legitimacy flowed from the dynasty, the greatness of which transcended biological difference.[19]

21

CENSORS, JACOBINS, AND
THE MAGIC FLUTE

*C*ensorship was originally the prerogative of the Catholic Church and was exercised by bishops, usually working in tandem with commissions composed of Jesuits. In Vienna, the university fulfilled the role of censor, which meant that the Jesuits employed there were again in charge. Well before the suppression of the Jesuits by Pope Clement XIV in the 1770s, Maria Theresa had pared back their influence, cracking down on their monopolies and on their over-elaborate processions. In 1752, she removed Jesuits from their professorial posts in the university and as censors, entrusting the task of vetting publications to a ten-man committee, headed by Gerhard van Swieten. The lists of condemned books that the committee drew up were circulated and acted as guidelines throughout the Habsburg lands.

Van Swieten's influence with the empress was formidable. As her personal doctor he was allowed considerable intimacy in respect to her physical body, and he used his privileged access and the confidence Maria Theresa had in him to put pressure on the censorship committee. So Montesquieu's *Spirit of the Laws* was eventually let through, alongside works by Montaigne, Lessing, and Diderot. Van Swieten principally censored works of a 'superstitious' religious content, French pornography, and only the most egregious attacks on the political order and on the Catholic Church. Even so, copies of prohibited books were kept and might be made available to scholars upon request—only a few were condemned outright.[1]

Joseph II took matters further, removing most restrictions after 1780. Whereas under Maria Theresa some five thousand works were still listed as banned, Joseph reduced the number to nine hundred. (The number looks large, but often the same work was published under different titles.) He also relaxed controls on the news press. The consequence was a proliferation of pamphlet literature and an effervescence of debate. Previously, only two twice-weekly newspapers had circulated in Vienna—the short-lived *Gazette de Vienne* and the *Wienerisches Diarium* (renamed the *Wiener Zeitung*, it claims to be the world's oldest newspaper still in production). Both reported foreign news without comment and reprinted court communiqués. New dailies and twice-weeklies now appeared, churning out gossip, political opinion, and reports of (literally) hair-raising experiments with electricity, magnets, and amber. Captain James Cook's voyages in the Pacific also provided a fund of good stories.[2]

Some seventy coffee shops provided venues for reading and discussion in Vienna, with the one on the Charcoal Market (Kohlmarkt), just next to the Hofburg, setting up eighty additional seats in the narrow street. Vienna began to acquire what it had hitherto lacked—a public sphere that was separate and critical of government. From the coffee shops, a new species of 'idler' (*Müssigganger*) drifted between salons, lodges, theatres, the parks, and meetings of learned societies, the variety and number of which astonished one visiting French nobleman. Libraries, too, opened. Vienna's imperial library and the library of the university were already open to the public, but aristocrats now welcomed visitors to their private collections. Booksellers and printers also functioned as lending libraries.

There was a seedy side to Vienna. A city of about two hundred thousand people, it had ten thousand 'common prostitutes', four thousand 'higher-class' courtesans, twelve thousand persons registered with syphilis, and an infant mortality of 40 per cent. The 'Stretch' (Strich) along which prostitutes touted for business extended from St Stephen's Cathedral, along the Graben thoroughfare and the Charcoal Market, and thence to the city wall and the grounds of the Hofburg. Plenty of churches along the Stretch had dark corners inside. The cheaper sex workers kept to the parks. Maria

Theresa ordered recidivist prostitutes to be deported to Hungary, where as one wag put it, 'they can only debauch Turks and infidels.' But Joseph was kinder. He had the bushes in the parks uprooted, the churches locked, and made convicted streetwalkers work as street cleaners. He instructed their heads to be shaved and that they be deprived of the broad hoop skirts by which they advertised their trade.[3]

Morality mattered. Maria Theresa instituted a Chastity Commission (Keuschheitskommission) to prosecute prostitutes in Vienna and the countryside beyond the city, but it fell into ridicule—when walking alone, honest and disreputable women alike now carried rosaries as if on their way to Mass. Even so, a chastity court under the oversight of the city council lingered on in Vienna until the beginning of the nineteenth century. The theatre was also a concern, both to Maria Theresa and to her son. Actresses were thought by vocation to be of loose morals, and itinerant players were suspicious because of their rootlessness. On top of this, the theatre was believed to communicate easy messages that influenced impressionable audiences. The ribaldries of the harlequin Jack Sausage, a mix of earthy innuendo and social satire often delivered impromptu, were considered especially harmful.[4]

Whereas the press became freer, the theatre faced increasing censorship. Joseph von Sonnenfels, who briefly served as a censor, imagined that the theatre might act to inculcate 'manners, courtesy, and language' and thus promote Enlightenment values. The censor with special responsibility for the theatre, the long-serving Karl Franz Hägelin, also defined the theatre as 'a school for manners and taste.' This meant interfering with plots that concluded unsatisfactorily. Most notoriously, a succession of playwrights rewrote the ending of Shakespeare's *Hamlet* to satisfy the censors by giving the tragedy a more uplifting and less bloody final scene. So the dying Queen Gertrude confesses to conspiring against her first husband and saves her soul, and although Hamlet still slays Claudius, he fights no deadly duel with Laertes but succeeds as king.[5]

Other productions saw lines and stage directions cut, so that lovers did not exit without chaperones, a woman's virtue was not tested in the bedroom, and dishonest conduct was never rewarded. Political constraints applied too, with words like 'liberty', 'equality', 'despotism', and 'tyrant' expunged. In Mozart's *The Marriage of Figaro*, the line 'Because you are a great lord, you believe yourself to be a great genius' had to be excised before the censor allowed the opera to be performed. The finale to act one of Mozart's

Don Giovanni, which premiered in Vienna in 1788, was also altered so that the important line 'Long Live Freedom' was replaced by the anodyne 'Long Live Jollity.'

There were originally just two theatres in Vienna. The Burgtheater (Castle Theatre) in the Hofburg was the descendant of the old wooden theatre erected by Leopold I but since transferred several times to new venues until ending up in a converted indoor tennis court. The Kärntnertortheater (Carinthian Gate Theatre), on the site of what is now the Hotel Sacher, had been taken over by the court following a fire in 1761. The two venues had different repertoires. In the Burgtheater, French and Italian opera were mostly performed, while the Kärntnertortheater showed more popular productions and ballets. Although there was some overlap of genres, comedies were almost exclusively shown in the Kärntnertortheater. During the 1770s, a few commercial theatres were given licenses. Mostly showing comedies, they were subject to the same censorship as the Burgtheater and Kärntnertortheater.

Children famously like the same story to be read out to them. The Viennese too expected the popular theatre to rehearse the same plot—a hero, attended by a harlequin, goes through various trials in a magical country. He outwits his adversaries using magical instruments, assisted by the harlequin, and they both find brides. The harlequin may be Jack Sausage, Pulcinella (a forebear of Mr Punch), or the umbrella maker Staberl—it is only important that he be ludicrously dressed, coarse, cunning, and drawn from the lower orders to act as a foil to the hero. As for setting, the main requirement was frequent shifts of set, each as exotic as the last. The changes of scenery, delivered by cranes and pulleys, earned productions of this type the name of 'mechanized comedies' (*Maschinenkomödien*).

Mozart's *The Magic Flute* premiered in 1791 in the Wieden Theatre, just outside the city wall. It is typical of 'magic opera' as well as conforming to the principles of German *Singspiel*, which interwove singing with dialogue. The story is set in ancient Egypt and involves a mysterious brotherhood, headed by an apparently evil man, Sarastro. But at the end the brotherhood turns out to be benign and Sarastro to be kindly and wise. Over two acts, the hero, the prince Tamino, aided by his companion, the bird catcher and harlequin Papageno, goes through various tests to see if he is worthy of the princess whom Sarastro keeps hidden for her own safety. Thanks to his magic flute, Tamino passes these and wins the princess. She is the daughter of the Queen of the Night, whose attempts to prevent the marriage fail. Papageno meanwhile earns Papagena, transformed by magic from a hag to a fine woman of 'eighteen years and two minutes.' They sing the famous allegro 'Pa-pa' duet together. The Queen of the Night attempts to destroy Sarastro's temple but is thrown into darkness (usually through a trap door on stage). As the sun rises, Sarastro celebrates the victory over night and a new age of wisdom and brotherhood.

The plot is elaborate and repetitive, but it comprises scarcely concealed allegories of freemasonic ritual and beliefs, loosely strung together to make an incoherent but charming whole. The principals sing only one or two arias each, since individuality counts for less than the messages the opera is intended to convey. Temples (of Reason, Nature, and Wisdom), pyramids, rites of initiation, hierophants, and other masonic symbols abound, and it may be that several of the characters are based on real freemasons—the Archduchess Maria Anna's collaborator Ignaz von Born is a plausible Sarastro. The plot crams in so much because Mozart and the librettist, Emanuel Schickaneder, wanted the opera to combine the popular idioms of German magic opera and *Singspiel*, some stunning scene sets, and the veiled messages of freemasonry.[6]

The score is also heavy with freemasonic allusions. The number three, which is the defining key in masonic ritual, is announced in the three loud chords at the beginning of the overture and in the three flats of the signature key of E flat. Slurred notes in pairs stand for the chain of brotherhood; harmony is denoted using parallel thirds and sixths, and the reconciliation of apparent opposites by counterpoint or the simultaneous playing of two melodies. The orchestral arrangement also includes the clarinet, familiar in freemasonic rituals, and relies upon the full range of instruments. As Mozart explained to his fellow freemason, Joseph Haydn, 'If each instrument does not consider the rights and properties of other instruments in relation to its own rights . . . the aim, which is beauty, will not be achieved.' Masonic views on brotherhood and equality thus influenced not only the score but also the orchestra pit.[7]

Freemasonic allusions were not confined to *The Magic Flute* but can also be found in *The Marriage of Figaro* and works by other contemporary playwrights and composers. This is not unexpected, for many theatre managers and playwrights were freemasons, including Mozart's collaborator, Schickaneder (he also played Papageno in the premiere performance of *The*

Magic Flute). Playwrights in search of inspiration most frequently turned to the prolific author of magical romances, Christoph Wieland, who was also a freemason—his collected works published in Leipzig between 1794 and 1811 run to forty-five thick volumes. The readiness of the censors to let through freemasonic works should come as no surprise either. Sonnenfels, Hägelin, and most probably van Swieten were all freemasons too.[8]

Joseph II was not a freemason, regarding freemasonry's rituals as nonsense. He was, however, alert to the way secrecy could provide a cover for sedition, on which account he required the names of lodge members to be forwarded to the police. He also rationalized the lodges, forcing them to combine, so the thirteen in the capital were reduced to three. The provincial lodges of Bohemia, Transylvania, Hungary, and the Austrian Lands were then made subordinate to the central direction of the Grand Lodge of Vienna. As one grand master noted at the time, Joseph's reforms had 'built a coordinated and ordered whole out of all the masonic bodies of the Austrian monarchy.' It is an irony that Joseph's most successful attempt at institutional unification should have been with the organization of freemasonry, which he otherwise ridiculed, and not with the apparatus of government, which he revered.[9]

As Joseph's reforms began to unravel in the second half of the 1780s and opposition to his rule gathered, the emperor toughened censorship in both the press and the theatre. Joseph now banned the improvised routines of the harlequin, imposed a special tax on newspapers, and instructed the police to investigate potential troublemakers who sought 'to undermine all religion, morality, and social order.' He also played fast and loose with the criminal law, sanctioning retrospective punishments and introducing 'precautionary custody' as a way of imprisoning without trial. The police were now made into a separate ministry and their powers defined by decrees that were never made public. The 'well-regulated state', for which reformers had striven, became in the last years of Joseph's reign a police state.

Joseph II was succeeded in 1790 by his brother Leopold II (1790–1792). Cynical and manipulative, Leopold convinced both contemporaries and subsequent generations of historians that he was thoroughly at ease with the Enlightenment, advertising to all who would listen his interest in conveying happiness and in meeting 'the general needs of humanity.' True, as grand duke of Tuscany from 1765 to 1790, he had abolished the death penalty, and he undertook his own chemical experiments with the aim of finding new compounds that would be useful to industry (his stained workbench is on view in the Museum for the History of Science in Florence). But his earnest discussions over constitutions never resulted in a constitution for Tuscany, while his promise to give a full financial reckoning of his rule amounted to the publication of just one year's budget. In a review of his government of Tuscany, he praised his prudential elimination of the state debt, but he had achieved this only by cancelling three-quarters of government bonds. His doctrinaire embrace of free trade had, meanwhile, wiped out much of Florence's nascent manufacturing industry.[10]

Leopold mounted a ruthless campaign to suppress the opposition. He made peace with the Turks, returning Belgrade, and used the released troops to restore his sister Mimi and her husband in the Low Countries. To settle the Hungarians, he threatened the division of the kingdom but sweetened them by affirming that Hungary 'shall be a free kingdom and independent in respect of its entire lawful administration, that is not subject to any other kingdom or people but having its own political existence and constitution.' He went on to establish ten committees of the Hungarian diet to work out exactly what the Hungarian constitution was. Confusing a constitution with legislation, the committees produced ten volumes of laws that they regarded as either fundamental or desirable, but it was not until the 1830s that any of these were converted into statute.[11]

Leopold had initially greeted the French Revolution as providing for a constitutional monarchy in France, but he was shocked by its descent into demagoguery and violence. The revolutionary leaders voided all the remaining rights of German princes in Alsace, which amounted to a repudiation of the terms of the Peace of Westphalia, and they kept Leopold's sister, Marie Antoinette, in what amounted to imprisonment. The integrity of the Holy Roman Empire and brotherly instinct pushed Leopold into the arms of Prussia, whose king, Frederick William II, reckoned that by launching a war on France he could expand his territories on the Rhine. In August 1791, Leopold met Frederick William at Pillnitz, near Dresden. The two rulers, joined by the elector of Saxony, declared the fate of the French monarchy to be of concern to all monarchs. Unless the National Assembly in Paris restored Louis XVI's rights, they would use force.

The Declaration of Pillnitz produced an outcry in France, propelling the Girondist 'war party' into power. As one Girondist deputy exclaimed, 'The mask has fallen. Our enemy is now known—it is the emperor.' The French foreign minister demanded an assurance that Leopold wished 'to live in peace' with France, but Prince Kaunitz in Vienna gave no such undertaking. Meanwhile, companies of French aristocratic émigrés ostentatiously mustered in the Rhineland, adding to the war fever in Paris. On 1 March 1792, Leopold II unexpectedly died of a stroke, to be succeeded by his son, the young Francis II (ruled 1792–1835). The next month, France declared war.[12]

The French Revolutionary Wars were a vortex that drew in most of Europe and led to more than two decades of fighting. The revolutionary identification of state, nation, and people proved equally giddying, capturing idealists and malcontents alike in its undertow. Some, like the pastor's son on the Swiss border who in his Sunday best addressed the arriving French troops with a speech extolling republican virtues, were just naïve—the soldiers promptly divested him of his pocket watch, boots, and waistcoat. Others, like the 'clubbists' and Cisrhenans in Mainz and the Rhineland, were a real danger, for they intrigued to found revolutionary republics and welcomed what they called 'the reception of that blissful happiness, which French arms have offered us.' So too was the popular revolutionary movement of the Carbonari in Italy. A sort of freemasonry resting upon the supposed rites of charcoal burners, the Carbonari looked forward to founding an 'Ausonian Republic' free of foreign rule and to the overthrow of all tyrants.[13]

Governments throughout Europe were convinced that French revolutionary sentiment, known by the catch-all term of 'Jacobinism', constituted a real threat. The guillotining of both Louis XVI and Marie Antoinette in 1793 was especially shocking, for it showed what might be expected of Jacobin rule. But the authorities lacked the mechanisms by which to establish just how large the domestic threat was. Within the Habsburg lands, the police exaggerated the scale of opposition, confusing the 'itch to criticize' with subversion. Not a few of the plots they uncovered were of their own making and intended to trap would-be conspirators. Others were the fanciful inventions of attention seekers. Nevertheless, Francis II and his ministers strengthened police powers, permitted detention without trial, and applied an indiscriminate censorship that eventually caught Bunyan's *Pilgrim's Progress*, Defoe's *Gulliver's Travels*, and Mary Shelley's *Frankenstein*.

Instructions to the police circulated in 1793 included the closure of all 'secret conventicles', because of which all freemasonic lodges were shut. A few lodges lingered on, posing as societies, but their extravagant names often gave them away. Even so, there were periodic panics in government at the discovery of lodges in areas that were thought to have been cleansed. The ostensible collapse of freemasonry in the 1790s is the more remarkable given its recovery and efflorescence first in 1848 and then in the 1860s, when controls were relaxed. Perhaps, as seems to have been the case in Transylvania, freemasonry had never really been rooted out but only become dormant.[14]

Clearly, some plotting was going on. A few Austrian and Hungarian Jacobins opened channels to the French, but most confined their activity to writing manifestoes and vulgar ditties, such as:

> *The people aren't just bog roll but can do their own thinking.*
> *If you won't learn good manners, you'll be hanged like a lout.*
> *Off to the guillotine, blood for blood.*
> *Had we a guillotine here, a lot of big men would pay.*[15]

One of the earliest plots involved the distribution of proclamations by '100,000 specially trained dogs' (even the authorities did not take it seriously). Another included the construction of a war machine of spikes mounted around an axle, for use by peasants against mounted attack. Since the conspirators had no contacts in the countryside, it was never built, let alone used. In 1794, several score of the more prominent Jacobins were arrested and put on trial. Embarrassingly, it turned out that several had been enlisted by Leopold II to write revolutionary tracts as a way of intimidating the Hungarian nobility. There was one execution in Vienna and seven in Hungary. Most of those tried were either found not guilty or pardoned. The long prison terms given to the remainder were subsequently commuted.[16]

The significance of the Jacobin trials was larger than the paltry threat posed by the conspirators, for they proved that some plotting was indeed going on and justified the extension of censorship and police powers. Discussion of politics now became dangerous. With its cultivation of manners and of the art of conversation, Vienna's salon society fostered educated opinion on music, literature, philosophy, and the theatre. While gossip about politicians was permitted, however, controversial political opinions were not. A public sphere continued to exist, but the gristle of political criticism had been stripped from it, leaving it flabby and intellectually unchallenging.

Educated society turned away from the salon and towards domesticity and the simplicities of the Biedermeier (so-called after a fictional petit bourgeois), with its Schubert *Lieder* sung around a piano, uncomplicated furniture, bright waistcoats, and innocuous amusements. French, long prized as the métier of the educated and culturally sophisticated, gave way to everyday German, while family outings to the park at weekends or to eat cake replaced days spent in coffee houses, libraries, and lodges. As much as anything, the war with France that had begun in 1792 had left everyone poorer, while rents in Vienna had more than trebled in the 1780s and 1790s. Even so, the number of prostitutes continued to climb, reaching twenty thousand in the capital by 1820.[17]

The monarchy also became respectably middle class. Whereas Joseph II had always worn a military uniform, Emperor Francis went shopping in a frock coat, while the empress, Caroline Augusta, cultivated the image of a dutiful housewife. Court artists responded to the new style, composing portraits of the imperial family at leisure, with babies squabbling at their feet and infants engaged in dangerously unsupervised scientific experiments. In Peter Fendi's 'Archduchess Sophie praying', Emperor Francis's daughter-in-law is shown gathering her children before a crucifix, with discarded toys on the floor. Stripped of its Baroque ornamentation, the traditions of Austrian piety were also absorbed into the Biedermeier.

The theatre changed as well, towards romantic opera, heralded by Weber's *Der Freischütz* ('The Marksman'), which was performed in Vienna in 1821, the same year as its Berlin premiere. Italian opera, and Rossini in particular, was also favoured. Mozart, however, fell out of fashion, even though the press continued to laud him as 'the Shakespeare of music.' Back in 1790, Mozart's comic opera *Così fan tutte* had the highest box office receipts of the season. In the new century, it was seldom performed and, when revived in 1840, went through only seven performances. Even *The Magic Flute* lost its popularity. When after a four-year gap it opened in the Kärntnertortheater in 1827, it was only because another production had been cancelled. By this time, however, it is doubtful that anyone in the audience understood the allegories in its libretto and score. Censorship and the police had drained Mozart's greatest opera of both meaning and intention.[18]

22

METTERNICH AND THE
MAP OF EUROPE

*C*lemens von Metternich came to office as Austrian foreign minister in 1809. A Rhinelander who had lost all to revolutionary France and Napoleon, his debts were at the time of his appointment reckoned at 1.25 million gulden. His master, Emperor Francis II (1792–1835), was bankrupt too. Unable to redeem the state bonds he had issued, Francis survived financially only by printing money and by the expedient of confiscating his subjects' silverware in exchange for lottery tickets. The debt owed by the imperial treasury in 1809 amounted to 1,200 million gulden, to which should be added a further 1,000 million gulden in unbacked paper notes. Two years later, Francis would declare bankruptcy, reneging on all but 20 per cent of the state debt, busting in the process many manufacturing and agricultural enterprises.[1]

Francis's territorial capital had withered too. At first, Francis's armies, led by the emperor's brother, Archduke Charles, had almost held their own against the French during the long War of the First Coalition (1792–1797), bearing the brunt of the land war in alliance with Great Britain, Prussia, and the Dutch Republic. Although obliged to give up the Austrian Low Countries and Lombardy, the Habsburgs were compensated by the terms of the Peace of Campo Formio (1797) with Venice and its hinterland of Venetia, Istria, and Dalmatia. Venice's strategically vital Ionian Islands in the Adriatic went, however, to France, with the island of Corfu now having Europe's largest fort. Its enlargement presaged the major expansion of French power into the Eastern Mediterranean that led to Napoleon's invasion of Egypt in 1798.

Napoleon became first consul of France in 1799 and, five years later, emperor of the French. His ambition was to enlarge France beyond its natural boundaries, to create a barrier beyond it of satellites, and to maintain on the periphery a cordon of enfeebled and compliant states. In pursuit of this goal, he pulled the Habsburg territories apart. As the British prime minister William Pitt the Younger presciently observed in 1805, upon hearing of the Habsburg and Russian defeat at Austerlitz, 'Roll up that map, it will not be needed these ten years.' Following Francis II's participation in the wars of the Second and Third Coalition against Napoleon (1798–1802; 1803–1806), in both of which Francis was obliged to sue for an early peace, the Habsburgs not only lost almost all they had gained at Campo Formio but also surrendered the Tyrol to Napoleon's Bavarian ally and the remaining Austrian possessions in the old duchy of Swabia (Further Austria) to Baden and Württemberg. The only consolation was Salzburg, which Francis annexed in 1805.[2]

Francis stood aside from the War of the Fourth Coalition (1806–1807), but hoping to take advantage of Napoleon's discomfiture in Spain, where the French were bogged down in a long war of attrition, he joined with Britain in April 1809 to renew the struggle. Napoleon reacted, however, by speedily taking Vienna. Then, building a pontoon bridge across the Danube, he caught Archduke Charles unawares, forcing him to commit to battle prematurely. The Battle of Wagram, fought on a fifteen-mile front over two days in July 1809, was not decisive, and the archduke was able to withdraw his troops in good order, but it had used up the whole of Habsburg resources, obliging Francis to seek peace. The Treaty of Schönbrunn was devastating. Croatia together with Trieste, Gorizia (Görz-Gradisca), Carniola, and a part of Carinthia were now transformed into the Illyrian Provinces, which Napoleon made a part of France. West Galicia, which Francis had taken in the final Third Partition of Poland (1795), was absorbed into the puppet Duchy of Warsaw, and a further slice of Galicia was ceded to Napoleon's latest ally, Alexander I of Russia.

But Francis's losses in the wars with Napoleon were more than territorial. In May 1804, Napoleon had crowned himself emperor of the French in Paris. In order, so he claimed, to maintain parity with Napoleon, Francis II now declared himself to be emperor of Austria, thus adding a hereditary imperial title to the elected dignity of Holy Roman Emperor. It was a wise move. Just two years later, Napoleon established the Confederation of the Rhine, appointing himself as its president. Bavaria, Württemberg, Baden, and thirteen smaller states promptly defected from the Holy Roman Empire to join the confederation. Noting that 'circumstances have rendered it impossible to discharge the commitments made at my imperial election', Emperor Francis now formally declared the bond that joined him to the 'state entities of the German Empire to be dissolved.'

Without a ruler, the thousand-year-old Holy Roman Empire came to an end. Even so, Francis's decree of dissolution, published on 6 August 1806, commenced by reciting his titles as Holy Roman Emperor, including the designation 'at all times Enlarger of the Empire.' Fortunately, by having previously instituted the title of emperor of Austria, the Habsburgs were able to keep hold of an imperial title. But their numbering changed. So Holy Roman Emperor Francis II became Austrian Emperor Francis I; his successor became Ferdinand I rather than Ferdinand V, and so on.[3]

Francis did, however, take over the double-headed imperial eagle, in use since the fifteenth century, and the imperial colours of black and yellow, making these purely Habsburg symbols. In the case of yellow, it curiously became a Brazilian one too. In 1817, Francis's daughter, Leopoldine (1797–1826), married Prince Pedro of Portugal during his family's exile in Brazil. Following Pedro's declaration of Brazilian independence in 1822, it fell to her to design the country's flag. Leopoldine duly combined the yellow of the Habsburg flag with the green of the Portuguese and Brazilian house of Braganza. Brazil's football team still plays in Habsburg colours.[4]

As ambassador to Paris, Metternich had warned against a new war with the French, considering it reckless. Vindicated by Wagram and by the harsh terms Napoleon imposed, it was no surprise that Emperor Francis should have appointed him foreign minister in 1809. Metternich's main concern at this point was to buy time, on which account he urged a policy of peace towards France. The emperor concurred, to the extent of sacrificing his daughter Marie Louise by having her marry the upstart Corsican commoner. Even she was third best, for Napoleon had previously been looking at two Russian princesses, but the first turned him down, and the second never obtained her father's approval.

An elegant dandy, Metternich was as much at home in the boudoir as the conference hall. But Metternich's liaisons allowed him intimacies of more than one kind. A notorious and indiscreet gossip, he also traded secrets. When he needed to know more, he simply arranged for the diplomatic mail to be opened. Most spectacularly, after 1808 Metternich had the former French foreign minister and state councillor Talleyrand in his pocket. The information which Talleyrand passed on, including military dispositions, went straight to Emperor Francis as evidence obtained from 'Monsieur X.'[5]

Between March and September 1810, Metternich was in Paris, officially as part of the delegation attending Napoleon's marriage. He used the opportunity to fathom Napoleon's intentions, frequently staying up with him until four AM while Napoleon rehearsed his genius. It was clear to Metternich that Napoleon's ambition had not yet been sated, but his next move was uncertain. On 20 September, in Napoleon's palace at St Cloud, the emperor of the French disclosed his aim to conquer Russia. 'I had at last obtained light,' Metternich later recalled. 'The object of my stay in Paris was attained.' Four days later, he left for Vienna.[6]

Metternich planned carefully. The outcome of a Franco-Russian war was uncertain, and to back either or neither side invited danger. So Metternich opted instead for 'armed neutrality': he would support Napoleon, but only against Russia and not in the main assault. Behind the scenes, he advised Tsar Alexander that the Habsburg army would only play a supporting role. As it turned out, the army led by Prince Schwarzenberg acquitted itself so well that the tsar lodged a protest with Francis.

The campaign of 1812 saw Napoleon commit what was then the largest ever army in the history of warfare—about six hundred thousand men, of which only thirty thousand were under Schwarzenberg's command. Although the French reached Moscow, they were by October in headlong retreat and eating their horses. Generals January and February did the rest. In the wake of the retreat from Moscow, Napoleon's adversaries regathered, joining together in 1813 to form the Sixth Coalition. Although Napoleon managed to organize a new army, he was decisively defeated at Leipzig at the so-called Battle of the Nations by a combination of Habsburg, Russian, Swedish, and Prussian forces (Saxony and Württemberg defected halfway through the four-day battle to join the winning coalition).

As the allies pressed westwards into France and British forces crossed the Pyrenees from Spain, Talleyrand in Paris seized the initiative. Leading what was left of the French senate, he declared himself head of a provisional government and Napoleon to be deposed. Talleyrand then proclaimed the Bourbon dynasty restored by the people of France 'of their own, free will.' Louis XVIII objected to Talleyrand's interpretation, for he considered himself to rule by divine right, irrespective of his people's wishes, but the restoration of the Bourbon monarchy was entirely to Metternich's satisfaction. With Russian troops deployed as far west as Calais and thus within eyeshot of the English coast, Metternich had already discerned that Russia was now the leading continental power; he saw a strong and stable France as a counterweight.

The map of Europe was repaired at the great international conference, or congress, which met in Vienna from November 1814 to July 1815. The congress was by every measure an apogee of Habsburg power, however much the long wars had also been fought by others. Its proceedings were halted for several months during the 'Hundred Days', when Napoleon escaped from Elba (as Metternich had predicted) briefly to recapture power in France. The Congress of Vienna brought together two emperors, four kings, eleven ruling princes, and two hundred plenipotentiaries. There were daily banquets, either in the Hofburg or in Metternich's chancellery building, balls, hunting expeditions, portrait sittings, operas, and concerts. Beethoven conducted in person his Seventh Symphony—it was an expiation of sorts for his Third, the *Eroica*, which he had ten years earlier dedicated to Napoleon.

Metternich got much of what he wanted. Most of the Habsburg territories were returned, and although the Low Countries were lost, there was compensation in the form of Lombardy and Venetia, which were now combined to make the Kingdom of Lombardy-Venetia within the Austrian Empire. Along with Venetia came Dubrovnik and Venice's other possessions on the Dalmatian coast. Tuscany and Modena, although not incorporated in the Habsburg lands, continued to be governed by archdukes drawn from the Habsburg line, while Parma was given over to Francis's daughter, Marie Louise, the estranged wife of Napoleon. The congress additionally recognized the annexation of Salzburg and gave over a sliver of Bavaria. It further restored Galicia and Lodomeria to Habsburg rule, although with some territorial adjustments, including the loss of Cracow, which now became a free city.

Importantly too, France was not punished but returned to its borders in 1792, and Saxony was not sacrificed to Prussia. The Holy Roman Empire was not restored either, but a German Confederation, which included the Austrian lands, was put in its place under Habsburg presidency. The royal titles bestowed by Napoleon on the rulers of Saxony, Bavaria, and Württemberg were retained, and Hanover was given one too. The congress also permitted the bigger German principalities to keep the smaller ones that they had gobbled up during the recent war, reducing the new confederation to just thirty-four members (several others joined later). In so doing, Metternich ensured that the German Confederation had enough capacity to resist French and Russian encroachments, as well as to hem Prussia in.[7]

The overall result of these changes was that the new Austrian Empire comprised a concentrated block of territory in Central Europe, with extensive influence northwards over the German Confederation, and southwards into Italy. It was enough to keep Russia and France apart and for the Austrian Empire to hold the balance between the two. It was a masterful redrawing of the map of Europe. A grateful Emperor Francis rewarded Metternich with the castle of Johannisberg in the Rhineland—he had in 1813 been given the honorific title of prince and would in 1821 receive the equally honorific office of chancellor.

Metternich was never less than duplicitous. Notoriously, in communicating with his ambassadors abroad, Metternich would send three letters. The first would announce a policy position; the second would indicate to whom it should be disclosed, and the third would give the real policy. Metternich continually referred to his principles, his interest in maintaining the rule of legitimate monarchs, and his goal of a lasting peace and balance of power in Europe. Like so much else, none of these were his true aims. Metternich's interest was to maintain the influence of his master and of the newly proclaimed Austrian Empire, particularly in respect of the German Confederation and Italy. His stress on legitimacy was a cover for maintaining the status quo, which he had stacked to Austria's advantage. When it came to the legitimate rights of Spain to its rebellious Latin American colonies, of the Poles to their historic kingdom, or of the city of Cracow to independence (he sent in troops to occupy it in 1846), Metternich was uninterested.[8]

Metternich always stood close to the emperor, generally keeping him abreast of events and policy, although often filtered and filleted in such a way as to earn his approval. Metternich advertised his relationship to Francis as if they were political twins. As he remarked, 'Heaven has placed me next to a man who might have been created for me, as I for him. The Emperor Francis knows what he wants and that never differs in any way from what I most want.' Francis seems to have concurred, although he explained that Metternich was the kindlier of them. In truth, Francis had better things to do than pore over dispatches. His interest was instead to examine the sealing wax that had been used on them. An eager student of wax production, he reputedly delayed opening letters from Napoleon until he had scrutinized the wax used to close them. Making bird cages, lacquer boxes, and toffee also occupied his time, as did the glasshouses of the Schönbrunn.[9]

The 'Big Four' at the congress were Tsar Alexander, Metternich, Prince Hardenberg for Prussia, and Lord Castlereagh for Great Britain, but Talleyrand also had an influence that was often decisive. Following the Congress of Vienna, the four agreed to meet periodically 'for the purpose of consulting upon their common interests . . . for the repose and prosperity of nations, and for the maintenance of the peace of Europe.' Tsar Alexander added to this his own plan for a brotherly bond of peoples, based on the 'sublime truths' of Christianity. Metternich famously described the tsar's Holy Alliance as a 'resounding nothing', but he deftly changed the text of the tsar's plan from a union of peoples to a union of sovereigns, thus once more stamping the monarchical status quo on the map of Europe.[10]

Defending the status quo and upholding the rights of legitimate rulers obliged the four powers and France to intervene whenever the threat of revolution presented itself. This suited Metternich, since it permitted Austria to march into Piedmont and Naples in 1821 to defend their monarchs, thereby enlarging Habsburg influence in the peninsula. It was, however, unwelcome to politicians in Britain and France, who found themselves committed to support all established governments, including those which resisted even the slightest reforms. Metternich's attempts to extend the guarantee to include Ottoman Turkey exemplified the British predicament—that, as Castlereagh foresaw, a 'general European police' was intended to act as 'the armed guardians of all thrones.'[11]

Four congresses met between 1818 and 1822, at Aachen, Opava (Troppau) in Austrian Silesia, Ljubljana (Laibach) in Carniola, and Verona in Venetia. The last three were held within the Austrian Empire, thus acknowledging Metternich's influence and making it easier for him to open the diplomatic mail. But unlike Russia, Britain and France were increasingly unwilling to be drawn into the business of defending unpopular rulers against their subjects. With the main powers divided on the principle of intervention, the congress system fell apart. A precedent of sorts had, however, been established that international crises might be better resolved through conferences than by going to war.

After 1822, Metternich increasingly relied for support on Prussia and Russia, cementing an uneasy alliance of the three 'northern courts' of Vienna, Berlin, and St Petersburg. (Europe was still at this time thought to be divided north-south rather than east-west). Meeting at Münchengrätz and Berlin in 1833, Emperor Francis, Tsar Nicholas of Russia, and Prince Frederick William of Prussia agreed to maintain 'the conservative system as the unquestionable basis of their policies', and they affirmed that all rulers were entitled to call upon one another for military aid.

With the acquisition of Venice and its Adriatic possessions, the Habsburgs had inherited a navy, comprising in 1814 ten ships of the line with several gun decks, and nine smaller frigates. At first, the fledgling fleet languished in disrepair, being mainly used to carry mail and ferry sightseers along the coast. Gradually, however, its value became apparent: to convey the archduchess Leopoldine to Brazil in 1817 and a few years later to cement a new commercial treaty with China. So unused were the Chinese to Habsburg vessels that they did not recognize the red-and-white naval standard introduced by Joseph II, obliging the captain to hoist instead the old black and yellow flag of the Holy Roman Empire with the double-headed eagle.[12]

The fleet proved its value in 1821 when it supported land operations in the invasion of Naples. It was also deployed against Greek corsairs who plundered merchant shipping to support an insurrection in the Peloponnese. By the late 1820s, the Habsburgs had more than twenty vessels patrolling the Aegean Sea and Eastern Mediterranean. It was, however, the activities of Moroccan pirates that gave the navy sudden importance. In 1828, the sultan of Morocco repudiated his agreement not to molest Habsburg shipping and began attacking commercial vessels passing through the Mediterranean on their way to Brazil. One of these was the *Veloce* bound for Rio de Janeiro out of Trieste, whose crew were held for ransom. To rescue the men, Metternich ordered two corvettes and a two-masted brig with several hundred troops aboard to sail to the Moroccan coast. The expedition was a resounding success, culminating in the bombardment of the port of El Araich. Shortly after, the sultan renewed his treaty with Emperor Francis.[13]

The navy remained, nevertheless, small, comprising in 1837 just four frigates with single gun decks, five corvettes, a paddle steamer, and some smaller vessels. The merchant marine, by contrast, comprised five hundred large commercial vessels, and from Venice, Trieste, and Rijeka (Fiume) it dominated commerce with the Ottoman Empire and North Africa. Many of its ships belonged to two companies in the establishment of which Metternich was active: the Danube Steamship Company, founded in 1829, and the Austrian Lloyd, which was incorporated in 1836.[14] Both were engaged in the Black Sea and East Mediterranean trade, and Metternich pushed the Ottoman sultan to grant preferential terms to Austrian merchants in the trade in cotton and silk. When the pasha, or governor, of Egypt, Mohammed Ali, attacked Ottoman Syria in 1839, Metternich instructed the Austrian fleet to join the British navy in bombarding Beirut and blockading the Nile delta in support of the sultan. The pasha subsequently agreed to open his territories to European merchants, of which the Austrians were the first to establish themselves.

Austrian ships not only transported cotton and silk but also took charge of much local commerce in the Eastern Mediterranean, including the movement of grain and other agricultural produce. They were also deeply implicated in the slave trade, transporting captives from Alexandria in Egypt to the markets of Istanbul and Izmir (Smyrna). Although figures on the slave trade are speculative, about a million Africans were transported to the Eastern Mediterranean in the nineteenth century. Of these, many tens of thousands travelled in ships of the Austrian Lloyd. Indeed, investigations as late as the 1870s disclosed that there was not a single Austrian Lloyd vessel working the Alexandria to Istanbul route that was not carrying slaves. A few of the wretches ended up in Vienna, working there as household servants under the description of 'persons of unclear legal status.'[15]

Austrian commercial expansion in the East Mediterranean was a colonial venture without territories. It bore many of the hallmarks of the more visible colonial empires in terms of its economic exploitation of indigenous resources and the paternalistic zeal of the diplomats and entrepreneurs who oversaw its expansion. They came not only to found trading depots but also to convert, bringing an iron gunboat down the White Nile in support of Catholic missionaries. Since the Habsburg emperor also acted as the protector of Catholics in Egypt and the Sudan, the extension of the faith increased his political weight there. The Geographical Society in Vienna was happy to record in 1857 that the Austrian flag had been planted only three degrees north of the Equator and looked forward to the steady development under its shadow of 'Christianity and civilization.'[16]

As Habsburg merchants pressed southwards into Africa, they found the local population uninterested in the manufactured wares, textiles, and umbrellas that they put up for sale. So they traded currency instead, mostly the large silver coins known as Maria Theresa thalers. First minted in 1741, the thaler stabilized in design and content in 1783, bearing the date 1780 to commemorate the year of the empress's death. Of a good silver content and impressively sculpted, the Maria Theresa thaler became the medium of exchange in Ethiopia, the Horn of Africa, and the Indian Ocean, being used to buy gold, ivory, coffee, civet oil (for perfumes), and slaves. It was, as one Ethiopian slave girl remarked in the 1830s, the coin 'which serves to buy children and men', but it was also, when threaded on a wire, a neck ornament and the medium through which local rulers collected tax. The Maria Theresa thaler remained an official currency in Ethiopia until 1945, in Muscat and Oman until 1970, and continues to this day in informal circulation as far afield as Indonesia.[17]

Metternich himself observed that he 'may have governed Europe occasionally, but Austria never.' His principal sphere was foreign policy and, since they were regarded as almost foreign countries, Hungary and Lombardy-Venetia. The plans he put forward for the administrative reform of the Austrian Empire were neglected by the emperor. Metternich's bugbears were the committees of state, which examined policy in laborious detail and proceeded by taking votes. Far better, he thought, to have ministers with real power, who coordinated policy between themselves. But Emperor Francis opposed him. 'I want no changes, our laws are sound and sufficient' and 'The time is not suitable for innovations' were comments typical of Francis's political immobility.[18]

Both Francis and Metternich agreed that there was a revolutionary threat to the Austrian Empire and to the established order in Europe. They were mistaken only in one respect, for the revolutionary threat was not coordinated by a secret committee in Paris, as they and many other statesmen imagined, but operated more loosely, almost in the manner of modern terrorist 'franchises.' Many of the revolutionary leaders in Naples, Spain, Russian Poland, the Balkans, and Latin America knew each other, fought in each other's wars, and circulated to one another draft constitutions and revolutionary manifestoes. They operated secretively through cells and so-called societies of friends, which borrowed from freemasonry their rites of admission, system of passwords, and bloodthirsty oaths.[19]

Metternich used Austria's presidency of the German Confederation to push through a programme of censorship that applied throughout its territory, exempting only works of more than 320 pages, since these were thought too tiring for readers and censors alike (not 20 pages as historians often allege, but 20 *Bogenseiten*—that is, folded quires of 16 printed sides). He additionally forced the German rulers to clamp down on political organizations, demonstrations, and representative institutions that trespassed on their sovereignty. In the Austrian Empire, however, censorship was patchy, since there were only twenty-five censors employed in Vienna with responsibility for ten thousand titles a year. The liberal *Allgemeine Zeitung*, published in Augsburg, and the Leipzig *Grenzboten* circulated freely, with only occasional issues being confiscated, while the official *Wiener Zeitung* published foreign news both extensively and impartially.[20]

Generally, repression was light, since Metternich preferred to monitor opinion through informers and surveillance than to prevent it forming. He recalled fondly his childhood tutor, 'one of the best of men', who had gone over to revolutionary republicanism, and he had no wish to punish errant convictions. There were political prisoners, but they had usually done something wrong, either through belonging to a banned society or by actively plotting insurrection, rather than just holding the wrong opinions. Even in Lombardy-Venetia, a hotbed of conspiracy, Metternich's officials put more trust in La Scala than in the police, reckoning that just as the circus had tamed the ancient Romans, so the opera might make Italians more pliant. In Hungary and Transylvania, Metternich had the ringleaders of the liberal opposition—Louis Kossuth, László Lovassy, and Nicholas Wesselényi—gaoled in 1837 on charges of sedition. But they were held in fairly comfortable conditions in the Špilberk (Spielberg) prison in southern Moravia and amnestied after three years.[21]

The most determined opposition to Metternich's rule came, however, from within government itself. The bureaucracy continued to be infused with reformist zeal and to push for the improvement of society. Despite Emperor Francis's resistance to innovation, the bureaucracy's achievements were remarkable: a new code of criminal law in 1803; a civil code in 1811, which removed the distinctive legal status of the nobility; new technical and mining colleges; and support for ambitious commercial and industrial undertakings, particularly railway construction and the laying of telegraph lines. Obliged to take an annual oath that they were not members of secret societies, the bureaucrats joined the next best thing, which were the reading clubs, where foreign newspapers and banned books circulated with police approval. Of the thousand or so senior officials in Vienna, some two hundred were members of the Legal and Political Reading Union, where they could read Rousseau, the works of the early Swiss communists, and even *Il Progresso*, the mouthpiece of revolutionary Young Italy.[22]

The bureaucrats pressed for the abolition of peasant servitude and for tenant farmers to be given the land they cultivated. But that meant compensating the landlords, which would use up resources otherwise earmarked for the army. Metternich's foreign policy rested on the possibility of intervention, so he was in favour of a large military budget. The bureaucrats accordingly looked to Metternich's rival in the administration, Count Kolowrat-Liebsteinsky, who had the main responsibility for financial affairs. Kolowrat was no reformer, but he was no fool either. As he remarked to Metternich, 'Your instruments are force of arms and the rigid maintenance of existing conditions. In my view, this will lead to revolution.' By cutting military expenditures, Kolowrat briefly balanced the budget for 1830–1831, on which account his political influence grew disproportionately.[23]

In 1835 Francis was succeeded by his son, Ferdinand. Childhood rickets had left Ferdinand with epilepsy and a deformed skull, but his principal disability as a ruler was his complete lack of interest in affairs of state. Like several of his forebears, Ferdinand's preoccupation was botany—the genus of flowering tropical plants called *Ferdinandusa* was named in his honour. On his deathbed, Francis advised Ferdinand 'to govern and not to change', but he wisely instituted a regency council or state conference to act on Ferdinand's behalf. The state conference became the vehicle whereby Kolowrat consistently impeded Metternich, blocking any expansion of the military budget but failing also to relieve the condition of the peasantry for fear of unravelling the state's finances. Following a bloody uprising in Galicia in 1846, in which the peasants massacred their lords, collecting their heads by the wagon load, the need for reform in the countryside became urgent, but the state conference was frozen by wrangling and by its inability to reach decisions.

During Ferdinand's reign (1835–1848), Metternich lost control of internal policy, to such an extent that many of the repressive features of the period were not of his creation but the work of Kolowrat or of his close allies in the state conference. Even so, it was Metternich who was identified with all the shortcomings of government as well as of the international order. In Stendhal's *The Red and the Black* (1830), the exiled Count Altamira discards the beautiful Mathilde at a ball to speak instead to a Peruvian general, because 'he so despairs of Europe as Metternich had organized it.' Anton von Auersperg's political poem *Walks of a Viennese Poet* (1831) has the Austrian people hammering on Metternich's door begging to be let free. Indeed, by 1848 Metternich had in popular discourse become 'the chief blood-sucker of all blood-sucking ministers', 'the wicked demon', and 'money swallowing, drinking the blood of the people.'[24]

Yet Metternich's achievement lies on the map of Europe. Cast aside by Napoleon, it was restored by him, and he gave the new Austrian Empire a commanding position in the centre, from which it might even spill Maria Theresa thalers into Africa. The borders that Metternich helped draw up in Vienna in 1814–1815, and that he strove to maintain, survived to the extent of forming the broad outline of the European state system until 1914. With a stable core, Europe's great-power conflicts were 'peripheralized', and moved eastwards to the Ottoman Empire and southwards into colonial rivalries. Between 1815 and 1914 there were just four European wars, all of them short, whereas between 1700 and 1790 there had been at least sixteen major wars involving several or more leading powers. Metternich did not bring peace to Europe, but he gave Europe the foundation on which its statesmen might choose peace if they wanted it. Guided by Metternich, the Austrian Empire emerged from the marginal status accorded it by Napoleon to the main arbiter of Europe and, for almost forty years, a bastion against revolutionary disorder.[25]

1848: VON NEUMANN'S DIARY AND RADETZKY'S MARCH

*B*aron Philipp von Neumann was an Austrian diplomat cast in Metternich's mould. With his coiffed hair and prominent nose, he even resembled his master. For more than three decades, Neumann was councillor and chargé in the Austrian embassy at Chandos House in London. After a string of affairs, he married in his early sixties Lady Augusta Somerset, who was the great niece of the Duke of Wellington. At the end of 1844, Neumann took Augusta to Florence, where he had been appointed ambassador. It was, however, in nearby Modena that he learned in February 1848 of the outbreak of revolution in France. The entries in his diary, normally a recitation of balls attended and important people met, became increasingly agitated as the ferment crossed Europe: 'In France the revolutionary party has proclaimed a republic (1 March). . . . It is added that Belgium is made a republic and King Leopold has left Brussels (3 March). . . . The police report that a rising is planned for tomorrow at Modena, Reggio, and Parma (6 March). . . . Bad news from Germany where the revolutionary movement is spreading (14 March).' Finally, Neumann received the message he had been dreading: 'The Archduke Ferdinand

(Prince of Modena) sent for me and communicated very sad news from Vienna . . . (18 March).'[1]

As Neumann's diary suggests, the outbreak of revolution in Vienna was no less shocking because it was expected. As governments and monarchs were toppled across Europe, the vulnerability of the established order stood exposed, demands for reform became shriller, and copycat uprisings more likely. When on 13 March the diet of Lower Austria convened in its magnificent new palace in the centre of Vienna, everyone expected trouble, and many made sure that they were there to see it. Much of what followed had been planned. Having stormed the building and dispersed the diet's deputies, students harangued the crowds below from a first-floor balcony. Groups of thugs recruited from the suburbs added muscle, turning a noisy demonstration into a riot. The military commander on the spot, Emperor Ferdinand's cousin Archduke Albrecht, implored the crowds to disperse but was hit on the head. For several hours his troops put up with a hail of rocks until a group of Italian soldiers broke rank and opened fire. Four people were shot dead, a law student was bayonetted, and an old woman was crushed to death in the panic.

By nightfall, Vienna was in chaos. Mobs looted shops and workplaces in the suburbs, assaulting the well-to-do, and breaking into bakeries and tobacconists. In the centre, rioters pulled up the street lights to use them as battering rams and lit the escaping gas at pavement level to send sheets of flame into the darkness. Outside the Hofburg, crowds eerily gathered, cheering the emperor. But another drama was going on inside the palace. For several days, Metternich's enemies in the imperial family had been planning to use any disturbance as a pretext for forcing him from power. In a choreographed action organized by Emperor Ferdinand's sister-in-law, Archduchess Sophie, the foes now closed in, pressing Metternich for his resignation. With his political ally, Ferdinand's uncle Archduke Ludwig, now siding with Sophie (Ludwig feared the Hofburg would soon be invaded), Metternich reluctantly gave way. At nine PM, he wrote his letter of resignation. The next day he took the train out of Vienna's Nordbahnhof, destined for London. His summer palace on the outskirts of Vienna burnt behind him.[2]

Unexpectedly, Emperor Ferdinand now set the pace with these simple words: 'I'm the sovereign and the decision lies with me. Tell the people I agree to everything.' His ministers fell into line. On 14 March, Ferdinand withdrew troops to their barracks and tasked militias of citizens and students with keeping order, but there was no need to arm them—the arsenal had already been invaded and weapons distributed. At the same time, Ferdinand authorized the abolition of censorship. Within hours, booksellers had moved to shop windows their previously hidden stocks of banned publications. The next day, a herald dressed like a playing card announced in front of the Hofburg that Ferdinand had committed himself to a constitution and a parliament. The emperor then toured the centre of the city in an open-topped carriage, amidst much popular applause.[3]

Ferdinand's ministers, meanwhile, picking up the current vocabulary of reform, decided that they ought to form a 'responsible ministry', which meant that they would assume responsibility for all the activities of government (rather than leave decision making to whoever had the emperor's ear). They now refashioned the various offices and councils of state into ministries, which in most cases only amounted to changing the name plates on doors. Even so, decisions continued to be taken in the court, mostly by Ferdinand's brother and uncle, the archdukes Franz Karl and John, who gave instructions in the emperor's name that bypassed his ministers.[4]

But the revolution was not over. Across the Austrian Empire, groups began framing petitions, drawing up constitutions, and pushing for changes in the local administration. Metternich had fallen, and all those implicated in his regime were now deemed redundant. In places, agitators used violence, physically ejecting officers from town halls or, in some cases, forcing their resignation by howling and screeching fiddles outside their homes until they complied—the din was known as 'caterwauling' or *Katzenmusik*. More soberly, reformers set up committees which coordinated and amalgamated agendas of a quite different complexion, framing each in the manner of a loyal address to the throne. In mental asylums, inmates also began composing petitions and constitutions.

The demands laid might be trivial—in the case of one village in the Bukovina in eastern Galicia, that the peasant petitioners not be expected to do so much logging for the army. Others were more comprehensive. Over the last decades, many of the ideas of liberalism—with its stress on the rule of law, press freedom, political representation, and the rights of the citizen—had acquired a following. So too had nationalism, which emphasized the nation. The idea of the nation was at this time based mainly on language and, to a lesser extent, on religion. Although intellectually opposed, liberal individualism and nationalist collectivism worked together, and both embraced similar social programmes that had at their heart the abolition of peasant serfdom. The universalism of the reformers' demands was demonstrated in the students' flag in Vienna, which adopted the colours of the rainbow.[5]

A succession of governments collapsed, each unable to respond convincingly to the pressures that Metternich's resignation had released. Philipp von Neumann, now in Vienna, found only chaos. As he wrote at the end of March 1848, 'The whole chancellery is in a complete state of disorganization; agitation and uncertainty prevail everywhere; God only knows what future is in store for my country.' Count Kolowrat, appointed minister president on 20 March, survived a month. His successor lasted no longer. In the meantime, the minister of the interior, Franz von Pillersdorf, published a draft constitution as the basis for discussion in a new imperial parliament or Reichstag, scheduled to meet at the end of June with elected representatives.[6]

But Pillersdorf's initiative was overtaken by events. In May, an elected assembly, which included representatives from the Austrian lands, convened in Frankfurt to work out a constitution for a new Germany that would unite all German speakers. The next month, a self-appointed Pan-Slav Congress convened in Prague to represent Slavonic speakers from across the empire— Czechs, Slovaks, Poles, Ruthenes (or Ukrainians), and so on—with the aim of building 'a confederation of nations.' Developments elsewhere were even bleaker for the empire. At the beginning of April, Ferdinand had conceded to the Hungarians the right to have their own government, on the back of which a newly appointed Hungarian ministry started selling state bonds, recruiting troops, and embarking upon its own independent foreign policy. Meanwhile, in Lombardy and Venetia, rebels had seized control, declaring their own democratic republics and forcing the withdrawal of the Habsburg army northwards.

The danger was that the Habsburg Empire would be broken up. Its German-speaking Austrian parts would join a new Germany, while Bohemia formed the core of a new Slav state, and Lombardy-Venetia seceded, perhaps to join the kingdom of Piedmont. A greatly reduced Hungary would then become an independent country. By the middle of 1848, it looked as if the dissolution of the Habsburg Empire was certain. On the streets of Vienna, meanwhile, power passed into the hands of increasingly radicalized militias, whose numbers had been swollen by 'bearded elements' (a beard was considered the revolutionary's badge). Amidst fresh violence, the imperial family fled the capital for Innsbruck in May.[7]

In Vienna, the ministry struggled, desperately seeking to raise money by a fire sale of state assets and by selling government bonds at double the usual interest rate. Its initial inclination was to concede, giving way to pressure from the streets, even to the extent of embarking on a public works programme whereby many thousands of unemployed were rewarded for undertaking useless work in the city parks. They typically spent the days shirking and the nights looting. Gradually, however, the government's resolve stiffened, largely because of the leadership shown by the minister of war, General Latour. It was Latour who increasingly spoke first and longest at cabinet meetings. Latour was opposed to concessions and was convinced that there was a military way out of the disarray. He was not wrong.

But the bombshell that landed at three forty-five AM in Vienna on the morning of 13 June had nothing to do with Latour. The veteran military commander of Bohemia, General Windischgrätz, announced by telegraph that his troops had been ambushed in Prague, that a revolution had broken out there, with barricades put up in the streets, and that he was taking urgent counter-measures. The ministers in Vienna were appalled by Windischgrätz's message but could do little except follow the telegraph traffic. One of these, sent on the morning of 16 June, was from the telegraph clerk: 'Prague is in complete uproar. I can't stay here.' In fact, the clerk managed a further brief dispatch that night—'Prague is in flames.' Shortly after that, the ministers learned, the line had gone dead.[8]

The uproar in Prague was partly Windischgrätz's own work. Resentful of Latour's instruction that he release some of his troops for service in Italy, he had provocatively deployed close to Prague. In this tense atmosphere, an outdoor religious service conducted unusually in Church Slavonic by a Serbian priest (to celebrate the unity of all Slavs) became on the evening of 12 June the occasion for rioting and for armed attacks on the garrison. A mob gathered in front of Windischgrätz's lodgings, shouting abuse. Shots were fired into the windows, killing the general's wife. With extraordinary courage, Windischgrätz faced the crowd, warning them, 'Notwithstanding my wife now lies behind me in her own blood, I conjure you in all kindness to depart and not compel me to use against you all the force and power at my command.' Ruffians dragged the old general to a lamp post, preparing to hang him, but he was rescued by troops.[9]

True to his word, Windischgrätz commenced the bombardment of Prague. Behind a rolling artillery barrage, his troops advanced through the streets and squares of the Old Town, demolishing the barricades put up against them. After three days of fighting, all opposition was crushed. Windischgrätz closed the Pan-Slav Congress, abolished the government of Bohemia, cancelled the next meeting of the diet, and proclaimed martial law. Emperor Ferdinand, under pressure from Archduchess Sophie, who stood close politically to Windischgrätz, retrospectively sanctioned the general's high-handed measures by giving him full military and civilian authority in case of emergency, backdated to May 1848.

In Lombardy-Venetia, Habsburg rule had almost completely collapsed. After five days of fighting in March, the Habsburg commander in Italy, the octogenarian field marshal Radetzky, had abandoned Milan. Then, on 22 March, the workers in the Venice Arsenal rebelled, distributing arms to insurgents and inciting the (mainly Italian) garrison to mutiny. The king of Piedmont, Charles Albert, who was as much a reluctant soldier as he was a reluctant constitutional monarch, now declared war on the Austrian Empire and invaded Lombardy, which voted in a plebiscite to join Piedmont. Radetzky had had enough experience of war to know when one was winnable. Without reinforcements, he prudently withdrew south of Lake Garda to the square of fortresses known as the Quadrilateral, from which he refused to budge.

In Vienna, the government was convinced that the Habsburg position in Italy was untenable. The ministers only held back from completely abandoning Lombardy-Venetia for fear of exciting calls for secession elsewhere. By the end of May, however, Latour had succeeded in having the first reinforcements reach the Quadrilateral. Even so, the ministry urged Radetzky to keep his troops in barracks, while simultaneously seeking an armistice with Charles Albert. Coolly reporting through Latour, Radetzky announced that he would find it hard to respect any truce that the government might arrange. Instead, he broke out of the Quadrilateral, overrunning Venetia in June, after which he turned against Charles Albert's forces to the west. After several days of battle, fought at Custoza in late July, Radetzky forced Charles Albert to retreat and then to sue for peace. Venice, however, held out for more than a year, suffering the first aerial bombardment in history when Radetzky launched several hundred unmanned balloons laden with explosives against the city.[10]

News of Radetzky's victory at Custoza prompted widespread jubilation in Vienna and was celebrated in August with the premiere of Johann

Strauss's *Radetzky March*. In Lombardy, meanwhile, all democratic government was torn up, military rule imposed, and a reign of terror released on
the countryside. Habsburg troops hunted down insurgents and sympathiz-
ers alike, handing them over for public floggings and the hangman's noose.
Concertgoers today who clap and stomp to the beat of the *Radetzky March*
should recall just what they are cheering.[11]

Vienna remained in uproar. Even so, elections went ahead in June for
the imperial parliament that the emperor had promised. There had already
been elections in German-speaking areas for the German parliament that
was meeting in Frankfurt, as well as for many of the local diets, which had
remodelled their franchises to be more inclusive of the population, so procedures were by this time established and known. Elections followed, therefore, a largely uniform two-tier pattern, with voters meeting in (generally
peaceful) assemblies where by majority vote they chose a deputy. Groups of
deputies then cast their votes for a representative, with one representative for
every fifty thousand or so first-tier voters. The two-tier process together with
the requirement that voters be householders over twenty-four years of age
(and male) ensured that most representatives were of a politically moderate
persuasion.[12]

The imperial parliament met in Vienna in July and immediately pe-
titioned for the return of the emperor from Innsbruck, which duly took
place. Thereafter, it busied itself with drafting a constitution and working
out the terms of peasant emancipation. Although the abolition of servile
conditions on the land had been promised by Ferdinand in April, there was
no agreement on what land the peasants might receive or on how landlords
were to be compensated. Meanwhile, Emperor Ferdinand's uncle, Archduke
John, was elected imperial regent by the German parliament in Frankfurt.
Although it was still uncertain who would hold the title of emperor in the
new Germany that the Frankfurt parliament purported to represent, the
selection of John suggested that a Habsburg might indeed fill this role.

Bohemia had been subdued, Habsburg rule restored to Lombardy, the
emperor had returned to the capital, a Habsburg was regent in Germany,
and an imperial parliament was meeting in Vienna. To that extent, some
sort of order was emerging out of the chaos. Hungary, however, was still
bent on a course that would lead to its independence and the breakup of
the Austrian Empire. It was to Hungary that the generals now turned their
attention. No friend of representative institutions, Windischgrätz planned to

cow revolutionary Vienna by military means as the preliminary to an assault on Hungary. To this, he added at the end of August a further aim—the replacement of the emperor by his nephew, the young Franz Joseph. In Windischgrätz's opinion, Emperor Ferdinand had already conceded too much and had to be removed from office. Young and a firm champion of the army and its generals, Franz Joseph was his obvious successor.

In April 1848, Ferdinand had conceded a constitution to Hungary, known as the April Laws. It had established a separate Hungarian government and made it responsible for the kingdom's internal arrangements, including its military and financial affairs. The conviction remained in Vienna that Hungary was bound inseparably to the Austrian Empire and constituted part of a 'common state.' But the Hungarian leaders believed that they owed their sole allegiance to the king of Hungary, who just happened to be the emperor of Austria. Accordingly, they acted as if Hungary was independent and refused Austrian requests for cash and troops to assist in the war in Italy.[13]

The kingdom of Hungary was multinational in the sense that less than half of the population were Hungarian speakers. The rest were mostly Romanians, Serbs, Slovaks, Germans, Ruthenes, and Croats. The extent to which members of the various national groups were aware of their separate identities, or regarded them as politically significant, differed. There were plenty of people, including Hungarian speakers, who when asked their identity simply explained that they were Catholics or 'the people from here.' Slovaks in northern Hungary alternated between a regional identity and a broader Slavonic one. Many Ruthenes in north-eastern Hungary considered themselves completely Hungarian, although they spoke not a word of the language, while Romanian intellectuals in the Banat preferred to describe themselves as 'Hungarians of Romanian language.'[14]

The events of 1848 hastened the process whereby individuals made choices as to who they were and where they belonged. Many repudiated the authority claimed by the new Hungarian government, holding to a larger Austrian identity, or they sought a separate physical space for the nationality of their adoption, either through autonomy or statehood. The minutes of the first meeting of the Hungarian cabinet, on 12 April, testify to the way attitudes were hardening. Reports were received of unrest in the Slovak highlands and in Bratislava, which were being egged on by Serb and Croat agitators and fanned, so it was claimed, by Russian government propaganda. Meanwhile, in Croatia, the governor or ban, Baron Josip Jelačić, was known to have summoned a national assembly in Zagreb, thereby exceeding his powers. The ministers agreed that loyal Hungarian-speaking troops should be sent in, but there were few available. Some, they learned, could be deployed from Linz if a steamship were found.[15]

The minutes of that first cabinet meeting disclose the fears and heavy-handed responses of the Hungarian government to disaffection. Compromises could certainly have been struck, but distrust opened breaches between the emerging national groups that made confrontation inevitable. Political competition pitted Hungarians against Serbs, Romanians, and Slovaks; Banat Romanians against Serbs; Transylvanian Germans against Hungarians, and so on. By July 1848, open warfare flared across Hungary. To meet the challenge of revolt, the Hungarian prime minister, Count Louis Batthyány, ordered the construction of a national army. To pay for it, the finance minister, Louis Kossuth, introduced a Hungarian paper currency.

Batthyány and Kossuth's actions took Hungary even further down the road to independence. Although the measures they had adopted were consonant with the April Laws, the court in Vienna dug in its heels, affirming that 'the existence of a Kingdom of Hungary separate from the Austrian Empire must be described as politically impossible.'[16] To rein Hungary in, the government appointed the Hungarian general Ferenc Lamberg to take control of all armed forces operating within Hungary. Lamberg's arrival in Pest was greeted with handbills in the manner of 'Wanted' posters. Identified by a mob, Lamberg was on 28 September hacked to pieces with scythes on the pontoon bridge that linked Pest to Buda.

The ban of Croatia, Josip Jelačić, was an accomplished pianist, indifferent poet, and poor general. He was also a dedicated Croatian nationalist who was determined to break Croatia's historic connection to Hungary. Over the preceding decades, the Hungarian diet had gradually established Hungarian as the official language of the kingdom, quite ignoring the fact that most of the population did not speak Hungarian. The April Laws sealed this trend by making Hungarian the only language that might be spoken in the diet, thus both inconveniencing and insulting the Croatian deputies there, who had previously communicated in Latin. Jelačić demanded that the Hungarian ministry give Croatia its own constitution and parliament, where all business would be conducted in Croatian. Hungarian politicians were typically disdainful of Croatian ambitions, with Kossuth egregiously declaring that he could not find Croatia on a map.[17]

But sections of the court were also opposed to Jelačić's agenda, and they prevailed upon Ferdinand to declare that he 'would never allow the legal bond between the Lands of the Hungarian Crown to be loosened by arbitrary orders or unilateral decisions', on which account Jelačić should conform to instructions given by the Hungarian government. Jelačić continued to muster troops regardless, assumed dictatorial powers in Croatia, and returned unopened all communications from the Hungarian ministry. On 10 June, Ferdinand stripped Jelačić of all his offices and declared him a traitor. But Jelačić had friends in high places. Archduchess Sophie wrote to Jelačić, imploring him to stand firm, while Latour sent the ban money from the War Ministry to fund his army. In complete panic, the Hungarian ministry offered Jelačić in late August independence for Croatia—'but', as Kossuth added, 'let's be good friends.' It was too late. On 11 September, Jelačić crossed the Drava River and invaded Hungary.[18]

Everything now fell into place, just as Windischgrätz intended. The government collapsed in Hungary, to be replaced by a Committee of National Defence. Headed by Kossuth, it was bent on safeguarding Hungary's independence by military means, thus giving Windischgrätz the war he wanted. Appalled by the murder of Lamberg, Ferdinand was convinced to reinstate Jelačić, thus approving the war he had begun with Hungary. Despite the steady flow of troops and cash from Vienna, Jelačić was militarily outmanoeuvred. He retreated from Hungary into Lower Austria, pursued westwards by a Hungarian army. Then, in October, Vienna itself exploded when crowds attempted to block the entrainment of soldiers to the front by pulling up the railway tracks. Bands of labourers and students invaded the War Ministry, where the government was in session, causing the ministers to flee. Latour remained at his post, but the mob dragged him outside and butchered him in the street, hanging his body from a street lamp. Revolutionaries also invaded the Spanish Riding School, where the imperial parliament was in session, intimidating the deputies with firearms.

Following a prearranged plan, Windischgrätz evacuated the imperial family to Olomouc in Moravia and ordered the imperial parliament to the castle of Kroměříž (Kremsier), also in Moravia. Having warned honest citizens to leave the city, Windischgrätz subjected Vienna to a cannonade, beginning on 26 October. Some two thousand people were killed in the bombardment, which Jelačić joined with gusto, notching up the victory that had eluded him in Hungary. After four days, resistance collapsed in the besieged city. Windischgrätz rode in, imposing martial law, making arrests, and executing several dozen revolutionaries. In the meantime, he also dispersed at Schwechat a Hungarian army that was marching on Vienna to assist the rebels there.

Philipp von Neumann was back in England in the autumn of 1848, visiting the Devonshires at Chatsworth, calling on the exiled Metternich in Hove (he had found London too expensive), and enjoying a house party in Richmond. As the news came through from Vienna, Neumann's diary entries became increasingly staccato: 'A horrible assassination has taken place in Pest' (8 October). 'It is reported from Vienna that there has been a frightful revolution there. . . . They have killed Latour with hatchets and hammers and then hanged his body. . . . The ministry is in a state of panic' (13 October). 'It appears that Windischgrätz occupied Vienna on 1 November. . . . The Imperial Palace and Library caught fire' (6 November). Then, on 9 December, Neumann recorded laconically, 'Today I received the news of the abdication of our emperor on the 2nd instant, in favour of his nephew the Archduke Franz Joseph, son of the Archduke Franz Karl, who has renounced his rights to the crown. The ex-emperor has retired to Prague.'[19]

What Neumann describes was in fact a military coup. To settle the affairs of Hungary, Emperor Ferdinand had to go, for he had agreed to the April Laws. He was, moreover, manifestly incapable of the tough rulership needed in hard times. This was the conviction of Windischgrätz and of his brother-in-law, Prince Schwarzenberg, who had been appointed prime minister in November. Schwarzenberg was politically aligned to Radetzky and Jelačić, and the generals were setting the political pace. Satirical pamphlets published in Vienna played on the imperial 'We'—WIR, now standing for Windischgrätz, Jelačić, and Radetzky.

The emperor's entourage, having fled Vienna, was now in Olomouc. Its members received at short notice an invitation to convene on 2 December at the archbishop's palace, where the imperial family was staying. There, in the audience chamber, they witnessed an act unprecedented in Habsburg history. First, Emperor Ferdinand formally abdicated, which he did with good grace. Then, the next in line to the throne, his brother Franz Karl, gave up his rights. A decent man, with liberal instincts, Franz Karl was no friend of the generals, and in any case, his wife, the tiresome Archduchess Sophie, insisted. The mantle thus passed, literally, to Franz Karl's son, the eighteen-year-old Franz Joseph. A surviving watercolour shows the teenager being led forward by his mother and aunt, with Ferdinand and Franz Karl in the background. Around an improvised throne stand Schwarzenberg, Jelačić, and Windischgrätz. As Schwarzenberg noted, by their insubordination the generals had saved the Austrian Empire. It was they too, and the ghost of the murdered Latour, who now determined the succession.[20]

FRANZ JOSEPH'S EMPIRE, SISI, AND HUNGARY

O n 6 October 1849, the former prime minister of Hungary, Count Louis Batthyány, was taken into the courtyard of the main gaol of Pest. An Austrian military court had condemned him to hang for treason on account of his role in promoting Hungary's independence, but he had slit his throat several days earlier in an unsuccessful attempt at suicide. So the court changed the penalty to death by firing squad. Batthyány was so weak that he had to be carried to the place of execution; he died slumped on a chair. Several hours before, at five thirty AM, thirteen generals in what had been the army of independent Hungary were also executed in Arad Castle on the same grounds of treason, the majority by hanging. The noose was a harsh punishment, for death came not from the sudden breaking of the neck but from slow suffocation. It was intended to be humiliating, too, for the victim writhed in his agony and, at expiry, his bowels usually opened.

The executions of Batthyány and the generals came at the end of a bloody war between Hungary and the Habsburgs that had begun with Jelačić's invasion. The country had held out for almost a year—its resources and Hungarian population ably mobilized by Kossuth and its armies expertly commanded. Even so, it was only in April 1849 that the Hungarian government proclaimed the country's formal independence, deposing 'the perjured house of Habsburg' and appointing Kossuth governor and regent. Until then, Hungary's politicians had held by the conviction that they were acting lawfully, in accordance with the terms of the April Laws, as granted by Emperor Ferdinand.

Finally, in June 1849 a Russian army invaded Hungary at the request of the new emperor, Franz Joseph (1848–1916). With the Austrian general von Haynau pressing from the west and General Paskevich's Russians from the north, resistance collapsed. Kossuth meanwhile escaped into the Ottoman Empire. For the remainder of his long life (he died in 1894), Kossuth inveighed against Habsburg rule in Hungary, electrifying audiences in Great Britain and the United States with his oratory. His claim that he had learned English from reading Shakespeare in prison may not be true, but the story enhanced his reputation and the cause of a free Hungary. Visiting England in 1851, Kossuth received a rapturous welcome, feted by tens of thousands in every city in which he spoke. By contrast, when Haynau came to London, he was set upon by the draymen of Barclay and Perkins brewery, pelted with dung, and chased down Borough High Street.[1]

The killing of Batthyány and the generals was the work of the young Franz Joseph, who rejected his ministers' proposal of a comprehensive amnesty. But the emperor was not yet finished with 'the scaffold and the bloodbath', as one former prime minister put it, and he gave Haynau free rein in Hungary. A hundred executions followed, and several thousand long gaol sentences. Even when the Austrian prime minister, Prince Schwarzenberg, ordered Haynau to desist from killing, he carried on, until finally dismissed in July 1850. Haynau was sufficiently insensitive to buy on retirement an estate in Hungary. He never understood why his neighbours did not invite him to dinner.[2]

Emergency rule continued in Hungary until 1854, and some offences remained under the jurisdiction of military courts for several years longer. On top of this, Hungary's counties were abolished and replaced by administrative districts headed by appointees of the interior ministry in Vienna. Croatia, Transylvania, and the Banat together with the neighbouring Vojvodina were additionally ruled separately from Vienna as crown lands. All institutions of self-government were abolished, and German was made the language of administration. Tasks previously performed by the counties and noble landlords were now undertaken by bureaucrats, many of whom were recruited from elsewhere in the Austrian Empire.

The breakup of Hungary into districts ruled from Vienna was part of a plan that Schwarzenberg (or at least someone close to him) had hatched as early as December 1848. Developments elsewhere were more haphazard. As one of his first acts, Franz Joseph had closed the imperial parliament that had been meeting in Kroměříž. In the early hours of 7 March 1849, troops with bayonets had entered the castle where the parliament met and blocked the entrances, after which they had scoured the city, arresting several of the more radical deputies. In place of the constitutional proposals the parliament had devised, Franz Joseph imposed a constitution of his own, which as he explained was more suited to the times and less influenced by remote and theoretical ideas.[3]

The Decreed or March Constitution was in some respects a good one. It was centralist in the sense that it envisaged one elected parliament for the whole of the Austrian Empire, including Hungary, a single central government, and one coronation. Although the emperor retained strong powers, there were layers of elected bodies, which possessed a devolved authority. The constitution additionally confirmed the abolition of serfdom previously agreed by the imperial parliament, legal equality, and that 'all national groups are equal and that every national group has an inviolable right to the use and cultivation of its language and nationality.'[4]

For all its merits, the constitution was a cynical ploy. Franz Joseph was out to make his mark, and he was lured by Schwarzenberg's dream of joining the entire Austrian Empire to the German Confederation to create a massive new territorial bloc in Central Europe, in which the Habsburg emperor would be politically dominant. To win over the German princes to the scheme, Franz Joseph needed to appear as a constitutionalist who was ready to be bound by legal constraints. But by the middle of 1851, it was clear that the German rulers would not agree to a merger with the Austrian Empire, preferring to renew the Confederation set up after the defeat of France in 1814. By this time, too, Franz Joseph was casting envious eyes on Napoleon III of France, who had, as the emperor admiringly described, 'seized the reins of power in his hands' and made himself much more than 'a machine for writing his signature.'[5]

Implementation of the March Constitution went at a snail's pace, and its provisions on local elected government were drastically pared back. Finally, on New Year's Eve 1851, Franz Joseph issued a series of instructions, known collectively as the Sylvester Patent, that abolished the March Constitution outright and gave himself the sole right to make laws. (31 December is St Sylvester's Day; a patent was a type of decree.) The coup was completed after the death of Schwarzenberg in April 1852, when Franz Joseph declared that he would now act in the capacity of prime minister.

The Sylvester Patent introduced a decade of neo-absolutism or neo-Caesarism, when Franz Joseph ruled as a dictator. Both terms are recent ones—at the time, the type of government practised by Franz Joseph was known simply as absolutism or more tellingly as bureaucratic absolutism, for the emperor imposed his will through the administrative apparatus. But the bureaucrats also had their own political agenda, which was to maintain the reforming programme of Joseph II, with its belief in the wisdom of state management and in social and economic progress directed from above. They even had a name for themselves: the 'party of Enlightenment.'[6]

Altogether, the Habsburg civil service numbered in the 1850s around fifty thousand persons, but this included junior and ancillary staff. About ten thousand belonged to the higher 'policy service' (*Konzeptdienst*), and almost all of these had received a university education, mostly in law. Those in the higher branches were overwhelmingly liberal in disposition and outlook, and disproportionately represented in the reading clubs and, during 1848, in the politics of reform. They were liberals in the sense of believing in individual empowerment, through education, legal equality, freedom of the press and of association, and the removal of economic constraints. They saw a strong state as the vehicle for a liberal programme of reform and were prepared to make concessions to it—press freedom was an early casualty. But by endorsing state intervention, the bureaucrats 'fattened the state up', turning it into a Leviathan that devoured the individual freedoms that their liberalism had originally championed.[7]

The achievements of bureaucratic absolutism were massive—as one historian has put it, 'a Josephinist fantasy come true.' There were new institutes of science, regulations on safety in mines and the workplace, a penny-stamp postal service, new roads, telegraphs, and railways. By 1854, a thousand kilometres of track had been laid, and the Linz to České Budějovice (Budweis) line, originally built in 1832, was converted from horse to steam power. For the roads, almost ten million cubic metres of stone were laid in just three years. Experts recruited from the London Board of Works helped to dredge and canalize the Danube and Tisza rivers. Infrastructural expansion was underpinned by burgeoning coal and iron production, by a developing banking sector for commercial loans, and by the removal of customs barriers that made the Austrian Empire into a common market. Vienna, too, was transformed, with the old city walls torn down and a spacious 'Ring' built in its place to house the new class of entrepreneurs and industrialists created by economic modernization.[8]

The peasantry had been freed by Joseph II in the sense that they were able to leave the land and marry without the lord's consent. But the land they farmed still belonged to the lord, on which account they owed him dues and services performed by hand. In the early months of the revolution, the Hungarian diet had committed itself to giving the peasants the lands they farmed, but elsewhere promises were vague and piecemeal, with the terms of emancipation deferred until the imperial parliament met. The difficulties were that the lords needed some sort of compensation for their loss and that the land that the peasants farmed was of varying legal quality—some was ancestral peasant property, farmed over generations; other land was leased from the lord under contract, or else it was common land or had been cleared by the peasant personally from scrub.

The imperial parliament had shirked its obligation to facilitate emancipation by hiding behind generalities. After 1849, however, the government made a determined attempt to resolve the issues arising from emancipation. Ancestral land became the peasants', in its entirety, with no compensation paid to landlords. All the rest was compensated for, with the state bearing the brunt of the burden, which it did through the expedient of printing bonds and distributing them slowly. The terms of compensation were worked out by commissions, and the new landowning peasants were obliged to enter details of their properties in land registers. These also recorded liens—whether the property was now leased out or mortgaged—and neighbours, kinsmen, and lenders frequently challenged the contents of the registers. The courts in Hungary alone were in the second half of the century handling seldom fewer than three hundred thousand cases a year of disputed entries, with a backlog extending to over a million.[9]

In the past, minor disputes such as these would have gone in the first instance to manor courts, but with the abolition of landlordism had also gone the landowners' courts and their gratis contribution to the administration of the countryside. The state had now to fill the gap, establishing across the empire 1,500 new courts and supervisory offices. Bureaucrats were despatched to the countryside to see to the implementation of directives from the centre. Their task was a hard one. The interior minister, Alexander Bach, ordered civil servants in Hungary to buy an uncomfortable uniform based on a Hungarian cavalryman's, but it cost half a year's salary and earned them ridicule as 'Bach hussars.' Underresourced and living in shabby conditions, they found it impossible to reconcile their obligations with the day-to-day realities of the countryside. Arriving in one Hungarian village, a 'Bach hussar' found there to be no prison: convicts were instead lodged unguarded in an inn and given a daily allowance for food.[10]

Bach's instructions for the civil service stressed the importance of stability, routine, and predictability of outcome in the legal and administrative process. To that end, the Austrian civil law was extended in the 1850s across the whole of the Austrian Empire, replacing in Hungary and Transylvania the arcane and largely unwritten customary law. But to meet local circumstances, the law had to be modified and adapted, thus robbing it of its regularity and uniformity. On top of this, the medley of official circulars, formulary books, clarifications, edicts, and modifications emanating from the centre rendered the law even less certain and its application in individual circumstances unpredictable. Bewildered bureaucrats frequently referred up, so that even trivial matters ended up on Bach's desk, never to be resolved.[11]

But there was uncertainty at the top too. Franz Joseph was unaccountable, unconstrained by either institutions or a constitution. He was inept but convinced in his own superior wisdom. In an example that shocked the British ambassador, he insisted in early 1852 that a cavalry parade take place on the cobblestones before the Schönbrunn Palace in a deep frost, even though warned of the danger. The horses toppled, killing two cuirassiers. Franz Joseph's handling of foreign policy was equally calamitous. He did not support Tsar Nicholas in the Crimean War (1853–1856), thus letting down the ally who had come to his rescue in 1849, but neither did he back the British and the French against Russia. Diplomatically isolated, he was now prey for Napoleon III of France, whose army swept through Lombardy in 1859, assigning the province to the kingdom of Piedmont in exchange for France taking Nice and Savoy. It did not help that halfway through the campaign Franz Joseph appointed himself commander. His generalship led directly to the bloodbath of the Battle of Solferino. Two years later, having overrun the

Habsburg-ruled duchies of Parma, Modena, and Tuscany, the king of Piedmont was proclaimed king of Italy.[12]

In April 1859, the Austrian National Bank collapsed, refusing to honour its own currency. Franz Joseph had treated the bank as a 'grand state treasury', taking what he needed, and he simply did not understand what it meant when earlier that year his agents had been refused a loan on the London market. The bankers would not lend to an unaccountable monarch. Anselm Rothschild put it bluntly: 'No constitution, no money.' Franz Joseph's own finance minister, Karl Ludwig von Bruck, went further. The absolutist experiment had not lived up to expectations and had failed to harness the energies of the Austrian Empire, he wrote. Centralization should be 'cooled down' and a 'sound, enduring constitution' imposed, but not one that revived the antique arrangements of the past.[13]

Typically, Franz Joseph did exactly what Bruck advised him not to do. Casually commenting to his mother that 'we will now have a little parliamentarism', he resuscitated an older institution, the imperial council or Reichsrat, packing it with his aristocratic chums in the hope that it would be mistaken for a parliament. To further the deception, he also recalled the diets so that they might send representatives to join the imperial council, but only ones whom he approved. In the October Diploma of 1860 (a diploma is a solemn decree, stronger than a patent), Franz Joseph declared this Pinocchio's nose of a constitution to be 'permanent and irrevocable', but the bankers still refused to lend. Ignaz von Plener, who had replaced Bruck as finance minister, was adamant in his advice to Franz Joseph. Financial stability could only be assured, he explained, when the National Bank was freed from governmental interference and when borrowing was subject to oversight by genuinely representative institutions.[14]

Franz Joseph gave way. Setting aside the 'permanent and irrevocable' October Diploma, he issued the so-called February Patent of 1861. Technically explanatory of the October Diploma, the patent gave the Austrian Empire a real parliament, even though it retained the old name of the imperial council. It was made up of two houses—an Upper House of high aristocrats and churchmen and a Lower House comprising deputies sent by the diets—whose consent was needed for all legislation. New regulations published at the same time laid down qualifications for voting to the diets, extending the franchise to about a quarter of the adult male population and introducing a complicated procedure for casting ballots that advantaged the German-speaking population.

The February Patent kept many of the emperor's powers, including over the army and foreign policy. Most importantly, the emperor chose the government, and ministers were responsible to him. Invariably, Franz Joseph appointed bureaucrats and not politicians to the ministries. Having served in the administration, they were more likely to be loyal to him, and in any case he valued expertise more than political posturing. A bureaucratic elite, therefore, still made most of the important political decisions. On top of this, legislation was frequently enacted in the form of administrative decrees that bypassed the parliamentary process entirely. Bureaucratic absolutism thus gave way not to government by democratic institutions but instead to bureaucratic constitutionalism.[15]

At the head of the apparatus remained the man who described himself as his empire's 'first civil servant.' At work by five in the morning, Franz Joseph busied himself with paperwork, often correcting ministerial drafts or rewriting them entirely. His office routine was broken by meetings with his ministers and, twice a week, with general audiences at which any of his subjects might petition to see him. Here his bureaucratic routines proved their worth, for a filing system meant that he could keep up with every petitioner—whether he had visited before and, if so, what his concerns had been, and the remedies given. Franz Joseph kept going throughout the day on Virginia cigarettes and coffee, which he replaced in old age with mild cigars and tea. The knowledge he acquired of matters of state was formidable, but it lay unsorted in his mind, with trivial matters of protocol often uppermost.[16]

Franz Joseph treasured the Austrian presidency of the German Confederation, for it provided a vehicle for projecting power as far afield as the Baltic and North Sea, as well as suggesting dynastic continuity with the old Holy Roman Empire. As late as 1863, Franz Joseph was still hoping to be offered the German imperial crown. But Prussia also had ambitions to leadership in Germany, which the Prussian ambassador to the Confederation, Otto von Bismarck, expressed with typical forcefulness. In 1862, on the eve of his appointment as the prime minister of Prussia, Bismarck explained to the Conservative politician Benjamin Disraeli in London how he planned to reorganize the Prussian army. Then, he went on, 'I shall seize the first best pretext to declare war against Austria, dissolve the German Confederation, subjugate the minor states and give national unity to Germany under Prussian leadership. I have come here to say this to the Queen's ministers.' But Bismarck did not just say it to the British government—the Austrian ambassador was also in the room with Disraeli.[17]

In Franz Joseph's case, forewarned was not forearmed. On the flimsiest of pretexts, Prussia declared war on the Austrian Empire, defeating the Habsburg army in a lightning campaign waged over seven weeks in 1866. The kingdom of Italy, Prussia's ally, counted on the winning side, even though defeated at sea at Lissa (Vis) in the Adriatic in the first fleet battle to involve ironclad warships. Italy was now rewarded with Venice, while Bismarck rolled up all the states north of the River Main into a new North German Confederation under Prussian presidency. Less than five years later, the South German states gave way, joining Bismarck's newly proclaimed German Empire. The Habsburg link to the German lands, which had persevered throughout the history of the dynasty and had survived both Napoleon and 1848, was now finally severed.

In less than twenty years, Franz Joseph had lost Lombardy, Venice, and the German Confederation. The Austrian Empire had shrunk back into Central Europe. On top of this, it stood to lose even more, for Hungary was far from pacified. Rumours of insurrection circulated there, fanned from abroad by Kossuth. The roughness of Austrian rule was summed up in 1858 by the governor of Hungary, Archduke Albrecht. When asked by a Hungarian delegation to restore the kingdom's ancient constitution, Albrecht grabbed his sword, exclaiming, 'This is my constitution.' Unsurprisingly, the diet summoned in 1861 to select deputies for the parliament in Vienna refused point-blank to cooperate and even questioned whether Franz Joseph was Hungary's lawful king. The imperial parliament that met in Vienna, in a temporary wooden structure on the new Ring, was accordingly eighty-five deputies short. Hoping to break Hungary's will, Franz Joseph ramped up the politics of coercion, only to be faced by a tax strike.[18]

Hungary was saved for the Habsburgs by the intervention of two people. The first was the lawyer and politician Ferenc Deák. Deák argued that the public law of Hungary rested on two instruments—the April Laws of 1848 that had granted Hungary independence and Charles VI's Pragmatic Sanction that had declared Hungary an 'inseparable and indivisible' part of the Habsburg lands. The trick was to arrive at a compromise that bridged the two documents, and Deák saw how this could be done. The second to intercede on Hungary's behalf was more unexpected—Franz Joseph's wife, Empress Elizabeth, whom he had married in 1854, when she was just sixteen.

Elizabeth or 'Sisi' was, in the words of Franz Joseph's valet, 'a world away from being the ideal wife.' Wilful and self-obsessed, she luxuriated in her own beauty. Having done her duty by providing a male heir, she travelled, flitting between health spas, Corfu, and England. There were visits in between to Monte Carlo, where she played the tables, and long cruises in the Mediterranean, in token of which she sported an anchor tattoo on her shoulder. Much has been said of her that is not true. For most of her life, she kept her waist at 16.5 inches in diameter (42 centimetres), but she was neither too thin for the corsets of the time nor anorexic. Although she periodically dieted, she normally ate a healthy breakfast with wine, a meat dish for lunch, but little for supper, since coffee and cigarettes had by the evening robbed her of her appetite (she chain-smoked, including in the state carriage). Even so, she exercised vigorously, having her own gymnasium in the Hofburg, where her high bar and balancing rings survive, and she was a distinguished equestrian. In England, she rode to hounds with the Northamptonshire Hunt, but it is unlikely that she had an affair with the Scottish huntsman Bay Middleton, despite a tantalizing aside in one of her daughters' diaries. Franz Joseph's valet hinted at liaisons, and she did sometimes behave peculiarly with men, but beyond that we know nothing.[19]

Sisi's education in Bavaria had been erratic, since her father had eccentrically imagined that she would in time join a circus troupe, so she was largely self-taught. She spoke fluent English, Hungarian, and demotic Greek, and composed some exquisite romantic poetry in the manner of Heinrich Heine, on whose works she was an acknowledged expert. Her husband by contrast was a bore. It is not true that he only read the *Army List*—he also read the newspapers' military supplements. Franz Joseph was a stickler for etiquette, mainly because in its absence he did not know what was appropriate. Although he may not have presented himself to his bride on their wedding night in full regimental uniform (as has been alleged), he did attend one of his wife's hunts dressed in *Lederhosen*. Franz Joseph had affairs, but probably not with the burly actress Frau Schratt, with whom he is usually associated. His preference was for married middle-class women with a home to go to, the husbands having been bought off.

Franz Joseph's letters to Sisi (his survive, but not hers to him) are extraordinary in their affection and intimacy. She is 'my heavenly angel', 'my darling', 'sweet soul', and he signs off 'your little one' or 'the manikin' (*Männeken*)—he was shorter than she. They share family news, gossip, and private jokes, so Schratt is either 'the girlfriend' or on account of her tantrums 'the minister of war.' In his study, Franz Joseph hung a portrait of Sisi in a loose robe, with her hair cascading to her waist and giving only the faintest smile. (In fact, her hair reached to her ankles, and she never opened her mouth to smile for fear of showing her irregular teeth.) Yet their meetings were often tempestuous and even violent, with furniture thrown. Clearly, the relationship succeeded best at a distance.[20]

Sisi first visited Hungary in 1857 and was charmed by the lack of stiff ceremony there. Free from oversight, she was able to disport with Gypsies and jugglers, and to enjoy the effusive attentions of the Hungarian aristocracy. She also came to know the leading Hungarian nobleman, Count Andrássy, and the lawyer Ferenc Deák, both of whom were willing to negotiate with Franz Joseph. Sisi recommended them to Franz Joseph. Although Andrássy had only recently been amnestied for his part in the Hungarian War of Independence, Sisi succeeded in having Franz Joseph meet him. To his surprise, the emperor found the count to be 'brave, honourable, and highly gifted.' At Sisi's insistence too, he met secretly with Deák, reporting their conversation back to her in cipher. For more than a year, the empress acted as an intermediary, relaying messages between her husband and the Hungarian political leaders, and stiffened the resolve of the two sides to make a deal. Behind the scenes, she pressed the emperor to show flexibility, in letters that told him explicitly what to do.[21]

Sisi's intervention was not decisive, for Franz Joseph would eventually have had to come to terms with Hungary, but she facilitated the meetings that led to a solution and worked on her husband to be better disposed to the Hungarian leaders. The result was the Compromise or Settlement of 1867. Devised by Deák, it gave Hungary independence while keeping it in the Habsburg Empire, thus squaring the April Laws with the Pragmatic Sanction. The Compromise gave the kingdom its own government and parliament, with an Upper House of dignitaries and an elected Lower House, but the emperor as king of Hungary appointed the government. To satisfy Hungarian demands, Transylvania was also fully absorbed into Hungary, and Hungarian law replaced the Austrian civil code. In June 1867, Franz Joseph and Elizabeth were crowned king and queen of Hungary, with the Holy Crown being placed on their heads consecutively, and she, too, was invested with the royal sceptre and orb. It was an honour never given before to a queen of Hungary.[22]

In 1867, Franz Joseph published constitutions for both halves of the empire. From this point onwards, the Habsburg Empire comprised two equal parts—a Hungarian part and a part for all the rest, which included the Austrian lands, Bohemia, Polish Galicia, the Adriatic coastline, and so on. The second had no obvious name and was officially known as the Lands and Kingdoms Represented in the Imperial Council, and unofficially as 'this side of the Leitha' (Cisleithania: the River Leitha marked Hungary's western border). The two halves remained, however, 'inseparable and indivisible', in the understanding of the Pragmatic Sanction. Foreign policy and the army were regarded as 'common matters' and were overseen by 'common ministries' of foreign affairs and war, to which was added a third ministry of finance, with responsibility for funding the other two. In all other respects, the two governments were separate, with the prime minister of Hungary regarding his counterpart in Vienna as only a 'distinguished foreigner.' Since Hungary now had its own government, the name of the empire changed from the Austrian Empire to the Austro-Hungarian Empire (or Austria-Hungary for short). The adjective 'imperial-royal' (*kaiserlich-königlich*, or *k.k.*) was also replaced with 'imperial and royal' (*kaiserlich und königlich*, or *k.u.k.*), signalling Hungary's new status.

Above the ministries sat the Crown Council, made up of the three common ministers, the prime ministers of Hungary and Cisleithania, and whomever else Franz Joseph chose to invite. The Crown Council was the emperor's instrument and how he kept control of foreign policy and the army. The new Austro-Hungarian Empire or 'dual monarchy' had parliaments; and 'this side of the Leitha' also had elected diets, but its government was not parliamentary. The emperor conducted his own foreign policy and military deployments, with minimal parliamentary oversight. Franz Joseph also kept the right to legislate by decree, again with few constraints, which meant that he could bypass or substitute for the parliamentary process. When the going was tough, he even had the power to close the parliament in Vienna (but not the one in Hungary) and to impose ministries without parliamentary approval. To that extent at least, absolutism survived.

More importantly, the empire survived, but it was not just a matter of finding a constitutional formula to satisfy Hungarian aspirations. Franz Joseph was unloved in Hungary, not least for killing the kingdom's generals, but Sisi had the glamour and passion for Hungary that reconciled Hungarians to Habsburg rule. She was their queen, who spoke their language, wore their national dress, and went to hunt in their fields. Back in 1866, Sisi had asked Franz Joseph to buy her Gödöllő Palace, just outside Pest. He had grumpily refused, explaining that 'in these hard times, we must save mightily.' The next year, the newly installed Hungarian government led by Count Andrássy bought it for her, as the gift of the nation on her coronation.[23]

Andrássy had no doubt of Sisi's contribution to the 1867 settlement between the monarch and Hungary. But for the other nations of the new Austro-Hungarian Empire, Sisi showed little interest, being particularly disdainful of Czechs and Italians. Her inconsistency and eccentricities should not, however, conceal the way her intervention in Hungarian affairs fitted into a larger pattern of queenly conduct. Because of Queen Victoria (1837–1901), Maria Theresa, and Catherine the Great of Russia (1762–1796), we tend to think of the eighteenth and nineteenth centuries as a period when female rulers prospered. In fact, there were fewer regnant queens then than in preceding centuries, and females were expressly barred from the succession in Bourbon France and Spain, Sweden (after 1720), and Prussia.[24]

It was, instead, as consorts that queens became influential, directing matters of state behind the scenes and rebuilding the image of monarchy. Leopoldine of Brazil set the pace, for, besides designing the Brazilian flag, she pushed her cautious husband into declaring independence in the first place. But in some ways the closest parallel to Sisi was Queen Alexandra, the consort of Britain's Edward VII (1901–1910). Elegant, striking in appearance, and a meddler in politics, Alexandra too had a husband whose reign as King Edward the Caresser had commenced amongst the lowest of expectations but whose eventual acceptance and rehabilitation owed much to her own reputation.

25

MAXIMILIAN, MEXICO, AND ROYAL DEATHS

*A*s a boy, Franz Joseph had delighted in his toy castle with its miniature soldiers and cannons, and he remained all his life passionate about the army, his soldier's uniforms, and parades. His younger brothers received an almost identical education and training, but each turned out differently. Karl Ludwig was a zealous Catholic of no special talents. He was later known as the 'exhibition archduke', since the only task he could perform competently was to represent the ruler at public events. Ludwig Viktor ('Luzi Wuzi') was mostly distinguished by his overt homosexuality and cross-dressing. He favoured silk frocks and was eventually declared insane. In contrast to his three siblings, Maximilian (more properly Ferdinand Maximilian), who was the oldest of Franz Joseph's three younger brothers, was outgoing, charismatic, adventurous, and balanced. The archduchess Sophie contrasted her two eldest sons when they were just ten and eight years old respectively: 'I must say that of all my boys Franz Joseph is the best behaved . . . but Maxi wins everyone's hearts. . . . Maxi has the richest spirit.'[1]

Franz Joseph remained jealous of Maximilian even after he became emperor. Aware that he owed his position to a coup that had forced his uncle from office, Franz Joseph feared that he might in turn be overthrown and replaced by his brother. Although no liberal, Maximilian opposed the harsh regime imposed by his brother, and his criticisms were gleefully reported to Franz Joseph by the emperor's advisors. Accordingly, Franz Joseph kept Maximilian away from Vienna and out of the political limelight. Whereas his two younger brothers received governorships and infantry regiments, Maximilian was appointed in 1850 to command of the sailing sloop *Minerva*, based in Trieste. As he wrote generously to his mother, 'I am just a corvette captain, the last in rank of all the archdukes, but I stand on my own two feet and really hope to serve my revered emperor.'[2]

Like the empress, Maximilian was thrilled by the lyrical verse of Heinrich Heine. Whereas Sisi was moved by Heine's melancholic songs of lost love and worldly disillusionment, Maximilian read them for their vivid tales of travel. Both adopted Heine's style in their writing, but Maximilian's descriptions were unfailingly wooden. For him, meadows were always 'emerald green', cliffs were 'mighty', and the sea was 'deep blue.' Maximilian travelled extensively, mostly around the Mediterranean but also down the Atlantic coast and across the sea to Brazil, and he recorded his experiences in his 'Travel Sketches' (*Reiseskizzen*), which were themselves modelled on Heine's 'Travel Pictures' (*Reisebilder*).

It was in Spain that mission and travel fused. There Maximilian encountered, as he explained at the time, 'memories of the time when Spain was under the wings of the double-headed eagle, eternally embroidered by the sun, at the highest summit of its power and the greatest empire in the world.' Attending a bull fight in 1851, he imagined the onlookers paying him homage, and he 'dreamt back to the fine times when the Habsburgs were rulers of this noble people.' In Granada he knelt before the tomb of Ferdinand of Aragon, grandfather of Emperor Charles V, 'as a traveller in a foreign land . . . but as the closest legal descendant of the dead man.' He mused that the 'golden sceptre' of the Habsburgs had been broken in Spain but, addressing himself, 'that it shines plus ultra to you.'[3]

Despite his appeal to the Plus Ultra of Charles V, the destiny that Maximilian sought was not founded on ideas of world empire and of service to the faith. It rested instead on a wistful reading of the past, learned from Washington Irving's romantic histories of Spain, and on frustration at his own situation. After the birth of a son, Rudolf, to Franz Joseph and Sisi in 1858, the chance of Maximilian succeeding his brother became virtually nil.

Instead, he had to make do with his naval duties. Appointed rear admiral and overall commander of the fledgling Habsburg fleet in 1854, he pushed for naval expansion and was responsible for the introduction of screw-driven ironclads. He sponsored the circumnavigation of the globe by the *Novara* in 1857–1859. Maximilian was sufficiently reconciled to a career in the margins to begin the construction in 1856 of a 'fairytale building' just outside Trieste. It was to the battlements and lavish state rooms of Miramare, with its park laid out to receive exotic gingkoes and giant sequoias, that Maximilian brought his new wife, Princess Charlotte (Carlota) of Belgium, in 1857.

Maximilian and Charlotte's marriage was one of love. It came, however, at a high price to Charlotte's father, King Leopold I of Belgium, who had to make over a sizeable dowry, which went immediately into the depleted Austrian treasury. In return, Leopold asked Franz Joseph to find his new son-in-law a more suitable vocation, on which account Franz Joseph appointed Maximilian governor of the province of Lombardy-Venetia. This was a poisoned chalice laced with gunpowder. Habsburg rule was deeply resented in the province, yet the terms of Maximilian's appointment forbade him from engaging in any course of action that might have made his government acceptable to most Italians. Even so, he ignored Franz Joseph's instruction that he should use 'severity in the event of the smallest revolt.' On 19 April 1859, Franz Joseph dismissed Maximilian. Within two months, Austrian rule had collapsed in Lombardy.[4]

Maximilian was not the only prince who believed that he had a historic mission to play on the world stage. Napoleon III of France was equally convinced of the part to which he, as the nephew and namesake of the first Napoleon, was predestined. In Europe, he championed Italian independence and support for Turkey against Russia. North Africa, the African coast, the Middle East, and South-East Asia were in turn the other targets of Napoleon III's ambition. The Americas offered him, however, an opportunity which might be justified as much by strategy as by vanity. French policy had long opposed the expansion of the United States as endangering the balance of power in the New World. On this account, France had in the 1840s backed an independent Texas and in the next decade made naval demonstrations in support of Mexico in its war with the United States.

The outbreak of the American Civil War in 1861 temporarily removed the geopolitical threat posed by the United States. But Napoleon was determined to put an end to future expansion from the north. Just as Britain and

France's earlier intervention in the Crimea in support of Ottoman Turkey had stopped the Russian movement along the Black Sea coast, so France would now make Mexico the stumbling block. Napoleon considered French intervention there not to be enough. To defend itself in the long term, Mexico needed stable rule—in the forty years since independence Mexico had had no less than fifty different governments, most of them military. In Napoleon's view, only a monarchy could rebuild the Mexican nation and forge the unity needed to prevent further losses of its territory to the United States.

Maximilian was an obvious choice for ruler. After his dismissal as governor of Lombardy-Venetia, Maximilian had languished in frustration, spending most of his time either travelling or developing the Miramare estate. Both he and Charlotte were convinced that they had by birth and aptitude a right to more. Already, on a visit to Brazil in 1860, Maximilian had felt a surge of emotion when standing as the first Habsburg prince on the shores of the New World, and he had at once pontificated on the scheme of government most suited to Latin America—'a wise tyrant', who melded iron discipline with justice. He was ready for the part allotted by fate. For Napoleon, the Habsburg was an ideal candidate. Franz Joseph's cooperation was, furthermore, guaranteed, for the scheme of making Maximilian ruler of Mexico would both enhance Habsburg prestige and rid the emperor of his brother's shadow. The problem was that Mexico already had a government under the presidency of the Republican politician Benito Juárez.[5]

Mexican historians have conventionally seen the attempt to establish a monarchy in Mexico as a vain attempt to halt the country's progress towards a modern republic. In fact, as one of Mexico's greatest scholars, Edmundo O'Gorman, long ago argued, there was also in Mexican politics a conservative tradition upon which a monarchical movement could build. Mexican Conservatism was strongly Catholic and opposed the Republican programme of closing monasteries, seizing church land, and harrying priests. Yet it was ready to embrace moderate reforms in the interests of sound administration. It certainly had a following that was larger than the handful of military men, clerics, and landowners described in the accounts of most Mexican historians. As O'Gorman argued, there was thus nothing quaint about installing a Habsburg as Mexico's ruler, but this was 'an authentic possibility for the national being.'[6]

Maximilian was formally offered the throne of Mexico in 1863 by a delegation of Conservative leaders, who addressed him in Miramare as the worthy descendant of Emperor Charles V. His monarchy was also to be an empire, and he thus to be an emperor, because this was thought to be the developing style in the New World. Having accepted the title, Maximilian busied himself with diplomatic and practical preparations. He was under no illusion about the scale of the task before him, having received from the Austrian ambassador in Washington ominous warnings about the difficulties he would face. Accordingly, he sought military guarantees of support from Napoleon, which the French ruler readily gave. Franz Joseph was less accommodating. While he promised some limited financial support and allowed Maximilian to enlist a volunteer force from the Habsburg lands, he unnecessarily demanded that his brother repudiate his rights and titles as a Habsburg. Should the venture fail, Maximilian would thus return to Europe as less than an archduke—and any children he and Charlotte might have would also be deprived of rank. The stakes were high, and Maximilian almost threw in his hand. As he remarked in April 1864, only a few days before he was due to embark, 'For my part, if someone were to tell me that everything was off, I would shut myself up in my room and jump for joy! But Charlotte?'[7]

In the intervening time, French troops had invaded Mexico on the pretext of recovering loans owed to the French government and banks. Landing in Veracruz in December 1861, a six-thousand-strong force made its way inland. The French commanders were convinced that they would face a rabble, but the forces mustered by the Republicans were disciplined; when outnumbered, they took to guerrilla tactics. Napoleon's response to the slowness of the French advance was to throw an increasing number of troops into the fray. By the middle of 1863, he had committed almost forty thousand men. In June that year, Mexico City fell, and a new regency government took over on Maximilian's behalf. Still in Miramare, Maximilian expressed concern that the Republicans had been ousted by force, and he questioned whether there was genuine support for a monarchy. Accordingly, in every territory that the French forces overran, they held plebiscites, which were neither free nor fair. As one of the Mexican politicians disingenuously stated in a letter to Maximilian, these confirmed that 'three-quarters of the total territory of Mexico and four-fifths of her whole population have declared for a monarchy.'[8]

On 28 May 1864, Maximilian and Charlotte disembarked at Veracruz with more than five hundred pieces of luggage—including carriages, crates of bone china bearing the Mexican imperial arms that Maximilian had designed, crystal goblets, furnishings, and fine wines. The progress to Mexico City took a fortnight on a narrow-gauge railway and along rutted tracks. During the six-week voyage from Trieste, Maximilian had composed a monumental guide to court etiquette, the *Reglamento para el Servicio y Ceremonial de la Corte*. Consisting of seating plans for dinners and other ceremonies and orders of precedence involving one hundred separate ranks, and with minute attention to detail, the *Reglamento* amounted to almost six hundred pages:

> The delicacies will be laid out in the Dining Room. As soon as the imperial couple approach the table, the Secretaries of Ceremonies will enter the Dining Room followed close behind by the men of the Palace Guard. . . . The First Secretary of Ceremonies will attend the table of the gentlemen and the Second Secretary the table of the ladies. At this point, the Emperor will hand his sombrero to the attending Field Adjutant, and the Empress her handkerchief and fan to the attending Maid of Honour.[9]

Maximilian also prescribed a minimum height for the troops of the Palace Guard. They were to be no less than six foot, six inches tall. Twelve-inch-high silver helmets, each crowned with an imperial eagle, topped them off.

It is easy to be scornful of Maximilian's endeavours, but the *Reglamento* had a greater purpose than just etiquette. Maximilian intended to make his court the centre of all political life in Mexico, which united 'all parties and opinions' in the common performance of rituals and obeisance.[10] The grand ball held in June 1866 brought together eight hundred guests, and Charlotte noted with approval the Paris finery that they wore. Even the native population was not left out: one of the empress's ladies-in-waiting was Josefa Marela, a Mexican of dark complexion, who was reputed to be a descendant of the last Aztec ruler. Likewise, where their content affected the indigenous population, Maximilian published his decrees in the Nahuatl language, which is the only occasion in Mexico's history when its government has done so.

For those not invited to Maximilian's new Chapultepec Palace outside Mexico City, he gave a redesigned capital, with parks, fountains, gas lighting, and a broad boulevard modelled on Paris's Champs Élysées. Yet Maximilian's endeavours to reconcile the factions and broaden his support went beyond ceremony and symbolism. On first entering the National Palace, which housed the ministries, he had found complete disarray—no filing systems, correspondence unregistered, documents heaped on the floor, and no set hours for work. Appointing and promoting on the basis of merit, without regard for party affiliation, he put together an administration that embarked on a programme of radical reform. Universal elementary education was mandated, debt servitude and child labour abolished, hours of work and lunch breaks regulated, and the communal property and water rights of the indigenous people protected.[11]

No less significant were Maximilian's reforms of government and the law. In order to break the power of the regional bosses or caudillos, he divided the country into fifty provinces, each headed by a prefect appointed by him. Administrative courts took over from the slow-moving judiciary the resolution of disputes between individuals and agencies of government. At the end of 1865, the fruits of a committee made up of lawyers drawn from across the political spectrum were published in the form of a Civil Code that regulated family law, inheritance, property, and contracts. Declared abolished by the Republican government in 1867, three-quarters of the 1865 code was, nonetheless, included in the 'new' Civil Code of 1870.[12]

The Civil Code illustrates the difficulty that Maximilian faced. In order to make his regime acceptable to most Mexicans, he embraced an essentially Republican programme of modernization. In so doing, he jettisoned the Conservatives, not restoring the oppressive rights of landowners or the Catholic clergy to their property. Indeed, Maximilian went further, entrenching civil marriage and full religious toleration in the Civil Code of 1865. And yet Maximilian was not acceptable to the Republican camp on account of his imperial title and the symbols of royalty that he so assiduously burnished. The consequence was that instead of creating unity beneath the crown, he manufactured a void.

The end came swiftly. At its height, the French military contribution to Maximilian amounted to forty-five thousand French troops, plus the pay and equipping of seven thousand Mexican regulars and about twenty thousand auxiliaries, including Austrian and Belgian volunteers. With the end of the American Civil War in 1865, the Republican forces were able to reequip with surplus weaponry and take out international loans. At the same time, Napoleon III came under pressure at home to rein in the French finances and to prepare an army for the expected war against Prussia. During 1865,

Republican tactics ominously changed from guerrilla attacks to broad offensives. The next year, the French withdrawal commenced. A desperate voyage by the Empress Charlotte to France, where she pleaded with Napoleon to delay the evacuation, proved hopeless. Distraught and convinced that Napoleon was trying to poison her, Charlotte took temporary refuge in the Vatican as the most unwelcome guest of Pope Pius IX. Her descent into madness had begun.

Back in 1862, the Spanish general Juan Prim had warned Napoleon III that a foreign monarch imposed on the Mexicans by force of French arms 'will have nothing to sustain him; on the day that this support is withdrawn . . . he will fall from the throne erected by Your Majesty.' And so it came to pass. Left with only twenty thousand volunteer troops after the French withdrawal, Maximilian was first pushed out of the countryside and then out of the towns. Much of what remained of the imperial army either deserted or changed sides. Early on in 1867, Maximilian abandoned Mexico City and made his headquarters at Querétaro, 200 kilometres (125 miles) north-west of the capital. Three months later, the city fell, and Maximilian was betrayed. After a brief trial and notwithstanding the previous abolition of the death penalty in Mexico, he was condemned to the firing squad along with two of his generals. As he went to his execution on 19 June 1867, he remarked on the weather—'What a beautiful day! I have always wanted to die on a day like this.'[13]

As he stood before the firing squad, Maximilian delivered a final oration: 'Mexicans! Men of my class and origins are appointed by God to be the happiness of people or their martyrs. Called by some of you, I came for the good of the country, I did not come for ambition. . . . I hope that my blood will be the last to be spilled and I pray that it regenerates this unhappy country. Viva Mexico! Viva la Independencia!' As previously agreed, the two generals stood on either side of Maximilian, to recall Christ's crucifixion.[14]

This was a choreographed death, which played on the themes of mission and of Christ-like martyrdom and redemption. Stories abounded to lend credence to the simulacrum—that the bullets that tore into Maximilian had formed on his shirt the sign of the cross, that a crown of thorns had materialized over his portrait in Miramare, and so on. Images and sketches of the execution were reproduced across America and Europe, as well as one of the first faked photographs. Most famously, the death of Maximilian was the subject of four paintings and a lithograph by Édouard Manet. In all but one of these, the troops performing the execution are dressed not as Mexicans but as French soldiers, thus pointing to Napoleon III's responsibility for Maximilian's death.[15]

Franz Joseph was unmoved by his brother's death, commenting only that his skills as a huntsman would be missed at the next shoot, but even so 'we may still look forward to good sport.' Across the Habsburg Empire, however, the story of Maximilian's death was retold, particularly in the pages of the new illustrated weeklies. The Hungarian mass-circulation *Sunday News* (*Vasárnapi Újság*) thus rehearsed Maximilian's biography and his betrayal by Napoleon. It reported the drama of Charlotte's intervention and hinted at the madness brought on by her 'broken spirit' (she died in 1927). For those wanting more, an anonymous French text that dwelled at length on Maximilian's dignity, courage, and martyrdom was soon rushed out in German and Hungarian translations. More than anything else, the circumstances of Maximilian's death constituted his posthumous reputation.[16]

Monarchs were the first modern celebrities. They were objects of spectacle, whose image was through the photograph and mass-produced engraving made into a commodity that lent them a 'larger than life' quality. Their deaths, too, gave meaning and intensity to existences that were remote from everyday experience. Maximilian's death in 1867 was the first murder of a sovereign in a line of assassinations across Europe that resumed the next year with the murder of Prince Michael of Serbia. It was followed by the killings of Alexander II of Russia (1881), Umberto I of Italy (1900), King Alexander and Queen Draga of Serbia (1903), Carlos I and Crown Prince Luiz Felipe of Portugal (1908), and George I of Greece (1913).[17]

Among the Habsburgs, violent death also became familiar after 1867. In 1889, Crown Prince Rudolf took his own life. Sisi was killed in Geneva in 1898 by an Italian anarchist eager to murder anyone royal—'O no! What's happened to me now?' were her dying words. On each of these occasions, the press gave extensive coverage not only of the life but also of the death. In Rudolf's case, editors had to be careful, but even so readers were treated to minute accounts of how the news had been first reported, confirmation of death by a doctor, the situation of the body and the first obsequies, the peaceful expression on Rudolf's face, and so on. Sisi's death in 1898 consumed as much as a month's coverage in some of the illustrated weeklies.

Her murder was described in tasteless detail, including her black dress being weighed down with her own blood, and was sometimes accompanied by graphic sketches of the moment of her death.

Monarchs and royalty had once crafted their own images. The Habsburgs had been most assiduous in their self-fashioning, piling on mythological conceits and evidence of their divinely ordained rule. But dynasties had lost their power to cultivate the popular imagination, and the days of triumphal arches and soaring catafalques were past. In most of Europe, it was now the press that framed the way dynasties were represented. In the case of the Habsburgs, the most powerful and resonating images communicated in the new media were spectacles of death. Soon it would be another photograph, this time of a murder in the making—a plumed archduke descending a flight of steps towards a car—that would both capture and symbolize the start of the events that led to the death of Habsburg rule in Europe.

26

THE POLITICS OF DISCONTENT
AND THE 1908 JUBILEE

ranz Joseph's absolutism was the incubator of nationalism. Before 1848, nationality had been just one social bond among many, vying with religion, region, and kindred, and whether a noble, peasant, townsman, or priest. Now it became the predominant force, its potency enhanced by an oppressive regime bent on centralization and uniformity. The events of 1848 provided a story around which ideas of nationhood clustered—of a heroic struggle for freedom, of champions of the national cause, and of martyrs who had suffered on the nation's behalf. Portraits on walls, homespun verse embroidered on samplers, and even haircuts recollected their example, magnetizing new communities of identity. The advent of constitutional rule in the 1860s did not diminish nationalism's appeal. Instead, the new parliaments provided vehicles for its articulation, thus contributing to its potency and spread.

Tokens of belonging were also markers of difference. Czechs distinguished themselves from others with elaborately buttoned jackets, Slovenes with dormouse pelts, and Hungarians with moustaches, of which one diligent observer counted no fewer than twenty-three types, each indicating a different affinity to the nation. Items of dress popular in parts of the countryside were seized upon and declared to be national—the gaudy Hungarian 'Kalocsa' embroidery was taken from a style originally favoured in Serbian-populated villages in the south of the country. Sexual connoisseurs elaborated checklists of foreign women in a descending order of depravity, their debasement evident from the degree to which they deviated from the observer's own supposed national norm of femininity.[1]

Space too was demarcated. In the 1860s (and after a decade-long discussion), the market place of Zagreb, previously a gathering place for peoples from across the Balkans, was made Croat by the insertion of a giant statue of Jelačić on horseback. In Prague, a cordon of monuments to Czech saints and German heroes divided the Czech from the German residential quarters. Streets and shops were also sites of belonging, the different national groups displaying their allegiance by where they chose to live and shop. In Hungary, the taverns were differentiated by the alcohol they served—beer for Germans, wine for Hungarians, and cheap brandy for the rest. Even in their cups, the different national groups were reported to be different, the Hungarian becoming melancholy, the German talkative, the Romanian violent, and the Ruthenian incoherent.[2]

Nationhood was not a matter of fact but of decision. Although his mother was German, Kossuth chose to be Hungarian, but his uncle became a notable Slovak patriot. Many, however, had no obvious grounds for embracing a single identity. One soldier at the beginning of the twentieth century wrote his diary in four different languages—German for regimental matters, Slovene when thinking about his girlfriend, Serbian for songs he recalled, and Hungarian for his sexual fantasies. Others changed what they said they were according to circumstance and financial advantage, or were indifferent, often conversing in several languages or in a blended argot. Shunning a strong national identity, they too were shunned, disparaged as 'hermaphrodites' and 'amphibians' who did not fit into the increasingly conventional categories of belonging.[3]

Identities were impressed by neighbours, parents, friends, and schoolteachers. But government and the bureaucracy were also involved. The constitution for the non-Hungarian part of the empire, the so-called Cisleithania, published in December 1867, guaranteed nationalities the right to 'preserve and cultivate their nationality and language' including through education. This was fleshed out two years later in a law that mandated the provision of public funds for schools teaching in national languages when there were more than forty pupils requesting it. But the definitions of nationality and national language were restrictive, and they did not acknowledge many of the vernaculars that people spoke—Lemko, Hutsul, Yiddish, Friulian, Dalmatian Italian, and so on. Finally, in the censuses taken after 1880 in Cisleithania, participants had to choose their 'everyday language' (*Umgangssprache*) from a prescribed list of German, Bohemian-Moravian-Slovak, Polish, Ruthenian, Slovene, Serbian-Croat, Italian-Ladino, Romanian, and Hungarian.

The 1881 Hungarian census was more flexible, permitting respondents to name their 'mother tongue' if it was missing from the list. It also included on this occasion categories for Romani speakers, Armenians, and mutes. Even so, the consequence was much the same, forcing people into linguistic blocks and effacing the intermediate identities which made nationality fuzzier and so more permeable. Along with the censuses came ethnic maps, which showed the populations in stark blocks of colour, with no in-between shades, and ethnographic museums, which made tumbledown cottages into markers of national specificity.[4]

As individual lives were swept up into bureaucratic categories, more and more became seen through the prism of nationality. Where several nationalities lived side by side, relations were often marked by competition, with rival choirs, fire brigades, parishes, athletics clubs, savings banks, veterans' associations, and schools. Conflicts over funding made schools battle-grounds, with governing boards in mixed regions seeking to recruit above the forty-pupil threshold to meet the quota for state support, even if that meant bribing students of another nationality to attend. In Prague, the university split down the middle into German and Czech sections; only the botanical garden remained common to both, since the names of the plants were written in Latin.

The ethos of the bureaucracy taught that civil servants should stand above nationality, but here too the politics of difference prevailed. In the provinces, governors' offices were rapidly 'nationalized', and local officials often promoted the interests and funding of their own linguistic community. In the central reaches of the bureaucracy, a balance was sought, but ministries often became the preserve of individual nationalities, with Poles dominant in the finance ministry and Czechs in education and commerce. German remained, however, the only official language of internal communication in Cisleithania. Hungary had its own civil service after 1867, which was solidly Hungarian, but Hungarians were disproportionately represented in the common foreign ministry in Vienna.[5]

In Hungary, the government pursued a relentless policy of 'Magyarization', cracking down on the organizations of the non-Hungarian nationalities, gerrymandering constituencies to keep their representatives out of the parliament, and closing secondary schools that taught in any language except Hungarian. The Hungarian prime minister put it bluntly in 1908: 'We have only one single categorical imperative, the Hungarian state idea, and we demand that every citizen should acknowledge it and subject himself unconditionally to it. . . . The Hungarians conquered this country for the Hungarians and not for others. The supremacy and hegemony of the Hungarians is fully justified.' The rector of Budapest University put it even more boldly: the purpose of Magyarization was assimilation, and 'we shall just keep on at it until there is not a Slovak left.'[6]

In Cisleithania, where no one nationality had a majority, policy aimed instead at regulation through the law. Disputes were channelled through administrative courts, which usually came down on the side of whichever group constituted the minority. To begin with, the administrative courts held by the principle of subjectivity—an individual's nationality was whatever he or she declared it to be. But they confronted so many patently false declarations that they had to apply 'objective tests', based on checklists of language, parentage, membership of societies, and daily routines. Identity became a measurable quality and the pigeonholing of individuals into categories of belonging now constituted part of the business of government. Nazi Germany would take this process one stage further, compiling menus of identity that were also death warrants.[7]

Nationalism rendered parliamentary politics in Cisleithania unworkable. To begin with, the electoral system favoured the German middle class. They elected respectable liberal spokesmen, but Franz Joseph disliked liberals. They baulked at spending money on the army, and they also forced him to abandon the concordat he had reached with the pope in 1855 that had put most schools under clerical supervision. The liberals' reputation was destroyed by the banking collapse of 1873, in which too many fingers were caught in tills. The emergence of a non-German bourgeoisie and electorate weakened them further. The newcomers voted for their own national parties, but these were also split on ideological grounds. The consequence was a proliferation of parties and a succession of weak coalitions.

The solution was, as one prime minister put it, 'to muddle through', trading piecemeal concessions with the aim of keeping the national parties in 'a condition of even and well-modulated discontent.' So the Poles were kept quiet by giving them control of Galicia, and the Slovenes by handing over to them the government of Carniola. German Catholics were won over by legislation on pensions and the workplace that gave Cisleithania the best labour laws in Europe after Germany and Switzerland. But the Czechs proved harder to convince. To buy their support, Franz Joseph planned to grant Bohemia the same self-government as Hungary, but Hungary's leaders vehemently opposed any watering down of their country's special status. Instead, Franz Joseph backed a solution whereby the higher civil service in Bohemia would conduct business in Czech rather than German. The result was chaos. Rioting over several days on the streets of Vienna and Prague forced the measure to be indefinitely postponed.[8]

Franz Joseph believed nationalism to be a middle-class infection, so he promoted the extension of the franchise to bring in the working class. The system of voting which gave higher taxpayers an advantage was also abandoned in elections to the imperial parliament (but not to the diets), so that by 1907 every adult male in Cisleithania had an equal vote. The largest party in the parliament became the socialists, who spoke the rhetoric of class and whose leaders denounced nationalism as 'false consciousness', of no more relevance than hair colour. Even so, the socialists split along national lines, into competing German and Czech organizations. Their affiliated trade unions were similarly divided. National rivalries continued to be an endemic part of the political system.

The result was a stalemate. Even minor matters such as the provision of language classes in a Styrian secondary school paralysed the imperial parliament, with noisy interruptions and inkpots thrown. This suited Franz Joseph. It showed that constitutional rule was unworkable and justified his appointment of bureaucratic ministries headed by civil servants that stood above the hurly-burly of nationalist discontents. Increasingly, he suspended parliament, legislating instead by decree and only summoning the parliament to give retrospective sanction to what he had ordered. Notwithstanding periodic elections and an expansive franchise, bureaucratic absolutism prevailed. Cisleithania may have had a parliament, but its politics was not parliamentary.

The faults in the structure were obvious even at the time, and plenty of solutions were proposed—to reconfigure the empire into units based on nationality, or to organize people into loose national associations, which would oversee educational and cultural policy, while territorial units looked after less contentious administrative matters. Although a few writers recommended simply ditching Hungary from the empire in the interest of the rest, nobody envisaged breaking the empire up into separate states. Writers and politicians as diverse as the Czech historian František Palacký, Karl Marx, Lord Palmerston, and the Austrian socialist Otto Bauer were unanimous in their opinion that to destroy the Habsburg Empire would leave a dangerous vacuum in the heart of Europe, which Russia was only too likely to fill. As Palacký put it, if the Austrian Empire did not exist, it would be necessary to invent it.

For nationalist politicians the goal was to maintain the empire as a shield while yet manipulating it in the interests of their own national group. For Franz Joseph and his ministers, the task was to foster a sense of unity that inspired loyalty. The novelist Robert Musil, writing in the 1920s, poked fun at the endeavours of government, describing a so-called Parallel Action Campaign desperately searching for an idea that would give meaning to empire. (Set in 1913, the campaign eventually embraced the formula 'Empire means peace.') The solution which government chose was, in fact, the only one available. As a dynastic enterprise, it was the dynasty that held the empire together: by feting Habsburg history, the empire might be given a common story around which the parts could coalesce.

A framework had been given by the Tyrolean historian and state archivist Joseph von Hormayr (circa 1781–1848). Hormayr wrote big books, not least his *Pocket Book on National History*, which ran to forty-two volumes. His shorter, twenty-volume *Austrian Plutarch*, published between 1807 and 1814, was devoted to 'the lives and portraits of all the princes and most famous generals, statesmen, scholars, and artists of the Austrian Empire', but it endeavoured to balance Habsburg heroes with national champions, interweaving their achievements. For Hormayr, national sentiment was not at odds with the idea of empire, since Habsburg rule guaranteed that 'the smaller, weaker and less stable nations feel their possessions to be safe from more powerful neighbours.' But the Habsburgs also gave unity, he explained, binding peoples together in strength and prosperity in a single enterprise.[9]

Hormayr's view of Habsburg history influenced successive school textbooks, which presented national history in the context of a larger, imperial undertaking. So the history of the Slovenes was integrated into the narrative of a greater 'Austrian homeland', while for Czechs their medieval history slid effortlessly into Habsburg dynastic history, with embarrassing features such as the revolt of 1618 simply left out. The elision of the national and the dynastic also influenced the way the Habsburgs chose to present history in two of their greatest cultural undertakings. The first of these was the official multivolume account of the empire, known as the Crown Prince's Work, since it was initially edited by Franz Joseph's son, Rudolf. The second was the celebration of Franz Joseph's sixtieth anniversary as emperor, which fell in 1908. Both, however, also demonstrated the weakness of the glue that held the empire's parts together.[10]

Crown Prince Rudolf was drawn towards both liberalism and socialism. Critical of his father's conservatism, he penned angry letters to the press under pseudonyms. It was to keep him out of politics, and away from the brothels, that Franz Joseph entrusted Rudolf in 1883 with the editorship of the massive *Austro-Hungarian Monarchy in Word and Image* (*Die österreichisch-ungarische Monarchie in Wort und Bild*), the first volume of which appeared in 1886. The full set, which took sixteen years to complete, ran to twenty-four volumes, which were released in 397 fortnightly instalments, and consisted of more than twelve thousand pages and 4,500 illustrations, drawing on the work of some 430 contributors. A parallel Hungarian-language version appeared simultaneously with the German original, although by merging sections it only came to twenty-one volumes. The venture survived Rudolf's suicide in 1889, its editorship passing nominally to his widow, Princess Stephanie of Belgium, who is otherwise remembered as the inventor (and patent holder) of the hostess trolley.[11]

The series was arranged province by province, starting with Vienna and Lower Austria and concluding with Croatia. Each volume described the geography, flora and fauna, ethnography, culture, and history of a province, combined with frothy praise for the ruler and the benefits of empire. So from the volume on Austrian Silesia: 'Thanks to the wise government of our emperor, who has brought peace, our little land has flourished beneath his wings as never before . . . so that our province now stands in the first rank of Crownlands in this our common fatherland.' All this comported with Rudolf's aim, which was pure Hormayr: 'Let the peoples of these lands love, respect, and support each other as they come to learn about one another through this work; let them ponder how they may loyally serve the throne and the fatherland.'[12]

The Hungarian government insisted upon complete editorial control of the six volumes dedicated to Hungary, which were uncritically overseen by the novelist Maurice (Mór) Jókai. Jókai's contribution on Budapest presented the capital as a city of leisure, overlooking its warped economy which made it both the 'Chicago of the Balkans' and, in the title of Ferenc Molnár's contemporary novel, *Hungry City* (*Az éhes város*, 1901). More pointedly, the volumes on Hungary deliberately downplayed national minorities, giving as much space to the insignificant Hungarian-speaking Palóc people of northern Hungary as to the millions of Romanians in Transylvania and the Banat. Contributions on the Jews of Hungary also contained antisemitic asides that were omitted in the German version of the series.[13]

The Cisleithanian volumes were each composed under the direction of scholars drawn from the relevant province. Mostly academics who had been educated in Vienna, they dwelled on the exotic and alien. Hence, in Galicia fathers placed garlic beneath the pillows of their children, and midwives spat three times on the newborn to ward off the evil eye; among the South Slavs the kidnapping of brides and the blood feud still prevailed; the Slovenes of Styria wore wooden clogs, and so on. Far from aiding mutual comprehension among the peoples of the Habsburg Empire, the great undertaking achieved the reverse, emphasizing the stark cultural differences and gradations of backwardness that prevailed despite the beneficence of imperial rule.

Plans for a jubilee to celebrate Franz Joseph's fiftieth anniversary as emperor had to be pared back in 1898 on account of the empress's assassination. The sixtieth-anniversary celebrations were thus planned on a scale that was unprecedented. Two processions would pass through the centre of Vienna to do homage to Franz Joseph. The first would provide tableaux of the history of the dynasty, and the second would display the allegiance of the empire's peoples to their ruler in a parade that brought to life the multi-volume Crown Prince's Work. Dynasty, nation, and empire would fuse in a collective affirmation of loyalty to the aged emperor.

Difficulties arose from the start. The Hungarian government refused to be involved on the grounds that as king of Hungary, Franz Joseph had begun his reign in 1867 and not 1848. The Vienna city council had recently banned a performance of *Hamlet* because it was to be delivered in Czech, so the Czechs were already disaffected. Then the choice of historical tableaux caused rancour. The organizers of the pageant had decided to commence the procession with King Rudolf of Habsburg, but his defeat of King Ottokar of

Bohemia made him unacceptable to the Czechs, who now absented themselves entirely. A tableau commemorating Radetzky's defeat of rebellion in Lombardy led in turn to an Italian boycott. The Croats almost walked out too upon learning that their role in the tableau recalling 1848 was to play the part of looters, and the programme had to be adjusted at the last minute.[14]

The procession of the peoples made up in numbers for the missing Hungarians, Czechs, and Italians, with some eight thousand participants parading past the emperor, who stood for three hours beneath a massive mock-up of Rudolf II's crown that had been set up on the Ring, Vienna's circular thoroughfare. National costumes had been devised for the occasion, which often had little to do with what people really wore, although the homage of the city of Vienna was led by gentlemen in white tie and top hats. After them came, according to an eyewitness report, 'Styrians in Loden coats and hats with green bands, South Tyrolean marksmen with grey jackets, Ruthenes, and here and there a Polish Jew in a kaftan, with a velvet cap on his head.' One feature of the procession was the disproportionately large number of participants coming from the poorer parts of the empire. Paid a pittance to attend, they flocked in their thousands from Bukovina, Dalmatia, and Galicia, often clad in only the crudest garments. 'Rustic simplicity as urban spectacle' was the verdict of the leading socialist newspaper.[15]

The jubilee celebration was at the time deemed a success, with three hundred thousand spectators lining the Ring, no serious accidents, and the emperor 'visibly moved.' But as the liberal newspaper the *Neue Freie Presse* observed, a parade was all it had been, and the cacophony of languages spoken by the participants only emphasized their mutual incomprehension. On top of language, the contrasting levels of development between nations were all too obvious. Some spectators reported shock at confronting the uncouth representatives of the poorer parts of the empire, who frightened children, so one journalist remarked, with their weather-beaten and haggish faces. The architect Adolf Loos felt he was witnessing barbarian tribes from the Middle Ages.[16]

Despite the praise it received at the time, the jubilee was a double flop. Not only did the recitation of Habsburg history prompt a boycott by Czechs, Hungarians, and Italians, but the procession of the peoples also highlighted difference, division, and cultural hierarchy. Indeed, once the procession was over, fights and bullying erupted between the various national groups camped out in Prater Park.[17] Nevertheless, as they had progressed before the imperial dais, set up outside the Hofburg, the participants saluted the emperor. Ultimately, it was his person alone that excited loyalty.

The emperor had grown old with his reign. By 1870, his hair was receding and his moustache greying. Over the next decade, his whiskers whitened, and he went completely bald. Except for the spreading lines around his eyes, he looked almost the same for the next thirty-five years, thus conveying a sense of his own timelessness. On every public occasion, he said the same thing: 'It was nice. We enjoyed it.' His dress seldom changed either, being invariably a military tunic and red cavalry trousers. But it was as the 'emperor of peace' that he was most frequently portrayed, on the grounds that he had after 1866 kept the empire out of war. Peace went hand in hand with his piety and with his studious performance of time-honoured Catholic rituals. A letter circulated by the Catholic hierarchy in Cisleithania drew attention to his example 'of faithfulness to the truth . . . of the conscientious observance of religious duties . . . and of selfless forbearance.'[18]

The tragedies that dogged Franz Joseph and the violent deaths of his brother, son, and wife yielded a further image of the emperor as 'the man of sorrows.' He was, as one popular biography put it, 'one of the most sorely tried bearers of human pain.' Despite his tribulations, he remained 'a mighty rock in the middle of surging waves', ever devoted to the needs of his peoples and working deep into the night, not resting so that his subjects might sleep safely. Franz Joseph's personal sorrows and the burdens of rule were even compared to Christ's Crown of Thorns, confirming the emperor as not only the ruler of peoples but also their redeemer.[19]

Franz Joseph's virtues and portrait were communicated in a string of publications aimed at popular consumption and bearing such titles as *Our Emperor*, *Hooray Habsburg*, and *Austria's Days of Joy*. These were not restricted to German editions but went into most of the languages of the empire. There were also plaster busts, as well as ashtrays and aprons bearing Franz Joseph's likeness. The authorities attempted to keep track of the circulation of portraits, forbidding the emperor's face to appear on rubber balls. Most spectacularly, in 1908 hundreds of thousands of Galician Poles and Ruthenes bought from an enterprising merchant cheap transparencies of the emperor, putting them in their windows so that at night the streets of towns and villages shone with identical portraits of Franz Joseph.[20]

The emperor thus became the almost exclusive focus of loyalty and symbol of an idea that transcended nation. But much was invested in a mortal who had already exceeded his biblically appointed span. As the *Neue Freie Presse* warned in 1908, 'If we look beyond him, that is when our thoughts become troubled and anxious. Long may the fate of the Monarchy lie, therefore, in his experienced hands, so that he can lead the country to unity, peace and reconciliation.' Eight years later, the emperor would be dead, with these goals still unaccomplished. In this respect, Franz Joseph's final words, 'Why does it have to be now?' captured the meaning of his unfulfilled reign more precisely than his personal motto, 'With powers united' (*Viribus unitis*).[21]

27

EXPLORERS, JEWS, AND THE WORLD'S KNOWLEDGE

*I*t was an irony not lost on nineteenth-century observers that the Habsburgs had once been the world's foremost colonial dynasty but that their empire was now without any overseas colonies. There were plenty of suggestions and private initiatives aimed at securing territories abroad. Explorers and merchants variously proposed Sudan, Yemen, Borneo, and what is now Zambia as possible locations, but government support was lacking. It was almost by accident that Franz Joseph obtained a micro-colony in the treaty port of Tianjin (Tientsin) on the Chinese coast, for he had a warship at hand when the anti-Westerner Boxer Rebellion suddenly escalated in China in 1900. Measuring 108 hectares (0.7 square miles), the Tianjin concession lasted just fifteen years, until it was repossessed by the Chinese government in 1917. Depending on how the city's limits are defined, Tianjin is now either the eleventh or the thirteenth most populous city in the world. Former public buildings decorated with the twin pillars recall to this day the short time when Tianjin was for the Habsburg Empire 'our place in the sun.'[1]

Visitors to Habsburg Tianjin lamented Vienna's reluctance to exploit the city's commercial potential. Elsewhere, however, merchants from

Austria-Hungary were pressing ahead. In terms of tonnage, their ships ranked fourth in use of the Suez Canal, while in 1913 alone the Austrian Lloyd made fifty-four voyages to India and the Far East. The Austro-Americana line, founded in 1895, also conveyed annually about a million tons of cargo across the Atlantic. The Austro-Hungarian Colonial Society, which first met in 1894, pushed the government to build on this foreign trade by establishing colonies. They might, the society's spokesmen argued, also be good places to export the Habsburg Empire's surplus population. But the flag followed neither trade nor the 'demographic impulse' (*Lebensdrang*) advertised by the advocates of colonial expansion. Even when Austrian explorers discovered in the 1870s an unknown archipelago in the Arctic, naming it Franz Josef Land, they did not plant the imperial flag upon it. Had they done so, Austria today might be an exporter of gas and oil.[2]

Instead of planting the flag, Franz Joseph and his ministers chose to wave it, and Austrian and then Austro-Hungarian warships routinely sailed into the Pacific and to the Americas and Arctic. Franz Joseph and the empress travelled to Port Said in 1869 for the opening of the Suez Canal. Twenty-five years later, Archduke Franz Ferdinand joined the circumnavigation of the globe by the Austro-Hungarian warship *Kaiserin Elisabeth*, visiting Africa, Australia, and the Far East before returning home by commercial liner via the United States. Franz Ferdinand's observations were acute, and he was critical of colonial ventures overseas, not least on account of the harm done to the local population.[3]

The Austrian and, after 1867, Austro-Hungarian navy saw little action before 1914. In 1866, Vice Admiral Tegetthoff's ironclads had defeated the Italian navy at Lissa (Vis) in the Adriatic, and the fleet also engaged Greek rebels in the 1897 Cretan uprising. But Franz Joseph's interest in the navy was at best intermittent, since it drained funds that he preferred to invest in the army. One vice admiral complained that in his endeavours to release money from ministerial pockets, 'soirees, balls, and dinners are the order of the day.' Under Franz Ferdinand's patronage, the navy expanded in the run-up to the First World War, having three dreadnought-class warships, a further nine battleships, and eight cruisers. But it was still smaller than its Italian rival, which counted seventeen battleships, including six dreadnoughts, and no fewer than twenty-three cruisers.[4]

As part of its flag flying, the navy supported exploration and scientific ventures to remote corners of the world. It established an observation post on Jan Mayen, an island in the Arctic five hundred kilometres (three hundred miles) east of Greenland, and briefly attempted a settlement on the Solomon Islands in the South Pacific to investigate their nickel deposits. The navy also gave explorers weapons, training, and experienced officers, in return for which it expected cartographic and topographical information. Much of Central and East Africa was first charted by Austrian German, Czech, and Hungarian geographers, including the Congo River and its watershed with the Nile. Their contribution was stamped on the maps they drew: Lake Rudolph in Kenya and Lake Stephanie in Ethiopia, honouring the crown prince and his wife, and Mount Teleki in Kenya and Baumann Peak in Togo, named after two explorers.

Explorers sent back trophies and scientific and ethnographic material, which filled museums across the Habsburg Empire. The Czech Emil Holub, whose expedition north of the Zambezi River had been funded in the 1880s by the War Ministry, provided more than thirty thousand specimens, mostly flora and fauna. These were put on view in Prater Park in 1891 but were too numerous to be accommodated in any single museum. So Holub's collection was broken up and distributed to more than five hundred institutions and museums around the world. Sofia's Museum of Natural History acquired his dead birds, Admont Abbey in Styria his stuffed lions, Prague his pinned insects (and much else besides), London his marine plants, the Smithsonian in Washington some of his fossils, and so on.[5]

The most influential expedition was the circumnavigation begun by the naval frigate *Novara* in 1857. Over two years, the *Novara* covered more than fifty thousand nautical miles (ninety-two thousand kilometres), visiting every continent, including Antarctica and Australasia—hence New Zealand's Franz Josef Glacier. On board was a team of scientists, on whose behalf a part of the gun deck was cleared to make way for a library. The expedition gathered twenty-six thousand botanical, zoological, geological, and ethnographic specimens, as well as undertaking oceanographic measurements and calculations of the earth's gravitational field. The scientific report of the expedition ran to twenty-one volumes and took seventeen years to complete. Experiments on the coca leaves that the *Novara* brought back also yielded the first distillation of pure cocaine, which soon became one of the empress's preferred medications (she took it in a spritzer).[6]

Of the twenty-one volumes of the *Novara* works, three were dedicated to anthropology and ethnography with sections on skull types, body size, and material culture. The scientists aboard the *Novara* were mainly concerned with measurement and compiling tables. Although condescending, their descriptions were largely factual: 'The Javanese are in stature several inches smaller than the mid-sized European. Their bodies are well nourished, and their chests quite strongly built. Their limbs are refined and delicate, and their hands nimble. Their faces are normally long and broad, and both sexes retain a child-like expression.' But the information that the scientists relayed was soon filtered through the new field of 'racial science.' Using their records, Augustin Weisbach elaborated a scheme whereby the world's population was divided into nine white and nine black races, with the San or Bushmen of southern Africa occupying the lowest rank of all, since he considered them close to apes. Jews he put at the bottom of the white races. As a doctor attached to the military, Weisbach also traversed the Balkans, measuring skulls, but always in such a way as to support his theories.[7]

Weisbach's approach was championed by the Anthropological Society of Vienna, whose president emphasized the wealth of material already at hand, within Austria-Hungary, to support 'craniological and linguistic research' as well as investigations into character and customs that exposed the significance of race. The Anthropological Society sponsored studies of the supposedly superior 'Nordic type' in Central Europe and of the ways in which Darwinist principles of natural selection might be deployed to refine the region's racial stock. The First World War yielded an abundance of new specimens, in the form of refugees from eastern Galicia and Russian POWs, whose skulls, limbs, and blood types were duly analysed to show the supposed genetic inferiority of the East Slavonic and other 'races.' The influence of this approach persisted into the 1990s, being demonstrated in the Natural History Museum (Naturhistorisches Museum) in Vienna, which in part of its permanent exhibition invited visitors to compare the skulls of an australopithecine 'ape-man', a chimpanzee, and a Bushman.[8]

We may lament the misuses to which scholarly endeavour is put. But by supporting scientific activity, Franz Joseph and his ministers were returning to one of the meanings of AEIOU—that Austria and the Habsburg dynasty stood for a universal principle that was rooted in ideas of Christian leadership and global prestige. This principle was now made into a mission to amass the world's knowledge. The dedication of the new Natural History Museum in Vienna, carved in gold on its portico, spoke to this goal: 'To the Empire of Nature and its Investigation, Emperor Franz Joseph, 1881.'

Around the building were placed representations of the continents and on its facades stood statues of Columbus, Magellan, and Cook, along with Jason of the Argonauts, Alexander the Great, and Julius Caesar. The message was clear: explorers of the empire of nature were as much to be celebrated as the empire builders of classical antiquity. As Emil Holub's obituarist put it, other nations looked overseas for land, but Austrians went abroad 'for love of research and to broaden knowledge of others.'[9]

But the building was the dynasty's too. Together with the Museum of Art (Kunsthistorisches Museum), the Natural History Museum flanked a new Emperor Forum (Kaiserforum), which extended from the Hofburg over the Ring. The content of both museums originated in imperial collections that had previously been kept either in the Hofburg or in the Belvedere Palace, which Maria Theresa had bought from the heirs of Eugene of Savoy. The Museum of Art retained the arrangement given the Belvedere collection in the 1780s by Christian von Mechel, who was among the first to exhibit paintings by school as opposed to hanging them in a jumble. The two museums thus displayed the dynasty's 'court collections', accumulated over generations. The courtly and dynastic character of the Emperor Forum was amplified by the plan to situate a Court Theatre and Court Opera beside the two museums, with the ensemble leading to the Hofburg through two triumphal arches. Since the forum was never completed, the opera and theatre were relocated to sites along the Ring, weakening their association with the court. But a statue of Maria Theresa, planned for the space between the two museums, went ahead, stamping the dynasty at the centre of the complex.[10]

'Historicism' was the architectural convention in the middle decades of the nineteenth century, which meant that buildings should reflect the period most appropriate to their function. So Vienna's city hall was built in the Gothic style to recall the Middle Ages, when the city had received its privileges. The new parliament, by contrast, was given a classical facade that harked back to Periclean Athens, which was thought to be the birthplace of democracy. Friezes inside depicted Greek and Roman legislators and orators, while outside was raised a four-metre (thirteen-foot) statue of the Greek goddess Pallas Athene. The original intention had been to have in her place a statue of Austria, but no one could agree what she looked like. Still, it was hoped that as the goddess of wisdom, Pallas Athene might bestow some of her sagacity on the parliament's bickering politicians.

In accordance with the conventions of historicism, the two museums were completed in the style of the High Renaissance, which was intended to recall the flourishing of the arts and learning in the sixteenth century and to celebrate their rebirth under the patronage of Franz Joseph. By the time they were opened, however, architectural fashion had changed in favour of the revived or neo-Baroque. In an influential pamphlet published in 1880, the art historian and curator in the Museum of Art, Albert Ilg, praised the Baroque style for its universality and versatility. First, he explained, it was suitable for all manner of buildings, from the monumental down to the middle-class villa and working-class apartment blocks, with theatres and churches in between. Second, the Baroque comported with a style already established in the capital. Lively and witty, it was more in tune with Vienna than the 'cold classicism' and restraint of Berlin. Finally, it was supra-national, which meant that it served 'to merge peoples.' By providing a unifying architectural language, the Baroque had the power, Ilg went on, 'to dissolve the individualities of each people to embrace the whole globe in a single rule.'[11]

The neo-Baroque became during the last decades of the century the style of choice. The design of the St Michael's wing of the Hofburg, completed in the 1890s, was based on plans originally devised by the foremost Baroque architect of the early eighteenth century, Joseph Emanuel Fischer von Erlach. With its four great statues of Hercules, twin fountains, and green copper dome, it is now the most photographed part of the palace complex. The new Imperial War Ministry building, whose massive 200-metre (650-foot) frontage dominates the north-eastern stretch of the Ring, was also constructed in the style of the neo-Baroque. So too were most of the six hundred or so blocks of flats that fronted the Ring. The facades of these 'rental palaces' (*Mietpalais*) were typically 'ennobled' in a grand Baroque style, to give the impression of aristocratic living, but behind them were middle-class apartments and, lower down, offices and stockrooms for ground-floor shops.[12]

The neo-Baroque style was not confined to the capital. In the decades before the First World War, the architectural studio of Fellner and Helmer built more than forty opera houses, concert halls, and hotels, reaching from Prague and Zagreb to Chernivtsi (Czernowitz) in Bukovina and Timişoara in the Banat. All were constructed in the language of the neo-Baroque, communicating a common civic code and visual identity for the cities of the Habsburg Empire. Yet in both Chernivtsi and Timişoara the designs of Fellner and Helmer confronted an alternative code that spoke to national difference and singularity: the new Romanesque church in Timişoara that exemplified Hungarian hegemony and in Chernivtsi the recently built Residence of the Metropolitans, which wonderfully combined Byzantine and Romanesque forms with elements of Ukrainian folk art. Chernivtsi and Timişoara were not exceptional. While the neo-Baroque sought a universal language, local artists and architects across the empire toiled to develop national styles that emphasized particularity and difference.[13]

With its excessive ornamentation and elaborate facades, the neo-Baroque invited criticism. The modernist architect Adolf Loos compared its unnecessary accretions to tattoos, which he suggested were only worn by cannibals and criminals—hence the title of his celebrated essay, *Ornament and Crime* (1908). Along with a new generation of architects, Loos proposed a simpler and more honest style of architecture, shorn of distraction and false historicism. The Loos House in Vienna, which looks across to the St Michael wing of the Hofburg and was built as a department store, adopted a deliberately stark exterior—even the window boxes were not part of the original plan. Loos's Café Museum, designed in 1909, was similarly bare of decoration, with elegantly curved chairs that were free of the contemporary fashion for elaborate carving. As Loos himself put it, 'The evolution of culture is synonymous with the removal of ornament from utilitarian objects.'[14]

Loos was connected to the artists of the Secession and of its arts and crafts twin, the Wiener Werkstätte. Both movements looked abroad for inspiration—to impressionist and expressionist art and to the type of design that would later be known as Art Deco. The Secession was also at odds with the conservatism of the controlling Austrian Association of Artists, from which its members ostentatiously seceded (hence the name). No single style defined the Secession. It included the gilded portraits and sinuous female forms of Gustav Klimt, the bold colours and flat surfaces of Oscar Kokoschka, and the twisted figures of Egon Schiele, which verge on the pornographic. In architecture too, the principles of Loos were often subverted by a return to historicism and to elaborate embellishment. Even the Secession Building, put up in 1897 to house exhibitions by Secession artists, had at its front entrance reliefs of forest leaves and Gorgon heads; it was crowned by a neo-Baroque dome of interwoven gold boughs.

The Vienna Secession spoke to universal values. Unlike art and architecture in contemporary Hungary, it was not dedicated to a rustic national style and to celebrating a crowded pantheon of national heroes. Consequently, government and public institutions supported it as, in the words of one prominent Secessionist, 'a form of art that would weld together all the characteristics of our multitude of constituent peoples into a new and proud unity.' Shortly before his death in 1889, Crown Prince Rudolf agreed that art could bond 'different nations and different races under a united rule', and the Arts Council founded by the Ministry of Culture ten years later also noted how 'works of art speak a common language and . . . lead to mutual understanding and reciprocal respect.'[15]

Artists and architects associated with the Secession were commissioned to build hospitals, post offices, and even an astronomical observatory, decorate the interiors of public buildings, and plan parks and whole suburbs. They also designed the posters advertising Franz Joseph's 1908 jubilee. But Franz Joseph himself had little understanding of the new art. One expressionist painting convinced the emperor that the artist must be colour blind, and so he advised him to give up his vocation. Franz Ferdinand, who oversaw the construction of the new Ministry of War building, also favoured traditional forms. He rejected Adolf Loos's design for the building in favour of one that mixed a palace with a military barracks in neo-Baroque style to project martial power.

Fin de siècle Vienna experienced an efflorescence not only in art and architecture but also in a wide variety of disciplines and fields of scholarly endeavour. This was the city that produced Sigmund Freud; the philosopher Ludwig Wittgenstein; Arnold Schoenberg, the leader of the twentieth century's musical revolution; and Karl Renner and Otto Bauer, who made revolutionary Marxism compatible with the salon. Their endeavours shared a common feature: to strip back their objects of enquiry to expose the intellectual building blocks beneath and to establish the laws that governed each. Language, modern art and music, logic, and mathematics were thus distinguished by their 'rule-governed-ness', which for Wittgenstein meant that the whole of philosophy might be reduced to a handful of theorems or propositions. Only what could be observed and sensed was true, which put ethics and aesthetics into the realm of the unverifiable. But it also put ideas of the nation and national identity there as well, for these, too, were aesthetic conceits that rested on untestable propositions—hence the interest in race, which was thought to be scientifically demonstrable.[16]

Many of the prominent figures in fin de siècle Vienna were of Jewish descent. Besides Freud, Wittgenstein, Loos, Schoenberg, and Bauer, they include Gustav Mahler, the writers and dramatists Hugo von Hofmannsthal and Arthur Schnitzler, and the two scholars who transformed the study of economics and law, Ludwig von Mises and Hans Kelsen. Others, like Klimt, Kokoschka, and Schiele were not Jewish, and the Jewish contribution in art and architecture was less than in other fields. Even so, the gallery owners, dealers, and patrons of artists were often Jewish, as were the subjects of many of Klimt's portraits. Of these, the most famous was a sugar-baron's wife, Adele Bloch-Bauer, whom Klimt painted several times and who was also the model for his disturbingly seductive *Judith*.

Central European Jewry was more numerous than in Western Europe. Its population stood in the mid-eighteenth century at around 150,000 in the Austrian lands, Bohemia, and Hungary. The acquisition of Galicia in 1772 brought with it a further 200,000 persons, most of whom were rural *Landesjuden*, cultivating small plots. The small province of Bukovina, which lay to the east of Galicia and was obtained from the Turks two years later, also had a burgeoning Jewish population, enlarged by immigration from Russia. The capital of Bukovina, Chernivtsi, which was one-third Jewish in 1900, became one of the great centres of Central European Jewish culture, including of the Yiddish theatre. Politicians in Chernivtsi and Vienna worked out in 1910 a new electoral law for Bukovina that guaranteed Jews representation in the local diet, although in such a way as not to acknowledge that they were anything other than a religious minority.[17]

In order to render Jews 'more useful and serviceable to the State', Joseph II had removed many of the disabilities which hindered their social and economic advancement. Emancipation coincided with the Jewish *Haskalah* or Enlightenment, which stressed secular values and the importance of integration. Even so, there were several Jewish paths to modernity—through ennoblement and state service, manufacturing and commerce, the professions, and emigration. Assimilationist strategies were rejected in parts of Galicia, where Hassidism stressed fidelity to Talmudic traditions. Elsewhere, however, Jews abandoned the countryside for integration and advancement in the cities. By the 1880s, 10 per cent of the population of Vienna was Jewish. In Budapest, the proportion was higher still, exceeding 20 per cent in 1910. In both cities, Jews dominated business and the professions, making up in Vienna three-quarters of the lawyers and half of medical doctors.

But Vienna's politics was ugly. The city council was dominated by the Christian Socials, who combined social reform with Jew baiting. Vienna had the distinction of electing in 1895 the cynical and opportunistic Karl Lueger as Europe's first antisemitic mayor. The Christian Socials kept Vienna German by the simple expedient of denying residence permits to outsiders, especially Slavs and poor Jews from the countryside. More than two-thirds of the urban population of almost two million comprised 'illegals', without access to welfare, decent housing, and the vote. On the streets, proto-fascist groups mustered. Although insignificant in the parliament, the Pan-Germans, whose members greeted their tinpot leader with loud *Heils*, forced by their violence the collapse of at least one ministry. The Vienna of Freud and Wittgenstein was also the Vienna of the young Adolf Hitler.[18]

It may well be that under these circumstances Jews and other members of the educated middle class in Vienna were overwhelmed by a sense of alienation, anomie, disenchantment, and rootlessness and so retreated into a temple of art, but the proposition is hard to test. What is certain is that cultural creativity in Vienna was strongly non-national and that it owed much to Jews. Some of these would in time embrace the Jewish nationalism of Herzl's Zionism, and a few made curious forays into the politics of intolerance, compiling long lists of deviants and degenerates. But most stood above the hurly-burly of nationalist politics. Like the neo-Baroque and the art and architecture of the Secession, they embraced instead a universalism that rejected the simplicities and reductionism of romantic nationalism. Along with the dynasty, Jews were part of the cement that kept the Habsburg Empire together. As one Jewish rabbi and Reichsrat deputy put it, 'we are neither Germans nor Slavs, but Austrian Jews or Jewish Austrians.'[19]

Franz Csokor's drama *3 November 1918* premiered in Vienna in 1937. In one scene, soldiers gather to bury their colonel, who has shot himself upon news of the Habsburg Empire's collapse. They each heap soil upon his corpse—'earth from Hungary . . . earth from Carinthia . . . Czech earth', symbolically burying the empire with him. The colonel's Jewish comrade is last, stuttering, 'Earth from, earth from . . . Austria.' As Csokor suggests, Jews in Vienna stood for something larger than the nation, and they may come close to representing a universal 'Austrian idea' that stood above the embittered politics of nationalism. But by 1914 that idea was fast running out.[20]

THE HUNTER AND THE HUNTED:
FRANZ FERDINAND AND BOSNIA

*I*n the early hours of 30 January 1889, the thirty-year-old Crown Prince Rudolf shot dead his teenage mistress, Maria Vetsera, in a hunting lodge at Mayerling in the Vienna Woods. He had some years before disclosed to a friend that he was looking for an opportunity to watch someone die, so it was only after several hours that he put the revolver to his own head. The impressionable Maria had agreed to a suicide pact with Rudolf, but she was not the first whom Rudolf had asked to join him in death. Besides his wife and a male secretary, Rudolf had also invited his long-term mistress, Mizzi Caspar, who was an *horizontale* and graduate of Madame Wolf's celebrated bordello in Vienna. Caspar was sufficiently alarmed to report the matter to the police. Rudolf spent the night before his death in Caspar's bed.[1]

The imperial court came clean almost at once over Rudolf's death, admitting that the crown prince had killed himself in a moment of insanity. It did, however, seek to cover up Maria's involvement, but the press had the story. Censorship in the Austrian half of the Habsburg Empire was governed by a contradiction. The 1867 constitution guaranteed press freedom, but an earlier decree of 1850 was still in force that allowed provincial governors to suppress news stories and theatrical performances that were deemed seditious, indecent, or offensive. The censors managed a compromise. Having ordered a newspaper article to be blacked out prior to distribution, they often published its title 'for the record', so it was not hard for readers to work out what had happened at Mayerling. Within weeks of Rudolf's death, books speculating on the tragedy were also available by mail order from Germany.[2]

After Rudolf, the next in line to the throne was Franz Joseph's brother, the 'exhibition archduke' Karl Ludwig. The pious Karl Ludwig died in 1896 on pilgrimage to the Holy Land, having contracted dysentery by drinking from the River Jordan. Karl Ludwig's son, Franz Ferdinand, thus took his place as the emperor's heir. Franz Ferdinand had been a close companion of Crown Prince Rudolf, and their several escapades had provoked outraged speeches in the parliament. The two cousins had also shared the prodigal favours of Mizzi Caspar. But after Rudolf's death, Franz Ferdinand learned responsibility, circumnavigating the globe in 1892–1893, and thereafter diligently performing the duties of heir presumptive. (Since Franz Joseph might, however improbably, have still sired a male heir, who would then be his successor, Franz Ferdinand did not qualify as his heir apparent.)

In 1900, Franz Ferdinand married Sophie Chotek. What Franz Ferdinand described as 'some triviality' in his wife's family tree was, in fact, a colossal problem. Although the Choteks were of old aristocratic descent, they did not count as 'princely' and even less as royal. Franz Joseph refused to permit the marriage unless it was morganatic, which meant that neither the wife nor the couple's heirs were raised to royal status. Franz Joseph's master of etiquette enforced the protocol with cold diligence, making Sophie stand with the ladies-in-waiting at receptions and sit in a separate box in the opera. Franz Ferdinand did not forgive these slights.[3]

Crown Prince Rudolf had been a keen ornithologist, and his published observations are still cited in the specialist literature. But instead of watching birds, Franz Ferdinand preferred to shoot them. As a huntsman, he was indiscriminate in his targets, bagging two elephants and a tiger in India and Sri Lanka, flamingos in Egypt, kangaroos and a duck-billed platypus in Australia, and even his own cat. The Central European style of hunting involved birds and deer being driven close to the hunters, who then blasted away at the game, while servants filled bags. Over his lifetime, Franz Ferdinand managed 274,889 kills, mostly of partridges (his game books survive).

When not murdering small animals, Franz Ferdinand tended his rose garden at Konopiště Castle in Bohemia and pressed wild flowers. He was also a loving father and faithful husband who doted on his family.[4]

Franz Ferdinand's politics were as ambiguous as his personality. He hated Hungarians and saw Hungary's special status within the Habsburg Empire as an obstacle to the changes he wanted. For a time, he thought to build up Croatia territorially at Hungary's expense and to convert dualism to trialism, with Austria-Hungary becoming Austria-Hungary-Croatia. He realized, however, that the Czechs would press for equal rights and, after them, the Poles. So he began thinking about how to reconfigure the empire from scratch, either by creating new national homelands or by keeping the existing provinces but giving the national minorities control of their own educational and cultural arrangements. Yet he had no intention of allowing his powers as the future emperor to be diminished, on which account his goal was, as one historian has put it, 'not the equality of nations but their non-equality' beneath the throne.[5]

By 1900, Franz Joseph was seventy years old and ailing. He kept oversight of government but allowed it to run its course, only intervening to mediate the squabbles of his ministers. Franz Ferdinand occupied the space that the emperor vacated—almost literally. First, he moved the collection of seventeen thousand ethnographic and other items he had gathered on his round-the-world tour into the Upper Belvedere, which was conveniently empty following the removal of its paintings to the Museum of Art History. Then, he prevailed upon Franz Joseph to give him the palace as his headquarters and military chancellery. As heir to the throne, Franz Ferdinand was copied into all the most important military correspondence, and he regularly interfered in the appointment of officers. He also had his stooges in the civil service who passed him information in a childish code. As one prime minister complained, 'We not only have two parliaments, we also have two emperors.'[6]

Franz Ferdinand was a close friend of the German emperor Wilhelm II, who always took care to treat Princess Sophie with the highest marks of esteem. Like Wilhelm II, Franz Ferdinand was opinionated in his conversation, railing against 'the Jewish press' and freemasons, but circumspect in his undertakings—'much decisiveness in talking; little in acting' was one contemporary verdict. For all his bluster, Franz Ferdinand was a strong advocate for peace. His knowledge of the army convinced him that it could not sustain a sizable war. Even so, Franz Ferdinand urged the modernization of the armed forces to include aeroplanes, mechanized units with armoured cars, telephone communications, and up-to-date battleships.[7]

Franz Joseph was not averse to innovation. Although he disliked telephones and refused to introduce lifts into the Hofburg, he had an electric cigar lighter, and he looked forward to car rides with almost childish anticipation. Unlike Franz Ferdinand, he was ready to go to war, but he needed a theatre in which to wage it. By the 1870s, traditional fields of expansion in Italy and Ukraine had been blocked. The emperor toyed with a war of revenge against Germany and even instructed his generals to come up with a war plan called 'Event D' (for Deutschland), but he settled instead for a military alliance in 1879. In Germany's place, the Balkans beckoned, with ministers pushing the emperor for a resumption of 'Austria's old policy in this part of the Near East.' The Ottoman Empire was falling apart, they explained, and he should pick up the pieces before others did so. By degrees, the Habsburg Empire was drawn into the 'Eastern Question', which was about how to manage and divide up the disintegrating Ottoman Empire.[8]

The Habsburg frontier with the Ottoman Turks was a broad militarized zone that ran 1,200 miles (1,850 kilometres) from the Adriatic to eastern Transylvania. Originally manned by soldier-farmers, who held land in exchange for military service and other duties, it was still organized into frontier regiments that took their orders from the War Ministry in Vienna. The frontiersmen were a mix of migrants and refugees, mostly Serbs, Croats, and Romanians who had settled over centuries in a mosaic of different national groups. Their officers were largely German—or, at least, Germanized Slavs and Romanians—and appointed by the War Ministry. The main task of the frontier troops was to guard the border against Turkish attacks, but they were also deployed in Italy and used to threaten Hungary. Many of the troops gathered by Jelačić in 1848 to invade Hungary were recruited from frontier regiments.[9]

There had been a spate of raiding by renegade Turkish captains from Ottoman Bosnia into Hungary around 1830, but after that the military frontier was mostly quiet. The significance of the military frontier was, however, as much symbolic as defensive, marking a transitional zone between civilization and 'oriental' backwardness. Travellers passing beyond the frontier noticed a quite different landscape on the Balkan side, describing minarets, tumbledown houses, and idlers sitting in the dirt drinking coffee. In their imagination, the frontiersmen occupied a culturally intermediate place between civilization and barbarity. Habsburg ethnographers and statisticians accordingly found the frontiersmen to be indolent, disorganized, and inclined to violence, but they had, so they explained, picked up some elements of German culture and refinement. Their women at least were industrious, and they kept the houses neat.[10]

The military frontier also served to enforce quarantine regulations. Travellers from the Turkish side were kept in isolation for up to twenty days at yellow-flagged checkpoints, while commercial cargoes of cotton and wool had to be aired and tested by having a servant sleep on the bales, after which he would be checked for symptoms. Commercial exchanges on the border were done from behind screens, with coins disinfected in vinegar. Much of this rigmarole was unnecessary. The Ottoman Empire had been among the first in Europe to introduce inoculation for smallpox (later replaced by cowpox vaccination), and it had in the 1830s undertaken far-reaching sanitary reforms. The problem in the Ottoman Empire was not epidemic disease, of the type that quarantine was intended to catch, but endemic disease, mostly gastro-intestinal and respiratory. The purpose of the quarantine was not only to safeguard health, however, but also to demonstrate the superior hygiene of a higher civilization. So quarantining continued on the military frontier even after it had been recognized as unnecessary elsewhere.[11]

In 1875 the oppression of mainly Christian peasants by mainly Muslim landlords caused an uprising in Herzegovina, which spilled over into the other Ottoman provinces of Bosnia and Bulgaria. Habsburg agents and officers fanned the flames. In June that year, a steamer unloaded at the Habsburg naval port of Kotor (now in Montenegro) eight thousand Austrian service rifles and two million rounds of ammunition for distribution to the rebels. Turkish reprisals, mostly against civilians, provoked outrage across Europe. The principalities of Serbia and Montenegro took up arms against Ottoman Turkey but were speedily vanquished. But Russia was an entirely different foe. In the summer of 1877, three hundred thousand Russian troops poured across the Danube in support of the rebels. Within just a few months, they had reached the outskirts of Istanbul.[12]

The scale of the Russian victory tipped the international balance of power. Gyula Andrássy, the former prime minister of Hungary and current foreign minister of Austria-Hungary, had initially backed the Russian invasion, having been promised that the Habsburg Empire would have a share of the spoils. Now he pushed for war against Russia. For a time, it looked as if the emperor would back Andrássy, but the treasury was empty. Absurdly, Andrássy suggested a staggered mobilization so that the costs could be spread. Common sense was restored to the discussions of the Crown Council by the intervention of Colonel Friedrich von Beck, who was there only by special invitation of the emperor. 'For what purpose is this war to be fought?' he asked Franz Joseph. Unable to give a convincing reply, the emperor backed down and agreed to negotiations instead. At the Congress of Berlin, held in 1878, Bismarck for Germany, Disraeli for Britain, and Andrássy for the Habsburg Empire obliged the tsar to abandon the 'Big Bulgaria' that he wanted as a Russian satellite in the Balkans.[13]

The Congress of Berlin awarded the provinces of Bosnia and Herzegovina to the Habsburgs, but only as a temporary military protectorate. Franz Joseph had hoped to gain the provinces in full sovereignty, but Andrássy convinced him otherwise. By bringing Bosnia-Herzegovina (as the provinces were now known) into the Habsburg Empire the delicate balance between Slavs, Germans, and Hungarians would be upset. But not to bring Bosnia-Herzegovina in, Andrássy explained, left it exposed to a takeover by Serbia. Far better to leave the status of Bosnia-Herzegovina ambiguous. For that reason, Franz Joseph did not join the newly acquired territory to either the Cisleithanian or the Hungarian halves of the Habsburg Empire but put it under the supervision of the common Ministry of Finance.

The Congress of Berlin also recognized Serbia as a fully independent state and no longer a theoretical vassal of the sultan. With Bosnia occupied and the Ottoman shadow removed from the face of Serbia, the military frontier was wound up. Many of its officers often went on to distinguished service in the regular army, not least in the Balkans. But the mentality of the military frontier lived on in the idea that Balkan peoples were culturally impoverished and medically diseased. As an article tellingly entitled 'On the Degeneration of the People of Bosnia-Herzegovina' explained, Balkan society had been 'cut off from civilization for centuries.' It was the task of the Habsburg authorities in Bosnia to bring culture and sanitation to the backward people of the Balkans. Over centuries, it was argued, they had intermixed, decayed physically and mentally, and become particularly susceptible to disease and hysteria. Their supposedly lower moral level and unhygienic customs had also made syphilis and skin diseases endemic.[14]

Unsurprisingly, the Habsburg civilizing mission in the Balkans was first marked by sanitation laws and the introduction of a sanitary police. The new government of Bosnia-Herzegovina imposed by the Finance Ministry required all midwives, dentists, surgeons, and veterinary staff to show qualifications that conformed to Austrian law, so most lost their jobs. It also instructed prostitutes to register and undergo regular medical check-ups. In fact, Bosnian bodies were soon shown to be healthy and the incidence of venereal infection to be about the same as within the Habsburg Empire. Undaunted, Habsburg physicians identified among the Bosnian Muslim population an entirely new variant of syphilis (called *škrljevo*) and a narrowing of the pelvis in Muslim women, which was thought to originate from moving on all fours. Ventures to colonize and civilize often start by identifying female differences.[15]

Ottoman rule had distinguished between Muslim, Catholic, and Orthodox, with each group paying different taxes and having separate courts. Habsburg rule reinforced these divisions. Whereas elsewhere in the Habsburg Empire censuses made language the marker of identity, in Bosnia-Herzegovina religious criteria were used. The reason was straightforward. Linguists had already identified the Štokavian dialect of South Slav as predominant in Bosnia-Herzegovina, Serbia, Montenegro, and eastern Croatia. The influential Serbian scholar Vuk Karadžić had gone so far as to call this dialect Serbian—hence the title of his celebrated article 'Serbs, All and Everywhere' (1849). Politicians in Belgrade imagined all South Slavs—including Bosnians, Croats, Dalmatians, and Slovenes—to be either Serbs or their close kinsmen, and they looked forward to building a Greater Serbia that would unite them in a single state. A Bosnian census that revealed Štokavian or Serbian to be the language most people spoke would give them a powerful weapon.

The census of 1879 showed no one group holding an absolute majority, giving the Orthodox Church 500,000 souls, the Catholic 200,000, and Islam 450,000. Each of these groups had co-religionists across the border with whom they identified—Orthodox Serbs in Serbia, Catholic Croats in Croatia, and Muslims throughout the Balkans. The danger was that Bosnia-Herzegovina would be pulled apart or thrust into a civil war, in which each side received outside reinforcements. From the first, however, Habsburg administrators recognized the Serbian threat to be the greater. As one finance minister observed, the Serbs would be content with nothing less than a complete takeover of the province and the expulsion of its Muslim population.[16]

Habsburg policy towards Bosnia-Herzegovina rested on two principles. The first was economic modernization, which it was hoped would civilize the province and reduce tensions between the religions. As Crown Prince Rudolf remarked upon visiting Bosnia in 1888, 'Our mission here is to bring western culture to the orient.'[17] So the province was given schools, hospitals, technical colleges, and industry in the form of coal and iron mining, tobacco cultivation and processing, and paper manufacturing to exploit its forests. Most spectacularly, the Habsburg administration in Bosnia-Herzegovina laid down more than six hundred miles (one thousand kilometres) of railway track. The North Bosnian line, which ran through mountainous terrain east of Sarajevo, included ninety-nine tunnels and thirty iron bridges in a stretch of just a hundred miles (160 kilometres). The so-called Bosnian narrow gauge (of 760 millimetres) subsequently became an international benchmark and was adopted across Europe as well as in the Congo and Argentina.

The second principle was to promote a Bosnian identity that would bind together the various religions, but this was only ever undertaken piecemeal. Successive governors encouraged a Bosnian style of architecture that blended secessionist forms with 'neo-orientalist' motifs. Most strikingly, Sarajevo's new city hall mimicked the Moorish Alhambra Palace in Granada, with elaborate tracery, horseshoe arches, and motifs in stained glass that derived from Islamic art. Curators at the Provincial Museum (Zemaljski Muzej), meanwhile, set about giving Bosnia a new history, demonstrating that in the Middle Ages there had been a Bosnian religious tradition that was neither Catholic nor Orthodox but derived instead from a heresy called Bogomilism. According to this theory, Bosnian Muslim landowners were the descendants of Bogomil nobles who had embraced Islam. When the curators discovered archaeological remains that disproved this thesis, they either smashed or hid them.[18]

The skull measurers were also enlisted to the task. Craniologists working in the museum conveniently found that there was a 'pure' Bosnian skull belonging to the Aryan-Nordic type that was brachycephalic, or shortened, and common to both Muslims and Catholic Croats. By contrast, Orthodox Serbs had skulls that were long, exhibiting 'extreme dolichocephaly', which suggested a more primitive racial group that had migrated to Bosnia from elsewhere. In wandering like Jews, Serbs were, according to the museum curator Ćiro Truhelka, marked by a tendency towards 'tuberculosis and sterility, and then feebleness of the psychic and physical constitution', and by a rootlessness that made for 'cultural parasitism.'[19]

As these examples suggest, the Bosnian nation-building project left out the Serbs, who now vied with Muslims at the bottom of the cultural hierarchy. But Muslims did not encounter the same hostility as Serbs, and they integrated more successfully into the new structures, holding successively the office of mayor in Sarajevo and dominating the city council. The president of the Bosnian diet, which met for the first time in 1910, was also a Muslim. Over time, Bosnian Muslims evinced a loyalty to the Habsburg Empire that was matched only by Jews, providing the army with the core of four regiments recruited from the province. Like the British Gurkha regiments, the Bosnian regiments were celebrated for their courage. 'The Bosnians Are Coming' (*Die Bosniaken kommen*), composed in 1895, is still one of the most popular military marches in the Austrian army.

Economic development benefited the Muslim merchant elite but barely touched the Serbs. Instead, they remained the peasant tenants of mainly Muslim landlords, for the government lacked the money to pay compensation for their freedom. The benefits of modernization thus passed by most Serbs, with the consequence that they remained overwhelmingly illiterate. On top of this, Serbian organizations and newspapers were frequently banned, and Serbian schoolteachers inconvenienced by having to give stricter proof of 'political reliability.' Manipulation of the electoral system meant that the Serbian representatives in the Bosnian diet belonged to the conservative wing of the Serbian national movement, being mostly agents of a small group of Orthodox businessmen.

The Habsburg military occupation of Bosnia-Herzegovina was intended only as a temporary solution. In what might be considered a masterstroke, had it not been performed in such a botched manner, the province was formally annexed in October 1908 and incorporated within the Habsburg Empire. The Habsburg foreign minister believed he had the agreement of his Russian counterpart to the annexation, but this was a misunderstanding. The consequence was a breakdown in diplomatic relations, which drew Russia closer to Serbia. Serbian expansion southwards into Ottoman Macedonia during the Balkan Wars of 1912–1913 fuelled the suspicion in Vienna that, with Russia's backing, Serbia would soon seek to 'liberate' the Serbs who lived within the Habsburg Empire.

Serbia had a parliament, elected on a wide franchise, but its government was not democratic. The institutions of state had been eviscerated by secret societies and terrorist groups operating from within the army and the security services. At their heart was the formation called Union or Death or the Black Hand, headed by the chief of Serbian military intelligence, Dragutin Dimitrijević. The group comprised the conspirators who had assassinated the unpopular King Alexander and Queen Draga of Serbia in 1903, dividing up their body parts as spoils. Ten years later, with his career enhanced by murder, Dimitrijević was grooming young men of a type all too familiar today—puny, sexually frustrated, and yearning for a cause that would bring meaning to their lives. The task given them was to free Bosnia-Herzegovina from Habsburg rule by terrorist means as the prelude to its incorporation into Serbia.

It was into this cauldron that Franz Ferdinand stepped. The archduke hated Serbs almost as much as Hungarians, but he counselled peaceful relations with Serbia. He was particularly successful in hemming in Conrad von Hötzendorf, the chief of the General Staff, who over the course of 1913 recommended a preventive war on Serbia on no fewer than twenty-five occasions. He had no wish, Franz Ferdinand explained to the foreign minister, Leopold Berchtold, to see the Habsburg Empire dragged into Conrad's 'witches' kitchen of war.' Nor did he believe that there was any great demand for war in Serbia itself, which already had difficulties enough swallowing the territories it had acquired in the recent Balkan Wars.[20]

Franz Ferdinand's solution was a great deal cleverer. His plan was a modified version of the trialism that he had previously espoused. Croatia would be reconstructed as a South Slav state and an alternative magnet to Serbia. It would receive Bosnia-Herzegovina, which Franz Ferdinand regarded as the logical next step after the province's annexation, and Dalmatia, which although once a part of Croatia had been incorporated in Cisleithania. The result would be the marginalization of Serbia, and the vanguard role in South Slav unification would pass from Belgrade to Zagreb. Franz Ferdinand's plans were well known in Belgrade, on which account it was decided that he had to go, and the plot to kill him went right to the top of the Serbian political establishment. Franz Ferdinand's assassin Gavrilo Princip later explained the singling out of the archduke on the grounds that 'as future sovereign, he would have prevented our union by carrying through certain reforms.'[21]

Franz Ferdinand visited Sarajevo on 28 June 1914 to open the new building of the Provincial Museum. Waiting for him were the spindly young

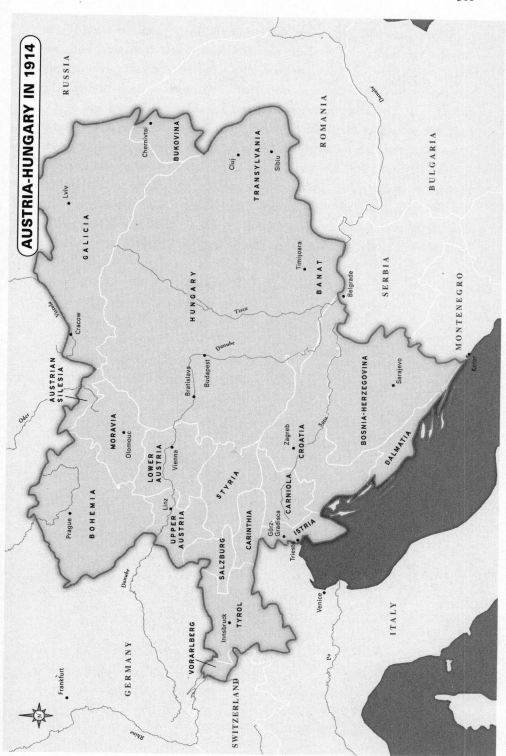

men with guns and bombs, all of them armed in Belgrade by Dimitrijević and his hoodlums. Three of the six conspirators were teenagers, and two were in their twenties. All but one were Bosnian Serbs, and they were equally incompetent. As the archduke and his wife proceeded sedately through the streets of the city in an open-top Gräf and Stift Double-Phaeton motor car, only one of the six managed to throw a bomb. Forgetting that the bomb had a time delay, he missed his target entirely. By chance, Gavrilo Princip, having previously lost his nerve, was on the pavement when the Double-Phaeton reappeared half an hour later, carrying the couple to the hospital to visit those wounded in the earlier bomb blast. Confused over the route to take, the driver stalled the car next to Princip. With the same luck as Lee Harvey Oswald fifty years later, the youth fired two lethal shots.

29

WORLD WAR AND DISSOLUTION

*N*ews of Franz Ferdinand's death was seen throughout Europe as another tragedy in the house of Habsburg, to go alongside the violent deaths of Maximilian of Mexico, Crown Prince Rudolf, and the empress. The 12 July 1914 issue of the Parisian *Le Petit Journal*, at the time France's largest circulation newspaper, carried on its front cover a colour image of Franz Joseph, head in hand, while above him floated ghostly images of previously slain Habsburgs. The illustration carried the inscription 'Tragedy of the Old Emperor: Nothing has been spared him', thus rehearsing Franz Joseph's own words on hearing sixteen years before of his wife's assassination. *The Times* in Britain commented similarly: 'The first thoughts of all men will turn to the venerable emperor, whose lot it has been to endure manifold and terrible sorrows, such as mortal man has rarely known.'[1]

Had Franz Joseph launched a war of revenge on Serbia in the days immediately after the murder, he would have had the understanding, if not the complete support, of the European powers, including perhaps even of Russia (whose foreign minister had no time for Serbian aggression). As Prime Minister Ion Brătianu of Romania explained to Franz Joseph, he might 'have had the sympathies of Europe on your side.' But Franz Joseph delayed. Since it was the summer, much of the army was on leave to help bring in the harvest, so Austria-Hungary was militarily unready. As there was the possibility of

Russian intervention on Serbia's side, Franz Joseph also wanted to make sure that his German ally would stand by their 1879 treaty of mutual defence.[2]

Over the previous decades, exchanges between the German and Habsburg general staffs had consisted mostly of Christmas cards. But Wilhelm II honourably promised to stick by Franz Joseph, even though he was already thinking that any ensuing war might be a large one, fought on several fronts. On 6 July, the Austro-Hungarian ambassador in Berlin received the guarantee that the emperor 'may rest assured that His Majesty will faithfully stand by Austria-Hungary, as is required by the obligations of his alliance and of his ancient friendship.' Having given Franz Joseph a 'blank cheque' of unconditional support, Wilhelm II left Berlin to go on his annual yacht trip around Scandinavia. The initiative returned to Vienna, but the troops were still in the fields.[3]

By delaying, Franz Joseph not only lost control of the master narrative but also allowed Habsburg war aims to escalate so that Austria-Hungary looked the aggressor. Balkan specialists in the foreign ministry no longer pushed for just a punitive war against Serbia but now talked of Serbia's complete erasure, and they did not care that a larger conflict might follow. In fact, they counted on one, believing that to postpone it would give Austria-Hungary's enemies an advantage. Some hotheads in the ministry conceived of a war in Social Darwinist terms, as an inevitable battle for supremacy in which weakness would be punished, and they looked forward to a 'totally new epoch' in which the Habsburg Empire's fortunes were restored. Without the controlling influence of Franz Ferdinand, the chief of the general staff, Conrad von Hötzendorf, also pushed again for a war, even though it might bring Russia in. He confidently reported that the Habsburg armies could defeat Serbia in days, after which they would be wheeled round to block any Russian offensive.[4]

Franz Joseph spent most of July at Bad Ischl in the Austrian Alps. He received telegraphs and reports from Vienna but did not attend the meetings of the crown council, where policy was made. To begin with, the Hungarian prime minister, István Tisza, urged caution, but he was soon won over to the opinion that a belligerent Serbia also posed a threat to Hungary's territorial integrity. Foreign minister Berchtold held to a hard line, fearful lest he show any weakness before his colleagues. Franz Joseph backed Berchtold's solution of an ultimatum to Serbia with which its government could not comply, thus handing Austria-Hungary an excuse for war. Even so, policy in

Vienna was still predicated on 'waging a bit of war' and on a limited theatre of operations.[5]

On 23 July, the Austro-Hungarian ambassador in Belgrade delivered the ultimatum to the Serbian government, which among much else demanded that Austrian police head up the investigation into the archduke's murder. It was an assault on Serbia's sovereignty that its government had to refuse, amounting, in the words of the British foreign minister Sir Edward Grey, to 'the most formidable document that was ever addressed from one state to another.' The Russian foreign minister put it even more succinctly: 'This is war.' Two days later, the Serbian government rejected the ultimatum. Within hours the staff of the Austro-Hungarian embassy left Belgrade, taking the train to Budapest. At three AM, shortly after crossing the border into Hungary, the train was halted by rejoicing crowds and the ambassador forced to give an impromptu address. At every station through which it passed, the train was cheered.[6]

Five days later, Austria-Hungary declared war on Serbia. Sitting at his desk at Bad Ischl, Franz Joseph signed the fateful order, remarking, 'I can't do anything other.' The next day, he published a proclamation explaining the decision to 'my peoples.' The war was being fought, he said, for 'the greatness, the honour, and the might of the fatherland.' Privately he told Conrad, 'If we must perish, we should do so with honour.' His words were prescient. The Russians did after all back Serbia, Germany paid on its blank cheque to Austria-Hungary, and Britain and France stood by Russia. Within a week Europe was at war.[7]

Posters written in fifteen languages announced the mobilization of the armed forces in the Habsburg Empire. From the very first, the problem was not only the logistical one of how to move over a million and a half men to the front, but also one of morale—of how to inspire the very different national groups to fight. The officer corps of the Habsburg army may well have been enthused by an 'imperial patriotism' that looked beyond nationality, but the rank and file were not so motivated. The solution was to appeal to national sentiments. Recruits were accordingly allowed to mass under their own national flags, and they were lured by the prospect of going to war against their nation's traditional enemy—Poles against Russians, Croats against Serbs, Hungarians against Slavs of all types, and so on. Appeals to nationalism seemed to work, and some commentators noted with surprise 'the frenetic rejoicing, with music and song' that greeted troops on their way to war.[8]

Motivated more by national hatreds than by a sober patriotism, Habsburg forces frequently ran amok, slaughtering civilians and burning villages. One typical order, issued in September 1914 in response to a report that some villagers had ambushed troops, read: 'Pull out the mayor, priest, assistant priest and a few others, principally Jews, and shoot them immediately. Then burn the place and try to knock down the church steeple.' As this instruction suggests, even the hostility of the officer corps to antisemitism (17 per cent of Habsburg officers were Jews) was breaking down.[9]

Desperation fed excess. The Habsburg armies were ill-equipped and poorly trained: only one in twenty adult males had received any military instruction before 1914, and for most this had been perfunctory. The trains that conveyed the men to the front travelled no faster than bicycles; provisioning was haphazard, and tin lids substituted for spades. Much can be blamed on financial constraints. The government had only managed to keep within its budget in the prewar years by cutting back on military expenditure. The generals, however, were also incompetent. Halfway through mobilization in August 1914, Conrad reversed his plans, leaving an entire army stranded on the Serbian as opposed to the Russian front, where it should have been. The campaign against Serbia, launched in August, was conducted according to a battle plan which, when it was war-gamed, had been shown to fail.[10]

The war on the Eastern Front was more mobile than on the Western, and Habsburg forces were deployed along a thousand-kilometre (six-hundred-mile) line. To begin with, the Russians made rapid gains, coming to within a day's march of Cracow in Galicia and destroying half the Austro-Hungarian army's regular troops—it would now depend on hastily trained conscripts. Then came the Italian declaration of war in May 1915, which forced the deployment of Habsburg troops to the Alps, and in the summer of 1916 a crushing Russian offensive, which convinced Romania to enter the war against the Habsburgs. To withstand the Russians, the Habsburg armies depended on German reinforcements, which had to be rushed from the siege of the French fortress of Verdun to support their ally. The Habsburg Empire became the military appendage of Germany, the strategic command of its forces passing in September 1916 to Emperor Wilhelm II.

Gradually, however, the Habsburg armies regathered their poise. Conscription brought under arms some three million men and swept up even those with medical exemptions, who were deployed in special units like the

Hungarian 'intestinal ailments battalion.' Army divisions were fitted out with proper supporting trains and field batteries, with the Škoda works in Plzeň in Bohemia producing super-heavy 'Big Bertha' howitzers. An artillery unit and three thousand men were sent in 1915 to prop up the Ottoman army in Jerusalem; mostly comprising Hungarian troops, it arrived with its own Gypsy band. Austro-Hungarian scientists, working with Ferdinand Porsche at Austro-Daimler to design six-cylinder aero-engines and four-wheel-drive armoured cars, also built the first working helicopter. In 1915, Czech cryptographers cracked the new Russian military code in three days.

Backed by the Germans, the Habsburg armies notched up military successes. The Serbian army, already in retreat, abandoned the Balkan mainland in 1915–1916 for the Greek Ionian Islands. The Romanians were defeated and forced in December 1917 to sue for peace, while Russia simultaneously collapsed into revolution. The Italian front held, and Venice lay within the Habsburg military grasp. Austrian troops fighting on the Italian front were now sufficiently confident to feel sorry for the enemy, refusing to machine-gun their advance and begging them instead to return to their dugouts. As the Habsburg foreign minister reported in November 1917, 'the war can be regarded as won.'[11]

But the politicians overlooked the home front. The demands of the army, the allied blockade, and the loss of most of the granary of Galicia to the Russians squeezed the food supply. Communications and agriculture were further disrupted by bands of deserters, who operated in quasi-military formations in the countryside. Flour and bread were rationed in 1915; sugar, milk, and coffee the next year, and then potatoes. By 1918, the weekly ration of potatoes was just half a kilo (one pound). Even with rationing, food was frequently unavailable or unaffordable. At weekends, workers poured into the countryside, foraging for food and digging up potato fields. To provide for their own communities, mayors halted supply trains destined for the big cities and offloaded their cargoes. A shortage of coal in the winter of 1917–1918 resulted in the closure of many theatres, cinemas, and other places of recreation, since they were found impossible to heat.[12]

To rally the population, cinemas (when open) showed films of an uplifting content, with cheerful troops, busy factories, and relaxed street scenes. The censors forbade scenes of fighting or casualties, and they 'cleaned up' feature films imported from France to conceal their origin. Before the war, film production in Vienna had comprised almost entirely pornography produced by Saturn Films (it is hard nowadays to consider the output as other than burlesque). With the war, the initiative passed to Sascha Films, which made melodramas, weekly news bulletins, and comedy. The 1916 *Vienna at War* (*Wien im Krieg*) is a comic masterpiece, which interweaves social satire with an interlude that uses a distorting lens to show the city through the eyes of two drunks.[13]

To raise civilian morale, the government and military authorities organized in 1916 a special War Exhibition (Kriegsausstellung). Occupying a site several hundred metres square on Vienna's Prater Park, the exhibition comprised fifty halls and pavilions. The exhibits included an open-air reconstruction of trenches, a field hospital, and a large trophy hall, which showed captured artillery and planes. The exhibition had been set up on the site of the old theme park, and its intention was as much for recreation as instruction. So there was a theatre, cinema, several restaurants, and booths selling souvenirs, including the handiwork of prisoners of war.

The War Exhibition sanitized the conflict. It showed 'boys' toys' in the form of huge howitzers and mobile bridges. The enemy were represented with samples of their weaponry, pictures of them surrendering, and 'models of the most interesting racial types of Russian soldiers.' Displays and glass cabinets showed typical rations at the front, including the daily quantity of fodder given to horses, as well as the latest wireless telegraphy, the work of war artists, X-ray machines, and so on. A whole building was given over to prosthetics. Disabled survivors often showed to the public what they might still achieve in terms of carpentry, playing musical instruments, and typewriting. For those who had not survived, a section was given over to war graves. Grieving relatives were assured that their loved ones were resting in well-tended cemeteries.[14]

The War Exhibition was opened in July 1916 by Archduke Franz Salvator, the emperor's son-in-law. He had married in 1890 Franz Joseph's youngest daughter, Marie Valerie, who looked almost identical to her mother. Typically, Franz Joseph had insisted that she be deprived of rank upon marriage, as Franz Salvator was not of royal stock. On the first day, twenty thousand people came through the turnstiles, and over the next five months close to a million. The War Exhibition was so successful that after winter closure it reopened the next year. As one journalist later observed, the War Exhibition helped people forget about the war by looking at it. Visitors had been, he remarked, like the viewers in a cinema, their 'spirits suddenly removed from the world.'[15]

The catalogue of the exhibition could not conceal the everyday privations of wartime. At three hundred pages, the catalogue was kept cheap by sponsorship, and firms competed to show how they had altered production to serve the state. Other advertisements promised shoes made with wooden soles and nails, since leather and iron were scarce. The Imperial Fig-Tobacco Factory, meanwhile, proclaimed the merits of its ersatz coffee as 'better than beans.'[16] The War Exhibition did not reopen in 1918. In its place there was a much smaller Exhibition of Substitute Goods (Ersatzmittelausstellung). Purely didactic, it advised Viennese on how to make do with cardboard shoes, substitute eggs, and synthetic oil. Faced with a shortage of cloth, industrialists also investigated the production of uniforms by using stinging nettles, and the savings that might follow the introduction in the armed services of single-sex blouses.

With the delivery of the ultimatum to Serbia in 1914, emergency powers had come into effect which curtailed civil liberties (free speech, freedom of assembly, right to property and privacy, and so on), conscripted labour into industry, and handed over large areas of the empire to military authority. By the middle of 1915, martial law had been imposed across Cisleithania, except for Upper and Lower Austria, and Bohemia. Military tribunals frequently ignored procedures and meted out an arbitrary justice, with Slav minorities bearing the brunt of their prejudice. Altogether about three million people were prosecuted by military tribunals, many for trivial offences that amounted to just slips of the tongue. A group of Slovenes in Styria was arrested in August 1914 for having two years earlier contributed to a Red Cross fund in Ljubljana in Carniola. Martial law was often buttressed with 'emergency law' (Standrecht), which demanded a speedy trial with only two outcomes: acquittal or death.[17]

The armed forces additionally took control of heavy industry, appointing 'military directors' to oversee production. In fact, weapons and vehicle output rose throughout the war—four thousand machine guns in 1915 compared to over fifteen thousand in 1917; three hundred locomotives as against four hundred, and so on. But the rate of increase was less than its rivals managed. It also came at the cost of unbalancing the economy. Loans, mainly from German banks, and gold and foreign-currency reserves were used to import steel and coal but not food. A state monopoly on grain introduced in 1915 and the appointment of a 'General Commissariat' to coordinate food supplies did not help. Police reports on public opinion noted as early as 1916 long queues outside food stores that often started gathering at midnight. There was, the reports stated, no longer any interest in the military outcome, only the wish that the end would come soon.[18]

By 1918, provincial governments were withholding food supplies for their own populations. Even so, by the autumn food reserves had dwindled everywhere to almost nothing. Starvation, rationing, and food queues gave way to strikes and bread riots. In January 1918, seven hundred thousand workers downed tools for ten days, while tens of thousands more gathered to listen to agitators. In the spring of 1918, Cracow dissolved into mayhem, as Jewish shops were plundered and fights for food spilled onto the streets. Since a militarized bureaucracy now commanded both the law and the economy, it was increasingly the government and administration that were blamed for shortages. When the prime minister was assassinated in the autumn of 1916, the police reported little interest and few black flags. The death in November of Franz Joseph himself elicited mourning and rather more flags, but otherwise the streets of Vienna were said to be 'completely normal.' The historian and politician Joseph Redlich confided in his diary, 'The whole city is surrounded by a deep and intense tiredness; neither sorrow for the dead ruler, nor joy over his successor can be felt.' A government that fails to feed its population soon becomes first irrelevant and then illegitimate.[19]

By November 1918 one million of the eight million men recruited into the Austro-Hungarian armed forces were dead. Almost two million had been wounded, four million hospitalized through illness, and around one and a half million taken prisoner. This was out of a total population of just under thirty million. Although numerically depleted, the bulk of the Habsburg armed forces stayed if not loyal then at least disciplined. When in early November 1918 the Italian army took the surrender of around four hundred thousand Habsburg troops, it discovered that they included more than eighty thousand Czechs and Slovaks, sixty thousand South Slavs (mostly Croats), twenty-five thousand Transylvanian Romanians, and even seven thousand Italians from Istria and the Tyrol. It was the final irony that as the Habsburg Empire dissolved into national states, its army retained its multinational character.[20]

Franz Joseph's final words to his valet were: 'Tomorrow morning, at half past three.' Although sick, the eighty-six-year-old emperor was determined to rise at his usual time. Franz Joseph's successor was his nephew, Karl. The new ruler fell short of the standard set by his uncle. As a contemporary quip put it, 'You hope to meet a thirty-year-old man, but you find the appearance of a twenty-year-old youth, who thinks, speaks, and acts like a ten-year-old boy.' Notwithstanding these jibes, Karl was a decent man, committed to peace. But he lacked both the authority that age had lent his predecessor and the tenacity of Franz Ferdinand, into whose inheritance he had stepped. His commitment to the war seemed lukewarm. On a visit to the General Staff headquarters in spring 1915, he was reported to have said that he did 'not understand why we make so much effort, since everything is in any case pointless, for the war cannot be won.'[21]

On previous occasions, when faced with military disaster, the Habsburgs had made peace, even at the price of surrendering lands and the occasional princess. To win their support, the Western allies had promised Romania and Italy slices of the Habsburg Empire—Transylvania and the southern Tyrol and Dalmatia, respectively. The Habsburg Empire could have borne these losses. It might even have survived the sacrifice of part of Galicia, had this been the price of peace with Russia. By 1916, however, the Habsburg Empire's fate was bound to Germany's, and many of its troops were now under the command of German generals.

Starting in 1917, Emperor Karl put out feelers to the allies to test whether a peace might be obtained, promising (as if they were his to give) Istanbul to the Russians and the restoration of Alsace-Lorraine to France. But his overtures came to nothing and were leaked to the press. In order to reassure Wilhelm II, the Habsburg foreign minister publicly affirmed in April 1918 that Karl had no interest in making a separate peace. The next month, Karl visited Wilhelm at the German headquarters at Spa in Belgium. He agreed not only to the further coordination of the German and Austro-Hungarian armies under German command but also to the Habsburg Empire's subordination to Germany's expansive war aims and economic policy, even to the extent of merging Austria-Hungary into a German-led customs union. It was time for the 'blank cheque' to be repaid.

In April 1917, the United States had entered the war. To begin with, President Woodrow Wilson had no intention of breaking up the Habsburg Empire. His 'Fourteen Points', outlined in January 1918, spoke only of giving the peoples of the empire 'the freest opportunity of autonomous development.' Lloyd George, the British prime minister, also declared that the dismantling of the empire was 'no part of our war aims.' But with little prospect of detaching the Habsburg Empire from Germany, the allied position hardened. The US secretary of state demanded that the empire 'be wiped off the map of Europe', and in June 1918 Wilson declared that 'all branches of the Slav race must be completely liberated from German and Austrian domination.' Allied propaganda now openly supported the empire's dissolution and its replacement by independent nation states.[22]

In May 1917, Karl reconvened the parliament in Vienna, and two months later he declared a general amnesty, releasing over two thousand political prisoners. Many of these favoured the empire's comprehensive refashioning and even its obliteration. Ideas that had previously been marginal were now amplified on the floor of the parliament. The first was that all South Slavs should be united in a single state that would bring together Slovenes, Croats, and Serbs and be powerful enough to head off Italian claims to the Adriatic seaboard. Championed by a South Slav Committee, which operated in exile, the dream of a united Yugoslav state was endorsed in the summer of 1918 by the allies. The second was the vision of Tomáš Masaryk, the future president of Czechoslovakia, that Czechs and Slovaks should join a single state. Exiled in London, Masaryk convinced British politicians that his scheme was not fanciful.

The end came swiftly. In September 1918, the French-led Allied Army in the East smashed through the Macedonian front in the southern Balkans, forcing Bulgaria to sue for peace. The way lay open for the allies to attack Austria-Hungary from the south, but the Germans had insufficient manpower or resources to help. The latest German summer offensive on the Western Front had failed, by which time two million American troops had arrived in France to support the allied counter-offensive. By October, the Germans were in full-scale retreat.

Early on in October, the German government began negotiations with the Western allies for a ceasefire. In a vain attempt to accommodate the growing demands for self-government, Emperor Karl issued a manifesto that attempted to restructure the empire on national lines. But representatives of newly formed 'national committees' seized power in Prague, Zagreb, and Transylvania, claiming that they should be regarded as the governments constituted by the manifesto. At the end of the month, a revolution in Hungary brought into power the left-wing leader, the 'Red Count' Michael Károlyi.

Not much was left of the Habsburg Empire. Even in the Austrian lands, an independent German-Austrian state was proclaimed. On 11 November, Emperor Karl formally relinquished his involvement in public affairs (he did not abdicate). Shortly afterwards, the Austrian socialist leader Karl Renner visited Emperor Karl in the Schönbrunn Palace, bidding him speed with the words, 'Herr Habsburg, the taxi is waiting.' The next day, what was left of the imperial parliament declared a republic. As it turned out, Karl twice attempted in 1921 to seize power in Hungary as its rightful sovereign, but he was repulsed. He died the next year in Madeira, where he is buried. His heart, however, was extracted and brought to Muri Abbey— more than nine hundred years after Radbot and Ita, a Habsburg had at last returned in death to the dynasty's ancestral home in the Swiss Aargau.

The Habsburg Empire fell because it had tied its fate to Germany. Because it was unable to extract itself from the war, Germany's military defeat became its own. But Germany survived the war, as did Bulgaria and a greatly reduced Turkey, shorn of the trappings of the Ottoman Empire. The Habsburg Empire disintegrated completely, its lands being divided up into six states, and its ruin was the greatest. The glue of the dynasty had been found thin, and by 1918 it was insufficient to hold the parts together. Identities and allegiances had formed around nations, and they, and not the dynasty, became the containers in which people increasingly vested their hopes and loyalties. As the reputation of the dynasty tottered, there was no sense left of a common bond to keep the peoples of the Habsburg Empire together in some sort of political union or collective enterprise. The collapse of the Habsburg Empire in 1918 was for this reason final and entire. In the history of most European states, the year 1918 marks the end of a chapter (1917 in the case of Russia). For the Habsburg Empire, it is the end of the book.

Conclusion

When people meet celebrities, they often say afterwards that they were smaller than they expected, registering the difference between the imagined person and the real human being. It is the same with monarchs once they are 'undone' (to use Shakespeare's term in *Richard II*). Out of office, they are diminished and reduced to ordinariness. Their lives become visibly humdrum, marked by the same routines and petty cares as everyone else's. For a time, they may live off some vestigial charisma and, if lucky enough, the loot of their palaces. But once deprived of their regal address, most ex-monarchs become boring 'nonpersons', for their *persona*, which is the Latin for an actor's mask, has been taken from them. As the dethroned Richard II lamented in Shakespeare's play, 'I have no name. . . . And know not now what name to call myself' (*Richard II*, Act 4, Scene 1).

The fate of the Habsburgs has been no different. A thousand or more aspire to the name (some are plainly fraudulent), and there were at the last count about a hundred who claimed the rank of archduke. Titles still count for something in aristocratic circles, so most of the archdukes have managed 'society marriages.' Preferred careers are banking, farming, and art dealing. Other Habsburgs have been tiresome 'It girls', chat-show hosts, and dubious businessmen. A few have been recruited as 'roving ambassadors', usually on behalf of distasteful governments. Otherwise, the surviving members of the dynasty serve only as dull reminders of a lost world of empire.

Since 1918 the Habsburgs have produced one genuine celebrity. Otto (1912–2011) was the eldest son of the last emperor, Karl, and, to prolong a cliché, probably the best emperor the Habsburgs never had. Yet Otto's distinction has less to do with being a Habsburg than with his tireless dedication to European peace, the Catholic Church, and a host of causes that he championed as a member of the European Parliament. Otto was courageous and shrewd. He personally intervened in France in 1940 to save several thousand Jews, and he visited Sarajevo in 1997 in the aftermath of the Bosnian War, ignoring the death threats of Serbian gangsters. He would have nothing to do with Hitler in the 1930s and kept Mussolini at arm's length. Even so, he was never less than modest, explaining that he was happy to be called Dr von Habsburg or just Herr Habsburg. But when he was buried in the Capuchin Crypt in Vienna in July 2011, it was as 'Otto of Austria, former Crown Prince of Austria-Hungary, Prince Royal of Hungary and Bohemia, of Dalmatia, Croatia, Slavonia, Galicia, Lodomeria, and Illyria, Grand Duke of Tuscany and Cracow', and so on (his heart was separately interred in the Benedictine monastery of Pannonhalma in Hungary as a token of his commitment to both halves of the old Austro-Hungarian Empire).

Otto von Habsburg spoke seven languages to complete or near fluency. When an Italian politician thought to make a point in the European Parliament by delivering some faltering lines in Latin, Otto responded flawlessly in the same language. Unsurprisingly, he identified as 'a European' and thought a united Europe the best guarantor of the continent's peace. After 1989, he worked to have the former satellites of the Soviet Union become members of the European Union. But his experience of the Habsburg Empire had taught him that for the European idea to succeed, it needed to be held together culturally and to develop among its peoples a common identity. He saw Christianity as the cultural cement, on which account he opposed allowing Turkey to join the European Union, but he also recognized that secularism had diminished Christianity's power to unite.[1]

Otto never satisfactorily explained how to build a single political community out of different national communities. The story of multinational ventures in the twentieth century has not been a good one. In Czechoslovakia, the Soviet Union, and Yugoslavia, there was insufficient sense of common identity and purpose to build an enduring political project. In the twenty-first century, Spain, Belgium, the United Kingdom, and the European Union face a similar challenge, and the same anxieties attend their future as was once the case in the Habsburg Empire. But as Crown Prince Rudolf observed shortly before his death in 1889, 'Austria is a bloc of different nations and different races under a united rule . . . and it is an idea of enormous importance to the civilization of the world. Because the present execution of this idea is, to put it diplomatically, not altogether harmonious, it does not mean that the idea itself is wrong.'[2]

The Habsburg Empire collapsed in 1918, but the Habsburg idea was always about more than territory and politics. The Habsburg idea was complex. At its heart lay the inheritance of Rome and of the Roman Empire, renewed by Charlemagne and the Staufen emperors, whose heirs the first Habsburg rulers imagined themselves to be. The Holy Roman Empire embodied one aspect of this idea, hence the Habsburg ambition to fill the supreme office of emperor. So too did Austria, which under the Babenbergs had developed its own myth of exceptionalism. Over almost seven hundred years, impulses and emphases changed—service to the Catholic faith and leading the struggle against heresy and the Turks were the most consistent. But the Habsburgs also stood for the grand eloquence of the international Baroque, bringing enlightenment and care to subjects, empowering the state, making Europe safe from revolution, cultivating an architectural style as a universal idiom, and pursuing a civilizing mission within or beyond the territorial limits of its power. Over centuries, the Habsburgs also sought to build an empire of knowledge in the alchemist's laboratory, botanical adventures, and museum collections. Their legacy survives not only in architecture and great collections of art and natural history, but also as a vision that combined power, destiny, and knowledge, and blended earthly and heavenly realms in a universal enterprise that touched every aspect of humanity's temporal and spiritual experience.

The Habsburg idea embraced universality, which meant that the Habsburgs could never rest their identity on a single national group. Whereas the tsarist empire of the Romanovs took on Russianness and the Ottoman sultans in the last decades of the nineteenth century became increasingly Turkish, the Central European Habsburgs stood above nationality. Their style was to govern as if they were rulers of each land and people rather than masters of a composite whole or of a single national community. Even had they sought to do otherwise, the figures were stacked against them, for in their Central European lands no national group formed a majority upon which a single overarching identity might be built. Race was a different matter. Purity of the blood was part of the cosmic order that the Spanish Habsburgs exported to the New World, and the notion of civilization embraced in Central Europe in the nineteenth century was also partly bound up with ideas of racial hierarchy. But race never became a principle of Habsburg policy or developed into a coherent ideology. It remained just one aspect among many.

Among its former subjects, there was little regret for the empire's passing. A Hungarian 'Legitimist' party struggled for a Habsburg restoration in the 1930s but obtained only a single seat in the Hungarian parliament. In interwar Austria, where civil war periodically erupted against a backdrop of economic ruin, a 'Habsburg nostalgia' and 'wistfulness' (*Wehmut*) occasionally surfaced. But it was a false remembrance of things past that looked back to an idealized and timeless world of bumbling officials, frozen hierarchies, and Biedermeier clichés, with a song and a cake for every occasion. Elsewhere in the former Habsburg Empire, a politicized generation of historians and writers cast Habsburg rulers as the villainous gaolers of nations, from whose prison their subject peoples had broken free.

In the successor states of the fallen empire the 'liberated' nations affirmed their primacy, and since none of the new states was mononational, they frequently did so by bullying their national minorities. The reckoning was not long in coming. Without the shelter of the Habsburg Empire, and divided within themselves, the new states soon fell prey to the resurgent empires on their rim—Nazi Germany and Soviet Russia. Their borders were once more redrawn, and where people were found to be in the wrong place the cattle trucks stood ready to receive them. But the victims were also collaborators. The mass murder of Jews in Central Europe could not have been done without the connivance of local police and militias. Communist rule after the Second World War also depended on a web of informers. In all the countries of the old Habsburg Empire, only Austria maintained a democratic character, left free from Soviet control in return for sticking to a neutral course between the rival power blocs. Everywhere else, Communist rule persisted until finally overthrown in a series of popular revolutions in 1989.

Back in 1990, there was a moment when it seemed that Otto von Habsburg might be put forward as president of a new democratic Hungary. The veteran historian and political éminence grise Domokos Kosáry weighed up his nation's prospects. 'We could do a lot worse,' he observed.[3] Within little more than a decade, Hungarian public life had degenerated into the politics of the pig trough, dominated by a new breed of multimillionaire politicians who plundered state enterprises and international aid, loading family and friends with stolen money, sometimes in collaboration with organized crime. A similar pattern of political corruption was evident among Hungary's neighbours in the former Habsburg Empire. For some Western observers, it seemed so embedded to suggest that private interests had captured power in several Central European states. In recent years, there has been a return in parts of the region to censorship of the media, manipulation of the courts, and state-sponsored antisemitism and political violence.

Over more than nine centuries the Habsburgs produced simpletons and visionaries, dabblers in magic and freemasonry, fanatics in religion, rulers committed to the welfare of their peoples, patrons of art and champions of science, and builders of great palaces and churches. Some Habsburgs were dedicated to peace, while others embarked upon fruitless wars. Even so, as the politics of Central Europe continues to sour, it is hard to avoid the conclusion that the Hungarian historian was right after all—a Habsburg would have done no worse.

ACKNOWLEDGMENTS

My first thanks is to Adam Gauntlett of Peters, Fraser and Dunlop, who first suggested that I write this book. I had just completed a much shorter work on the Habsburg Empire for Oxford University Press's series of Very Short Introductions and felt frustrated by its brevity. I wanted to say more, and Adam made this possible. I am grateful, too, to my London and New York editors, Simon Winder and Brian Distelberg, whose detailed criticisms and ability to stand above the text and explain what I was struggling to say has made this book more coherent and its chapters more lucid. Roger Labrie did a painstaking line-by-line edit of the manuscript, and Beth Wright a most thorough copyediting of the text. If I have not always succeeded in balancing narrative with context, the fault is mine and not my editors.

I owe much to colleagues at University College London's School of Slavonic and East European Studies, not least to Rebecca Haynes, who read through the complete text, and to Simon Dixon, Egbert Klautke, Tom Lorman, and Trevor Thomas. I am beholden, too, to generations of PhD students, from whose research and ideas I have over several decades unabashedly borrowed—Jamie Bulloch, Alex Kazamias, Tom Lorman, Robert Gray, Eleanor Janega, Christopher Nicholson, and Philip Barker. In completing this book, my thanks are also due to Phil Cavendish for sharing his expertise on early cinema, to Anastazja Grudnicka for her advice on Emperor Matthias, and to Barbara Stollberg-Rilinger of the University of Münster for so promptly addressing my queries on the law of succession in Mecklenburg. My knowledge of the Banat owes much to Irina Marin and to Adrian and Livia Magina, and of Transylvania and Transylvanian freemasonry to Ion-Aurel Pop, Alexandru Simon, and Tudor Sălăgean.

Over the last two years I have benefited from involvement in the project organized by Tom Lorman and Ferenc Hörcher of Budapest's Pázmány University on the history of the Hungarian constitution. I am grateful, too, to Richard Butterwick-Pawlikowski and the College of Europe in Natolin for their invitation in 2018 to lecture on Austria-Hungary and the First World War, which helped me refine my thoughts on the dissolution of the Habsburg Empire. Several talks given recently at UCL by Alexander Maxwell of Victoria University Wellington proved characteristically thought-provoking.

A Freak Brothers cartoon has one of its characters sitting and smoking until he himself becomes a pile of ash, at which point the brothers roll up the ash and smoke it. Ann's steadfast love has over the years prevented me succumbing to a similar fate. My parents have always shown unfailing interest in whatever I have been writing, and I am indebted to their encouragement and support. My first book, published in 1985, was dedicated to them. This one is too.

July 2019
Ramsgate, Kent

CREDITS FOR ILLUSTRATIONS

Muri Abbey, circa 1650: From Matthäus Merian, *Topographia Helvetiae*, 2nd ed. (Frankfurt/M., 1654).

Heraldic Wall of St George's Cathedral: Courtesy of Thomas Ledl, licensed under a Creative Commons Attribution-Share Alike 4.0 International license.

The family of Emperor Maximilian I: Courtesy of the Kunsthistorisches Museum Vienna.

Maximilian inspects a haul of fish: From Michael Mayr, *Das Fischereibuch Kaiser Maximilians I.* (Innsbruck, 1901).

The 'People of Calicut': Courtesy of the Metropolitan Museum of Art, New York.

Emperor Charles V, circa 1550: Courtesy of the Mauritshuis, The Hague.

Escorial Palace, Spain: Courtesy of Yvon Fruneau, licensed under a Creative Commons Attribution-ShareAlike 3.00 IGO license.

Emperor Rudolf II: Courtesy of the Rijksmuseum, Amsterdam.

Emperor Rudolf II as Vertumnus: Courtesy of Skokloster Castle, Sweden.

***Melencolia I,* by Albrecht Dürer:** Courtesy of the Metropolitan Museum of Art, New York.

Fort San Domingo: Courtesy of Asimonlee at the English Language Wikipedia.

An example of Andean Baroque: Courtesy of McKay Savage, licensed under a Creative Commons Attribution 2.0 Generic License.

'Charles Church' (Karlskirche): Courtesy of Thomas Ledl, licensed under a Creative Commons Attribution-ShareAlike 4.0 International license.

Design for a Catafalque: Courtesy of Metropolitan Museum of Art, New York.

Horse Ballet in the Hofburg, 1667: Courtesy of the Rijksmuseum, Amsterdam.

Maria Theresa, circa 1745: Courtesy of the Mauritshuis, The Hague.

Prince Metternich in 1822: Courtesy of the Metropolitan Museum of Art, New York.

The Execution of Emperor Maximilian of Mexico: Courtesy of the Metropolitan Museum of Art, New York.

The Looshaus in Vienna: Courtesy of Thomas Ledl, licensed under a Creative Commons Attribution-Share Alike 4.0 International license.

The Hungarian explorer Count Samuel Teleki: Taken from Lieut. Ludwig von Höhnel, *Discovery of Lakes Rudolf and Stefanie*, vol. 2 (London, 1894).

War Ministry Building in Vienna: Courtesy of Bwag/CC-BY-SA-4.0.

ABBREVIATIONS

AHR	*American Historical Review*
AHY	*Austrian History Yearbook*
AS	*Austrian Studies*
HAHR	*Hispanic American Historical Review*
HR	*Hispanic Review*
HZ	*Historische Zeitschrift*
JGPÖ	*Jahrbuch der Gesellschaft für die Geschichte des Protestantismus in Österreich*
JWCI	*Journal of the Warburg and Courtauld Institutes*
MGH	Monumenta Germaniae Historica
MGH, Dt. Chron.	MGH Deutsche Chroniken
MGH SS	MGH Scriptores, in folio
MGH, SS rer. Germ.	MGH Scriptores rerum Germanicarum in usum scholarum
MGH SS rer. Germ. N.S.	MGH Scriptores rerum Germanicarum, Nova series
MGH, Staatsschriften	MGH Staatsschriften des späteren Mittelalters
MIÖG	*Mitteilungen des Instituts für Österreichische Geschichtsforschung*
MNL OL	Magyar Nemzeti Levéltár, Országos Levéltár, Hungarian State Archive, Budapest

OeStA/HHStA Austrian State Archive, Haus-, Hof- und
Staatsarchiv, Vienna

SEER *Slavonic and East European Review*

FURTHER READING

Digital resources include The World of the Habsburgs (www.habsburger .net/en) and AEIOU Encyclopedia of Austria (www.aeiou.at).

GENERAL WORKS

Jean Berenger, *A History of the Habsburg Empire*, 2 vols. (Harlow and London, 1994–1997).

Benjamin W. Curtis, *The Habsburgs: The History of a Dynasty* (London, 2013).

Paula Sutter Fichtner, *The Habsburgs: Dynasty, Culture and Politics* (London, 2014).

Martyn Rady, *The Habsburg Empire: A Very Short Introduction* (Oxford, 2017).

Adam Wandruszka, *The House of Austria: Six Hundred Years of a European Dynasty* (London, 1964).

Geoffrey Wheatcroft, *The Habsburgs: Embodying Empire* (London, 1996).

Simon Winder, *Danubia: A Personal History of Habsburg Europe* (London, 2013).

WORKS COVERING SHORTER PERIODS

Steven Beller, *The Habsburg Monarchy 1815–1918* (Cambridge, 2018).

F. R. Bridge, *The Habsburg Monarchy among the Great Powers, 1815–1918* (New York, Oxford, and Munich, 1990).

John Deak, *Forging a Multinational State: State Making in Imperial Austria from the Enlightenment to the First World War* (Stanford, CA, 2015).

R. J. W. Evans, *Austria, Hungary, and the Habsburgs: Central Europe c. 1683–1867* (Oxford, 2006).

R. J. W. Evans, *The Making of the Habsburg Monarchy, 1550–1700: An Interpretation* (Oxford, 1979).

Pieter M. Judson, *The Habsburgs: A New History* (Cambridge, MA, and London, 2016).

Robert Kann, *A History of the Habsburg Empire, 1526–1918* (Berkeley, CA, 1974).

C. A. Macartney, *The Habsburg Empire 1790–1918*, 2nd ed. (London, 1971).

Robin Okey, *The Habsburg Monarchy c. 1765–1918: From Enlightenment to Eclipse* (Basingstoke and London, 2001).

Alan Sked, *The Decline and Fall of the Habsburg Empire, 1815–1918* (London, 1989).

A. J. P. Taylor, *The Habsburg Monarchy, 1809–1918* (London, 1948, and many subsequent editions).

INTRODUCTION: AN EMPEROR'S LIBRARY

Anna Coreth, *Pietas Austriaca* (West Lafayette, IN, 2004).

Robert Folz, *The Concept of Empire in Western Europe from the Fifth to the Fourteenth Century* (London, 1969).

Anke Holdenried, *The Sibyl and Her Scribes: Manuscripts and Interpretation of the Latin Sibylla Tiburtina c.1050–1500* (Aldershot and Burlington, VT, 2006).

Johanna Rachinger, *The Austrian National Library*, 2nd ed. (Munich, London, and New York, 2015).

Marie Tanner, *The Last Descendant of Aeneas: The Hapsburgs and the Mythic Image of the Emperor* (New Haven, CT, 1992).

1. CASTLE HABSBURG AND THE 'FORTINBRAS EFFECT'

Benjamin Arnold, *Princes and Territories in Medieval Germany* (Cambridge, 1991).

Clive H. Church and Randolph C. Head, *A Concise History of Switzerland* (Cambridge, 2013).

William Coxe, *History of the House of Austria*, vol. 1 (London, 1864).

Peter Felder, *Muri Abbey* (Berne, 2002).

Jane Louisa Willyams, *Tower of the Hawk: Some Passages in the History of the House of Hapsburg* (London, 1871).

2. THE HOLY ROMAN EMPIRE AND THE GOLDEN KING

Benjamin Arnold, *Medieval Germany, 500–1300: A Political Interpretation* (Basingstoke, 1997).

Noel Denholm-Young, *Richard of Cornwall* (Oxford, 1947).

England and Europe in the Reign of Henry III (1216–1272), ed. Björn K. U. Weiler and Ifor W. Rowlands (Aldershot, 2002).

Joachim Whaley, *The Holy Roman Empire: A Very Short Introduction* (Oxford, 2018), 44–66.

3. LOSING PLACE AND FORGING A PAST

Reinhard H. Gruber, *St. Stephan's Cathedral in Vienna* (Vienna, 1998).

Gerhart B. Ladner, 'The Middle Ages in Austrian Tradition: Problems of an Imperial and Paternalistic Ideology', *Viator*, 3 (1972), 433–62.

Len Scales, *The Shaping of German Identity: Authority and Crisis, 1245–1414* (Cambridge, 2012).

Andrew Wheatcroft, *The Habsburgs: Embodying Empire* (London, 1995), 39–68.

4. FREDERICK III: SATURN AND MARS

F. R. H. Du Boulay, *Germany in the Later Middle Ages* (London, 1983).

Frances Courtney Kneupper, *The Empire at the End of Time: Identity and Reform in Late Medieval German Prophecy* (Oxford, 2016).

Peter Moraw, 'The Court of the German King and of the Emperor at the End of the Middle Ages, 1440–1519', in *Princes, Patronage and the Nobility: The Court at the Beginning of the Modern Age c. 1450–1650*, ed. Ronald G. Asch and Adolf M. Birks (Oxford, 1991), 103–37.

Gerald Strauss, *Manifestations of Discontent in Germany on the Eve of the Reformation* (Bloomington, IN, and London, 1971).

Richard Vaughan, *Charles the Bold: The Last Valois Duke of Burgundy* (London, 1973).

5. MAXIMILIAN AND THE COLOUR-CODED KINGS

Giulia Bartrum, *Dürer* (London, 2007).

Gerhard Benecke, *Maximilian I (1459–1519): An Analytical Biography* (London, 1982).

Darin Hayton, *The Crown and the Cosmos: Astrology and the Politics of Maximilian I* (Pittsburgh, 2015).

Harald Kleinschmidt, *Ruling the Waves: Emperor Maximilian I, the search for islands and the transformation of the European world picture c. 1500* (Utrecht, 2008).

Larry Silver, *Marketing Maximilian: The Visual Ideology of a Holy Roman Emperor* (Princeton, NJ, 2008).

6. CHARLES V: RULER OF THE WORLD

Rebecca Ard Boone, *Mercurino di Gattinara and the Creation of the Spanish Empire* (London, 2014).

Karl Brandi, *The Emperor Charles V* (London, 1939).

John M. Headley, *The Emperor and His Chancellor: A Study of the Imperial Chancellery Under Gattinara* (Cambridge, 1983).

William Maltby, *The Reign of Charles V* (Basingstoke and New York, 2002).

Martyn Rady, *The Emperor Charles V* (London and New York, 1988).

Hugh Thomas, *The Golden Age: The Spanish Empire of Charles V* (London, 2010).

7. HUNGARY, BOHEMIA, AND THE PROTESTANT CHALLENGE

Kenneth J. Dillon, *King and Estates in the Bohemian Lands 1526–1564* (Brussels, 1976).

Paula S. Fichtner, *Ferdinand I of Austria: The Politics of Dynasticism in the Age of the Reformation* (Boulder, CO, and New York, 1982).

Howard Louthan, *The Quest for Compromise: Peacemakers in Counter-Reformation Vienna* (Cambridge, 1997).

Karin J. MacHardy, *War, Religion and Court Patronage in Habsburg Austria: The Social and Cultural Dimensions of Political Interaction, 1521–1622* (Basingstoke and New York, 2003).

Orsolya Réthelyi, *Mary of Hungary: The Queen and Her Court, 1521–1531* (Budapest, 2005).

8. PHILIP II: THE NEW WORLD, RELIGIOUS DISSENT, AND ROYAL INCEST

Henry Kamen, *The Escorial: Art and Power in the Renaissance* (New Haven and London, 2010).

Henry Kamen, *Philip of Spain* (New Haven and New York, 1997).

Geoffrey Parker, *The Dutch Revolt* (Harmondsworth, 1985).

Geoffrey Parker, *Imprudent King: A New Life of Philip II* (New Haven and London, 2014).

Hugh Thomas, *World Without End: The Global Empire of Philip II* (London, 2014).

9. DON JOHN AND AND THE GALLEYS OF LEPANTO

Jack Beeching, *The Galleys at Lepanto* (New York, 1983).

Gigi Beutler, *The Imperial Vaults of the PP Capuchins in Vienna (Capuchin Crypt)* (Vienna, 2003).

Niccolò Capponi, *Victory of the West: The Story of the Battle of Lepanto* (London, 2006).

Estella Weiss-Krejci, 'Restless Corpses: "Secondary Burial" in the Babenberg and Habsburg dynasties', *Antiquity*, 75 (2001), 769–80.

Margaret Yeo, *Don John of Austria* (London, 1934).

10. RUDOLF II AND THE ALCHEMISTS OF PRAGUE

R. J. W. Evans, *Rudolf II and His World: A Study in Intellectual History, 1576–1612* (Oxford, 1973).

Paula Sutter Fichtner, *Emperor Maximilian II* (New Haven, CT, and London, 2001).

Peter French, *John Dee* (London, 1987).

Peter Marshall, *The Theatre of the World: Alchemy, Astrology and Magic in Renaissance Prague* (London, 2006).

Sally Metzler, *Bartholomeus Spranger: Splendor and Eroticism in Imperial Prague* (New York, 2014).

11. THE TRIUMPH OF THE HERETICS

A Companion to the Reformation in Central Europe, ed. Howard Louthan and Graeme Murdock (Boston, 2015).

Ferdinand II: 450 Years Sovereign Ruler of Tyrol, ed. Sabine Haag and Veronika Sandbichler (Vienna, 2017).

Valentine Penrose, *The Bloody Countess: Atrocities of Erzsebet Bathory* (London, 1970).

Regina Pörtner, *The Counter-Reformation in Central Europe: Styria 1580–1630* (Oxford, 2001).

Martyn Rady, 'Bocskai, Rebellion and Resistance in Early Modern Hungary', in *Resistance, Rebellion and Revolution in Hungary and Central Europe*, ed. László Péter and Rady (London, 2008), 57–66.

12. FERDINAND II, THE HOLY HOUSE, AND BOHEMIA

Robert Bireley, *Ferdinand II, Counter-Reformation Emperor, 1578–1637* (Cambridge, 2014).

Bohdan Chudoba, *Spain and the Empire 1519–1643* (Chicago, 1952).

Geoff Mortimer, *The Origins of the Thirty Years War and the Revolt in Bohemia, 1618* (Basingstoke and New York, 2015).

Jaroslav Pánek et al., *A History of the Czech Lands* (Prague, 2009).

Brennan C. Pursell, *The Winter King: Frederick V of the Palatinate and the Coming of the Thirty Years' War* (Aldershot and Burlington, VT, 2003).

13. THE THIRTY YEARS 'WORLD WAR'

The Ashgate Research Companion to the Thirty Years' War, ed. Olaf Asbach and Peter Schröder (London and New York, 2014).

Robert Bireley, *Ferdinand II, Counter-Reformation Emperor, 1578–1637* (Cambridge, 2014).

Geoff Mortimer, *Wallenstein: The Enigma of the Thirty Years War* (Basingstoke and New York, 2010).

Geoffrey Parker, *Thirty Years' War* (London and New York, 1984).

Peter H. Wilson, *The Thirty Years War: Europe's Tragedy* (Cambridge, MA, 2011).

14. THE ABNORMAL EMPIRE AND THE BATTLE FOR VIENNA

Maria Goloubeva, *The Glorification of Emperor Leopold I in Image, Spectacle and Text* (Mainz, 2000).

Irina Marin, *Contested Frontiers in the Balkans: Habsburg and Ottoman Rivalries in Eastern Europe* (London and New York, 2013).

John P. Spielman, *Leopold I of Austria* (London, 1977).

Barbara Stollberg-Rilinger, *The Emperor's Old Clothes: Constitutional History and the Symbolic Language of the Holy Roman Empire* (New York and Oxford, 2008).

John Stoye, *The Siege of Vienna* (London, 1964).

Andrew Wheatcroft, *The Enemy at the Gate: Habsburgs, Ottomans and the Battle for Europe* (London, 2009).

15. SPAIN'S INVISIBLE SOVEREIGNS AND THE DEATH OF THE BEWITCHED KING

Alejandro Cañeque, *The King's Living Image: The Culture and Politics of Viceregal Power in Colonial Mexico* (New York and London, 2004).

J. H. Elliott, *The Count-Duke of Olivares: The Statesman in an Age of Decline* (New Haven and London, 1986).

Festival Culture in the World of the Spanish Habsburgs, ed. Fernando Checa Cremades and Laura Fernández-González (London and New York, 2016).

Alan Knight, *Mexico: The Colonial Era* (Cambridge, 2002).

Alejandra B. Osorio, *Inventing Lima: Baroque Modernity in Peru's South Sea Metropolis* (Basingstoke and New York, 2008).

16. THE THEATRE OF THE BAROQUE

Michael Kitson, *The Age of Baroque* (London, 1966).

Paul Koudounaris, *The Empire of Death: A Cultural History of Ossuaries and Charnel Houses* (London, 2011).

Evonne Levy, *Propaganda and the Jesuit Baroque* (Berkeley, Los Angeles, and London, 2004).

Derek McKay, *Prince Eugene of Savoy* (London, 1977).

J. W. Stoye, 'Emperor Charles VI: The Early Years of the Reign', *Transactions of the Royal Historical Society*, 12 (1962), 63–84.

17. MARIA THERESA, AUTOMATA, AND BUREAUCRATS

Edward Crankshaw, *Maria Theresa* (London, 1969).

P. G. M. Dickson, *Finance and Government Under Maria Theresia*, 2 vols (Oxford, 1987).

Michael Hochedlinger, *Austria's Wars of Emergence: War, State and Society in the Habsburg Monarchy 1683–1797* (Abingdon and New York, 2003).

C. A. Macartney, *Maria Theresa and the House of Austria* (London, 1969).

Michael Yonan, *Empress Maria Theresa and the Politics of Habsburg Imperial Art* (University Park, PA, 2011).

18. MERCHANTS, BOTANISTS, AND FREEMASONS

Eva H. Balázs, *Hungary and the Habsburgs 1765–1800: An Experiment in Enlightened Despotism* (Budapest, 1997).

Derek Beales, *Joseph II: Against the World, 1780–1790* (Cambridge, 2009).

Derek Beales, *Joseph II: In the Shadow of Maria Theresa, 1741–1780* (Cambridge, 1987).

Paula Findlen, *Possessing Nature: Museums, Collecting, and Scientific Culture in Early Modern Italy* (Berkeley, CA, 1996)

Franz A. J. Szabo, *Kaunitz and Enlightened Despotism, 1753–1780* (Cambridge, 1994).

19. VAMPIRISM, ENLIGHTENMENT, AND THE REVOLUTION FROM ABOVE

The Austrian Enlightenment and Its Aftermath, ed. Ritchie Robertson and Edward Timms (Edinburgh, 1991).

Derek Beales, *Property and Plunder: European Catholic Monasteries in the Age of Revolution, 1650–1815* (Cambridge, 2003).

T. J. Hochstrasser, *Natural Law Theories in the Enlightenment* (Cambridge, 2000).

Dorinda Outram, *The Enlightenment*, 3rd ed. (Cambridge, 2013).

Andre Wakefield, *The Disordered Police State: German Cameralism as Science and Practice* (Chicago and London, 2009).

20. ARCHDUCHESSES AND THE HABSBURG LOW COUNTRIES

Paul Arblaster, *A History of the Low Countries*, 2nd ed. (Basingstoke, 2012).

Luc Duerloo, *Dynasty and Piety: Archduke Albert (1598–1621) and Habsburg Political Culture in an Age of Religious Wars* (London and New York, 2012).

Early Modern Habsburg Women, ed. Anne J. Cruz and Maria Galli Stampino (Abingdon and New York, 2016).

Geoffrey Parker, *Spain and the Netherlands, 1559–1659: Ten Studies* (London, 1979).

Caroline Weber, *Queen of Fashion: What Marie Antoinette Wore to the Revolution* (London, 2007).

21. CENSORS, JACOBINS, AND *THE MAGIC FLUTE*

David J. Buch, *Magic Flutes and Enchanted Forests: The Supernatural in Eighteenth-Century Musical Theater* (Chicago, 2008).

Kurt Honolka, *Papageno: Emanuel Schikaneder, Man of the Theater in Mozart's Time* (Portland, OR, 1990).

Ernst Wangermann, *The Austrian Achievement, 1700–1800* (London, 1973).

Ernst Wangermann, *From Joseph II to the Jacobin Trials: Government Policy and Public Opinion in the Habsburg Dominions in the Period of the French Revolution*, 2nd ed. (Oxford, 1969).

W. E. Yates, *Theatre in Vienna: A Critical History, 1776–1995* (Cambridge and New York, 1996).

22. METTERNICH AND THE MAP OF EUROPE

Mark Jarrett, *The Congress of Vienna and Its Legacy: War and Great Power Diplomacy After Napoleon* (London and New York, 2013).

Prince Clemens von Metternich, *Metternich: The Autobiography* (Welwyn Garden City, 2004).

Alan Sked, *Metternich and Austria: An Evaluation* (Basingstoke and New York, 2008).

Lawrence Sondhaus, *The Habsburg Empire and the Sea: Austrian Naval Policy, 1797–1866* (West Lafayette, IN, 1989).

Bairu Tafler, *Ethiopia and Austria* (Wiesbaden, 1994).

23. 1848: VON NEUMANN'S DIARY AND RADETZKY'S MARCH

Istvan Deak, *The Lawful Revolution: Louis Kossuth and the Hungarians 1848–1849* (London, 2001).

Josef Polišenský, *Aristocrats and the Crowd in the Revolutionary Year 1848* (Albany, NY, 1980).

Mike Rapport, *1848: Year of Revolution* (London, 2008).

R. J. Rath, *The Viennese Revolution of 1848* (Austin, TX, 1977).

Alan Sked, *Radetzky: Imperial Victor and Military Genius* (London and New York, 2011).

24. FRANZ JOSEPH'S EMPIRE, SISI, AND HUNGARY

Steven Beller, *Francis Joseph* (London, 1996).

Jean-Paul Bled, *Franz Joseph* (Oxford, 1992).

Ágnes Deák, *From Habsburg Neo-Absolutism to the Compromise 1849–1867* (Boulder, CO, and New York, 2008).

John Deak, *Forging a Multinational State: State Making in Imperial Austria from the Enlightenment to the First World War* (Stanford, CA, 2015).

Brigitte Hamann, *The Reluctant Empress: A Biography of Empress Elisabeth of Austria* (Berlin, 1986).

25. MAXIMILIAN, MEXICO, AND ROYAL DEATHS

René Chartrand and Richard Hook, *The Mexican Adventure, 1861–67* (Oxford, 1994).

John Elderfield, *Manet and the Execution of Maximilian* (New York, 2006).

Joan Haslip, *The Crown of Mexico: Maximilian and His Empress Carlota* (New York, 1972).

M. M. McAllen, *Maximilian and Carlota: Europe's Last Empire in Mexico* (San Antonio, TX, 2014).

The Oxford History of Mexico, ed. William H. Beezley and Michael C. Meyer (Oxford, 2010).

26. THE POLITICS OF DISCONTENT AND THE 1908 JUBILEE

Gwen Jones, *Chicago of the Balkans: Budapest in Hungarian Literature, 1900–1939* (Leeds, 2013).

The Limits of Loyalty: Imperial Symbolism, Popular Allegiances, and State Patriotism in the Late Habsburg Monarchy, ed. Laurence Cole and Daniel L. Unowsky (New York and Oxford, 2007).

Alexander Maxwell, *Patriots Against Fashion: Clothing and Nationalism in Europe's Age of Revolutions* (Basingstoke and New York, 2014).

Staging the Past: The Politics of Commemoration in Habsburg Central Europe, 1848 to the Present, ed. Maria Bucur and Nancy M. Wingfield (West Lafayette, IN, 2001).

Understanding Multiculturalism: The Habsburg Central European Experience, ed. Johannes Feichtinger and Gary B. Cohen (New York and Oxford, 2014).

27. EXPLORERS, JEWS, AND THE WORLD'S KNOWLEDGE

Steven Beller, *Vienna and the Jews, 1867–1938: A Cultural History* (Cambridge, 1989).

Allan Janik and Stephen Toulmin, *Wittgenstein's Vienna* (London, 1973).

Martina Pippal, *A Short History of Art in Vienna* (Munich, 2001).

Walter Sauer, 'Habsburg Colonial: Austria-Hungary's Role in European Overseas Expansion', *Austrian Studies*, 20 (2012), 5–23.

Carl E. Schorske, *Fin-de-siècle Vienna: Politics and Culture* (London, 1980).

28. THE HUNTER AND THE HUNTED: FRANZ FERDINAND AND BOSNIA

Gordon Brook-Shepherd, *Victims at Sarajevo: The Romance and Tragedy of Franz Ferdinand and Sophie* (London, 1984).

Cathie Carmichael, *A Concise History of Bosnia* (Cambridge, 2015).

Brigitte Hamann, *Rudolf, Crown Prince and Rebel* (New York, 2017).

Robin Okey, *Taming Balkan Nationalism* (Oxford, 2007).

Gunther E. Rothenberg, *The Army of Francis Joseph* (West Lafayette, IN, 1976).

29. WORLD WAR AND DISSOLUTION

Mark Cornwall, *The Last Years of Austria-Hungary: A Multi-National Experiment in Early Twentieth-Century Europe*, ed. Mark Cornwall, 2nd ed. (Liverpool, 2005).

Maureen Healy, *Vienna and the Fall of the Habsburg Empire: Total War and Everyday Life in World War One* (Cambridge, 2004).

Manfried Rauchensteiner, *The First World War and the End of the Habsburg Monarchy, 1914–1918*, 2nd ed. (Vienna, Cologne, and Weimar, 2014).

Norman Stone, *The Eastern Front 1914–1917* (London, 1998).

Alexander Watson, *Ring of Steel: Germany and Austria-Hungary at War, 1914–1918* (London, 2014).

CONCLUSION

Gordon Brook-Shepherd, *Uncrowned Emperor: The Life and Times of Otto von Habsburg* (London and New York, 2003).

NOTES

I have been sparing with notes, using these mainly for quotations and unusual details, and to acknowledge scholarly debts. Information readily available in the standard accounts is generally not referenced.

INTRODUCTION: AN EMPEROR'S LIBRARY

1. Friedrich B. Polleross, 'Tradition und Recreation. Die Residenzen der österreichischen Habsburger in der frühen Neuzeit', *Majestas*, 6 (1998), 91–148 (100).

2. Matthias Müller, 'Der Anachronismus als Modernität. Der Wiener Hofburg als programmatisches Leitbilds für den frühneuzeitlichen Residenzbau im Alten Reich', in *Krakau, Prag und Wien. Funktionen von Metropolen im frühmodernen Staat*, ed. Marina Dmitrieva and Karen Lambrecht (Stuttgart, 2000), 313–29 (323); Luis Weckmann, *The Medieval Heritage of Mexico*, vol. 1 (New York, 1992), 577–81.

3. Ignaz von Mosel, *Geschichte der kaiserl. königl. Bibliothek zu Wien* (Vienna, 1835), 73–4, 96, 104–5.

4. Johannes Frimmel, '"Verliebte Dummheiten und ekelhafte Nuditäten." Der Verleger Johann Mösle, die *Priapische Dichterlaune* und der Erotika-Vertrieb im josephinischen Wien', *Das achtzehnte Jahrhundert*, 42, no. 2 (2018), 237–51.

5. Werner Telesko, *Geschichtsraum Österreich. Die Habsburger und ihre Geschichte in der bildenden Kunst des 19. Jahrhunderts* (Vienna, Cologne, and Weimar, 2006), 178; Mosel, *Geschichte der kaiserl. königl. Bibliothek*, 123–4.

6. Alphons Lhotsky, 'AEIOU. Die Devise Kaiser Friedrichs III. und sein Notizbuch', in Lhotsky, *Aufsätze und Vorträge*, vol. 2 (Vienna, 1971), 164–222 (172).

7. Mosel, *Geschichte der kaiserl. königl. Bibliothek*, 132.

8. Anna Coreth, *Pietas Austriaca* (West Lafayette, IN, 2004), 13–6.

9. The statuette is now in the main dining room of Castle Habsburg.

10. Marie Tanner, *The Last Descendant of Aeneas: The Hapsburgs and the Mythic Image of the Emperor* (New Haven, CT, 1992), 122.

11. Paul Gwynne, "*Tu alter Caesar eris*": Maximilian I, Vladislav II, Johannes Michael Nagonius and the Renovatio Imperii', *Renaissance Studies*, 10 (1996), 56–71.

12. For Erasmus and the universal ruler, see Margaret Mann Phillips, *The 'Adages' of Erasmus: A Study with Translations* (Cambridge, 1964), 224–5, 243.

13. *Urkundenbuch der Stadt Braunschweig*, vol. 1, ed. Ludwig Hänselmann (Brunswick, 1873), 294.

14. Martyn Rady, *Emperor Charles V* (Harlow, 1988), 36.

CHAPTER 1: CASTLE HABSBURG AND THE 'FORTINBRAS EFFECT'

1. Otto Forst, *Ahnen-Tafel seiner kaiserlichen u. königlichen Hoheit des durchlautigsten Herrn Erzherzogs Franz Ferdinand von Österreich-Este* (Vienna and Leipzig, 1910).

2. Harold Steinacker, 'Zur Herkunft und ältesten Geschichte des Hauses Habsburg', *Zeitschrift für die Geschichte des Oberrheins*, NF 19 (1904), 181–244, 359–433 (233–8).

3. For Muri's relics, see *Acta Murensia. Die Akten des Klosters Muri mit der Genealogie der frühen Habsburger*, ed. Charlotte Bretscher-Gisiger and Christian Sieber (Basle, 2012), 73–123.

4. *Acta Murensia*, 23; Albert Brackmann, *Zur Geschichte der Hirsauer Reformbewegung im XII. Jahrhundert* (Berlin, 1928), 6.

5. *Acta Murensia*, 300–3; Jean Jacques Siegrist, 'Die Acta Murensia und die Frühhabsburger', *Argovia. Jahresschrift der Historischen Gesellschaft des Kantons Aargau*, 98 (1986), 5–21 (11).

6. *Acta Murensia*, 35–7; Brackmann, *Zur Geschichte der Hirsauer Reformbewegung*, 27; the modern description is by Hans-Ulrich Stoldt, 'Rehpfeffer Radbot', in *Spiegel Geschichte*, 2009, no. 6 (digital edition).

7. J. Müller, *Der Aargau. Seine politische, Rechts-, Kultur- und Sitten-Geschichte* (Zurich, 1870), 418–46.

8. C. H. Herford, *The Age of Wordsworth* (London, 1945), 41.

9. Grete Klingenstein, 'The Meanings of "Austria" and "Austrian" in the Eighteenth Century', in *Royal and Republican Sovereignty in Early Modern Europe*, ed. Robert Oresko et al. (Cambridge, 1997), 423–78 (440); for the earls of Denbigh, see J. H. Round, *Studies in Peerage and Family History*, vol. 2 (London, 1901), 14–5.

10. For toll places, see Fritz Glauser, 'Der internationale Gotthardtransit im Lichte des Luzerner Zentnerzolls von 1493 bis 1505', *Schweizerische Zeitschrift für Geschichte*, 18 (1968), 177–245 (182); for Windisch, see *Das Habsburg-österreichische Urbarbuch*, ed. Franz Pfeiffer (Stuttgart, 1850), 149.

11. Jörg Wettlaufer, *Das Herrenrecht des ersten Nacht. Hochzeit, Herrschaft und Heiratzins im Mittelalter und in der frühen Neuzeit* (Frankfurt a/M. and New York, 1999), 251; Johannes von Müller, *Die Geschichten Schweizerischer Eidgenossenschaft*, vol. 2 (Stuttgart and Tübingen, 1832), 157; Konrad Glaettli, *Sagen aus den Zürcher Oberland* (Winterthur, 1951), 20; Le Doyen Bridel, *Glossaire du Patois de la Suisse romande* (Lausanne, 1866), 121. More generally here, Tom Scott, 'Liberty and Community in Medieval Switzerland', *German History*, 13 (1993), 98–113 (101–2).

12. Werner Wild, 'Habsburger und Burgenbau in den "Vorderen Länden"', in *Die Habsburger zwischen Aare und Bodensee*, ed. Peter Niederhäuser, 2nd ed. (Zurich, 2010), 34–60.

13. Oswald Redlich, *Rudolf von Habsburg* (Innsbruck, 1903), 11, 17.

14. Peter Blickle, *Von der Leibeigenschaft zu den Menschenrechte. Eine Geschichte der Freiheit in Deutschland*, 2nd ed. (Munich, 2006), 76–8; Hans Erich Feine, 'Die Territorialbildung der Habsburger im deutschen Südwesten', *Zeitschrift der Savigny-Stiftung für Rechtsgeschichte (Germanistische Abteilung)*, 67 (1950), 176–308 (188).

CHAPTER 2: THE HOLY ROMAN EMPIRE AND THE GOLDEN KING

1. For the Kaiserswerth inscription, see Barbara Haupt, *Das Fest in der Dichtung. Untersuchungen zur historischen Semantiken eines literarischen Motivs in der mittelhochdeutschen Epik* (Dusseldorf, 1989), 40.

2. Len Scales, *The Shaping of German Identity: Authority and Crisis, 1245–1414* (Cambridge, 2012), 234.

3. H. Salvador Martínez, *Alfonso X, the Learned: A Biography* (Leiden and Boston, 2010), 121–35; Armin Wolf, *Die Entstehung des Kurfürstenkollegs 1198–1298* (Idstein, 1998), 43–6; Björn Weiler, 'Image and Reality in Richard of Cornwall's German Career', *English Historical Review*, 113 (1998), 1111–42.

4. MGH SS, xxv, 350.

5. *Die Geschichtschreiber der deutschen Vorzeit. Annalen und Chronik von Kolmar*, ed. H. Pabst (Berlin, 1867), 10–13.

6. For the German monarchy and its links to Swabia and Franconia, see Peter Moraw, 'Franken als königsnahe Landschaft im späten Mittelalter', *Blätter fur deutsche Landesgeschichte*, 112 (1976), 123–38 (137–8).

7. Oswald Redlich, *Rudolf von Habsburg* (Innsbruck, 1903), 160–1.

8. For Rudolf's nose, see MGH, SS rer. Germ. in usum schol., xxxvi, Part 1, 247.

9. For contemporary verdicts on Rudolf, see Othmar Schönhuth, *Anekdoten und Sprüche zur Charakteristik von König Rudolphs von Habsburg* (Canstatt, 1841), and *Die Geschichtschreiber der deutschen Vorzeit*, 122. For Rudolf's chess playing, see Wilhelm Wackernagel, 'Das Schachspiel im Mittelalter', in Wackernagel, *Kleinere Schriften*, vol. 1 (Leipzig, 1872), 107–27 (113). For his speech, see Redlich, *Rudolf von Habsburg*, 168.

10. For the imperial style, see Eckhard Müller-Mertens, 'Imperium und Regnum im Verhältnis zwischen Wormser Konkordat und Goldener Bulle', *Historische Zeitschrift*, 284 (2007), 561–95 (578).

11. Winfried Dotzauer, *Die deutschen Reichskreise (1383–1806)* (Stuttgart, 1998), 23–4; *Handbuch der Bayerischen Geschichte*, vol. 3 (*Franken, Schwaben, Oberpfalz*), ed. Max Spindler (Munich, 1971), part 2, 904 (by Adolf Layer).

12. *Handbuch der Bayerischen Geschichte*, vol. 3, part 1, 163 (by Alois Gerlich).

13. For Ottokar's treasure, see MGH SS, xviii, 571. See further, Jörg K. Hoensch, *Přemysl Otakar II. von Böhmen. Der goldene König* (Graz, 1989), 64, 80; MGH SS, ix, 187; Scales, *The Shaping of German Identity*, 92.

14. Jiří Kuthan, *Přemysl Ottokar II. König, Bauherr und Mäzen* (Vienna, Cologne, and Weimar, 1996), 31–49.

15. Johann Franzl, *Rudolf I. Der erste Habsburger auf dem deutschen Thron* (Graz, 1986), 120.

16. MGH SS, xvii, 249.

17. For Ottokar's tomb, see *Prague: The Crown of Bohemia 1347–1437*, ed. Barbara Drake Boehm and Jiří Fajt (New York, 2005), 195.

18. Augustin Demski, *Papst Nikolaus III* (Münster, 1903), 175.

19. Dante, *Purgatorio*, 7.97–102.

CHAPTER 3: LOSING PLACE AND FORGING A PAST

1. Armin Wolf, *Die Entstehung des Kurfürstenkollegs 1198–1298* (Idstein, 1998), 59–60.

2. For Albert as a 'boorish man', see MGH, Dt. Chron., ii, 331.

3. For Boniface VIII, see Robert Folz, *The Concept of Empire in Western Europe: From the Fifth to the Fourteenth Century* (London, 1969), 207. For the papal tiara, see Edward Twining, *A History of the Crown Jewels of Europe* (London, 1960), 377–8. For Albert and Rudolf, see here MGH SS, xiii, 58.

4. MGH SS, xxx, part 1, 651; Peter Browe, 'Die angebliche Vergiftung Kaiser Heinrichs VII', *Historisches Jahrbuch*, 49 (1929), 429–38.

5. *Die Goldene Bulle. Politik, Wahrnehmung, Rezeption*, ed. Ulrike Hohensee et al., vol. 1 (Berlin, 2009), 150 (by Eva Schlotheuber).

6. For Albert the Lame, see Karl-Friedrich Krieger, *Die Habsburger im Mittelalter*, 2nd ed. (Stuttgart, 2004), 128–30. For the Habsburgs as Austrians, see MGH SS rer. Germ. N.S., iv, 382. For governors, see Dieter Speck, *Kleine Geschichte Vorderösterreichs*, 2nd ed. (Karlsruhe, 2016), 48.

7. Gerhart B. Ladner, 'The Middle Ages in Austrian Tradition: Problems of an Imperial and Paternalistic Ideology', *Viator*, 3 (1972), 433–62 (436–40).

8. For quaint descriptions, see MGH, Dt. Chron., iii, 706–29. For Norix, see MGH SS, ix, 535.

9. For Colonna, see Alphons Lhotsky, *Aufsätze und Vorträge*, vol. 2 (Munich, 1971), 7–102. For the two brothers, see MGH, SS rer. Germ. N. S., iv, 8–9. For the Königsfelden Chronicle, see Martin Gerbert, *De translatis Habsburgo-Austriacarum principum* (St Blasien, 1772), 86–113. See also *Deutsches Archiv für Erforschung des Mittelalters*, 28 (1972), 432–4.

10. The fraudulent texts are given in *Archiv für Kunde österreichischer Geschichtsquellen*, 8 (1852), 108–19.

11. For Petrarch, see *Quellensammlung zur österreichischen und deutschen Rechtsgeschichte*, ed. Rudolf Hoke and Ilse Reiter (Vienna, Cologne and Weimar, 1993), 120–1.

12. For Charles IV's confirmation, see Renate Spreitzer, 'Die Belehnungs- und Bestätigungsurkunden König Sigismunds von 1421 für Herzog Albrecht V. von Österreich', *MIÖG*, 114 (2006), 289–328 (304). For the Habsburg style, see Eva Bruckner, *Formen der Herrschaftsrepräsentation und Selbstdarstellung habsburgischer Fürsten in Spätmittelalter*, PhD thesis (University of Vienna, 2009), 27–8, 141, 154, 160, 168, 178, 184, 217.

13. *Zeitschrift für bayerische Landesgeschichte*, 13 (1941–2), 210.

14. For the runes on the sarcophagus, see Bernhard Bischoff, 'Die nichtdiplomatischen Geheimschriften des Mittelalters', *MIÖG*, 62 (1954), 1–27 (12). For the dress of the canons, see MGH, SS rer. Germ. N.S., xiii, 282.

15. Samuel Steinherz, 'Margareta von Tirol und Rudolf IV', *MIÖG*, 26 (1905), 553–611. Margaret's inducements to her ministers are given in Alfons Huber, *Geschichte der Vereinigung Tirols mit Oesterreich* (Innsbruck, 1864), 215–9. For the charter recording the ministers' consent to Rudolf's succession, see OeSta/HHStA, UR AUR 1363. I. 26.

16. For the boiling of Rudolf's corpse, see Estella Weiss-Krejci, 'Restless Corpses: "Secondary Burial" in the Babenberg and Habsburg Dynasties', *Antiquity*, 75 (2001) 769–80 (775).

CHAPTER 4: FREDERICK III: SATURN AND MARS

1. Karl-Friedrich Krieger, *Die Habsburger im Mittelalter*, 2nd ed. (Stuttgart, 2004), 145.

2. For Alsace, see Georges Bischoff, *Vorderösterreich in der frühen Neuzeit*, ed. Hans Maier and Volker Press (Sigmaringen, 1989), 276. For peasant pretensions, see *Die Salzburger Lehen in Kärnten bis 1520*, ed. Alois Lang et al. (Vienna, 1971), 8–9.

3. *Regesta Imperii*, vol. 12 (Albrecht II), ed. Günther Hödl (Vienna, Cologne, and Weimar, 1975), 4 (no. f); Wilhelm Wostry, *Albrecht II. (1437–1439)*, vol. 1 (Prague, 1906), 61.

4. Frances Courtney Kneupper, *The Empire at the End of Time: Identity and Reform in Late Medieval German Prophecy* (Oxford, 2016), 7, 163.

5. Daniel Carlo Pangerl, 'Die Beinamputation an Kaiser Friedrich III. am 8. Juni 1493 in Linz', *Sudhoffs Archiv*, 94 (2010), 195–200. See further, Wilfried Knoche, *Prothesen der unteren Extremität. Die Entwicklung vom Althertum bis 1930* (Dortmund, 2006), 25; *Ausstellung. Friedrich III. Kaiserresidenz Wiener Neustadt* (Wiener Neustadt, 1966), 36.

6. Janus Pannonius, *Epigrammata–Epigramme*, ed. Josef Faber (Norderstedt, 2009), 82. See also Karl-Friedrich Krieger, *Die Habsburger im Mittelalter* (Stuttgart, 2004), 171.

7. For Frederick's itinerary, see Paul-Joachim Heinig, *Kaiser Friedrich III. (1440–1493). Hof, Regierung und Politik* (Cologne, Weimar, and Vienna, 1997), 1347–87. See also *Perzeption und Rezeption. Wahrnehmung und Deutung im Mittelalter und der Moderne*, ed. Joachim Laczny and Jürgen Sarnowsky (Cologne, 2014), 33–65.

8. *Gerichts- und Schlichtungskommissionen Kaiser Friedrichs III.* (regesta-imperii.de /dbkommissionen/ZentraleKomm.html), nos. 126, 1268, 1522, 1620, etc. For the council meetings and charters, see Heinig, *Kaiser Friedrich III.*, 152, and Paul Herold and Karin Winter, 'Ein Urkundenfund zu Kaiser Friedrich III. aus dem Stiftsarchiv Lilienfeld', *MIÖG*, 116 (2008), 267–90 (282–6).

9. *Erzählen und Episteme. Literatur im 16. Jahrhundert*, ed. Beate Kellner et al. (Berlin and New York, 2011), 351 (essay by Thomas Schauerte); Christoph J. Hagemann, *Geschichtsfiktion im Dienste territorialer Macht. Die Chronik von den 95 Herrschaften* (Heidelberg, 2017), 146.

10. MGH, Staatsschriften, viii, 199, 287, 293, 305; MGH, SS rer. Germ. N.S., xxiv, 2, 829.

11. Peter Moraw, 'The Court of the German King and of the Emperor at the End of the Middle Ages, 1440–1519', in *Princes, Patronage and the Nobility: The Court at the Beginning of the Modern Age c. 1450–1650*, ed. Ronald G. Asch and Adolf M. Birks (Oxford, 1991), 103–37 (118).

12. Petra Ehm, *Burgund und das Reich* (Munich, 2002), 151, 166, 198.

13. J. F. Kirk, *History of Charles the Bold, Duke of Burgundy*, vol. 3 (London, 1868), 490.

CHAPTER 5: MAXIMILIAN AND THE COLOUR-CODED KINGS

1. Gernot Michael Müller, *Die 'Germania generalis' des Conrad Celtis* (Tübingen, 2001), 11–18.

2. Hermann Wiesflecker, *Kaiser Maximilian I. Das Reich, Österreich und Europa an der Wende zur Neuzeit*, 5 vols. (Vienna, 1971–86), vol. 1, 133–4.

3. Kunsthistorisches Museum Wien, MSS, Kunstkammer no 5073.

4. Glenn Elwood Waas, *The Legendary Character of Kaiser Maximilian* (New York, 1941), 5.

5. *Der Weiss Kunig. Eine Erzehlung* (Vienna, 1775), 290–2.

6. Michael Mayr, *Das Fischereibuch Kaiser Maximilians I.* (Innsbruck, 1901); Mayr, *Das Jagdbuch Maximilians I.* (Innsbruck, 1901); Ludwig Baldass, *Der Künstlerkreis Kaiser Maximilians* (Vienna, 1923), 14.

7. For the proving of Maximilian's descent, see Hieronymus Gebweiler, *Epitome regii ac vetustissimi ortus* (Hagenau, 1530).

8. Walter L. Strauss, *Albrecht Dürer: Woodcuts and Wood Blocks* (New York, 1979), 726–31.

9. For Burgkmair and the Calicuttish folk, see Christian Feest, 'The People of Calicut: Objects, Texts and Images in the Age of Proto-Ethnography', *Boletim do Museu Paraense Emílio Goeldi: Ciências Humanes*, 9 (2014), 287–303.

10. Wiesflecker, *Kaiser Maximilian*, vol. 5, 637. See also ibid, vol. 4, 92; *Standen en Landen*, 40–41 (1966), 82.

11. The literature on the reform of the empire is extensively discussed in Karl-Friedrich Krieger, *König, Reich und Reichsreform in Spätmittelalter*, 2nd ed. (Berlin, 2010), especially 55–60. See also Joachim Whaley, *Germany and the Holy Roman Empire*, vol. 1 (Oxford, 2012), 86.

12. Inge Wiesflecker-Friedhuber, 'Die Austreibung der Juden aus der Steiermark unter Maximilian I.', *Wissenschaftliche Arbeiten aus dem Burgenland*, 92 (1993), 47–64. For Maximilian as pope, see Wiesflecker, *Kaiser Maximilian*, vol. 4, 91–2, and Hugh Trevor-Roper, 'The Emperor Maximilian I, as Patron of the Arts', in Trevor-Roper, *Renaissance Essays* (London, 1986), 13–23 (17).

13. For the marital reputation of Juan and Margaret, see *Dead Lovers: Erotic Bonds and the Study of Premodern Europe*, ed. Basil Duffalo and Peggy McCracken (Ann Arbor, MI, 2007), 121; Rachael Ball and Geoffrey Parker, *Cómo ser rey. Instrucciones de Carlos V a su hijo Felipe. Mayo de 1543* (Madrid, 2014), 149–53.

14. The couples were married in separate ceremonies and not at a single event, as often supposed. See *Magyarország történeti kronológiája*, ed. Kálmán Benda, vol. 1 (Budapest, 1983), 341–2.

15. Alfred Kohler, *Quellen zur Geschichte Karls V.* (Darmstadt, 1990), 287–8; Elisabeth Klecker, '*Bella gerant alii*, tu, felix Austria, nube. Eine Spurensuche', *Österreich in Geschichte und Literatur*, 41 (1997), 30–44.

CHAPTER 6: CHARLES V: RULER OF THE WORLD

1. Hermann Wiesflecker, *Kaiser Maximilian I.*, vol. 4 (Munich, 1981), 424.

2. For Charles's jaw and teeth, see *Charles V, 1500–1558, and His Time*, ed. Hugo Soly (Antwerp, 1999), 490; *Letters of David Hume*, ed. J. Y. T. Greig, vol. 1 (Oxford, 1932), 315.

3. Frank Graziano, *The Millennial New World* (Oxford, 1999), 33, 47.

4. Pierre Houart and Maxime Benoît-Jeannin, *Histoire de la Toison d'Or* (Brussels, 2006), 150, 161.

5. The charges on loans are given in Ramón Carande, *Carlos V y sus banqueros* (edición abreviada), vol. 2 (Barcelona, 1983), 290–301.

6. Henry Kamen, *Spain, 1469–1714: A Society of Conflict* (London, 1983), 69.

7. Earl Rosenthal, 'Plus Ultra, Non Plus Ultra, and the Columnar Device of Emperor Charles V', *JWCI*, 34 (1971), 204–28.

8. For Cervantes and Charles V, see Ana Maria G. Laguna, *Cervantes and the Pictorial Imagination* (Lewisburg, PA, 2009), 97.

9. Hubert Jedin et al., *Handbuch der Kirchengeschichte. Reformation, Katholische Reform und Gegenreformation* (Freiburg, 1967), 48.

10. Roy Strong, *Art and Power: Renaissance Festivals 1450–1650* (Berkeley and Los Angeles, 1984), 78–81.

11. Marcel Bataillon, *Erasmo y España, estudios sobre la historia espiritual del siglo xvi* (Mexico City, Madrid, and Buenos Aires, 1966), 227; Antonio Pérez-Romero, *The Subversive Tradition in Spanish Renaissance Writing* (Lewisburg, PA, 2005), 190–5.

12. Rebecca Boone, 'Empire and Medieval Simulacrum: A Political Project of Mercurino di Gattinara, Grand Chancellor of Charles V', *Sixteenth Century Journal*, 42 (2011), 1027–49; Prudencio de Sandoval, *Historia de la vida y hechos del emperador Carlos V* (Madrid, 1955), 91–2; Desiderius Erasmus, *The Education of a Christian Prince*, ed. Lester K. Born (New York, 1963), 133.

13. James Atkinson, *The Trial of Luther* (London, 1971), 177–8.

14. For the 're-ordering of the world', see J. A. Maravall, 'Las etapas del pensamiento político de Carlos V', *Revista del Estudios Políticos*, 100 (1958), 93–146 (96).

15. *Kaiser Karl V. erobert Tunis*, ed. Sabine Haag and Katja Schmitz-von Lederbur (Vienna, 2013).

16. For the painted maps, see James D. Tracy, *Emperor Charles V, Impresario of War: Campaign Strategy, International Finance, and Domestic Politics* (Cambridge, 2002), 213.

17. J. De Zulueta, 'La causa de la muerte del Emperador Carlos V', *Parassitologia*, 49 (2007), 107–9.

18. Hugh Thomas, *The Golden Age: The Spanish Empire of Charles V* (London, 2010), 40–2.

19. For 'for the honour of God . . .', see Thomas, *The Golden Age*, 364.

20. For Charles's abdication speech, see Edward Armstrong, *The Emperor Charles V*, 2nd ed., vol. 2 (London, 1910), 355.

CHAPTER 7: HUNGARY, BOHEMIA, AND THE PROTESTANT CHALLENGE

1. Kenneth J. Dillon, *King and Estates in the Bohemian Lands 1526–1564* (Brussels, 1976), 40–4; Martyn Rady, 'Fiscal and Military Developments in Hungary During the Jagello Period', *Chronica* (Szeged), 11, 2011, 85–98.

2. For battlefield tactics, see V. J. Parry, 'La manière de combattre', in *War, Technology and Society in the Middle East*, ed. Parry and M. C. Yapp (London, 1975), 218–56 (221). See also László Veszprémy, 'The State and Military Affairs in East-Central Europe, 1380–c. 1520s', in *European Warfare 1350–1750*, ed. Frank Tallett and D. J. B. Trim (Cambridge, 2010), 96–109. For the king of Hungary as 'one of the great rulers', see Feridun M. Emecen, 'A csata, amely a "Nagy Török" előtt megnyitotta a magyar Alföldet—Mohács, 1526', in *Mohács*, ed. János B. Szabó (Budapest, 2006), 412–34 (414–6).

3. See here *Decreta Regni Mediaevalis Hungariae—The Laws of the Medieval Kingdom of Hungary 1490–1526*, ed. Péter Banyó and Martyn Rady (Idyllwild, CA, and Budapest, 2012).

4. On Utraquist communion, see Zdeněk V. David, 'Utraquism's Curious Welcome to Luther and the Candlemas Day Articles of 1524', *SEER*, 79 (2001), 51–89 (76–7).

5. Benita Berning, *'Nach alltem löblichen Gebrauch'. Die böhmische Königskrönungen der Frühen Neuzeit (1526–1743)* (Cologne, Weimar, and Vienna, 2008), 105, 119.

6. On the royal succession in Hungary, see Martyn Rady, 'Law and the Ancient Constitution in Medieval and Early Modern Hungary', in *A History of the Hungarian Constitution*, ed. Ferenc Hörcher and Thomas Lorman (London and New York, 2019), 21–45 (30–5).

7. *Monumenta Spectantia Historiam Slavorum Meridionalium*, vol. 33 (Zagreb, 1912), 50–3.

8. Katherine Walsh, 'Eine Ketzerin im Hause Habsburg? Erzherzogin Maria, Königin von Ungarn und Böhmen', *JGPÖ* (2007), 7–25 (10–11).

9. For a 'Chosen People', see Graeme Murdock, *Calvinism on the Frontier: International Calvinism and the Reformed Church in Hungary and Transylvania* (Oxford, 2000), 6, 262.

10. For 'all Hungarians and Slavs should be able', see Géza Kathona, *Fejezetek a török hódoltsági reformáció történetéből* (Budapest, 1974), 50.

11. Grete Mecenseffy, *Geschichte des Protestantismus in Österreich* (Graz and Cologne, 1956), 10; Johann Loserth, 'Zu den Anfängen der Reformation in Steiermark. Die Visitation und Inquisition von 1528 und ihre Ergebnisse', *JGPÖ* (1933), 83–97; Johannes Jung OSB et al., *Das Schottengymnasium in Wien* (Vienna, Cologne, and Weimar, 1997), 29. Astrid von Schlachta, 'Protestantismus und Konfessionalisierung in Tirol', *JGPÖ* (2007), 27–42 (30).

12. 'With a heavy heart and sighing breast', see Anita Ziegelhofer, 'Die Religionssache auf den steierischen Landtage von 1527 bis 1564', *JGPÖ* (1994), 47–68 (56). For the diets, see Rudolf Leeb, 'Der Augsburger Religionsfrieden und die österreichischen Länder', *JGPÖ* (2006), 23–54 (45). For Ferdinand's advisors, see Alfred Kohler, *Ferdinand I. 1503-1564. Fürst, König und Kaiser* (Munich, 2003), 144–7. See also, Howard Louthan, *The Quest for Compromise: Peacemakers in Counter-Reformation Vienna* (Cambridge, 1997), 87–96.

13. Győző Ember, *Az újkori magyar közigazgatás története Mohácstól a török kiűzéséig* (Budapest, 1946), 55–7, 71, 124–5; Václav Bůžek, *Ferdinand von Tirol zwischen Prag und Innsbruck* (Vienna, Cologne, and Weimar, 2009), 52–3.

CHAPTER 8: PHILIP II: THE NEW WORLD, RELIGIOUS DISSENT, AND ROYAL INCEST

1. For the Escorial and the Old Fort, see Matthias Müller, 'Der Anachronismus als Modernität. Der Wiener Hofburg als programmatisches Leitbilds für den frühneuzeitlichen Residenzbau im Alten Reich', in *Krakau, Prag und Wien. Funktionen von Metropolen im frühmodernen Staat*, ed. Marina Dmitrieva and Karen Lambrecht (Stuttgart, 2000), 313–29 (323–4).

2. Henry Kamen, *The Escorial: Art and Power in the Renaissance* (New Haven, CT, and London, 2010), 117; Antonio Rotondo, *Descripcion de la Gran Basilica del Escorial* (Madrid, 1861), 71–2.

3. Henry Kamen, *Philip of Spain* (New Haven, CT, and London, 1997), 115.

4. 'Christian certitude and confidence', see Geoffrey Parker, *Imprudent King: A New Life of Philip II* (New Haven, CT, and London, 2014), 91–4; Marie Tanner, *The Last Descendant of Aeneas: The Hapsburgs and the Mythic Image of the Emperor* (New Haven, CT, and London, 1993), 217–8.

5. Charles E. Bennett, *Laudonniere and Fort Caroline* (Tuscaloosa, AL, 2001), 38.

6. Andrew C. Hess, 'The Moriscos: An Ottoman Fifth Column in Sixteenth-Century Spain', *AHR*, 74 (1968), 1–25.

7. Francois Soyer, 'The Anti-Semitic Conspiracy Theory in Sixteenth-Century Spain and Portugal and the Origins of the Carta de los Judíos de Constantinopla: New Evidence', *Sefarad*, 74 (2014), 369–88 (371).

8. Howard F. Cline, 'The *Relaciones Geográficas* of the Spanish Indies, 1577–1586', *HAHR*, 44, (1964), 341–74.

9. For the Manila trade, see Birgit Tremml-Werner, *Spain, China, and Japan in Manila, 1571–1644* (Amsterdam, 2015), 50, 143.

10. Hugh Thomas, 'Spain and the Conquest of China', *Standpoint* (March 2012). See also C. R. Boxer, 'Portuguese and Spanish Projects for the Conquest of Southeast Asia, 1580–1600', *Journal of Asian History*, 3 (1969), 118–36.

11. For 'too much filled and settled . . . ', see Gaspar Pérez de Villagrá, *Historia de la Nueva México, 1610*, ed. Miguel Encinias et al. (Albuquerque, NM, 1992), 39.

12. Henry Kamen, *Philip of Spain* (New Haven, CT, and New York, 1997), 179. For censorship in the New World, see Antonio Rodríguez-Buckingham, 'Change and the Printing Press in Sixteenth-Century Spanish America', in *Agent of Change: Print Culture Studies*, ed. Sabrina Alcorn Baron et al. (Amherst, MA, and Boston, 2007), 216–37.

13. Stacey Schlau, *Gendered Crime and Punishment: Women and/in the Hispanic Inquisitions* (Leiden, 2013), 26.

14. For 'not to save the souls . . . ', see Alejandra B. Osorio, *Inventing Lima: Baroque Modernity in Peru's South Sea Metropolis* (New York, 2008), 106. The Sicilian figures are given in C. A. Garufi, 'Contributo alla storia dell'Inquisizione in Sicilia nei secoli xvi e xvii', *Archivo storico Siciliano*, 38 (1913), 264–329 (278). See also Bartolomé Bennassar, 'Patterns in the Inquisitorial Mind as the Basis for a Pedagogy of Fear', in *The Spanish Inquisition and the Inquisitorial Mind*, ed. Angel Alcalá (New York, 1984), 177–86.

15. For Martin Cortés, see Hugh Thomas, *World Without End: The Global Empire of Philip II* (London, 2014), 76.

16. For 'it is important to rule each land . . . ', see *Correspondenz des Kaisers Karl V*, ed. Karl Lanz, vol. 2 (Leipzig, 1845), 526.

17. Ralph E. Giesey, *If Not, Not: The Oath of the Aragonese and the Legendary Laws of Sobrarbe* (Princeton, 1968).

18. Henry Kamen, *The Duke of Alba* (New Haven, CT, and London, 2004), 92.

19. On the possibility of pacification in 1568, see Violet Soen, *Adellijke en Habsburgse verzoeningspogingen tijdens de Nederlandse Opstand (1564–1581)* (Amsterdam, 2011), 80–3.

20. F. C. Ceballos and G. Álvarez, 'Royal Dynasties as Human Inbreeding Laboratories: The Habsburgs', *Heredity*, 111 (2013), 114–21 (116–7).

21. Gonzalo Alvarez, Francisco C. Ceballos, and Celsa Quinteiro, 'The Role of Inbreeding in the Extinction of a European Royal Dynasty', *PLoS ONE*, 4 (no 4) (April 2009).

22. On the history of the Black Legend, see Julián Juderías, *La leyenda negra: Estudios acerca del concepto de España en el extranjero* (Madrid, 1914).

23. Eva Botella-Ordinas, '"Exempt from Time and from Its Fatal Change": Spanish Imperial Ideology, 1450–1700', *Renaissance Studies*, 26 (2012), 580–604 (596–7), citing Juan de Garnica, *De Hispanorum Monarchia* (1595). For Philip II and tyranny, see now Jonathan Israel, 'King Philip II of Spain as a Symbol of "Tyranny" in Spinoza's Political

Writings', *Revista Co-herencia*, 15 (2018), 137–54; Ronald Mellor, 'Tacitus, Academic Politics, and Regicide in the Reign of Charles I: The Tragedy of Dr Isaac Dorislaus', *International Journal of the Classical Tradition*, 11 (2004), 153–93 (183).

CHAPTER 9: DON JOHN AND THE GALLEYS OF LEPANTO

1. For Barbara Blomberg's background, see Marita A. Panzer, *Barbara Blomberg. Bürgertochter, Kaisergeliebte und Heldenmutter* (Regensburg, 2017), 36–7.

2. For Margaret's famous *barbula*, see Famiano Strada, *De Bello Belgico Decas Prima* (Rome, 1648), 42. The book was written in collaboration with Margaret's son.

3. Gregory C. McIntosh, *The Piri Reis Map of 1513* (Athens, GA, 2000), 6, 87; Anthony Reid, 'Sixteenth Century Turkish Influence in Western Indonesia', *Journal of Southeast Asian History*, 10 (1969), 395–414; C. R. Boxer, 'Portuguese and Spanish Projects for the Conquest of Southeast Asia, 1580–1600', *Journal of Asian History*, 3 (1969), 118–36 (120).

4. Carmen Y. Hsu, 'Writing on Behalf of a Christian Empire: Gifts, Dissimulation, and Politics in the Letters of Philip II of Spain to Wanli of China', *HR*, 78 (2010), 323–44 (327–8); William Henry Scott, *Looking for the Prehistoric Filipino and Other Essays in Philippine History* (Quezon City, 1992), 24–5.

5. William G. Clarence-Smith and David Eltis, 'White Servitude' in *The Cambridge World History of Slavery*, vol. 2, ed. Eltis and Stanley L. Engerman (Cambridge, 2011), 132–59 (133).

6. Özlem Kumrular, 'Lepanto: antes y después. La República, la Sublime Puerta y la Monarquía Católica', *Studia historica. Historia moderna*, 36 (2014), 101–20.

7. For the stench of galleys, see Jack Beeching, *The Galleys at Lepanto* (New York, 1983), 16.

8. Giovanni Pietro Contarini, *Historia delle cose successe dal principio* (Venice, 1572), fol. 51v.

9. Niccolò Capponi, *Victory of the West: The Story of the Battle of Lepanto* (London, 2006), 289.

10. For 'the most neglected knight . . . ', see *Lettere di D. Giovanni d' Austria a D. Giovanni Andrea Doria*, ed. Alfonso Doria Pamphili (Rome, 1896), Nov. 1571, Messina.

11. Virgil, *The Eclogues*, ed. Guy Lee (London, 1984), 57 (Ecl. 4. 1–10).

12. Marie Tanner, *The Last Descendant of Aeneas: The Hapsburgs and the Mythic Image of the Emperor* (New Haven, CT, and London, 1993), 202, 216–7.

13. For Lepanto in French poetry, see Bruno Méniel, *Renaissance de l'épopée. La poésie épique en France de 1572 à 1623* (Geneva, 2004), 388–9.

14. For Acontius, see Paula Sutter Fichtner, *Emperor Maximilian II* (New Haven, CT, and London, 2001), 39–40.

15. Miguel Falomir, 'La Religión socorrido por el Imperio (hacia 1568)', in *Museo Nacional del Prado: Memoria de Actividades 2014*, (Madrid, 2015), 72–4.

CHAPTER 10: RUDOLF II AND THE ALCHEMISTS OF PRAGUE

1. King's College Library, Cambridge, Keynes MS 28, fol. 2 r–v (spelling adjusted).

2. *Hermetica: The Greek Corpus Hermeticum and the Latin Asclepius in New English Translation*, ed. Brian P. Copenhaver (Cambridge, 1992), 48.

3. For prime matter and the principles of alchemy, see Martyn Rady, 'A Transylvanian Alchemist in Seventeenth-Century London', *SEER*, 72 (1994), 240–51.

4. Viktor Bibl, *Maximilian II. Der rätselhafte Kaiser* (Vienna and Leipzig, 1929), 98.

5. Friedrich Edelmayer, 'Honor y Dinero. Adam de Dietrichstein al servicio de la Casa de Austria', *Studia Historica. Studia Moderna*, 11 (1993), 89–116 (101–2).

6. R. J. W. Evans, *Rudolf II and His World: A Study in Intellectual History 1576–1612* (Oxford, 1973), 84, 196.

7. M. W. Wallace, *The Life of Sir Philip Sidney* (Cambridge, 1915), 17.

8. For 'disturbed in his mind . . . ', see Evans, *Rudolf II*, 45.

9. Christian Sapper, 'Kinder des Geblüts—Die Bastarde Kaiser Rudolfs II.', *MIÖG*, 47 (1999), 1–116 (4–6, 10–19).

10. Raymond Klibansky, Erwin Panofsky, and Fritz Saxl, *Saturn and Melancholy: Studies in the Natural Philosophy, Nature and Art* (London, 1964), 284–365. For depression, see Robert W. Daly, 'Before Depression: The Medieval Vice of Acedia', *Psychiatry*, 70 (2007), 30–51 (38); Winfried Schleiner, *Melancholy, Genius, and Utopia in the Renaissance* (Wiesbaden, 1991), 233; Aristotle, *Problemata*, ed. E. Forster (Oxford, 1927), Book 30, at 953a.

11. Johannes Fabricius, *Alchemy: The Medieval Alchemists and Their Royal Art* (Copenhagen, 1976), 148; Leah DeVun, *Prophecy, Alchemy and the End of Time: John of Rupescissa in the Late Middle Ages* (New York, 2009), 112.

12. Noel L. Brann, 'Alchemy and Melancholy in Medieval and Renaissance Thought', *Ambix*, 32 (1985), 127–48 (128, 138).

13. For Rudolf's depression, see Harald Tersch, 'Melancholie in österreichischen Selbstzeugnissen des Späthumanismus', *MIÖG*, 105 (1997), 130–55 (142). For his alchemists, see Gertrude von Schwarzenfeld, *Rudolf II. Ein deutscher Kaiser am Vorabend des Dreissigjährigen Krieges*, 2nd ed. (Munich, 1979), 70. For his personal involvement in experiments, see Daniel Jütte, *Das Zeitalter des Geheimnissen. Juden, Christen und die Ökonomie des Geheimen* (Göttingen, 2011), 268. For the diary of Damiano, see Hans Holzer, *The Alchemist: The Secret Magical Life of Rudolf von Habsburg* (New York, 1974).

14. *The Diaries of John Dee*, ed. Edward Fenton (Charlbury, 1998), 142; C. H. Josten, 'An Unknown Chapter in the Life of John Dee', *JWCI*, 28 (1965), 223–57 (228); Glynn Parry, *The Arch Conjuror of England* (New Haven, CT, 2011), 179–93.

15. 'Wizards, alchemists, cabbalists . . . '. See Evans, *Rudolf II*, 196. For Rabbi Loew, see Edan Dekel and David Gantt, 'How the Golem Came to Prague', *Jewish Quarterly Review*, 103 (2013), 241–58.

16. Thomas DaCosta Kaufmann, 'Remarks on the Collections of Rudolf II: The Kunstkammer as a Form of Representatio', *Art Journal*, 38 (1978), 22–8.

CHAPTER 11: THE TRIUMPH OF THE HERETICS

1. Cited by Thomas Brady in *Luther zwischen den Kulturen*, ed. Hans Medick and Peer Schmidt (Göttingen, 2004), 96–7.

2. Fritz Byloff, *Hexenglaube und Hexenverfolgung in den österreichischen Alpenländer* (Berlin and Leipzig, 1934), 15–6.

3. Josef Hirn, *Erzherzog Ferdinand II.*, vol. 1 (Innsbruck, 1885), 90, 111–3.

4. For Neo-Stoicism, see A. A. Long, 'Stoicism and the Philosophical Tradition', in *The Cambridge Companion to the Stoics*, ed. Brad Inwood (Cambridge, 2006), 365–92 (379–82).

5. Silvia Petrin, 'Der niederösterreichische Klosterrat 1568–1629', *Wissenschaftliche Arbeiten aus dem Burgenland*, 102 (1999), 145–56; *Forschungen zur Landeskunde von Niederösterreich*, 21 (1974), 125.

6. Walter Sturminger, 'Der Milchkrieg zu Wien am Fronleichnamstag 1578', *MIÖG*, 58 (1950), 614–24.

7. Mathilde Windisch-Graetz, *The Spanish Riding School* (London, 1956), 7–21.

8. *Acten und Correspondenzen zur Geschichte der Gegenreformation in Innerösterreich*, vol. 1, ed. J. Loserth (Vienna, 1898), 31–41.

9. For 'no longer a matter of religion alone . . . ', see August Dimitz, *Geschichte Krains*, vol. 3 (Ljubljana, 1875), 13. For 'It is in the nature of false belief . . . ', see Joseph von Hammer-Purgstall, *Leben des Kardinals Khlesl*, vol. 1 (Vienna, 1847), 304. For Herebel, see Gustav Reingrabner, 'Zur Entwicklung der niederösterreichischen Luthertums im 17. Jahrhundert', *JGPÖ*, 119 (2003), 9–92 (15).

10. Hirn, *Erzherzog Ferdinand II*, vol. 1, 167–9.

11. Reiner Sörries, *Von Kaisers Gnaden. Protestantische Kirchenbauten im Habsburger Reich* (Cologne, Weimar, and Vienna, 2008), 23. For Graz in 1590, see Regina Pörtner, *The Counter-Reformation in Central Europe: Styria 1580–1630* (Oxford, 2001), 95.

12. Hammer-Purgstall, *Leben des Kardinals Khlesl*, vol. 1, 321.

13. For treason, see István Nagy, *A magyar kamara és a királyi pénzügyigazgatás fejlődése Mohács után 1528–1686* (Budapest, 2015), 28. For Rudolf's crown, see *Monumenta Comitialia regni Hungariae*, ed. Árpád Károlyi, vol. 11 (Budapest, 1899), 172–3.

14. Martyn Rady, 'Bocskai, Rebellion and Resistance in Early Modern Hungary', in *Resistance, Rebellion and Revolution in Hungary and Central Europe*, ed. László Péter and Rady (London, 2008), 57–66.

15. For 'to bite into a sour apple . . . ', see Rudolf J. Schleich, *Melchior Khlesl and the Habsburg Bruderzwist, 1605–1612*, PhD thesis (Fordham University, 1968), 232.

16. *The Correspondence of Sir Philip Sidney and Hubert Languet*, ed. S. A. Pears (London, 1845), 116; Schleich, *Melchior Khlesl*, 271.

17. For 'the three estates of Lords, Knights and Cities . . . ', see Hammer-Purgstall, *Leben des Kardinals Khlesl*, vol. 2 (Vienna, 1847), 121. For 'My God, what am I to do?', see Schleich, *Melchior Khlesl*, 426–7.

18. For Anna of the Tyrol, see A. B., *Die Gunstdamen und die Kinder von Liebe im Hause Habsburg* (Berlin, 1869), 31.

CHAPTER 12: FERDINAND II, THE HOLY HOUSE, AND BOHEMIA

1. Katrin Keller, *Erzherzogin Maria Anna von Innerösterreich (1551–1606). Zwischen Habsburg und Wittelsbach* (Vienna, 2012), 128–9.

2. *Guilielmi Lamormaini Ferdinandi II. Romanorum imperatoris virtutes* (Vienna, 1638), 4.

3. Keller, *Erzherzogin Maria Anna*, 135–6.

4. *Guilielmi Lamormaini Ferdinandi II.*, 77.

5. Keller, *Erzherzogin Maria Anna*, 140.

6. Edgar Krausen, 'Die Blutweihbriefe der Kurfürsten Maximilian I. und Ferdinand Maria von Bayern', *Archivalische Zeitschrift*, 57 (1961), 52–6.

7. For 'rest under the wings . . . ', see Ágnes R. Várkonyi, *A királyi Magyarország 1541–1686* (Budapest, 1999), 75.

8. Géza Pálffy, 'Egy elfelejtett kiegyezés a 17. századi magyar történelemben. Az 1622. évi koronázódiéta Sopronban', in *Egy új együttműködés kezdete. Az 1622. évi soproni koronázó országgyűlés*, ed. Péter Dominkovits and Csaba Katona (Sopron and Budapest, 2014), 17–58 (30–49).

9. For Matthias's skilful politicking, see Bernd Rill, *Kaiser Matthias. Bruderzwist und Glaubenskampf* (Graz, Vienna, and Cologne, 1999), 287.

10. Karl Völker, 'Die "Sturmpetition" der evangelischen Stände in der Wiener Hofburg am 5. Juni 1619', *JGPÖ*, 57 (1936), 3–50 (34–42).

11. Robert Bireley, *Ferdinand II, Counter-Reformation Emperor, 1578–1637* (Cambridge, 2014), 99–100.

12. For 'To dismiss the regiment . . . ', see Peter Brightwell, 'The Spanish Origins of the Thirty Years' War', *European Studies Review*, 9 (1979), 409–31 (422).

13. Carlos Gilly, 'The "Midnight Lion", the "Eagle" and the "Antichrist": Political, Religious and Chiliastic Propaganda in the Pamphlets, Illustrated Broadsheets and Ballads of the Thirty Years War', *Nederlands archief voor kerkgeschiedenis*, 80 (2000), 46–77 (52–4); Brennan C. Pursell, *The Winter King: Frederick V of the Palatinate and the Coming of the Thirty Years' War* (Aldershot and Burlington, VT, 2003), 76–9.

14. H. Forst, 'Der türkische Gesandte in Prag 1620 und der Briefwechsel des Winterkönigs mit Sultan Osman II.', *MIÖG*, 16 (1895), 566–81 (570).

15. Adolf Petersen, *Über die Bedeutung der Flugschrift die anhaltische Kanzlei vom Jahre 1621* (Jena, 1867), 8.

16. Bayerisches Hauptstaatsarchiv (Munich), Kurbayern Urkunden, no 22118.

17. Extracts from the Renewed Constitution are given in English translation in C. A. Macartney, *The Habsburg and Hohenzollern Dynasties in the Seventeenth and Eighteenth Centuries* (New York, 1970), 37–45.

18. For *in forma universitatis*, see Hasso Hofmann, *Rappresentanza-rappresentazione. Parola e concetto dall'antichità all'Ottocento* (Milan, 2007), 172.

19. For the origins of three-way burial, see Rill, *Kaiser Matthias*, 323. More generally, see Estella Weiss-Krejci, 'Heart Burial in Medieval and Early Post-Medieval Central Europe', in *Body Parts and Bodies Whole*, eds. Katharina Rebay-Salisbury et al. (Oxford, 2010), 119–34.

20. Anna Coreth, *Pietas Austriaca* (West Lafayette, IN, 2004), 13–23.

CHAPTER 13: THE THIRTY YEARS 'WORLD WAR'

1. Johannes Arndt, *Der dreissigjährige Krieg* (Stuttgart, 2009), 12.

2. For 'to divert the king of Spain's arms . . . ', see Jesús M. Usunáriz, 'América en la política internacional española', in *Discursos coloniales: Texto y poder en la América Hispana*, ed. Pilar Latasa (Madrid, 2011), 167–82 (181); J. H. Elliott, *The Count-Duke of Olivares: The Statesman in an Age of Decline* (New Haven, CT, and London, 1986), 57, 492.

3. Marcelo Szpilman, *Judeus: Suas Extraordinárias Histórias*, 2nd ed. (Rio de Janeiro, 2012), 117; Jonathan Israel and Stuart B. Schwartz, *The Expansion of Tolerance: Religion in Dutch Brazil (1624–1654)* (Amsterdam, 2007), 13–32.

4. Alia Lagamma, *Kongo: Power and Majesty* (New York, 2015), 89–92.

5. T. J. Desch-Obi, *Fighting for Honor: The History of African Martial Art Traditions in the Atlantic World* (Columbia, SC, 2008), 21–5; John K. Thornton, 'The Kingdom of Kongo and the Thirty Years' War', *Journal of World History*, 27 (2016), 189–213.

6. Linda Heywood and John K. Thornton, *Central Africans, Atlantic Creoles, and the Foundation of the Americas, 1585–1660* (Cambridge, 2007), 151; Frederick A. De Armas, 'Numancia as Ganymede', in *Echoes and Inscriptions: Comparative Approaches to Early Modern Spanish Literatures*, ed. Barbara Simerka and Christopher B. Weimer (Lewisburg, PA, and London, 2000), 250–70 (255); also, Hendrik J. Horn, 'The "Allegory of the Abdication of Emperor Charles V" by Frans Francken III', *RACAR: revue d'art Canadienne / Canadian Art Review*, 13 (1986), 23–30.

7. José Eugenio Borao Mateo, *The Spanish Experience in Taiwan 1626–1642* (Hong Kong, 2009).

8. Tonio Andrade, *How Taiwan Became Chinese: Dutch, Spanish, and Han Colonization in the Seventeenth Century* (New York and Chichester, Sussex, 2007).

9. Peter H. Wilson, *The Thirty Years War: Europe's Tragedy* (Cambridge, MA, 2011), 786–8.

10. For these reports, see Hans Medick and Pamela Selwyn, 'Historical Event and Contemporary Experience: The Capture and Destruction of Magdeburg in 1631', *History Workshop Journal*, 52 (2001), 23–48 (30); Karl Wittich, 'Magdeburg als katholisches Marienburg. Eine Episode aus dem Dreissigjährigen Kriege', *HZ*, 65 (1890), 415–64 (432–3).

11. Wittich, 'Magdeburg als katholisches Marienburg', 461–2.

12. For Kepler's horoscope of Wallenstein, see Klaudia Einhorn and Günther Wuchterl, 'Kepler's Wallenstein-Horoscopes', *Acta Universitatis Carolinae. Mathematica et Physica*, 46 Supp. (2005), 101–14.

13. Cf. Robert Bireley, *Ferdinand II, Counter-Reformation Emperor, 1578–1637* (Cambridge, 2014), 307. See further Christoph Kampmann, *Reichsrebellion und kaiserliche Acht. Politische Strafjustiz im dreissigjährige Krieg* (Münster, 1992), 34, 94; Johann Moser, *Einleitung zu dem Reichs-Hof-Raths-Process*, vol. 3, part 6: *Von Reichs-Lehen* (Frankfurt and Leipzig, 1742), 406–7.

14. For the extent of Protestant secularization, see Wilson, *The Thirty Years War*, 448.

15. *Alberti Fridlandi Perduellionis Chaos sive Ingrati Animi Abyssus* (1634; no author, no place of publication); Geoff Mortimer, *Wallenstein: The Enigma of the Thirty Years War* (Basingstoke and New York, 2010), 252.

16. Cited by Tryntje Helfferich in *The Ashgate Research Companion to the Thirty Years' War*, ed. Olaf Asbach and Peter Schröder (London and New York, 2014), 151.

17. For 'In winter we negotiate . . . ', see Geoffrey Parker, *Thirty Years' War* (London and New York, 1984), 179; B. Dudík, *Schweden in Böhmen und Mähren 1640–1650* (Vienna, 1879), 294–5.

18. For the extent of anti-Habsburg gains, see Konrad Repgen, 'Ferdinand III.', in *Die Kaiser der Neuzeit 1519–1918*, ed. Anton Schindling and Walter Ziegler (Munich, 1990), 142–67 (151).

19. Johannes Postma, *The Dutch in the Atlantic Slave Trade, 1600–1815* (Cambridge, 1990), 33–45. The text of the peace treaty is given in Latin and German in *Tractatus Pacis, Trigesimo Januarii, anno supra millesimum sexcentesimo quadragesimo octavo, Monasterii Westfalorum* (1648). For modern verdicts, see Johannes Arndt, 'Ein europäisches Jubiläum: 350 Jahre Westfälische Frieden', *Jahrbuch für Europäische Geschichte*, 1 (2000), 133–58.

CHAPTER 14: THE ABNORMAL EMPIRE AND THE BATTLE FOR VIENNA

1. Michael Stolleis, *Geschichte des öffentlichen Rechts in Deutschland*, vol. 1 (Munich, 2012), 234–6. The quotation is taken from Samuel Pufendorf (1632–94), *irregularis aliquod corpus et simile monstro*. The translation here avoids using 'monster' or 'monstrous', which are misleading. See Hanns Gross, *Empire and Sovereignty: A History of the Public Law Literature in the Holy Roman Empire, 1599–1804* (Chicago and London, 1973), 321–6.

2. Barbara Stollberg-Rilinger, *The Emperor's Old Clothes: Constitutional History and the Symbolic Language of the Holy Roman Empire* (New York and Oxford, 2008), 130.

3. For 'empty signs and shadowy conceits', see Hippolitus de Lapide (Bogislav von Chemnitz), *Dissertatio de Ratione Status*, 2nd ed. ('Freystadt' [= Amsterdam], 1647), 394–5.

On Ferdinand III, see here Mark Hengerer, *Ferdinand III. (1608–57). Eine Biographie* (Vienna, Cologne, and Weimar, 2012), 338–9, and Konrad Repgen, 'Ferdinand III.', in *Die Kaiser der Neuzeit 1519–1918*, ed. Anton Schindling and Walter Ziegler (Munich, 1990), 142–67 (163–5).

4. William O. McCagg Jr, *A History of the Habsburg Jews, 1670–1918* (Bloomington and Indianapolis, 1989), 15–18.

5. Cited in Tim Blanning, 'The Holy Roman Empire of the German Nation Past and Present', *Historical Research*, 85 (2012), 57–70 (65).

6. Antony Black, *The History of Islamic Political Thought* (Edinburgh, 2011), 262–7.

7. Georg Kraus, *Erdélyi Krónika 1608–1665*, ed. Sándor Vogel (Budapest, 1994), 504; John P. Spielman, *Leopold I of Austria* (London, 1977), 65–6.

8. For 'Your Imperial Majesty has conquered Hungary . . . ', see Árpád Károlyi, *A magyar alkotmány fölfüggesztése 1673-ben* (Budapest, 1883), 10; *Ausgewaehlte Schriften des Raimund Fürsten Montecuccoli*, ed. Alois Veltzé, vol. 3 (Vienna and Leipzig, 1900), 447–50.

9. Sándor Payr, *A magyar protestáns gályarabok* (Budapest, 1927), 41–2; Walter Wilson, *Memoirs of the Life and Times of Daniel De Foe*, vol. 1 (London, 1830), 91.

10. Graeme Murdock, 'Responses to Habsburg Persecution of Protestants in Seventeenth-Century Hungary', *AHY*, 40 (2009), 37–52 (50).

11. Tibor Iványosi-Szabó, *Irott emlékek Kecskemét XVII. századi nyilvántartásaiból (1633–1700)*, vol. 1 (Kecskemét, 2008), 521.

12. Dávid Manó, *Thököly viszonya a Portához* (Cluj, 1906), 24–5.

13. Giovanni Benaglia, *Relatione del viaggio fatta à Costantinopoli* (Venice, 1685), 139–47.

14. Karl Teply, *Türkische Sagen und Legenden um die Kaiserstadt Wien* (Vienna, Cologne, and Graz, 1980), 34.

15. For 'What mountains are there?', see John Stoye, *The Siege of Vienna* (London, 1964), 208.

16. For the slave auction, see Karl Teply, 'Türkentaufen in Wien während des Grossen Türkenkrieges 1683–1699', *Jahrbuch des Vereines für Geschichte der Stadt Wien*, 29 (1973), 57–87 (61–2).

17. As noted by Anton Schindling, *Die Anfänge des Immerwährenden Reichstags zu Regensburg* (Mainz, 1991), 224.

CHAPTER 15: SPAIN'S INVISIBLE SOVEREIGNS AND THE DEATH OF THE BEWITCHED KING

1. Francisco de la Maza, 'Iconografia de Pedro de Gante', *Artes de México*, 150 (1972), 17–32 (28).

2. See here Jean Baudrillard, *Simulacra and Simulation*, trans. S. H. Glaser (Ann Arbor, MI, 1994), 5–7.

3. Minou Schraven, *Festive Funerals in Early Modern Italy: The Art and Culture of Conspicuous Commemoration* (Abingdon and New York, 2016), 53–83.

4. Cervantes de Salazar, *Túmulo Imperial* (Mexico City, 1560), fols 4v, 14r; Elizabeth Olton, 'To Shepherd the Empire: The Catafalque of Charles V in Mexico City', *Hispanic Issues On Line*, 7 (2010), 10–26.

5. Isabel Cruz de Amenábar, 'Arte Festivo Barocco: Un Legado duradero', *Laboratorio de Arte*, 10 (1997), 211–31 (224).

6. For 'We may appropriately say . . . ', see Alejandro Cañeque, *The King's Living Image: The Culture and Politics of Viceregal Power in Colonial Mexico* (New York and London, 2004), 238; Patricio Hidalgo Nuchera, 'La entrada de los gobernadores en Manila', *Revista de Indias*, 75 (2015), 615–44 (626).

7. Christoph Rosenmüller, *Patrons, Partisans, and Palace Intrigues: The Court Society of Colonial Mexico, 1702–1710* (Calgary, 2008), 35–6.

8. *Memoirs of Prince Eugene of Savoy Written by Himself*, ed. F. Shoberl (London, 1811), 198.

9. For 'perfect . . . unchanging in majesty . . . ', see Salvador de Mallea, *Rey Pacifico y Governo de Principe Catolico* (Genoa, 1646), 2. For 'with such regularity . . . ', see J. H. Elliott, 'The Court of the Spanish Habsburgs: A Peculiar Institution?' in *Politics and Culture in Early Modern Europe*, ed. Phyllis Mack and Margaret C. Jacob (Cambridge, 1987), 5–24 (13, citing Antoine de Brunel).

10. Carlos Gómez-Centurión Jiménez, 'Etiqueta y ceremonial palatino durante el reinado de Felipe V', *Hispania*, 56 (1996), 965–1005 (973–4). For petitioning in Burgundy, see Richard Vaughan, *Charles the Bold: The Last Valois Duke of Burgundy*, 2nd ed. (Woodbridge, 2002), 182–3.

11. Reported by Edward Herbert (1583–1648), in *Life of Lord Herbert, of Cherbury* (London 1856), 252. For Philip IV's minister, see Alistair Malcolm, *Royal Favouritism and the Governing Elite of the Spanish Monarchy, 1640–1665* (Oxford, 2017), 42.

12. Patrick Williams, 'Philip III and the Restoration of Spanish Government, 1598–1603', *The English Historical Review*, 88 (1973), 751–69 (753–6).

13. For 'the misfortune of our century', see Alistair Malcolm, *Royal Favouritism and the Governing Elite of the Spanish Monarchy, 1640–1665* (Oxford, 2016), 13. For 'a simulacrum of God . . . ', see Sara Gonzalez, *The Musical Iconography of Power in Seventeenth-Century Spain and Her Territories* (London and New York, 2016), 93.

14. I. A. A. Thompson, 'Castile', in *Absolutism in Seventeenth Century Europe*, ed. John Miller (Basingstoke and London, 1990), 69–98, 239–43 (241).

15. Xavier Gil, 'Parliamentary Life in the Crown of Aragon: Cortes, Juntas de Brazos, and Other Corporate Bodies', *Journal of Early Modern History*, 6 (2002), 362–95 (372).

16. Christopher Storrs, *The Resilience of the Spanish Monarchy 1665–1700* (Oxford, 2006), 204.

17. Gonzalez, *The Musical Iconography of Power*, 69.

18. Alejandra B. Osorio, *Inventing Lima: Baroque Modernity in Peru's South Sea Metropolis* (Basingstoke and New York, 2008), 52–3.

19. John Leddy Phelan, *The Kingdom of Quito in the Seventeenth Century: Bureaucratic Politics in the Spanish Empire* (Madison, WI, 1967), 33–7.

20. James M. Córdova, *The Art of Professing in Bourbon Mexico: Crowned-Nun Portraits and Reform in the Convent* (Austin, TX, 2014), 169–70.

21. *European Urology Today*, 27, no. 2 (March/May 2015), 4.

22. Antonio Cánovas del Castillo, *Historia de la Decadencia de España* (Madrid, 1910), 617; Pedro Scotti de Agoiz, *El Cenotafio: Oracion Funebre en la Muerte del Senor Rey Don Carlos II* (Madrid, 1700), 45.

CHAPTER 16: THE THEATRE OF THE BAROQUE

1. For 'the superlative of the bizarre . . . ', see Marco Bussagli and Matthia Reiche, *Baroque and Rococo* (New York, 2009), 11, citing the eighteenth-century art historian

Francesco Milizia. For Croce, see René Wellek in *Dictionary of the History of Ideas*, ed. Philip P. Wiener, vol. 1 (New York, 1973), 188–95.

2. Peter Hersche, *Musse und Verschwendung. Europäische Gesellschaft und Kultur im Barockzeitalter*, vol. 1 (Freiburg, Basle, and Vienna, 2006), 583.

3. Mario Praz, *Studies in Seventeenth-Century Imagery*, 2nd ed. (Rome, 1975), 16.

4. For radiance, see Evonne Levy, *Propaganda and the Jesuit Baroque* (Berkeley, Los Angeles, and London, 2004), 160.

5. Christian Kleinbub, 'At the Boundaries of Sight: The Italian Renaissance Cloud Putto', in *Renaissance Theories of Vision*, ed. J. S. Hendrix and C. H. Carman (Farnham and Burlington, VT, 2010), 117–33 (117–9).

6. Trevor Johnson, 'Holy Fabrications: The Catacomb Saints and the Counter-Reformation in Bavaria', *Journal of Ecclesiastical History*, 47 (1996), 274–97.

7. Marc R. Forster, *Catholic Revival in the Age of Baroque: Religious Identity in South-West Germany, 1550–1750* (Cambridge, 2004), 127–9.

8. Given in *Apparatus regius, serenissimo ac potentissimo Ferdinando II* (Vienna, 1618). See also *Pietas Victrix—Der Sieg der Pietas*, ed. Lothar Mundt and Ulrich Seelbach (Tübingen, 2002), xii.

9. Franz Lang, 'Imagines symbolicae', *Dissertatio de Actione Scenica* (Munich, 1727), 107–54; see also Cesare Ripa, *Iconologia* (Siena, 1613); Philippo Picinello, *Mundus Symbolicus* (Cologne, 1687). See more generally *The Sopron Collection of Jesuit Stage Designs*, ed. Éva Knapp and István Kilián (Budapest, 1999).

10. Charles E. Brewer, *The Instrumental Music of Schmeltzer, Biber, Muffat and Their Contemporaries* (Farnham and Burlington, VT, 2011), 49–50.

11. Peter Davidson, *The Universal Baroque* (Manchester and New York, 2007), 2; Gauvin Alexander Bailey, *The Andean Hybrid Baroque: Convergent Cultures in the Churches of Colonial Peru* (Notre Dame, IN, 2010), 18–20, 322–31.

12. Leopold Auer, 'Der Übergang des Ordens an die österreichischen Habsburger', in *Das Haus Österreich und der Orden von Goldenen Vlies* (Graz and Stuttgart, 2007), 53–64.

13. Robert F. Rogers, *Destiny's Landfall: A History of Guam* (Honolulu, 1995), 77; William O'Reilly, 'Lost Chances of the House of Habsburg', *AHY*, 40 (2009), 53–70 (61).

14. Anton Höller, *Augusta Carolinae Virtutis Monumenta* (Vienna, 1733); for Rákóczi's slogan, see Imre Wellmann, 'Az ónodi országgyűlés történetéhez', in Wellmann, *18. századi agrártörténelem. Válogatás Wellmann Imre agrár- és társadalomtörténeti tanulmányaiból* (Miskolc, 1999), 391–421 (395).

15. For the history of the Banat, see Irina Marin, *Contested Frontiers in the Balkans: Habsburg and Ottoman Rivalries in Eastern Europe* (London, 2013).

16. Paul Shore, *Jesuits and the Politics of Religious Pluralism in Eighteenth-Century Transylvania* (Aldershot and Burlington, VT, 2007), 117–20; Zoltán Ferenczi, *A kolozsvári színészet és szinház története* (Cluj, 1897), 49.

CHAPTER 17: MARIA THERESA, AUTOMATA, AND BUREAUCRATS

1. Tom Standage, *The Mechanical Turk: The True Story of the Chess-Playing Machine That Fooled the World* (London, 2002), 105–7.

2. For 'a machine which winds itself up . . . ', see La Mettrie, *Machine Man and Other Writings*, ed. Ann Thompson (Cambridge, 1996), 7 (first published in 1747); Geraint Parry, 'Enlightened Government and Its Critics in Eighteenth-Century Germany', *Historical Journal*, 6 (1963), 178–92 (185).

3. Parry, 'Enlightened Government and Its Critics', 182, citing J. H. G. von Justi.

4. Elizabeth Bridges, 'Maria Theresa, "the Turk", and Habsburg Nostalgia', *Journal of Austrian Studies*, 47 (2014), 17–36 (27–8); Michael Yonan, *Empress Maria Theresa and the Politics of Habsburg Imperial Art* (University Park, PA, 2011), 135–6; Michel Foucault, *Discipline and Punish: The Birth of the Prison* (New York, 1979), 136.

5. August Fournier, 'Zur Entstehungsgeschichte der pragmatischen Sanktion Kaiser Karl's VI.', *HZ*, 38 (1877), 16–47; Peter Berger, 'Die österreich-ungarische Dualismus und die österreichische Rechtswissenschaft', *Der Donauraum*, 13 (1968), 156–70 (167).

6. For 'the work of a good charlatan', see Tim Blanning, *Frederick the Great, King of Prussia* (London, 2015), 78.

7. For the queen's title in Hungary, see Emericus Kelemen, *Historia Juris Hungarici Privati* (Buda, 1818), 440.

8. For 'the queen of Hungary's head . . . ', see Letter by A. B., *The Town and Country Magazine* (September 1769), 456.

9. For 'whatever one might think of France . . . ', see C. A. Macartney, *Maria Theresa and the House of Austria* (London, 1969), 82.

10. János Barta, *Mária Terézia* (Budapest, 1988), 166.

11. Blanning, *Frederick the Great*, 293–4.

12. J. C. Bisinger, *General-Statistik des österreichischen Kaiserthumes*, vol. 2 (Vienna and Trieste, 1808), 162.

13. István M. Szijártó, *A diéta. A magyar rendek és az országgyűlés 1708–1792* (Budapest, 2005), 361–2.

14. P. G. M. Dickson, *Finance and Government Under Maria Theresia*, vol. 1 (Oxford, 1987), 233.

15. Waltraud Heindl, *Gehorsame Rebellen. Bürokratie und Beamte in Österreich, 1780 bis 1848*, 2nd ed. (Cologne and Vienna, 2013), 229, 246.

16. For 'which is the greatest slavery . . . ', see Franz A. J. Szabo, *Kaunitz and Enlightened Absolutism 1753–1780* (Cambridge, 1994), 279. For 'Every citizen is a part and cog . . . ', see Barbara Stollberg-Rilinger, *Der Staat als Maschine. Zur politischen Metaphorik des absoluten Fürstenstaats* (Berlin, 1986), 121. See also Anton Tantner, 'Addressing the Houses: The Introduction of House Numbering in Europe', *Histoire & Mesure*, 24, no. 2 (2009), 7–30 (14–16).

CHAPTER 18: MERCHANTS, BOTANISTS, AND FREEMASONS

1. Beatrix Hajós, *Schönbrunner Statuen 1773–1780. Ein neuer Rom in Wien* (Vienna, Cologne, and Weimar, 2004), 12.

2. For 'a very unprofitable and unworthy servant', see William Bolts, *Considerations on Indian Affairs*, vol. 2 (London, 1775), 123–4. See also Franz A. J. Szabo, *Kaunitz and Enlightened Despotism, 1753–1780* (Cambridge, 1994), 144–5.

3. Mary Lindemann, *The Merchant Republics: Amsterdam, Antwerp, and Hamburg, 1648–1790* (Cambridge, 2015), 288–9.

4. *Verhandlungen des zoologisch-botanischen Vereins in Wien*, 5 (1855), 27 (Abhandlungen); Alfred Lesel, 'Neugebäude Palace and Its Gardens: The Green Dream of Maximilian II', *Ekistics*, 61, nos 364–5 (1994), 59–67 (62–3).

5. Paula Findlen, *Possessing Nature: Museums, Collecting, and Scientific Culture in Early Modern Italy* (Berkeley, CA, 1996), 30.

6. Findlen, *Possessing Nature*, 80; Markus Oppenauer, 'Soziale Aspekte der Anatomie und ihrer Sammlungen an der Wiener Medizinischen Fakultät, 1790–1840', *Sudhoffs Archiv*, 98 (2014), 47–75 (52).

7. Bernhard Koch, 'Das Münzkabinett des Kunsthistorischen Museums', *Österreichs Museen stellen sich vor*, 9 (1978), 49–62 (52).

8. Günther Hamann, *Die Geschichte der Wiener naturhistorischen Sammlungen bis zum Ende der Monarchie* (Vienna, 1976), 18–20.

9. Gerbert Frodl and Marianne Frodl-Schneemann, *Die Blumenmalerei in Wien* (Vienna, 2010), 10; Santiago Madriñán, *Nikolaus Joseph Jacquin's American Plants* (Leiden and Boston, 2013), 49–50; C. F. Blöchinger vom Bannholz, *Chevalier Jean de Baillou. Ein Beitrag* (Vienna, 1868), 28.

10. Renate Zedinger, *Franz Stephan von Lothringen. Monarch, Manager, Mäzen* (Vienna, Cologne, and Weimar, 2008), 241–58.

11. Gilbert Daynes, 'The Duke of Lorraine and English Freemasonry in 1731', *Ars Quatuor Coronatorum*, 37 (1924), 107–32 (109); *300 Jahre Freimaurer. Das wahre Geheimnis*, ed. Christian Rapp and Nadia Rapp-Wimberger (Vienna, 2017), 37.

12. For 'a temple for the benefit of all mankind . . . ', see L. Lewis, *Geschichte der Freimaurerei in Österreich* (Vienna, 1861), 4. See also Ludwig Abafi, *Geschichte der Freimaurerei in Österreich-Ungarn*, vol. 2 (Budapest, 1891), 262.

13. *Die Protokolle der Wiener Freimaurerloge 'Zum wahren Eintracht' (1781–1785)*, ed. Hans-Josef Irmen (Frankfurt a/M, 1994), 167, 312; Sándor Domanovszky, *József nádor élete*, vol. 1, part 1 (Budapest, 1944), 132–42.

14. For 'observation of the workings of nature . . . ', see R. William Weisberger, *Speculative Freemasonry and the Enlightenment: A Study of the Craft in London, Paris, Prague, and Vienna* (Boulder and New York, 1993), 128.

15. For 'into the society of citizens', see Ludwig Rapp, *Freimaurer in Tirol* (Innsbruck, 1867), 20.

16. Margaret C. Jacob, *Living the Enlightenment: Freemasonry and Politics in Eighteenth-Century Europe* (New York and Oxford, 1991), 12, 20; Eckhart Hellmuth, 'Why Does Corruption Matter? Reforms and Reform Movements in Britain and Germany in the Second Half of the Eighteenth Century', *Proceedings of the British Academy*, 100 (1999), 5–23 (17–9).

17. Friedrich Weissensteiner, *Die Töchter Maria Theresias* (Vienna, 1994), 33–56.

18. Julia Budka, 'Hieroglyphen und das Haus Habsburg: Der Dekor des neuzeitlichen Obelisken in Schönbrunner Schlosspark', *Kemet*, 15, no 4 (2006), 58–62 (61).

CHAPTER 19: VAMPIRISM, ENLIGHTENMENT, AND THE REVOLUTION FROM ABOVE

1. Voltaire, *Dictionnaire Philosophique*, vol. 6 (*Oeuvres complètes*, vol. 38, Paris, 1838), 449 (first published in 1764).

2. Michael Ranft, *Tractat von dem Kauen und Schmatzen der Todten in Gräbern, worin die wahre Beschaffenheit derer Hungarischen Vampyrs und Blut-Sauger gezeigt* (Leipzig, 1734).

3. Ferencz Xavier Linzbauer, *A magyar korona országainak nemzetközi egességügye* (Buda, 1868), 110.

4. Gerhard van Swieten, *Vampyrismus* (Augsburg, 1768). This is a translation of the original French version, published in 1755.

5. Joseph Linden, *Abhandlungen über Cameral- und fiskalämtliche Gegenstände* (Vienna, 1834), 191–3.

6. Peter Gay, *The Enlightenment: The Science of Freedom* (New York and London, 1968), 489.

7. Teodora Daniela Sechel, 'The Emergence of the Medical Profession in Transylvania (1770–1848)', in *Cultural Dimensions of Elite Formation in Transylvania* (1770–1950), ed. Victor Karady and Borbála Zsuzsanna Török (Cluj, 2008), 95–114 (99–101).

8. Andre Wakefield, *The Disordered Police State: German Cameralism as Science and Practice* (Chicago and London, 2009), 14.

9. For 'Every tradition which has no justifiable basis . . . ', see T. C. W. Blanning, *Joseph II and Enlightened Despotism* (London, 1970), 3.

10. Teodora Shek Brnardić, 'Modalities of Enlightened Monarchical Patriotism in the Mid-Eighteenth Century Habsburg Monarchy', in *Whose Love of Which Country? Composite States, National Histories and Patriotic Discourses in Early Modern East Central Europe*, ed. Balázs Trencsényi and Márton Zászkaliczky (Leiden, 2010), 629–61 (640–5).

11. For 'because there the choice was between ugly peasants . . . ', see Derek Beales, *Joseph II: Against the World 1780–90* (Cambridge, 2009), 430. For 'eternal audiences', see Beales, *Joseph II: Against the World*, 147; Paul von Mitrofanov, *Joseph II. Seine politische und kulturelle Tätigkeit*, vol. 1 (Leipzig, 1910), 275.

12. Wilfried Beimrohr, *Die Zillertaler Protestanten oder Inklinanten und ihre Austreibung 1837* (Innsbruck, 2007).

13. *Monachologia or Handbook of the Natural History of Monks arranged according to the Linnaean System by a Naturalist* (Edinburgh, 1852), 3, 47–8, 64 (first published in Latin in 1783). See further Elisabeth Kovács, 'Der Besuch Papst Pius' VI. in Wien im Spiegel josephinischer Broschüren', *Archivum Historiae Pontificiae*, 20 (1982), 163–217 (171–4).

14. Beales, *Joseph II: Against the World*, 233.

15. For 'with books that have no worth', see S. Laschitzer, 'Die Verordnungen über die Bibliotheken und Archiven der aufgehobenen Klöster in Oesterreich', *MIÖG*, 2 (1881), 401–40 (431).

16. For 'the love of reason and humanity', see Renate Blickle, *Politische Streitkultur in Altbayern* (Berlin and Boston, 2017), 105.

17. I owe the information on swearing and spitting to the late Domokos Kosáry.

CHAPTER 20: ARCHDUCHESSES AND THE HABSBURG LOW COUNTRIES

1. Benedikt Sauer, *The Innsbruck Hofburg* (Vienna and Bolzano, 2010), 45.

2. Charles W. Ingrao and Andrew L. Thomas, 'Piety and Patronage: The Empresses-Consort of the High Baroque', *German History*, 20 (2002), 20–43 (21).

3. For 'because my father had never been pleased . . . ', see C. A. Macartney, *The Habsburg and Hohenzollern Dynasties in the Seventeenth and Eighteenth Centuries* (New York, 1970), 97; *Sprachgeschichte. Ein Handbuch zur Geschichte der deutschen Sprache und ihrer Erforschung*, Part 3, 2nd ed., ed. Werner Besch et al. (Berlin and New York, 2003), 2974; Karl Vocelka, *Die Familien Habsburg und Habsburg-Lothringen. Politik, Kultur, Mentalität* (Vienna, Cologne, and Weimar, 2010), 106; Elisabeth Kovács, 'Die ideale Erzherzogin. Maria Theresias Forderungen an ihre Töchter', *MIÖG*, 94 (1986), 49–80 (50–1, 74).

4. Mercedes Llorente, 'Mariana of Austria's Portraits as Ruler-Governor and Curadora' in *Early Modern Habsburg Women*, ed. Anne J. Cruz and Maria Galli Stampino (Abingdon and New York, 2016), 197–224.

5. Luc Duerloo, *Dynasty and Piety: Archduke Albert (1598–1621) and Habsburg Political Culture in an Age of Religious Wars* (London and New York, 2012), 519.

6. Geoffrey Parker, 'New Light on an Old Theme: Spain and the Netherlands 1550–1650', *European History Quarterly*, 15 (1985), 219–36.

7. Klaas Van Gelder, 'The Investiture of Emperor Charles VI in Brabant and Flanders', *European Review of History: Revue européenne d'histoire*, 18 (2011), 443–63 (453–4, 460).

8. Derek Beales, *Joseph II: Against the World 1780–90* (Cambridge, 2009), 137.

9. Michèle Galand, *Charles de Lorraine, gouverneur général des Pays-Bas autrichiens (1744–80)*, (Brussels, 1993), 28–30; Heinrich Benedikt, *Als Belgien österreichisch war* (Vienna and Munich, 1965), 109.

10. Sandra Hertel, *Maria Elisabeth. Österreichische Erzherzogin und Statthalterin in Brüssel (1725–1741)*, (Vienna, Cologne, and Weimar, 2014), 222–33.

11. Derek Beales, *Prosperity and Plunder: European Catholic Monasteries in the Age of Revolution, 1650–1815* (Cambridge, 2003), 215.

12. Benedikt, *Als Belgien österreichisch war*, 110–11; Michèle Galand, 'Le journal secret de Charles de Lorraine, gouverneur-général des Pays-Bas autrichiens', *Revue belge de Philologie et d'Histoire*, 62 (1984), 289–301.

13. For 'I love you furiously . . . ', See Friedrich Weissensteiner, *Die Töchter Maria Theresias* (Vienna, 1994), 72–3; Krisztina Kulcsár, 'A helytartói státus. Albert szász herceg (1738–1822) kinevezése és évtizedei Magyarországon', *Aetas—Történéttudományi Folyóirat* (2002), 51–66 (57).

14. Beales, *Joseph II: Against the World*, 504.

15. Hanns Schlitter, *Die Regierung Josefs II. in den österreichischen Niederlandern*, vol. 1 (Vienna, 1900) 92.

16. For 'no need to be afraid . . . ', see T. C. W. Blanning, *Joseph II* (Harlow, 1994), 174.

17. Josef Hrazky, 'Die Persönlichkeit der Infantin Isabella von Parma', *Mitteilungen des Österreichischen Staatsarchiv*, 12 (1959), 174–239 (194–5, 199).

18. For 'eminently placid nymphs', see *The Feminist Encyclopedia of Italian Literature*, ed. Rinaldina Russell (Westport, CT, and London, 1997), 203.

19. See here the essays in *Marie-Antoinette: Writings on the Body of a Queen*, ed. Dena Goodman (New York, 2003).

CHAPTER 21: CENSORS, JACOBINS, AND *THE MAGIC FLUTE*

1. For unusual information on Van Swieten's relationship to the empress, see Stephan Rössner, 'Gerard van Swieten 1700–1772', *Obesity Reviews*, 14 (September 2013), 769–70.

2. Leslie Bodi, *Tauwetter in Wien. Zur Prosa der österreichischen Aufklärung 1781–1795*, 2nd ed. (Vienna, Cologne, and Weimar, 1995), 51.

3. For 'they can only debauch Turks . . . ', see *The Life of David Hume*, ed. E. C. Mossner, 2nd ed. (Oxford, 1980), 211. See also Rüdiger Nolte, 'Die josephinische Fürsorge- und Gesundheitspolitik', *Geschichte in Köln. Zeitschrift für Stadt- und Regionalgeschichte*, 21 (1987), 97–124 (117–20); F. S. Hügel, *Zur Geschichte, Statistik und Regelung der Prostitution* (Vienna, 1865), 68–9; A Traveller, 'Some Account of the Famous Commission of Chastity, Instituted at Vienna by the Late Empress', *Edinburgh Review* (November 1785), 275–6; *The Imperial Style: Fashions of the Hapsburg Era*, ed. Polly Cone (New York, 1980), 38; but see Wilhelm Kisch, *Die alten Strassen und Plaetze Wien's und ihre historisch interessanten Haeuser* (Vienna, 1883), 33–4.

4. For rosaries, see Giacomo Casanova, *The Story of My Life*, trans. Stephen Sarterelli and Sophie Hawkes (London, 2001), 193–4.

5. For 'a school for manners and taste', See W. E. Yates, *Theatre in Vienna: A Critical History, 1776–1995* (Cambridge and New York, 1996), 9–10.

6. Joscelyn Godwin, 'Layers of Meaning in "The Magic Flute"', *Musical Quarterly*, 65 (1979), 471–92 (473–4).

7. Katharine Thomson, 'Mozart and Freemasonry', *Music and Letters*, 57, (1976), 25–46 (43).

8. Francesco Attardi, *Viaggio intorno al Flauto Magico* (Lucca, 2006), 50; Sándor Domanovszky, *József nádor élete*, vol. 1, Part 1 (Budapest, 1944), 136; Ludwig Lewis, *Geschichte der Freimaurerei in Österreich* (Vienna, 1861), 27.

9. Karlheinz Gerlach, 'Österreichische und preussische Freimaurer im Jahrhundert der Aufklärung', in *Aufklärung, Freimaurerei und Demokratie im Diskurs der Moderne*, ed. Michael Fischer at al. (Frankfurt a/M, 2003), 1–32 (28).

10. For the 'the general needs of humanity', see Adam Wandruszka, *Leopold II.*, vol. 2 (Vienna and Munich, 1965), 193–7; for Leopold and Florentine industry, see Wandruszka, *Leopold II.*, vol. 2, 245.

11. For 'shall be a free kingdom and independent . . . ', see C. A. Macartney, *The Habsburg and Hohenzollern Dynasties in the Seventeenth and Eighteenth Centuries* (New York, 1970), 141; Martyn Rady, *Customary Law in Hungary: Courts, Texts, and the Tripartitum* (Oxford, 2015), 216–9.

12. For 'The mask has fallen . . . ', see Alphonse de Lamartine, *History of the Girondists*, vol. 1 (New York, 1849), 356.

13. For 'the reception of that blissful happiness . . . ', see Amir Minsky, *'In a Sentimental Mood': German Radicals and the French Revolution in the Rhineland, 1792–1814*, PhD thesis (University of Pennsylvania, 2008), 42; Joachim Whaley, *Germany and the Holy Roman Empire*, vol. 2 (Oxford, 2012), 583; R. John Rath, 'The Carbonari: Their Origins, Initiation Rites, and Aims', *American Historical Review*, 69 (1964), 353–70.

14. OeStA/HHStA, Kabinettsarchiv. Kabinettskanzleiakten, Karton 20, 1809: 1020; ibid., Karton 48, 1821: 137; *300 Jahre Freimaurer. Das wahre Geheimnis*, ed. Christian Rapp and Nadia Rapp-Wimberger (Vienna, 2017), 94; Tudor Sălăgean, 'Repere pentru o istorie a francmasoneriei în Transilvania în epoca modernă', *Ţara Bârsei*, 9 (2010), 214–221 (217–8).

15. Inge Stephan, *Literarischer Jakobinismus in Deutschland (1789–1806)* (Stuttgart, 1976), 173–4.

16. Martyn Rady, *The Habsburg Empire: A Very Short Introduction* (Oxford, 2017), 69–70.

17. Werner Sabitzer, 'Geschichte der Prostitution. Von "unzüchtigen Weibspersonen"', *Öffentliche Sicherheit*, 11–12 (2000).

18. Yates, *Theatre in Vienna*, 143.

CHAPTER 22: METTERNICH AND THE MAP OF EUROPE

1. For Metternich's debts, see Wolfram Siemann, *Metternich. Stratege und Visionär, Eine Biografie*, 2nd ed. (Munich, 2017), 742–4.

2. For "Roll up that map . . . ', see J. Holland Rose, *William Pitt and the Great War* (London, 1911), 580.

3. *Wiener Zeitung*, 15 August 1804; *Wiener Zeitung*, 9 August 1806.

4. Karl H. Oberacker, *Kaiserin Leopoldine. Ihr Leben und ihre Zeit (1797–1826)* (São Leopoldo, 1980), 343–4.

5. Siemann, *Metternich*, 278–9.

6. Prince Clemens von Metternich, *Metternich: The Autobiography* (Welwyn Garden City, 2004), 139.

7. Enno E. Kraehe, *Metternich's German Policy*, vol. 2 (Princeton, 1983), 368, 392–93.

8. For Metternich's three letters, see Mark Jarrett, *The Congress of Vienna and Its Legacy: War and Great Power Diplomacy After Napoleon* (London and New York, 2013), 315. Metternich's use of legitimacy as a cover for keeping the status quo is shrewdly noted by Julian Schmidt, *Die Grenzboten*, vol. 7 (Leipzig, 1848), 542.

9. For 'Heaven has placed me next to a man . . . ', see Alan Sked, *Metternich and Austria: An Evaluation* (Basingstoke and New York, 2008), 116; E. Vehse, *Memoirs of the Court, Aristocracy, and Diplomacy of Austria*, vol. 2 (London, 1856), 472.

10. For 'for the purpose of consulting . . . ', see Jarrett, *The Congress of Vienna*, 168.

11. C. K. Webster, *The Foreign Policy of Castlereagh 1815–23: Britain and the European Alliance* (London, 1925), 304, 309.

12. Lawrence Sondhaus, *The Habsburg Empire and the Sea: Austrian Naval Policy, 1797–1866* (West Lafayette, IN, 1989), 49.

13. J. L. 'Eine oesterreichische See-Expedition gegen Marokko vor fünfzig Jahren', *Oesterreichische Monatsschrift für den Orient*, 5, no 6 (1879), 118–9.

14. Miroslav Šedivý, *Metternich, the Great Powers and the Eastern Question* (Pilsen, 2013), 452–6, 606–11.

15. Alison Frank, 'The Children of the Desert and the Laws of the Sea: Austria, Great Britain, the Ottoman Empire, and the Mediterranean Slave Trade in the Nineteenth Century', *AHR*, 117 (2012), 410–44.

16. Helge Wendt, 'Central European Missionaries in Sudan: Geopolitics and Alternative Colonialism in Mid-Nineteenth Century Africa', *European Review*, 26 (2018), 481–91 (483–4).

17. Adrian E. Tschoegl, 'Maria Theresa's Thaler: A Case of International Money', *Eastern Economic Journal*, 27, no 4 (2001), 113–62.

18. *Tagebücher des Carl Friedrich Freiherrn Kübeck von Kübau*, ed. Max von Kübeck, vol. 1 (Vienna, 1909), 438, 508. For 'may have governed Europe . . . ', see Sked, *Metternich and Austria*, 116.

19. Maurizio Isabella, *Risorgimento in Exile: Italian Émigrés and the Liberal International in the Post-Napoleonic Era* (Oxford, 2009), 42–64; see also Richard Stites, *The Four Horsemen: Riding to Liberty in Post-Napoleonic Europe* (Oxford, 2014).

20. For the number of pages, see Siemann, *Metternich*, 682.

21. Siemann, *Metternich*, 92; Alan Sked, 'Metternich and the Ficquelmont Mission of 1847–48: The Decision Against Reform in Lombardy-Venetia', *Central Europe*, 2 (2004), 15–46 (20).

22. Waltraud Heindl, *Gehorsame Rebellen. Bürokratie und Beamte in Österreich 1780 bis 1848* (Vienna, Cologne, and Weimar, 1990), 139, 289; Friedrich Engel-Jánosi, 'Der Wiener Juridisch-Politische Leseverein', *Mitteilungen des Vereines für Geschichte der Stadt Wien*, 4 (1923), 58–66.

23. For 'Your instruments are force of arms . . .', see Kübeck, *Tagebücher*, vol. 2 (Vienna, 1909), 626; Isabella Schüler, *Franz Anton Graf von Kolowrat-Liebsteinsky (1778–1861)*, (Munich, 2016), 295–6.

24. Schüler, *Franz Anton Graf von Kolowrat-Liebsteinsky*, 232–43; Siemann, *Metternich*, 810–1; R. John Rath, *The Viennese Revolution of 1848* (Austin, TX, 1957), 114–6.

25. T. W. C. Blanning, *The Origins of the French Revolutionary Wars* (London and New York, 1986), 37.

CHAPTER 23: 1848: VON NEUMANN'S DIARY AND RADETZKY'S MARCH

1. *The Diary of Philipp von Neumann*, ed. E. Beresford Chancellor, vol. 2 (London, 1928), 276–8 (adjusted).

2. Wolfram Siemann, *Metternich. Stratege und Visionär, Eine Biografie*, 2nd ed. (Munich, 2017), 833–5; Friedrich Rückert, *Liedertagebuch 1848–1849* (Göttingen, 2002), 478.

3. For 'I'm the sovereign . . .', see C. A. Macartney, *The Habsburg Empire, 1790–1918*, 2nd ed. (London, 1971), 330.

4. Thomas Kletečka, 'Einleitung', in *Die Protokolle des österreichischen Ministerrates*, Abt. 1: *Die Ministerien des Revolutionsjahres 1848*, ed. Kletečka (Vienna, 1996), ix–xlviii (x)

5. *Deutscher Kalender für die Bukowina für das Jahr 1935* (Chernivtsi, 1935), 51–63; Theodor Gomperz, *Essays und Erinnerungen* (Stuttgart and Leipzig, 1905), 19.

6. For 'The whole chancellery is in a complete state . . .'. see *Diary of Philipp von Neumann*, vol. 2, 281.

7. *Die Protokolle des österreichischen Ministerrates*, Abt. 1, 273.

8. *Die Protokolle des österreichischen Ministerrates*, Abt. 1, 417, 440.

9. William H. Stiles, *Austria in 1848–49*, vol. 1 (New York, 1852), 385.

10. *Die Protokolle des österreichischen Ministerrates*, Abt. 1, 505.

11. Alan Sked, *Radetzky: Imperial Victor and Military Genius* (London and New York, 2011), 176.

12. Thomas Stockinger, 'Die Urwahlen zum konstituerenden Reichstag des Jahren 1848', *MIÖG*, 114 (2006), 96–122.

13. *Die Protokolle des österreichischen Ministerrates*, Abt. 1, 155, 192–3.

14. Alex Drace-Francis, 'Cultural Currents and Political Choices: Romanian Intellectuals in the Banat to 1848', *Austrian History Yearbook*, 36 (2005), 65–93 (90).

15. *Kossuth Lajos összes munkái*, ed. Aladár Mód et al. vol. 12 (Budapest, 1957), 22–34.

16. For 'the existence of a Kingdom of Hungary . . .', see Martyn Rady, 'Lajos Kossuth, Domokos Kosáry and Hungarian Foreign Policy, 1848–49', in *'Lajos Kossuth Sent Word . . . ' Papers Delivered on the Occasion of the Bicentenary of Kossuth's Birth*, ed. László Péter et al. (London, 2003), 105–17 (111).

17. László Péter, *Az Elbától keletre. Tanulmányok a magyar és kelet-európai történelemből* (Budapest, 1998), 75.

18. For 'would never allow the legal bond . . .', see Macartney, *The Habsburg Empire*, 385; Istvan Deak, *The Lawful Revolution: Louis Kossuth and the Hungarians 1848–1849* (London, 2001), 139. For 'let's be good friends', see Zoltán I. Tóth, 'The Nationality Problem in Hungary in 1848–1849', *Acta Historica* (Budapest), 4 (1955), 235–77 (237).

19. *Diary of Philipp von Neumann*, vol. 2, 297–302 (adjusted).

20. Eugene Bagger, *Franz Joseph. Eine Persönlichkeits-Studie* (Zurich, Leipzig, and Vienna, 1928), 136.

CHAPTER 24: FRANZ JOSEPH'S EMPIRE, SISI, AND HUNGARY

1. Tibor Frank, 'Marketing Hungary: Kossuth and the Politics of Propaganda', in *'Lajos Kossuth Sent Word . . . ' Papers Delivered on the Occasion of the Bicentenary of Kossuth's Birth*, ed. László Péter et al. (London, 2003), 221–49.

2. Ágnes Deák, *From Habsburg Neo-Absolutism to the Compromise 1849–1867* (Boulder, CO, and New York, 2008), 75–6; for the 'scaffold and the bloodbath', see Joseph Redlich, *Emperor Francis Joseph of Austria: A Biography* (London, 1929), 64, citing Baron Wessenberg-Ampringen; Róbert Hermann, 'Haynau táborszernagy', *Múlt és jövő*, no. 2 (1999), 89–107 (103).

3. HHStA Kabinettsarchiv. Kabinettskanzlei Geheimakten. Nachlass Schwarzenberg, Karton 10, fasc. 4, no. 200, fols. 97–108 (16 December 1848); *Allgemeine Zeitung* (Augsburg), 12 March 1849, 1085; *Wiener Zeitung*, 8 March 1849.

4. *Reichsverfassung für das Kaiserthum Österreich* (Vienna, 1849).

5. Rudolf Kiszling, *Fürst Felix Schwarzenberg. Der politische Lehrmeister Kaiser Franz Josephs* (Graz and Cologne, 1952), 128–9.

6. J. F. Faber, *Joseph II. und Franz Joseph I. Eine historische Parallel* (Stuttgart, 1863), 51; *Allgemeine Zeitung* (Augsburg), 15 January 1868, 212; Waltraud Heindl, *Josephinische Mandarine. Bürokratie und Beamte in Österreich* (Vienna, Cologne, and Weimar, 2013), 36.

7. Gyula Szekfű, *Három nemzedék. Egy hanyatló kor története* (Budapest, 1920), 239, 258–60.

8. For 'a Josephinist fantasy come true', see Robin Okey, *The Habsburg Monarchy c. 1765–1918: From Enlightenment to Eclipse* (Basingstoke and London, 2001), 166.

9. Lajos Králik, *A magyar ügyvédség. Az ügyvédi kar*, vol. 1 (Budapest, 1903), 265–8.

10. Anon. (Josef Wizdalek), *Acht Jahre Amtsleben in Ungarn von einem k.k. Stuhlrichter in Disponibilität* (Leipzig, 1861), 15, 23.

11. Heindl, *Josephinische Mandarine*, 56; MNL OL O142 Justizministerium. Akten-Ungarn, fasc. 1–2, *passim*.

12. For the British ambassador's report, see Jonathan Steinberg, *Bismarck: A Life* (Oxford, 2011), 152.

13. *The Bankers' Magazine and Statistical Register*, vol. 15 (New York, 1860–61), 720; Pieter Judson, *Exclusive Revolutionaries: Liberal Politics, Social Experience, and National Identity in the Austrian Empire, 1848–1914* (Ann Arbor, MI, 1996), 75; Plener's advice was subsequently published as Anon., *Die Aufgaben Österreichs* (Leipzig, 1860), 39, 70.

14. Fritz Fellner, 'Das Februarpatent von 1861', *MIÖG*, 63 (1955), 549–64 (552); for the National Bank, see the speech of Plener, reported in *Pressburger Zeitung*, 20 December 1861.

15. László Péter, 'The Hungarian Diaetalis Tractatus and the Imperial Constitutional Systems: A Comparison', *Central Europe*, 6 (2008), 47–64 (57).

16. Jean-Paul Bled, *Franz Joseph* (Oxford and Cambridge, MA, 1992), 200–2.

17. Steinberg, *Bismarck*, 174; A. J. P. Taylor, *Bismarck: The Man and the Statesman* (London, 1968), 39.

18. For 'This is my constitution', See Péter, 'The Hungarian Diaetalis Tractatus', 56.

19. For 'a world away from being the ideal wife', see Cissy Klastersky, *Der alte Kaiser wie nur Einer ihn sah* (Vienna, 1929), 37–8; Sabine Fellner and Katrin Unterreiner, *Morphium, Cannabis und Cocain. Medizin und Rezepte des Kaiserhauses* (Vienna, 2008), 108–17;

Exhibition 'Tabak beim Hof', Frastanz bei Feldkirch, 6–21 October 2007; John Welfare, *The Sporting Empress: The Story of Elizabeth of Austria and Bay Middleton* (London, 1975), 133; *Marie Valérie von Österreich. Das Tagebuch der Lieblingstochter von Kaiserin Elisabeth*, ed. Martha and Horst Schad (Munich, Berlin and Zurich, 2005), 141.

20. *Briefe Kaiser Franz Josephs an Kaiserin Elisabeth 1859–1898*, ed. Georg Nostitz-Rieneck, 2 vols. (Vienna and Munich, 1966).

21. *Briefe Kaiser Franz Josephs*, vol. 1, 38, 41.

22. Sándor Márki, *Erzsébet Magyarország kiralynéja 1867–1898* (Budapest, 1899), 57–8.

23. For 'in these hard times . . . ', see *Briefe Kaiser Franz Josephs*, vol. 1, 58.

24. For Andrássy's opinion, see Egon Cesar Corti, *Elisabeth, die seltsame Frau* (Graz, 1953), 162.

CHAPTER 25: MAXIMILIAN, MEXICO, AND ROYAL DEATHS

1. Tina Schwenk, *Maximilian I: A Habsburg on Montezuma's Throne*, PhD thesis (University of Stirling, 2010), 14.

2. Gabriele Praschl-Bichler, *"Ich bin bloss Corvetten-Capitän". Private Briefe Kaiser Maximilians und seiner Familie* (Vienna, 2006), 154.

3. Maximilian, *Aus meinem Leben*, 7 vols. (Leipzig, 1867), vol. 2, 24, 68–71, 159, 163–4.

4. For 'severity in the event of the smallest revolt', see M. M. McAllen, *Maximilian and Carlota: Europe's Last Empire in Mexico* (San Antonio, TX, 2014), 32.

5. For 'a wise tyrant', see *Aus meinem Leben*, vol. 6, 17, 164.

6. Edmundo O'Gorman, *La supervivencia política novo-hispana. Reflexiones sobre el manarquismo mexicano* (Mexico City, 1969), 83. See also Erika Pani, 'Dreaming of a Mexican Empire: The Political Projects of the "Imperialistas"', *HAHR* 82 no 1 (2002), 1–31 (1–4).

7. McAllen, *Maximilian and Carlota*, 124.

8. Joan Haslip, *The Crown of Mexico: Maximilian and His Empress Carlota* (New York, 1972), 206.

9. *Reglamento para el Servicio y Ceremonial de la Corte* (Mexico City, 1866), 509.

10. Érika Pani, 'El proyecto de Estado de Maximiliano a través de la vida cortesana y del ceremonial público', *Historia Mexicana*, 45, no. 2 (1995), 423–60 (427–9).

11. Robert H. Duncan, *For the Good of the Country: State and Nation Building During Maximilian's Mexican Empire, 1864–67*, PhD thesis (University of California, Irvine, 2001).

12. Rodolfo Batiza, 'Código Civil del Imperio Mexicano', *Boletín Mexicano de Derecho Comparado*, 41 (1981), 571–86.

13. For 'will have nothing to sustain him . . . ', see McAllen, *Maximilian and Carlota*, 65. For 'What a beautiful day', see Haslip, *Crown of Mexico*, 498.

14. McAllen, *Maximilian and Carlota*, 386–7.

15. John Elderfield, *Manet and the Execution of Maximilian* (New York, 2006).

16. For 'we may still look forward to good sport', see Donald W. Miles, *Cinco de Mayo* (Lincoln, NE, 2006), 243.

17. Dina Gusejnova, *European Elites and Ideas of Empire 1917–1957* (Cambridge, 2016), 3–10.

CHAPTER 26: THE POLITICS OF DISCONTENT AND THE 1908 JUBILEE

1. Alexander Maxwell, 'The Handsome Man with Hungarian Moustache and Beard', *Cultural and Social History*, 12 (2015), 51–76 (64); Alexander Maxwell, 'Nationalizing Sexuality: Sexual Stereotypes in the Habsburg Empire', *Journal of the History of Sexuality*, 14 (2005), 266–90.

2. Alexander Maxwell, 'National Alcohol in Hungary's Reform Era: Wine, Spirits, and the Patriotic Imagination', *Central Europe*, 12 (2014), 117–35 (129).

3. Oto Luthar, 'The Slice of Desire: Intercultural Practices Versus National Loyalties', in *Understanding Multiculturalism: The Habsburg Central European Experience*, ed. Johannes Feichtinger and Gary B. Cohen (New York and Oxford, 2014), 161–73 (166–7); Tara Zahra, 'Imagined Noncommunities: National Indifference as a Category of Analysis', *Slavic Review*, 69 (2010), 93–119.

4. *Az 1881. évi elején végrehajtott népszámlálás*, vol. 1 (Budapest, 1882), 222–3.

5. Heindl, *Josephinische Mandarine*, 99–120.

6. Gerald Stourzh, *Der Umfang der österreichischen Geschichte* (Vienna, Cologne, and Graz, 2011), 284; Hugh and Christopher Seton-Watson, *The Making of a New Europe: R.W. Seton-Watson and the Last Years of Austria-Hungary* (London, 1981), 33.

7. Gerald Stourzh, 'Die Idee der nationalen Gleichberechtigung im alten Österreich', in *Nationale Vielfalt und gemeinsamen Erbe*, ed. Erhard Busek and Stourzh (Vienna and Munich, 1990), 39–47.

8. For 'a condition of even and well-modulated discontent', see C. A. Macartney, *The Habsburg Empire, 1790–1918* (London, 1971), 615.

9. *National Romanticism: The Formation of National Movements*, ed. Balázs Trencsényi and Michal Kopecek (Budapest and New York, 2007), 27–32.

10. Ernst Bruckmüller, 'National Consciousness and Education in Imperial Austria', in *The Limits of Loyalty: Imperial Symbolism, Popular Allegiances, and State Patriotism in the Late Habsburg Monarchy*, ed. Laurence Cole and Daniel L. Unowsky (New York and Oxford, 2007), 11–35 (19–21).

11. Called at the time 'a chafing dish with spirit lamp'. See *New York Times*, 17 March 1908, 1.

12. For 'Thanks to the wise government of our emperor . . . ', see *Die österreichisch-ungarische Monarchie in Wort und Bild*, vol. 17: *Mähren und Schlesien* (Vienna, 1897), 542. For 'Let the peoples of these lands love . . . ', see Christiane Zintzen, 'Einleitung' in *Die österreichisch-ungarische Monarchie in Wort und Bild. Aus dem Kronprinzenwerk des Erzherzog Rudolf*, ed. Zintzen (Vienna, 1999), 9–20.

13. Erika Szívós, *Az öröklött város. Városi tér, kultúra és emlékezet a 19–21. században* (Budapest, 2014), 115–29.

14. *Neues Wiener Journal*, 12 June 1908, 5.

15. Steven Beller, 'Kraus's Firework: State Consciousness Raising in the 1908 Jubilee Parade in Vienna and the Problem of Austrian Identity', in *Staging the Past: The Politics of Commemoration in Habsburg Central Europe, 1848 to the Present*, ed. Maria Bucur and Nancy M. Wingfield (West Lafayette, IN, 2001), 46–71 (57), citing *Neue Freie Presse*, 11 June 1908 (PM edition), 4–5; *Arbeiter-Zeitung*, 12 June 1908, 1.

16. *Das interessante Blatt*, 25 June 1908, 3; Megan Brandow-Faller, 'Folk Art on Parade: Modernism, Primitivism and Nationalism at the 1908 *Kaiserhuldigungsfestzug*', *AS*, 25 (2017), 98–117 (110); Adolf Loos, 'Ornament and Crime' (1908), in Ulrich Conrads,

Programs and Manifestoes on 20th-Century Architecture, trans. Michael Bullock (Cambridge, MA, 1970), 21.

17. Karl Kraus, 'Nachträgliche Vorurteile gegen den Festzug', *Die Fackel*, 10, no. 257–8 (1908), 9.

18. *Wiener Diözesanblatt* (1898, no 22), 255–6.

19. James Shedel, 'Emperor, Church, and People: Religion and Dynastic Loyalty During the Golden Jubilee of Franz Joseph', *Catholic Historical Review*, 76 (1990), 71–92 (81–9).

20. Daniel L. Unowsky, *Pomp and Politics of Patriotism: Imperial Celebrations in Habsburg Austria, 1848–1916* (West Lafayette, IN, 2005), 120–44.

21. For 'If we look beyond him . . . ', see Beller, 'Kraus's Firework', 51.

CHAPTER 27: EXPLORERS, JEWS, AND THE WORLD'S KNOWLEDGE

1. Brigitte Fuchs, *'Rasse', 'Volk', Geschlecht. Anthropologische Diskurse in Österreich 1850–1960* (Frankfurt and New York, 2003), 127; Mathieu Gotteland, 'Les Conséquences de la Première Guerre mondiale sur la présence impériale austro-hongroise en Chine', *Guerres mondiales et conflits contemporains*, 256 (2014), 7–18 (8).

2. *Vasárnapi Újság*, 1 May 1904, 294–5; Ferdinand de Lesseps, *A History of the Suez Canal: A Personal Narrative* (Edinburgh and London, 1876), 23; Lawrence Sondhaus, *Naval Policy of Austria-Hungary, 1867–1918* (West Lafayette, IN, 1994), 186–7; Simon Loidl, 'Colonialism Through Emigration: Publications and Activities of the Österreichisch-Ungarische Kolonialgesellschaft (1894–1918)', *AS*, 20 (2012), 161–75.

3. Franz Ferdinand von Österreich-Este, *Tagebuch meiner Reise um die Erde 1892– 1893*, ed. Frank Gerbert (Vienna, 2013).

4. For 'soirees, balls, and dinners . . . ', see Sondhaus, *Naval Policy of Austria-Hungary*, 88.

5. Barbara Plankensteiner, 'Endstation Museum. Österreichische Reisende sammeln Ethnographica', in *k.u.k. Kolonial. Habsburgermonarchie und europäische Herrschaft in Afrika*, ed. Walter Sauer (Vienna, Cologne, and Weimar, 2002), 257–88 (271).

6. Sabine Fellner and Katrin Unterreiner, *Morphium, Cannabis und Cocain. Medizin und Rezepte des Kaiserhauses* (Vienna, 2008), 128–9.

7. For 'The Javanese are in stature . . . ', see *Reise der österreichischen Fregatte Novara um die Erde* (Anthropologischer Theil 3: Ethnographie), ed. Friedrich Müller (Vienna, 1868), 75; Ferdinand Khull-Kholwald, 'Dr Augustin Weisbach', *Mitteilungen des Naturwissenschaftlichen Vereines für Steiermark*, 51 (1915), 8–16.

8. Fuchs, *'Rasse', 'Volk', Geschlecht*, 132; Margit Berner, 'From "Prisoner of War Studies" to Proof of Paternity: Racial Anthropologists and the Measuring of "Others"', in *Blood and Homeland: Eugenics and Racial Nationalism in Central and Southeast Europe, 1900– 1940*, ed. Marius Turda and Paul J. Weindling (Budapest and New York, 2007), 41–53; Letter of Adam Kuper, *Nature*, 364 (26 August 1993), 754.

9. Georg Friedrich Hamann, 'Emil Holub. Der selbsternannte Vertreter Österreich-Ungarns im Südlichen Afrika', in *k.u.k. Kolonial*, 163–95 (171).

10. For Christian von Mechel, see Kristine Patz, 'Schulzimmer', in *Die kaiserliche Gemäldegalerie in Wien und die Anfänge des öffentlichen Kunstmuseums*, ed. Gudrun Swoboda, vol. 2 (Vienna, Cologne, and Weimar, 2014), 437–57.

11. Matthew Rampley, 'From Potemkin Village to the Estrangement of Vision: Baroque Culture and Modernity in Austria Before and After 1918', *Austrian History Yearbook*,

47 (2016), 167–81 (174–5); Evonne Levy, *Baroque and the Political Language of Formalism (1845–1945)*, (Basle, 2015), 26.

12. Carl E. Schorske, *Fin-de-siècle Vienna: Politics and Culture* (London, 1980), 48.

13. Rampley, 'From Potemkin Village to the Estrangement of Vision', 174.

14. Adolf Loos, 'Ornament and Crime' (1908), in Ulrich Conrads, *Programs and Manifestoes on 20th-Century Architecture*, trans. Michael Bullock (Cambridge, MA, 1970), 19–24.

15. Berta Zuckerkandl, *My Life and History*, trans. John Sommerfield (New York, 1939), 25, 179.

16. James K. Wright, *Schoenberg, Wittgenstein and the Vienna Circle* (Bern, 2007), 156.

17. John Leslie, 'Der Ausgleich in der Bukowina von 1910. Zur österreichischen Nationalitätenpolitik vor dem Ersten Weltkrieg', in *Geschichte zwischen Freiheit und Ordnung. Gerald Stourzh zum 60. Geburtstag*, ed. Emil Brix et al. (Vienna, 1991), 113–44.

18. Ulrike Harmat, 'Obdachlosigkeit, Wohnungselend und Wohnungsnot, 1848–1914', in *Poverty, Charity and Social Welfare in Central Europe in the 19th and 20th Centuries*, ed. Olga Fejtova et al. (Newcastle upon Tyne, 2017), 297–342.

19. Robert S. Wistrich, *Laboratory for World Destruction: Germans and Jews in Central Europe* (London and Lincoln, NE, 2007), 37, citing Joseph Bloch in 1886. For 'a temple of art', see Ernest Gellner, *Language and Solitude: Wittgenstein, Malinowski and the Habsburg Dilemma* (Cambridge, 1998), 45.

20. Jamie A. M. Bulloch, *The Promotion of an Austrian Identity 1918–1938*, PhD thesis (University of London, 2002), 207.

CHAPTER 28: THE HUNTER AND THE HUNTED: FRANZ FERDINAND AND BOSNIA

1. For Rudolf's desire to watch someone die, see Julius Szeps, 'Berliner und Wiener Hofgeschichten', *Neues Wiener Journal*, 18 November 1923, 6–7.

2. *Wiener Zeitung*, 28 February 1889, 17; *Wiener Zeitung*, 13 September 1889, 17; *Bukowinaer Nachrichtungen*, 3 March 1889, 9.

3. Gordon Brook-Shepherd, *Archduke of Sarajevo: The Romance and Tragedy of Franz Ferdinand of Austria* (Boston and Toronto, 1984), 42.

4. For Rudolf's published observations, see Maarten Bijleveld, *Birds of Prey in Europe* (London and Basingstoke, 1974, and many later editions), 187, 244. For Ferdinand's game books, see Wladimir Aichelburg, *Erzherzog Franz Ferdinand und Artstetten* (Vienna, 1983), 34.

5. Rudolf Kiszling, 'Erzherzog Franz Ferdinand und seine Pläne für den Umbau der Donaumonarchie', *Der Donauraum*, 8 (1963), 261–6; Robert A. Kann, *Erzherzog Franz Ferdinand Studien* (Vienna, 1976), 153.

6. Samuel R. Williamson Jr, 'Influence, Power, and the Policy Process: The Case of Franz Ferdinand, 1906–1914', *The Historical Journal*, 17 (1974), 417–43 (418). For the coded information, see Zoltán Szász, 'Über den Quellenwert des Nachlasses von Franz Ferdinand', *Acta Historica* (Budapest), 25 (1979), 299–315 (304).

7. For 'much decisiveness in talking . . . ', see Kann, *Erzherzog Franz Ferdinand Studien*, 20.

8. Ian D. Armour, *Apple of Discord: The 'Hungarian Factor' in Austro-Serbian Relations, 1867–1881* (West Lafayette, IN, 2014), 26–30.

9. József Thim, *A magyarországi 1848–49-iki szerb fölkelés története*, vol. 1 (Budapest, 1940), 19, 108.

10. OeStA/HHStA, Kabinettsarchiv Minister Kolowrat Akten, 1829: 1700; 1830: 577; 1830: 1645; András Vári, 'Etnikai sztereotipiák a Habsburg Birodalomban a 19. század elején', *Tabula*, 3 (2000), 50–76 (58–68).

11. *A Handbook for Travellers in Southern Germany*, 5th ed. (London, 1850), 514; Sam White, 'Rethinking Disease in Ottoman History', *International Journal of Middle East Studies*, 42 (2010), 549–67 (557); Andre Gingrich, 'The Nearby Frontier: Structural Analyses of Myths of Orientalism', *Diogenes*, 60 (2015), 60–6.

12. For supplying the rebels through Kotor, see Karl Went von Römo, *Ein Soldatenleben* (Vienna, 1904), 158–9.

13. Scott W. Lackey, *The Rebirth of the Habsburg Army: Friedrich Beck and the Rise of the General Staff* (Westport, CT, and London, 1995), 74–5; Gunther E. Rothenberg, *The Army of Francis Joseph* (West Lafayette, IN, 1976), 97.

14. Emil Mattauschek, 'Einiges über die Degeneration des bosnisch-herzegowinischen Volkes,' *Jahrbücher für Psychiatrie und Neurologie*, 29 (1908), 134–48.

15. Brigitte Fuchs, 'Orientalizing Disease: Austro-Hungarian Policies of "Race", Gender, and Hygiene in Bosnia and Herzegovina, 1874–1914', in *Health, Hygiene and Eugenics in Southeastern Europe to 1945*, ed. Christian Promitzer et al. (Budapest and New York, 2011), 57–85; more generally, Anne McClintock, *Imperial Leather: Race, Gender, and Sexuality in the Colonial Context* (London and New York, 1995).

16. József Szlávy in 1882, cited in Zoltán Fónagy, 'Bosznia-Hercegovina integrációja az okkupáció után', *Történelmi Szemle*, 56 (2014), 27–60 (33).

17. Diana Reynolds-Cordileone, 'Displaying Bosnia: Imperialism, Orientalism, and Exhibitionary Cultures in Vienna and Beyond: 1878–1914', *AHY*, 46 (2015), 29–50 (32).

18. Marian Wenzel, 'Bosnian History and Austro-Hungarian Policy: The Zemaljski Muzej, Sarajevo, and the Bogomil Romance', *Museum Management and Curatorship*, 12 (1993), 127–42.

19. Nevenko Bartulin, *The Racial Idea in the Independent State of Croatia: Origins and Theory* (Leiden, 2014), 53–6.

20. Christopher Clark, *The Sleepwalkers: How Europe Went to War in 1914* (London, 2012), 105, 291.

21. Clark, *The Sleepwalkers*, 49.

CHAPTER 29: WORLD WAR AND DISSOLUTION

1. *The Times* (London), 29 June 1914, 9.

2. Sean McMeekin, *The Russian Origins of the First World War* (Cambridge, MA, 2011), 27; Christopher Clark, *The Sleepwalkers: How Europe Went to War in 1914* (London, 2012), 403.

3. Alexander Watson, *Ring of Steel: Germany and Austria-Hungary at War, 1914–1918* (London, 2014), 105; Manfried Rauchensteiner, *The First World War and the End of the Habsburg Monarchy, 1914–1918*, 2nd ed. (Vienna, Cologne, and Weimar, 2014), 95–96.

4. John Leslie, 'Österreich-Ungarn vor dem Kriegsausbruch', in *Deutschland und Europa in der Neuzeit. Festschrift für Karl von Aretin*, ed. Ralph Melville (Stuttgart, 1988), 661–84 (675).

5. Rauchensteiner, *The First World War*, 108.

6. For 'the most formidable document . . . This is war', see Rauchensteiner, *The First World War*, 113.

7. Steven Beller, *The Habsburg Monarchy 1815–1918* (Cambridge, 2018), 248.

8. Watson, *Ring of Steel*, 91.

9. Watson, *Ring of Steel*, 153.

10. For conditions on the Eastern Front, see now Béla Zombory-Moldován, *The Burning of the World—A Memoir of 1914* (New York, 2014).

11. Mark Thompson, *The White War: Life and Death on the Italian Front 1915–1919* (London, 2008), 2; F. R. Bridge, *The Habsburg Monarchy Among the Great Powers, 1815–1918* (New York, Oxford, and Munich, 1990), 364.

12. Jakub S. Beneš, 'The Green Cadres and the Collapse of Austria-Hungary in 1918', *Past and Present*, 236 (2017), 207–41.

13. Available at https://vimeo.com/132427132 (last accessed 18 February 2019).

14. For 'models of the most interesting racial types . . . ', see *Offizieller Katalog der Kriegsausstellung* (Vienna, 1916), 125.

15. Maureen Healy, 'Exhibiting a War in Progress: Entertainment and Propaganda in Vienna, 1914–1918', *AHY*, 31 (2000), 57–85 (85).

16. *Offizieller Katalog der Kriegsausstellung*, C.

17. John Deak and Jonathan E. Gumz, 'How to Break a State: The Habsburg Monarchy's Internal War, 1914–1918', *American Historical Review*, 122 (2017), 1105–36 (1123); Martin Moll, 'Österreichische Militärgerichtsbarkeit im Ersten Weltkrieg—"Schwert des Regimes"?' *Mitteilungen des Steiermärkischen Landesarchivs*, 50 (2001), 301–55 (315, 323).

18. Wienbibliothek im Rathaus, Polizeidirektion, *Stimmungsberichte aus dem Kriegszeit*, vol. 1916, no 2, 6 July, 13 July.

19. For 'The whole city is surrounded . . . ', see Z. A. B. Zeman, *The Break-Up of the Habsburg Empire 1914–1918* (Oxford, 1981), 98. See further Wienbibliothek im Rathaus, Polizeidirektion, *Stimmungsberichte aus dem Kriegszeit*, vol. 1916, no 2, 26 October, 23 November; Maureen Healy, *Vienna and the Fall of the Habsburg Empire: Total War and Everyday Life in World War One* (Cambridge, 2004), 305–9.

20. Alan Sked, *The Decline and Fall of the Habsburg Empire 1815–1918* (London and New York, 1989), 261.

21. For 'You hope to meet a thirty-year-old man . . . ', see Holger H. Herwig, *The First World War: Germany and Austria-Hungary 1914–1918*, 2nd ed. (London and New York, 2014), 241. For 'not understand why we make so much effort . . . ', see Rauchensteiner, *The First World War*, 643.

22. For 'all branches of the Slav race . . . ', see Bridge, *The Habsburg Monarchy Among the Great Powers*, 368.

CONCLUSION

1. Richard Mullen, 'Otto von Habsburg', *Contemporary Review*, 293 (September 2011), 274–86.

2. Berta Zuckerkandl, *My Life and History*, trans. John Sommerfield (London, 1938), 133.

3. Personal conversation, March 1990.

INDEX

Achilles, 157

Acontius, 105, 110

Adolf of Nassau, king of the Romans, 32–33

Adolphus, Gustavus, king of Sweden, 143

Adrian VI, pope, 69

AEIOU (Austria is to rule the whole world)
  Charles V and, 74
  Frederick III and, 46, 50
  imperial sponsorship of science and, 191–192, 294
  Maximilian I, Holy Roman Emperor and, 56
  meaning, 4–5, 46–47, 74, 136, 191–192, 208
  use in heraldry, 46–47

Aeneid (Virgil), 68

Agnes (granddaughter of Rudolf I), 35

Albert (brother of Frederick III), 45–46, 49

Albert I, king of the Romans (son of Rudolf I), 31–32

Albert II, king of the Romans, 43

Albert the Rich, 15, 18

Albert of Saxony, 215–217

Albert the Lame, 34, 36, 43

Albert the Wise, 23

Albert, governor of the Low Countries, 211–212

Albrecht, duke of Teschen, 244, 263

alchemy, 107–109, 112–115, 120, 192–193, 327

Alexander I, emperor of Russia, 230, 232, 235

Alexander I, king of Serbia, 277

Alexander II, emperor of Russia, 277, 306

Alexander the Great, 108, 295

Alexandra, queen (wife of Edward VII), 267

Alfonso X, king of Castile, 22

Altdorfer, Albrecht, 52

Ampringen, Johann, 151–152

Andrássy, Gyula, 265, 267, 305–306

Anna, empress of Russia, 182

Annals of Basle, 23

Anna of the Tyrol, 125

Anne (daughter of Wladislas Jagiello), 60, 75

Anne, queen of Great Britain, 174

Anne Charlotte (sister-in-law of Maria Theresa), 213–214

Aragon, 7, 32, 53, 58, 60, 65, 67, 93, 165, 175, 211, 270

architecture
  Baroque, 173–177
  Belvedere Palace, 173
  Castle Habsburg, 14–15
  Central American, 160–161, 174
  Champs Élysées, 274

architecture (*continued*)
  classical, 295
  Escorial Palace, 85–86
  Fellner and Helmer (studio), 296
  Gothic, 38, 295
  Hall of Giants, 209
  historicism, 295–297
  Hofburg, Innsbruck, 57, 209
  Hofburg, Vienna, 1–5, 120, 173,
      175
  Innsbruck, 57
  mausoleums, 39–40, 55, 85, 135–136,
      215
  Mexico City under Maximilian I,
      emperor of Mexico, 274
  nationalist, 296–297
  neo-Baroque, 296–298, 300
  neo-Gothic, 25
  neo-orientalist, 308
  Renaissance, 296
  the Ring, Vienna, 259, 295–296
  Romanesque, 38, 297
  Schönbrunn Palace, 189–190,
      197–198
  St Stephen's Cathedral, 38, 46
  Vienna Secession, 297–298, 300,
      308
  See also castles; gardens; palaces
Arcimboldo, 114
Arminius, 132
Árpád dynasty, 31
Arthur, king of England, 55
art movements, 177, 227–228, 297–298,
    300, 328
  See also architecture; the Baroque Age
Ascanian dynasty, 31
assassinations, 277–278, 286, 288, 310,
    312–313, 320
Auersperg, Anton von, 241
Augustine, Saint, 108
Augustus, 35, 104
Austria, duchy of
  as Eucharistia, 137
  Habsburg move to, 34
  'Happy Austria', 61
  Inner Austria, 119

Ottokar II and, 26–29
  mythology, 34–37, 46–48, 55
  Pseudo-Henry and Greater Privilege,
      36–37
  partition into Upper and Lower,
      41–42, 45
  religion in, 81, 118, 120–121, 124,
      128, 137, 146, 171–172, 228
  rights and titles regarding, 36–38
  symbolism of, 47–48
  See also AEIOU
Austrian Empire
  budget, 240
  constitutional division, 266
  formation, 231, 233–234
  hopes of dominating German
      Confederation, 257
  insubordination of the generals,
      253–254
  preeminence in Europe, 241
  threat of partition in 1848, 246,
      250–251
Austrian East India Company, 190–191
Austrian Plutarch (Hormayr), 284
Austro-Hungarian Empire, 266
  Bosnia-Herzegovina, 306–309
  collapse, 300, 321–323, 327
  contested border with Ottomans,
      304–305
  Franz Ferdinand's planned
      reorganizations, 303, 310
  government, 266
  nationalist divisions, 280–284,
      286–287, 327
  World War I and, 315–316
Austro-Hungarian Monarchy in Word and
      Image. See Crown Prince's Work
      (edited by Rudolf, son of Franz
      Joseph)
automata, 179–181
autos-da-fé (burning at the stake), 91–92,
      161

Babenberg dynasty, 26, 34–35, 47, 327
Bach, Alexander, 260
Baillou, Jean de, 194

Barbarossa, Turkish admiral, 70
Baroque Age, 4, 152, 169–170
   architecture, 173–176, 296
   in churches, 170–171, 176–177,
     212–213
   court theatre, 172–173
   Habsburg promotion of, 327
   origin, criticism, 169
   Plague Column, as epitome of,
     173–174
   public piety, 171–172, 228
   religious plays, 172, 177
Báthory, Elizabeth, 123
Batthyány, Louis, 251, 255–256
Bauer, Otto, 284, 298
Bavaria, 24, 26–27, 35, 70, 117, 127,
     129, 133, 143–144, 146, 153,
     155–156, 183, 207, 230–231,
     233–234, 264
Beck, Friedrich von, 306
Beethoven, Ludwig, 233
Belgiojoso, Ludovico di, 215–216
Berchtold, Leopold, 310, 314
Bethlen, Gabriel, prince of Transylvania,
     133
Bianca Sforza (second wife of Maximilian
     I, Holy Roman Emperor), 58
the Bible
   apocalyptic readings, 6, 44, 123,
     132–133
   New Testament, 82
   Old Testament, 5, 54, 80, 86, 133
   Ten Commandments, 12
Bismarck, Otto von, 262–263, 306
Black Hand, 310, 312
'Black Legend' (literary genre), 95, 141
Bligh, William, 190
Bloch-Bauer, Adele, 299
Blomberg, Barbara, 97
Bocskai, Stephen, 123
Bodin, Jean, 147
Bohemia
   diets, 77–78, 124, 130, 132,
     134–135
   in 1848, 247–248
   religion in, 28, 43, 146

Thirty Years War and, 130–135, 137,
     141, 285
   wealth of, 27
   See also Ottokar II, king of Bohemia
Bolts, William, 190–192, 194
Boniface VIII, pope, 32
Born, Ignaz von, 196–197, 205, 211, 223
Bosnia, 43, 304–305
Bosnia-Herzogovina, 306–308
'The Bosnians Are Coming' (*Die Bosniaken
     kommen,* Wagnes), 309
botany, 191–194, 240, 281, 293, 303, 327
Bourbon dynasty, 174, 183, 233, 267
Brahe, Tycho, 113
Brătianu, Ion, 313
Brazil, 138–139, 231, 267
The Brothers' Quarrel (Grillparzer), 123
Bruck, Karl Ludwig von, 261
Brukenthal, Samuel von, 196
Bruno, Giordano, 113
Burgkmair, Hans, 56
burial and funerary practices, 136,
     160–161, 199–200, 204
   See also crypts
Burke, Edmund, 196

Caesar, Julius, 36–37, 40, 47, 55, 295
Calvin, John, 80
Calvinism, 80–82, 125–126, 132–133,
     146, 152, 204
   See also Protestantism
cameralism, 202–204, 206, 208, 210
Canova, Antonio, 215
Carlos (son of Philip II), 94, 110
Carlos I, king of Portugal, 277
Caroline Augusta (wife of Francis II), 228
cartography. *See* maps
Casanova, Giacomo, 214
Caspar, Mizzi, 301–302
Castile, 22, 64, 65, 90, 93, 94, 164, 166,
     211
Castlereagh (Lord Robert Stewart), 235
castles, 14–15
   See also architecture
Catherine the Great, empress of Russia,
     186, 204

Catholicism and Catholic Church
  the Baroque and, 170–174, 176–177,
    212–213
  Catholic Enlightenment, 214
  censorship and, 219–220
  colonial missionary activity, 88, 159,
    166, 213, 237
  Edict of Restitution, 142–143
  Enlightenment and, 201
  freemasonry condemned by, 195
  under Joseph II, 203–204, 207
  Mass (Eucharist), 5, 78, 81, 110, 118,
    136
  in Mexico, 272, 275
  in New World, 167
  papacy, 6, 22, 24, 29, 43, 59
  reconversion, 120–122, 134, 146
  Reformation and, 67–68
  See also Jesuits; Protestantism;
    religious conflict; religious
    toleration; Spanish
    Inquisition
Catholic League, 129, 133, 141
celebrity, 277–278, 288, 325
Celtis, Conrad, 52
censorship, 91, 205, 214, 219–224,
    226–228, 239–240, 245, 258,
    301–302, 309, 317–319
censuses, 187–188, 281, 307
  See also population demographics
Cervantes, 66
Charlemagne, 6, 132, 327
Charles, duke of Teschen, 229–230
Charles Albert, king of Sardinia-Piedmont,
    248
Charles Alexander of Lorraine, 213–215
Charles I, king of England, 95
Charles of Styria, archduke of Austria, 93,
    119–121, 127
Charles II the Bewitched, king of Spain, 3,
    156, 167–168, 174, 211
Charles IV of Luxembourg, Holy Roman
    Emperor, 33–34, 37–38
Charles of Lorraine, 154–155
Charles the Bold, duke of Burgundy,
    48–50, 162

Charles V, Holy Roman Emperor, 60–61,
    64–74, 85, 95, 119, 160
  Don John and, 97–98
  governance, 8, 64–67, 72, 74, 92
  list of titles, 7–8
  Maximilian I, emperor of Mexico and,
    270, 272–273
  regencies for, 57, 67, 98, 211
  world-rulership, 69, 175
Charles VI, Holy Roman Emperor, 169,
    174–177, 210, 213–214
  Court Library and, 3–4, 9, 191
  numismatic collection, 193–194
  succession, 174–175, 181–184
Charles VIII, king of France, 57
Charles VII of Bavaria, Holy Roman
    Emperor, 183–184
Charlotte (Carlota) of Belgium, 271–274,
    276–277
charters. *See* forgeries; inheritance
China, 90, 140, 191, 213, 236, 291
Chotek, Sophie, 302–303
'Chronicle of the Ninety-Five Lords',
    46–48
Churchill, John, duke of Marlborough, 156
Churchill, Winston, 156
civil service, 187, 201, 258–260, 281–283
  See also state bureaucracy and
    centralization
Clement VII, pope, 68
Clement XIV, pope, 219
Clusius (Charles de l'Écluse), 192
colonies and colonialism, 56, 72, 88–92,
    234, 292
  government, 67, 88, 159–161, 166
  Habsburg loss of, 168, 190, 291
  New World, 64, 65, 99, 192, 194
  racial hierarchy within, 166–167
  revenue and commerce, 65, 237–238
  Thirty Years War and, 138–140
  viceroyalties, 88, 161, 166
Columbus, Christopher, 99, 159, 295
Confederation of the Rhine, 231
confessionalization, 120–122
congress system, 235–236
  See also Metternich, Clemens von

Conrad of Teck, king of the Romans, 31
Constantine the Great, 104
constitutions
    April Laws, 250–251, 253, 256, 263,
      265
    Cisleithanian, 280
    Compromise (Settlement) of 1867,
      265–267
    February Patent, 261–262
    Leopold II's promises of, 225
    March (Decreed) Constitution,
      257–258
    Maria Theresa, 186
    October Diploma, 261
    Peace of Westphalia, 146
    Renewed Constitution, 134–135
    as response to revolutions of 1848,
      245–246, 249–251, 257
Cook, James, 190–191, 220
Cordier, Charles, 159
Cortes (of Castile), 65, 93, 164–165
Cortés, Hernando, 64, 90
Cortés, Martin, 92
Corts-General (of Aragon), 65, 93, 164,
    165
Così fan tutte (Mozart), 228
Council of Basle, 78
Council of Trent, 71, 170
The Count of Habsburg (ballad), 15
Court Library (Hofbibliothek), 3–5, 175,
    191–192, 194, 196, 220
Coxe, William, 14
Croce, Benedetto, 169
Crown Prince's Work (edited by Rudolf,
    son of Franz Joseph),
    285–286
crusades, 6, 24, 52, 59, 70
crypts
    Augustinian Church, 135, 215
    Capuchin Crypt, 12, 136, 326
    'catacomb saints', 171
    Escorial Palace, 85–86, 103, 168
    Ferdinand of Aragon's, 270
    Gaming (Lower Austria), 34
    Graz, 144
    Loreto Chapel, 135–136, 144

    Maximilian I, Holy Roman Emperor's
      in Innsbruck, 54–55
    Muri Abbey, 12, 323
    Speyer Cathedral, 31
    St George's Chapel, Wiener Neustadt,
      63
    St Stephen's Cathedral, Vienna,
      38–40, 136
    Yuste, 160
Csokor, Franz, 300
Cymburga (mother of Frederick III), 44–45

Dante Alighieri, 29, 68
Darwinism, 294, 314
Deák, Ferenc, 263, 265
Dee, John, 113
depression, 107, 111–112
Diet of Worms (1521), 67, 69, 74, 81
Dietrichstein, Adam von, 110
diets (German and Central European
    parliaments), 77, 79, 81,
    123–124, 128, 182, 309
    Bohemian, 43, 77–78, 124, 130, 132,
      134–135
    Carniolan, 120, 186
    Ferdinand II and, 128, 148
    Holy Roman Empire, 22, 34, 38, 59,
      147–149, 156
    Leopold I and, 150–151, 153, 156
    Maria Theresa and, 182–183, 186
    at Regensburg, 147–149
    revolutions of 1848 and, 244,
      248–249
    taxes and treasuries, 42, 56, 76, 119
diets, Hungarian, 77, 183, 186, 206–207,
    225, 251, 263–264
    religious freedom and, 122–125,
      129–130
    succession and, 77, 79, 123–124,
      129–130, 155, 183, 207
    See also Hungary
Dimitrijević, Dragutin, 310, 312
Diocletian, 152
Disraeli, Benjamin, 262–263, 306
divine right of kings and divinity of rulers,
    162, 164, 166–167, 202, 233

Don Giovanni (Mozart), 222
Don John, 97–98, 101–103, 211
Draga (wife of Alexander I, king of Serbia),
    277, 310
Dürer, Albrecht, 52, 55, 111–113
Dutch Republic. *See* Low Countries

Eclogues (Virgil), 104
economy
    Austrian Mediterranean commerce,
        237–238
    Austrian National Bank, 261
    banking collapse of 1873, 282
    Bosnia-Herzegovina, 308–309
    under Charles V, 65–66
    currency, 238, 241, 251
    under Francis II, 229
    under Franz Joseph, 258–259
    Habsburg income, early sources of,
        17–18
    Hungarian, 76, 251, 286
    under Joseph II, 206
    under Leopold II, 225
    lotteries, 229
    Low Countries, 213–214
    under Maximilian I, Holy Roman
        Emperor, 56–58
    merchant marine, 237
    mines, 27, 39, 57, 65, 76, 88, 121, 166,
        308
    under Philip II, 88–90, 93–94
    rents, 228
    shipping, 237, 292
    slave trade, 100, 138, 146, 155, 166,
        237–238
    spice trade, 99, 140
    tolls, 17, 19, 21, 23, 33, 39, 76
    trade companies, 138, 140, 146,
        190–191, 237, 292
    trade with China, 236
    wartime mobilization, 319–320
    World War I rationing, 317, 319–320
    See also taxation
education, 202–203, 210, 275, 280–281,
    308
Edward VII, king of Great Britain, 267

Eleonora Gonzaga of Mantua, 135
Elizabeth (daughter of Sigismund, Holy
        Roman Emperor, wife of Albert
        II), 43
Elizabeth (Sisi, wife of Franz Joseph),
        264–267, 270, 277–278, 286,
        288, 293
Elizabeth Christine of Brunswick,
        181–182, 210
Elizabeth I, queen of England, 98, 110
The Emerald Tablet (alchemical text),
        107–109, 115
England, Britain, 90, 184, 201, 213,
        235–236
    Napoleonic Wars, 229–230, 233
    Seven Years War, 185
    War of the Spanish Succession, 156,
        174–175
    World War I, 315, 321
Enlightenment, 200–201, 204, 214, 221,
        224–225
Erlach, Joseph Emanuel Fischer von, 296
Ernest of Babenberg, 36
Eroica (Beethoven), 233
Etichonid dynasty, 12
Eucharist (Host), 5, 78, 81, 171–172
    Habsburg devotion to, 5–6, 104, 136,
        167, 172, 212
Eugene of Savoy, 156, 162, 173, 176, 295
European Union, 326–327
excommunications, 22, 28, 39, 67, 131, 205
exploration, 271, 292–293, 302
Eyck, Jan van, 215

Farinelli, 217
fascism, 300
    See also nationalism
Fendi, Peter, 228
Ferdinand (son of Philip II), 104
Ferdinand, Cardinal-Infante (son of Philip
        III), 144
Ferdinand I, emperor of Austria, 231, 240,
        243–245, 248, 250, 252–254,
        256
Ferdinand I, Holy Roman Emperor, 11,
        60–61, 64, 67–68, 72, 74–83

Ferdinand of the Tyrol, archduke of
Austria, 119–121
Ferdinand II, Holy Roman Emperor,
126–136, 141–144, 146, 151,
172, 182
Ferdinand III, Holy Roman Emperor,
143–149
Ferdinand IV, king of the Romans,
148–149
Ferdinand of Aragon, 58, 60, 64, 270
Fischer, Ignaz, 196
forgeries, 13, 36–39, 41, 45, 47, 183
See also inheritance
Fortinbras effect, 18–19, 75, 181
Foucault, Michel, 181
France
Congress of Vienna's results for, 234
congress system, 235–236
French Revolution, 225–226
Low Countries occupation, 213
medieval wealth, 56
Mediterranean acquisitions, 230
religion in, 117, 119, 121
Seven Years War, 185
Thirty Years War, 143–144
United States of America and, 271
War of the Spanish Succession, 174,
213
World War I and, 315–316, 321–322
See also Louis XIV, king of France;
Napoleon I, emperor of the
French; Napoleon III, emperor of
the French; revolutions
franchise, 249, 261–262, 283, 300
Francis I, king of France, 66–67, 78
Francis I, emperor of Austria. *See* Francis
II, Holy Roman Emperor
Francis II, Holy Roman Emperor, 226,
228–231, 234–236, 238–239,
240
Francis Stephen I, Holy Roman Emperor,
193–195, 209
freemasonry, 194–195, 197, 213
Maria Theresa and, 179, 182, 184,
189
Frankenstein (Shelley), 226

Franz Ferdinand, archduke of Austria,
11–12, 19, 292, 298, 302–304,
314, 321
assassination, 310, 312–313
Franz Joseph, emperor of Austria, 11,
260–267, 282–287, 294–296,
298
bureaucratic absolutism and
constitutionalism, 258, 261–262,
279, 283
childhood, 269–270
colonies, 291–292
finances, 261, 306
foreign policy calamities, 260–263
Franz Ferdinand and, 302, 313
Maximilian I, emperor of Mexico and,
269–273, 277
old age and death, 288, 289, 303, 320
reprisals for revolution, 256–257
succession, 250, 253–254
World War I and, 313–315
Franz Karl, archduke of Austria, 245,
253–254
Franz Salvator (husband of Marie Valerie),
318
Frederick I, Barbarossa, Holy Roman
Emperor, 18, 21–22, 36–37
Frederick II of Babenberg, duke of Austria,
26, 35
Frederick II, Holy Roman Emperor, 22–24,
26, 35
Frederick II, king of Prussia, 181, 183–186
Frederick III, Holy Roman Emperor, 43–51
character, 44–45, 48
Charles the Bold and, 48–49
Chronicle of the Ninety-Five Lords
and, 46–48
governance, 45–46
heraldry and, 46–47, 50
Maximilian I and, 50–51
relations with Matthias Corvinus,
49, 60
succession, 43, 50–51
wars, 48–49
See also AEIOU (Austria is to rule the
whole world)

Frederick of the Tyrol ('of the Empty
    Pockets'), 42
Frederick the Fair, 33
Frederick the Wise of Saxony, 67
Frederick V, king of Bohemia, 132–134,
    141–142
Frederick William II, king of Prussia, 225,
    236
Freemasonry, 194–198, 223–224
    Albert of Saxony and, 215
    artistic allusions to, 223–224
    Francis Stephen I and, 194–195, 197,
        213
    Franz Ferdinand's hatred of, 303
    government and, 195–198, 208, 224
    repression and resurgence, 226–227
Der Freischütz (The Marksman, Weber),
    228
Freud, Sigmund, 298, 300
Freydal (Maximilian I, Holy Roman
    Emperor), 52–53
Fugger family (bankers), 57, 60

Garcia II, king of Kongo, 139–140
gardens
    the Belvedere's, 173
    Franz Ferdinand's, 303
    the Hofburg's, 3
    Maximilian II's, 192
    Miramare's, 271
    Prague university's, 281
    Rudolf II's, 112
    the Schönbrunn's, 189, 197
    universities', 203
    Wallenstein's, 142
genealogy
    Babenberg dynasty's, 35
    Franz Ferdinand's, 11–12, 19
    genealogical romances (literary genre),
        46–48
    hazards of incest, 94–95, 177, 181
    Maximilian I, Holy Roman Emperor
        and, 53–55, 86
    See also incest; marriages
George, David Lloyd, 321
George I, king of Greece, 277

George of Brandenburg, 80
Germaine of Foix, 60
German Confederation, 234, 239, 257,
    262–263
German Empire, 263, 314, 321–323
German Gothic script, 52
Germania, Tacitus, 52
Giovanni Andrea Doria, 101
Golden Bull of Charles IV, 33–34, 36–37
governmental systems
    absolutism (monarchical), 164, 258,
        261–262, 266, 279
    bureaucratic constitutionalism, 262
    cameralism, 202–203, 206, 208
    Enlightenment and, 201–202
    valido, valimiento (government by
        valido), 163–165, 168
    viceroyal, 88, 161, 166
    See also state bureaucracy and
        centralization
Gregory X, pope, 23
Grey, Edward, 315
Grillparzer, Franz, 123, 187
Gulliver's Travels (Defoe), 226

Habsburg Empire. *See* Austrian Empire;
    Austro-Hungarian Empire
Habsburgs' Catholic devotion
    ambitions of Christian dominion,
        68–69, 95
    differing visions of, 105
    Ferdinand I, Holy Roman Emperor
        and, 78
    Ferdinand II, Holy Roman Emperor
        and, 127–129, 135–136
    persecution of heretics, 6, 69, 74,
        85–86, 95, 327
    public displays of piety, 172
    veneration of the Eucharist, 5–6, 104,
        136, 167, 172, 212
    See also piety and saintliness
Hägelin, Karl Franz, 221, 224
Hahnemann, Samuel, 196
Hall of the Giants (Riesensaal), 209–211
Hamlet (Shakespeare), 18, 221, 286
Hardenberg, Karl August von, 235

Haro, Don Luis de, 163–164
Haugwitz, count, 186
Haydn, Joseph, 223
Haynau, Julius Jacob von, 256
Heine, Heinrich, 264, 270
Henry the Leper (son of Frederick II, Holy Roman Emperor), 26
Henry, king of Portugal, 90
Henry IV, Holy Roman Emperor, 36
Henry V, Holy Roman Emperor, 13
Henry VIII, king of England, 66–67
Henry VII of Luxembourg, Holy Roman Emperor, 32–33
Heraclides, Jacob, despot of Moldavia, 117
heraldry
    Aztec, Maya, 160–161
    double-headed eagle, 160, 231, 236, 270
    at Lepanto, 104
    Maximilian I, emperor of Mexico, 274
    monument at St George's chapel, 46–47
    at palace of Innsbruck, 57
    Pillars of Hercules of Charles V, 66, 140, 175, 177
    symbolizing Habsburg territorial unity, 182
    See also vexillology
Hercules, 35, 47, 156, 172, 191, 209, 296
Hermes Trismegistus, 108–109
Hermetic Corpus, 108–109
Hermeticism, 107–110, 112–115, 118, 192
    See also alchemy
Herzl, Theodor, 300
Hitler, Adolf, 300, 326
Hofburg, Vienna
    Albert the Lame's relocation to, 34
    architecture, 1–5, 85, 120, 173, 175
    Burgtheater, 222
    Chapel, 129
    collections in, 193–194, 295
    Emperor Forum, 295
    family partition, 42
    Revolutions of 1848 and, 244
    St Michael's wing, 296–297

symbolism of, 1–3
    See also Court Library (Hofbibliothek)
Hofmannsthal, Hugo von, 299
Hohenberg, Johann Hetzendorf von, 198
Holub, Emil, 293, 295
Holy League, 101–102, 105
Holy Roman Empire
    administrative reform, 59
    changing meanings of the titles of king and emperor, 59
    decentralized government, 21–22, 59
    dissolution, 231, 234
    formation of, 6
    Frederick III's administration, 45–46
    Great Interregnum 1250-1273, 22–24
    Habsburg possessions within, 7
    imperial electors, 33–34
    questions of sovereignty, 147–148, 157
Homburg dynasty, 18
Hormayr, Joseph von, 284–285
Hötzendorf, Conrad von, 310, 314–316
humanism
    Adrian of Utrecht (Adrian VI, pope), 69
    Alfonso de Valdés, 69–70
    Erasmus, of Rotterdam, 7, 68–69, 82
    religious toleration, 118
    relationship to Hermeticism, 110
Hume, David, 64
Hungary
    abolition of self-government, 256–257
    after Habsburgs, 328–329
    Albert II and, 43
    Charles VI and, 175–177
    Elizabeth (Sisi) and, 265–266
    Franz Joseph and, 263–266
    Joseph II and, 206–208
    Joseph II and the nobility of, 206–207
    land reform, 259–260
    Legitimist party, 328
    Leopold II and, 225, 227
    Louis II and, 60, 64, 75–77, 80
    Magyarization, 282
    Maria Theresa and, 183, 186
    Matthias, Holy Roman Emperor and, 123–125

Hungary (*continued*)
    Metternich and, 238–239
    Ottoman-Habsburg wars, 122–124,
        150–155
    rebellions, 123, 151, 156, 176, 225
    religious freedom and persecution in,
        81, 122–125, 129–130, 151–153
    Revolutions of 1848 and, 246,
        249–253, 255–256
    royal succession, 77, 79, 123–124,
        129–130, 155, 183, 207
    Rudolf II and, 122–125
    Sigismund, Holy Roman Emperor
        and, 43
    See also diets, Hungarian
Hungry City (*Az éhes város*, Molnár),
    286
Hus, Jan, 78
Hussites, 43, 82

Ilg, Albert, 296
Illuminati, 195
incest, 11, 94–95, 168, 181
Indonesia, 140, 238
inheritance law, 33–34, 37, 41, 167–168,
    267, 275
    See also Pragmatic Sanction
inheritance
    Croatia by Ferdinand I, 79
    by Ferdinand II, Holy Roman
        Emperor, 129–131
    by Ferdinand III, 144
    forgeries, 13, 36–39, 41, 45, 47, 183
    Fortinbras effect, 18–19, 75, 181
    Hungary and Bohemia by Albert II,
        43
    Hungary and Bohemia by Ferdinand
        I, 61, 75, 77–79
    by Matthias, 125, 129
    Ottokar II, 26
    Portugal by Philip II, 90, 138
    Pragmatic Sanction, 182, 263,
        265–266
    Rudolf I, 19, 23
    Spain, its colonies, and various other
        titles by Philip II, 85

Spain and its colonies by Philip V,
    168, 174–175
Spain by Charles V, 60, 64
Zähringen and Kiburg lands, 18–19
Innsbruck, Tyrol, 39, 43, 55, 56–57
Irving, Washington, 270
Isabella Clara Eugenia (daughter of Philip
    II), 211–212
Isabella I, queen of Castile, 60
Isabella of Parma, 215, 217
Isabella of Portugal, 68, 85, 90, 211
Ita (wife of Radbot), 12, 323
Italy
    Charles VI's possessions in, 175, 182
    gains in Austro-Prussian war, 263
    Habsburg invasions of, 57
    Risorgimento, 260–261
    Staufen conflict in, 22
    World War I and, 316–317, 320–321

Jacobinism, 226–227
Jacquin, Nikolaus, 194
Jagiello dynasty, 61, 75
James I, king of England, 133
James II, king of England, 175
James of Berwick, 175
James VI, king of Scotland, 104–105
Jansenism, 214, 216
Jason (mythological), 104, 132, 295
Jelačić, Josip, 250–255, 280, 304
Jesuits, 166, 172, 176–177, 212–214, 219
    education and, 82, 122, 124, 127,
        134, 177
Jews
    Albert II and, 43
    antisemitism in World War I, 316, 320
    in 'Chronicle of the Ninety-Five
        Lords', 46–47
    in Crown Prince's Work, 286
    Franz Ferdinand and, 303
    Joseph II and, 204, 299
    Kabbalah, 60, 113
    Leopold I and, 149
    Maria Theresa and, 202
    Maximilian I, Holy Roman Emperor
        and, 59–60

New Holland (Dutch Brazilian
    colony), 139
  Otto (son of Karl I, emperor of
    Austria) and, 326
  persecution, 43, 59, 87–88, 91, 139,
    149, 202, 328
  Philip II and, 87–88, 95
  'racial science' and, 294, 308
  in Vienna and Austro-Hungarian
    Empire, 298–300
  See also religious conflict
John (son of Henry VII), 33
John, archduke of Austria, imperial regent,
    197, 245, 249
John, king of England, 22
John George I, elector of Saxony, 133–134
John III Sobieski, king of Poland, 153–155
John II Sigismund, prince of Transylvania,
    80
John the Parricide, 32
John XXIII, antipope, 42
Jókai, Maurice (Mór), 286
Joseph I, Holy Roman Emperor, 169, 175
Joseph II, Holy Roman Emperor, 183,
    190–194, 197, 203–209,
    220–221, 228
  governance, 204, 206–208, 224
  Low Countries and, 214–217
  religious policy, 204–205, 216, 299
  revolutionary reforms, 180–181,
    186–187, 203, 258
Juan (son of Ferdinand of Aragon and
    Isabella I), 60
Juana the Mad, 60, 94
Juárez, Benito, 272
Julio (son of Rudolf II), 111

Kanzelin, 12
Kara Mustafa, 153–155
Karadžić, Vuk, 307
Karl I, emperor of Austria, 12, 320–323,
    326
Karl Ludwig, archduke of Austria, 269, 302
Károlyi, Michael, 322
Kaunitz (Wenzel Anton), 185, 187–188,
    190, 226

Kelley, Edward, 112–113
Kelsen, Hans, 299
Kempelen, Wolfgang von, 179–181
Kepler, Johannes, 113, 142
Khlesl, Melchior, 121–123, 131
Kiburg dynasty, 18–19, 23, 33
Klimt, Gustav, 297, 299
Kokoschka, Oscar, 297, 299
Kolowrat-Liebsteinsky, Franz Anton von,
    240–241, 246
Kongo, kingdom of, 139–140
Königsfelden Chronicle, 35
Köprülü family (viziers of Ottoman
    Empire), 150, 153
Kosáry, Domokos, 328–329
Kossuth, Louis, 239, 251–252, 255–256,
    263, 280
Kunigunda (wife of Ottokar II), 26

Ladislas, king of Hungary (son of Albert
    II), 45, 49
Lamberg, Ferenc, 251–252
Lanzelin. *See* Kanzelin
Latour, Theodor Franz von, 247–248, 252,
    254
Lawrence, Saint, 86
legal reform
  absolutism and, 164, 258
  bureaucratic, 239–240, 259–260
  Francis II and, 238–240
  Hungarian, 265
  Imperial Chamber Court of
    Maximilian I, 58–59
  Jews and, 298–299
  Maximilian I, emperor of Mexico and,
    275
  nationalism and, 280–283, 307
  natural law theory, 202
  Rudolf I and, 25, 59
  World War I and, 319–320
  See also censorship; constitutions;
    inheritance law; Roman law
Lenzburg dynasty, 18–19
Leopold (brother of Frederick the Fair), 33
Leopold (brother of Rudolf IV the
    Founder), 42

Leopold I, Holy Roman Emperor, 149–157, 169, 173–175, 222

Leopold I, king of Belgium, 243, 271

Leopold II, Holy Roman Emperor, 224–227

Leopold III the Good, duke of Austria, Saint, 35

Leopoldine (daughter of Francis II), 231, 236, 267

liberalism, 245–246, 258, 282

Linnaeus, Carl, 194, 205

Loew, Judah, 113

Lombardy-Venetia, kingdom of, 233, 238–239, 248

Loos, Adolf, 287, 297–298

Lothar III, Holy Roman Emperor, 18

Louis II, king of Hungary, 60, 64, 75–77, 80

Louis IV of Bavaria, king of the Romans, 33

Louis XI, king of France, 49

Louis XII, king of France, 58

Louis XIV, king of France, 145, 148–151, 153, 156–157, 162, 165

Louis XV, king of France, 185

Louis XVI, king of France, 225–226

Louis XVIII, king of France, 233

Lovassy, László, 239

Low Countries
    dissolution, 212–213
    Habsburg possession of, 49, 233
    Maximilian I, Holy Roman Emperor and, 51, 53, 57
    rebellions, 57, 93–94, 103, 123, 138, 207, 216–217
    regencies, 98, 103, 211–212, 215
    religion, 212–214, 216
    United Provinces of the Netherlands, 94, 138, 174, 229
    War of the Spanish Succession and, 175, 213
    See also United Provinces of the Netherlands

Ludovico Sforza of Milan, 58

Ludwig, archduke of Austria, 244

Ludwig Viktor, archduke of Austria, 269

Lueger, Karl, 300

Luiz Felipe (son of Carlos I), 277

Luther, Martin, 67, 69, 81

Lutheranism
    persecution of, 87, 128, 141, 152, 176
    spread, 80–83, 117
    theology, 81, 125
    toleration of, 71–72, 125–126, 204
    See also Protestantism; religious conflict; religious toleration

Luxembourg dynasty, 31, 39

Magdeburg, Sack of, 141

Magellan, Ferdinand, 64, 99–100, 295

The Magic Flute (Mozart), 222–224, 228

Mahler, Gustav, 299

Malory, Thomas, 54

Manet, Édouard, 277

maps
    Austria-Hungary in 1914, 311
    Charles V and, 71–72
    Columbus, 99
    ethnic maps, 281
    Habsburg possessions in 1600, 89
    Habsburg territories in Central Europe, 1648, 145
    Habsburg territories in Europe, 1555, 73
    lack of, in warfare, 143, 154–155
    naval sponsorship of cartography, 293
    Southern Swabia, 16

Marela, Josefa, 274

Margaret (daughter of Maximilian I, Holy Roman Emperor), 57, 60, 98, 211

Margaret (sister of Frederick II, Babenberg), 26

Margaret *Maultasch* (Big Mouth) of the Tyrol, 39

Margaret of Parma, 98, 211

Margaret Theresa (second wife of Leopold I), 149

Maria Amalia (niece of Charles VI), 183

Maria Anna (daughter of Maria Theresa), 197, 211, 223

Maria Anna (first wife of Ferdinand II), 129

Maria Anna (wife of Charles II of Styria), 127–129

Maria Christina (Mimi, daughter of Maria Theresa), 215–217, 225

Maria Elizabeth (daughter of Maria Theresa), 214

Maria Manuela of Portugal, 94

Mariana of Austria, 211

Maria Theresa, Holy Roman Empress, 179–190, 200–203, 207, 209–210, 221, 267
    censorship and, 219–220
    statue of, 295
    succession, 37, 179, 181–183, 210

Marie Antoinette (Maria Antonia), 217–218, 225–226

Marie Louise (wife of Napoleon I), 231, 233

Marie Valerie (daughter of Franz Joseph), 318

Marquis de Prié (Hercule-Louis Turinetti), 213

The Marriage of Figaro (Mozart), 221, 223

marriages
    Albert II to Elizabeth (daughter of Sigismund, Holy Roman Emperor), 43
    Charles VI to Elizabeth Christine of Brunswick, 181–182
    Charles V, children and nieces, 70
    Charles V to Isabella of Portugal, 68
    Ferdinand I to Anne (daughter of Wladislas Jagiello), 60, 75
    Ferdinand II, archduke of Austria to Philippine Welser, 119
    Ferdinand II, Holy Roman Emperor to Eleonara Gonzaga, 135
    Ferdinand II, Holy Roman Emperor to Maria Anna, 129
    Ferdinand of Aragon to Germaine of Foix, 60
    Franz Ferdinand to Sophie Chotek, 302
    Franz Salvator to Marie Valerie, 318
    Habsburgs into Staufen, Lenzburg, Pfullendorf, Homburg dynasties, 18
    Louis II of Hungary to Mary (granddaughter of Maximilian I, Holy Roman Emperor), 60, 75
    Margaret (daughter of Maximilian I, Holy Roman Emperor) to Juan (son of Ferdinand of Aragon), 60
    Maria Christina to Albert of Saxony, 215
    Maximilian I, emperor of Mexico and Charlotte of Belgium, 271
    Maximilian I, Holy Roman Emperor and Mary (daughter of Charles the Bold), 49
    Napoleon I to Marie Louise, 231–232
    Philip I to Juana the Mad, 60
    Philipp von Neumann to Augusta Somerset, 243
    Rudolf I's daughters, 27, 29
    See also genealogy; inheritances

Marx, Karl, 284

Marxism, 298

Mary (sister of Charles V), 71

Mary I, queen of Scotland, 98

Mary I Tudor, queen of England, 85–86

Mary of Burgundy, 49, 52–53, 57, 63

Mary of Hungary, 60, 75–76, 80, 85, 98, 211

Mary of Jesus of Agréda, 163–164

Masaryk, Tomáš, 322

Matthias, Holy Roman Emperor, 103, 123–125, 127, 129–131, 136

Matthias Corvinus, king of Hungary, 49–50, 60

mausoleums. *See* crypts

Maximilian, duke of Bavaria, 129, 133–134, 142

Maximilian Francis (son of Maria Theresa), 213

Maximilian I, emperor of Mexico, 269–277, 288, 313

Maximilian I, Holy Roman Emperor, 6, 49, 50–64, 211

Maximilian II, Holy Roman Emperor, 74, 105, 110, 113, 119, 125, 192
Mechel, Christian von, 295
medicine and hygiene, 305–307
melancholy. *See* depression
Mercurino di Gattinara, 69
Merovingian dynasty, 12
Metternich, Clemens von, 229, 231–241, 244–246, 253
Mexico (New Spain)
    absentee monarchs, 88, 159–161
    Charles V of Ghent, Holy Roman Emperor and, 64, 72
    French intervention, 272–273, 275
    Maximilian I's emperorship, 272–276
    Mexican-American war, 271
    Philip II, king of Spain and, 88, 90–92
    See also colonies and colonialism
Mexico City, Mexico, 88, 90–91, 159–161, 274, 276
Meytens, Martin van, 211
Michael, prince of Serbia, 277
Michael I Apafi, prince of Transylvania, 153
Mises, Ludwig von, 299
modernization, 275, 299, 304, 308
Mohammed Ali (Egyptian pasha), 237
Molnár, Ferenc, 286
Monachologia (Born), 205
monasteries
    Admont, 81, 293
    Babenberg foundations, 34–35
    decline, 81, 118, 205–206, 272
    Escorial Palace, 86
    Klagenfurt, 197
    Muri, 12–14, 323
    St Peter's, Ghent, 214
    Yuste, 72, 160
Monastic Council *(Klosterrat)*, 119, 121–122
Montecuccoli, Raimondo, 151, 154
Montesquieu, 219
Le Morte d'Arthur (Malory), 54
Moser, Johann Jacob, 147
Mozart, Wolfgang Amadeus, 221–223, 228

museums, 225, 281, 293, 308, 327
    origins, 193–194
    in Vienna, 193–194, 196, 294–296, 303
    See also Wonder Chambers
music, 148–149, 173, 221–223, 228, 239
Musil, Robert, 284
Muslims, 87–88, 98–100, 309
    See also religious conflict

Nádasdy, Thomas, 82
Napoleon I, emperor of the French, 180, 229–233, 241
Napoleon III, emperor of the French, 257, 260, 271–273, 275–277
nationalism, 246, 248, 257, 279–287, 307–310, 312, 315–316, 322, 327–328
    architecture and, 296–297
    See also revolutions
navy, Habsburg, 90, 101–102, 236–237, 263, 270–271, 292–293, 304
Nazi Germany, 206, 282, 328
Nebuchadnezzar, 122, 144
Neptune, 68, 114, 190
Nero, 36–37, 47, 55
Netherlands. *See* Low Countries
Neumann, Philipp von, 243, 246, 253
New Christians. *See* Jews; Muslims
New Spain. *See* Mexico (New Spain)
newspapers
    Allgemeine Zeitung, 239
    censorship of, 220–221, 224, 239–240, 258, 301–302, 309
    Franz Joseph and, 264, 287, 289, 313
    Grenzboten, 239
    Habsburgs' violent deaths in, 277–278, 301–302, 313
    Il Progresso, 240
    Le Petit Journal, 313
    Neue Freie Presse, 287, 289
    Sunday News (Vasárnapi Újság), 277
    Wiener Zeitung, 220, 239
Newton, Isaac, 107, 180
New World, 64–65, 99, 192, 194
    See also colonies; Mexico (New Spain)

Nibelunglied (epic), 35
Nicholas I, emperor of Russia, 236, 260
North German Confederation, 263
Nostitz, countess, 184

O'Gorman, Edmundo, 272
Old Fort (Alte Burg). *See* Hofburg
Olivares, Count-Duke of (Gaspar de
    Guzmán), 163–165
opera. *See* music
Order of the Golden Fleece, 65, 98, 174
Ornament and Crime (Loos), 297
Otrokócsi, Ferenc Fóris, 152
Otto (son of Karl I, emperor of Austria),
    326, 328
Ottokar II, king of Bohemia, 24–29, 31,
    286–287
Ottomans
    abortive negotiations with Frederick
      V, 133
    collapse, 323
    conquest of North Africa and
      Mediterranean, 100
    contested border with Habsburgs,
      304–306
    decline and reform after Lepanto, 150
    defeat of Hungary at Mohács, 75–76
    Eastern Question (division by
      European powers), 304
    exoticization of, 181
    expulsion from Hungary, 176
    history and limits to expansion, 99
    Leopold II and, 225
    occupation of Hungary, 80–81
    sieges of Vienna, 1, 68, 79, 154
    trade with Austrian Empire, 237
    war in Hungary 1593, 122–124
    wars with Charles V, 66
    war with the Holy League, 100–103
    World War I and, 317
Oxenstierna, Axel, 143

paintings
    Allegory of Lepanto (Titian), 104
    'Archduchess Sophie praying' (Fendi),
      228

Ghent Altarpiece (Van Eyck), 215
Judith (Klimt), 299
Las Meninas (Velázquez), 149
portraiture, 63–64, 167, 209–211, 228
Strigel's Habsburg family portrait,
    63–64, 75–76
'Succour of Religion' for Philip II and
    Maximilian II (Titian), 105
palaces
    Alhambra, 308
    Belvedere, 173, 295, 303
    Chapultepec, 274
    Coudenburg, Brussels, 212
    Escorial, 85–86, 103, 107, 168, 175
    Gödöllő, 267
    Heidelberg, 134
    Hofburg, Innsbruck, 57, 209
    Miramare, 271–273, 276
    Napoleon's, at St Cloud, 232
    National (Mexico), 275
    Schönbrunn, 179, 189–193, 197, 235,
      260, 323
    Star (Hvežda), 120
    Versailles, 189, 192
    See also architecture; Hofburg
      (Vienna)
Palacký, František, 284
Palmerston (Henry John Temple), 284
papacy, 6, 22, 24, 29, 43, 59
    See also excommunications; individual
      popes
parliaments, 246, 261–262, 265–266,
    282–283
    See also cortes (Spanish parliaments);
      Corts-General; diets (German,
      Central European parliaments);
      diets (Hungarian)
Partitions of Poland, 185–186, 230
Paskevich, Ivan, 256
Pázmány, Peter, 129–130
peace treaties
    Aachen, 184–185
    Augsburg, 71–72, 119–120, 142
    Campo Formio, 230
    Congress of Berlin, 306
    Congress of Vienna, 233–235

peace treaties (*continued*)
  Nijmegen, 153
  Prague, 144
  Rastatt, 175, 213
  Ryswick, 156
  Schönbrunn, 230
  Vasvár, 151, 153
  Vienna, 123–124, 130
  Westphalia, 145–147, 225
  Zsitvatörök, 123–124
peasantry, 17, 166, 176, 181
  abolition of serfdom, 206, 208, 240,
    246, 249, 257, 259–260
Pedro I, emperor of Brazil, 231
Pedro II, king of Kongo, 139
Penelope (mythological), 157
Peru, 64, 88, 174
Peter of Ghent (Pedro de Gante), 72,
    159–160
Petrarch, 37
Pfullendorf dynasty, 18
Philip I, king of Castile, 53, 57, 60
Philip II, king of Spain, 85–90, 92–98,
    129, 163, 211–212
  colonies and their economies, 64, 72,
    88–90
  Don John and, 97–98, 101, 103
  Holy League and Battle of Lepanto,
    100–101, 104
  Isabella Clara Eugenia and,
    211–212
  succession, 74, 85
Philip III, king of Spain, 132, 163, 166
Philip IV, king of Spain, 144, 162–165,
    167, 212
Philip of Swabia, 18
Philippines, 64, 88–90, 100
Philip V, king of Spain, 168, 174–175
piety and saintliness, 288
  'Austrian piety', 171–172, 228
  Habsburg absorption of Babenbergs'
    reputation, 35
  Habsburg piety in paintings, 212
  Ita (wife of Radbot), 12
  Maximilian I, Holy Roman Emperor's
    saintly genealogy, 54

Rudolf I, 24
  See also Catholicism; Habsburgs'
    Catholic devotion
Pilgrim's Progress (Bunyan), 226
Pillersdorf, Franz von, 246
Pitt, William the Younger, 230
Pius II (Enea Silvio Piccolomini), pope, 44
Pius IX, pope, 276
Pius V, pope, 100–102, 105
Pius VI, pope, 205
Plato, 108
Plener, Ignaz von, 261
Pliny the Elder, 192
Plus Ultra (motto of Charles V), 66, 160,
    270
Pocket Book on National History (Hormayr),
    284
Poland, 117, 137, 154, 185–186, 230
police, 224, 226–228, 239, 315
Pompadour, Madame de, 185
population demographics, 140–141, 166,
    220, 281, 299
  Austrian army, 315–316, 320
  Balkan, 304–305, 307
  census, 187–188, 281
  diversity in Hungary, 176, 250, 286
Portocarrero, cardinal, 168
portraiture, 63–64, 167, 209–211, 228
  See also paintings
Portugal, 99, 138–139, 144, 165
Pragmatic Sanction, 182, 263, 265–266
Prague, Bohemia, 111–112, 119, 130–131,
    247–248
Přemyslid dynasty, 31
Prim, Juan, 276
Princip, Gavrilo, 310, 312
prostitution, 214, 220–221, 228
Protestant Defenders (Bohemia), 130–131
Protestantism, 71, 87, 129–130, 174, 204
  Diet of Worms and, 67, 69
  dispute over Eucharist's meaning, 5,
    78, 81
  Ferdinand II, Holy Roman Emperor
    and, 129–130, 133
  Matthias and, 124–126
  Maximillian II and, 110

Peace of Westphalia and, 146
persecution under Habsburg rulers,
　87, 93, 95, 128, 134, 149,
　151–152, 176, 202
Rudolf II and, 110, 125–126
spread, 80–82, 117–118
suppression of, 6, 119, 121–123
See also Catholicism and Catholic
　Church; religious conflict;
　religious toleration
The Protocols of the Elders of Zion, 87–88
Prussia, 225, 236
French Revolutionary and Napoleonic
　Wars, 225, 229, 232, 234–235
German imperial ambitions, 207,
　262–263
See also German Empire
public sphere, 196–197, 220, 227
Purgatory (Dante), 29

race
demographics of Taiwan, 140
freemasonry and, 195
Habsburg racism, 327–328
New World hierarchy of, 166–167
racialized Ottoman-Habsburg frontier
　peoples, 304–307
'racial science', 294, 307–309, 318
Radbot (son of Kanzelin), 12, 14, 323
Radetzky, 248–249, 253, 287
Radetzky March (Strauss), 249
Rákóczi, Francis, 176
Ranft, Michael, 199–200
rebellions, 121, 139, 149, 234, 240,
　291–292, 305
Bohemian, 130–135, 137, 247–248,
　285
Hungarian, 123, 151, 156, 176, 225
under Joseph II, 206–207
Low Countries, 57, 93–94, 103, 123,
　138, 207, 216–217
Peasants' War, 68
in Spain, 64–65, 87, 93–94, 98, 144,
　165
Transylvanian, 123, 156, 206
See also revolutions; riots

Recife, 139
The Red and the Black (Stendhal), 241
Redlich, Joseph, 320
Reformation. *See* Protestantism
Reform Commissions, 122, 128, 134
*Reglamento para el Servicio y Ceremonial de
　la Corte* (guide to court etiquette,
　Maximilian I, emperor of
　Mexico), 274
religious conflict, 176, 202, 204
Diet of Worms, 67, 69
dispute over Eucharist's meaning, 5,
　78, 81
Ferdinand II, Holy Roman Emperor
　and, 128, 134
Leopold I and, 149, 151–152
Philip II and, 87, 93, 95
suppression of Protestantism, 6, 119,
　121–123
See also Catholicism and Catholic
　Church; confessionalization;
　Jesuits; Jews; Protestantism;
　Spanish Inquisition; Thirty Years
　War
religious toleration, 71, 124–126, 139, 146,
　176, 275
Ferdinand II, Holy Roman Emperor
　and, 129–130, 133
Joseph II and, 204, 208, 299
Leopold I, Holy Roman Emperor and,
　152, 155–156
Ottomans and, 81, 152
philosophical basis for, 188, 204
Rudolf II's Letter of Majesty, 125,
　130, 134
Renaissance, 7–8, 170
Renate of Lorraine, 11
Renner, Karl, 298, 323
Requesens, Luis de, 98 101, 103
revolutions
defence against after Congress of
　Vienna, 235–236, 238–239
of 1848, 243–253, 255–256, 287, 304
of 1820, 235–236
French, 225–226
of 1989, 328

revolutions (*continued*)
    revolutionary societies, 226, 238–239
    Russian, 317, 323
    See also Jacobinism; rebellions; riots
Richard II (Shakespeare), 325
Richard of Cornwall, 22–23, 26
Richelieu, cardinal, 143
Rilke, Rainer Maria, 19
riots, 119, 121, 244, 246–247, 251, 252,
    320
Roman Empire, 6, 36, 95, 327
Roman law, 128, 134–135, 142, 164
Romanov dynasty, 327
Romeo and Juliet (Shakespeare), 203
Rossini, Gioachino, 228
Rothschild, Anselm, 261
Rousseau, Jean-Jacques, 207
Rubens, Peter Paul, 212
Rudolf (son of Franz Joseph), 270, 285, 302
    suicide, 277, 285, 301–302, 313
    political views, 285, 298, 308, 327
Rudolf (son of Kanzelin), 12
Rudolf (son of King Rudolf), 32
Rudolf I, king of the Romans, 5, 19, 23–29,
    31–32, 59, 136, 286–287
Rudolf II, Holy Roman Emperor, 107–115,
    123–125, 127, 129, 144, 287
    religious policy, 119, 122–123, 125,
    130, 134
Rudolf IV the Founder, duke of Austria,
    36–41, 45, 50, 136
Rudolf the Old, 18–19
Russia, 185, 230, 232–235, 236, 256,
    271–272
    Poland-Lithuania partitions, 185–186,
    230
    Russo-Turkish wars, 182–183,
    305–306
    Serbian relations, 309, 313, 315
    World War I and, 314–317, 321, 323
    See also Soviet Union

Saadi dynasty, 99
Safavid Empire, 99
Sausage, Jack (Hans Wurst), 197, 221–222
Schickaneder, Emanuel, 223–224

Schiele, Egon, 297, 299
Schiller, Friedrich, 15
Schnitzler, Arthur, 299
Schoenberg, Arnold, 298
Schratt, Katharina, 264
Schubert, Franz, 228
Schwarzenberg, 253–254, 256–258
science, 192–196, 213–214, 224–225, 258,
    293–295, 317
Scipio Africanus, 140
Selim II, Ottoman Sultan, 100, 105
Sendivogius (Michał Sędziwój), 113
Serbia, 199–200, 306–310, 312, 313–317,
    319
serfdom. *See* peasantry
Shakespeare, William, 115, 132, 203, 221,
    256, 325
Sidney, Philip, 110, 123
Sigismund (cousin of Frederick III), 49
Sigismund of Luxembourg, Holy Roman
    Emperor, 42–43
simulacra of royalty, 66, 140, 148, 159–162
Social Contract (Rousseau), 207
socialism, 283, 285, 323
Socrates, 159
Soliman, Angelo, 195
Somerset, Augusta, 243
Sonnenfels, Joseph von, 203, 221, 224
Sophie of Bavaria, 228, 244, 252–254,
    269–270
Soviet Union, 326, 328
    See also Russia
Spain, 161–165, 168, 270
    Charles V and, 60, 64–68, 74, 85
    Habsburg loss of, 168, 174–175, 190
    Philip II and, 74, 85, 87–90, 92–95,
    105
    rebellions in, 64–65, 87, 93–94, 98,
    144, 165
    Thirty Years War and, 137–138,
    144–146
    War of the Spanish Succession, 156,
    175, 182, 213
    See also colonies and colonialism;
    cortes (Spanish parliament)
Spanish Inquisition, 90–93

Spirit of the Laws (Montesquieu), 219
Spranger, Bartholomeus, 114
state bureaucracy and centralization,
        180–181, 197–198, 256–260,
        275
    Joseph II and, 180–181, 186–187,
        203, 208, 224
    Maria Theresa and, 180–181,
        186–188, 201–203
    See also decentralization,
        governmental; governmental
        systems
Staufen dynasty, 18, 22–24, 31, 327
Stendhal, 241
Stephanie of Belgium, 285, 293
St George's Chapel, Wiener Neustadt, 46,
    63
St Michael's Church, 81, 176–177
Stöger, Ferdinand, 216
Stoss, Veit, 55
Strauss, Johann, 248–249
Strigel, Bernhard, 63–64, 75
St Stephen's Cathedral, 38–40, 45–46, 50,
    154
Styria, duchy of, 26, 38, 44, 118, 120–121
successions. *See* genealogy; inheritance law;
    inheritance; marriages
Suleiman I the Magnificent, Ottoman
    Sultan, 76, 99, 150
Swabia, duchy of, 22–24, 43, 51
    Habsburg possessions in, 12, 19, 24,
        26, 29, 34
Swieten, Gerhard van, 200–201, 224
Sylvester, Saint, 32
Szelepcsényi (primate of Hungary),
    151–152

Tacitus, 52
Taiwan, 140
Talleyrand (Charles Maurice de
    Talleyrand-Périgord), 232–233,
    235
taxation, 3, 17, 21, 36, 206–207, 263
    Habsburg diets and, 42, 56, 135, 186
    Habsburg rulers and, 81, 83,
        206–207

Low Countries, 56, 93, 212
    Spanish Cortes, 65, 164–165
    See also economy
Tegetthoff, Wilhelm von, 292
The Tempest (Shakespeare), 115
terrorism. *See* assassinations
Teutonic Knights, 27, 151
theatre, 148, 172–173, 177, 212, 214,
    221–224
    See also music
Theresa D'Avila, Saint, 171
Theuerdank (Maximilian I, Holy Roman
    Emperor), 52
Third Reich. *See* Nazi Germany
Thirty Years War, 137–146
Thököly, Imre, king of Hungary, 153,
    155
'A Thousand Regrets' (chanson), 68
3 November 1918 (Csokor), 300
Thurzó, Stanislas, 130
Tianjin, 291
Tilly (Johann Tserclaes), 133–134
Tirant lo Blanc (Martorell), 54
Tisza, István, 314
Titian, 68, 104–105, 113
tombs. *See* crypts
Transylvania, 79–80, 155, 176–177, 187,
    199, 265
    Ottomans and, 123, 150, 153, 155,
        176
    Protestantism in, 80–81, 122–123,
        126, 155, 176, 202
    rebellions, 123, 156, 206, 322
'Travel Pictures' (*Reisebilder,* Heine), 270
'Travel Sketches' (*Reiseskizzen,* Maximilian
    I, emperor of Mexico), 270
treaties. *See* peace treaties
'A Treatise on Man' (Isabella of Parma),
    217
*Treatise on the Chewing and Gnawing of the
    Dead in Their Graves, in Which
    Is Revealed the True Nature of
    the Hungarian Vampires and
    Bloodsuckers* (Ranft), 200
Trismegistus, Hermes, 108–109
Truhelka, Ćiro, 309

Tschernembl, George, 121
Tunis, 64, 66, 70
Tyrol, county of, 39–40, 42, 56–57, 118,
        120–121, 230

Ulysses, 157, 161
Umberto I, king of Italy, 277
Union or Death. *See* Black Hand
Unitarianism, 80–81, 126, 176, 204
United Provinces of the Netherlands, 94,
        138, 174, 229
    See also Low Countries
United States of America, 271, 321–322
United States of Belgium, 217
    See also Low Countries
Utraquists, 78, 80, 82–83, 125

vampires, 199–201
Vega, Lope de, 212
Velázquez, Diego, 149
Venice, Italy, 58, 100–101, 103, 230
Vetsera, Maria, 301
vexillology, 66, 138, 231, 236, 267
    See also heraldry
Victoria, queen of Great Britain, 267
Vienna, Austria, 47, 149, 220–222,
        227–228, 230, 298–300
    Ottoman sieges of, 1, 68, 79, 154
    Revolutions of 1848 and, 244–249,
        252–253
    See also architecture; Hofburg;
        museums; St Stephen's Cathedral
Vienna at War (*Wien im Krieg,* film), 318
Virgil, 68
Voltaire, 199, 205

Walks of a Viennese Poet (Auersperg), 241
Wallenstein (Albrecht Václav Eusebius z
        Valdštejna), 141–144
Walpole, Robert, 194–195
wars
    American Civil, 271, 275
    Austrian intervention in Naples 1821,
        235–236
    Austrian Succession, 183–184, 207
    Austro-Prussian, 263

Balkan Wars 1912-1913, 309–310
Bohemian Revolt, 130–135
Bosnian, 326
Charles Albert of Sardinia-Piedmont
        and Austrian Empire, 248
Charles the Bold's invasion of
        Lorraine and Swiss Vaud, 49
Charles V, various, 66, 68, 70–71
Charles VIII's invasion of kingdom of
        Naples, 57
Coalition Wars against France,
        229–230, 232–233
Crimean, 260, 271–272
Francis II and Morocco, 236
Frederick III and Charles the Bold, 49
Frederick the Fair against King Louis
        of Bavaria, 33
French religious, 117
French Revolutionary, 226–227
Holy League and Ottomans, 100–105
Hungarian, 75–77, 79–80, 122–124,
        150–155, 176, 251–253, 255–256
Joseph II and Ottomans, 208, 216
Leopold II and Ottomans, 225
Louis XIV and Habsburgs, 149–153,
        156
Matthias Corvinus' invasion of
        Austria, 49
Maximilian I, Holy Roman Emperor,
        Louis XII, the pope, and Venice,
        58
Mexican-American, 271
Napoleon I and Egypt, 230
Napoleon III and Franz Joseph,
        260–261
Oriental Crisis 1840, 237
Ottoman conquest of North Africa,
        100
Philip II's real and planned, 90
Poland-Lithuania partitions, 185–186,
        230
Polish Succession, 182
Rudolf I and Ottokar II, 28
Rudolf IV the Founder and the
        patriarch of Aquileia, 38
Russo-Turkish, 182–183, 305–306

Selim II and Knights of Malta, 100
Seven Years, 185, 207
Sigismund, Holy Roman Emperor and
Hussite heretics, 43
Spanish Succession, 156, 175, 182,
213
Swiss cantons and Habsburgs, 42–43
See also Thirty Years War
Washington, George, 3
Weber, Carl Maria von, 228
Weisbach, Augustin, 294
Weisskunig ('White King, allegory,
Maximilian I, Holy Roman
Emperor), 53–54, 58
Welser, Philippine, 119
Welser family, 57, 119
Wenceslas II, king of Bohemia, 29
Werner, bishop of Strasbourg, 13
Werner I, son of Radbot, 13
Werner II, 18
Wesselényi, Nicholas, 239
Westphalia, Peace of, 146–148
Wieland, Christoph, 224
Wilhelm II, emperor of Germany, 303, 314,
316, 321
William II, duke of Bavaria, 120
William III, king of England, 156

Wilson, Woodrow, 321–322
Windischgrätz, Alfred I prince of,
247–250, 252–254
Wittelsbach dynasty, 24, 26, 31, 39, 129
Wittgenstein, Ludwig, 298, 300
Wladislas Jagiello, king of Hungary and
Bohemia, 60, 64, 76
Wolf, Johanna, 301
women, 182, 210–218, 264, 267
See also Maria Theresa, Holy Roman
Empress
Wonder Chambers, 109, 114–115, 120, 144
woodcuts
Melencolia I (Dürer), 111–112, 114
The Triumphal Arch, 52, 55
The Triumphal Carriage, 55
The Triumphal Procession, 52, 55–56,
58, 61
world empire, 7, 69, 72, 95, 175
World War I, 12, 292, 294, 313–323
World War II, 328

Yugoslavia, 322, 326

Zähringen dynasty, 18–19
Zápolya, John, king of Hungary, 79–80
Zita (wife of Karl I), 12

Martyn Rady is Masaryk Professor of Central European History at University College London. He is the author of *The Habsburg Empire: A Very Short Introduction*, *The Emperor Charles V*, and other books on Central European history. He has honorary doctorates from Károli University in Budapest and Lucian Blaga University of Sibiu in Romania. He lives in Kent, UK.